# Western Law,
# Russian Justice

# Western Law, Russian Justice

*Dostoevsky, the Jury Trial, and the Law*

Gary Rosenshield

THE UNIVERSITY OF WISCONSIN PRESS

The University of Wisconsin Press
1930 Monroe Street
Madison, Wisconsin 53711

www.wisc.edu/wisconsinpress/

3 Henrietta Street
London WC2E 8LU, England

5     4     3     2     1

Printed in the United States of America

Library of Congress Cataloging-in-Publication Data

Rosenshield, Gary.
Western law, Russian justice: Dostoevsky, the jury trial, and the law /
Gary Rosenshield.
p. cm.
Includes bibliographical references and index.
ISBN 0-299-20930-X (cloth: alk. paper)
1. Dostoyevsky, Fyodor, 1821–1881—Knowledge—Law. 2. Law in literature.
3. Jury in literature. 4. Justice in literature. 5. Dostoyevsky, Fyodor, 1821–1881.
Bratia Karamazovy. I. Title.
PG3328.Z7L37 2005
891.73′3—dc22

2004024341

*For Jill*

# Contents

# Acknowledgments

Research for *Western Law, Russian Justice: Dostoevsky, the Law, and the Jury Trial* was supported by grants from the University of Wisconsin Graduate School. I owe a great deal to those who read the present study, in whole or in parts, through its various stages during the last decade, including Victor Terras, David Bethea, Andrew Weiner and anonymous readers from the *Slavic and East European Journal* and *Canadian-American Slavic Studies*. I was also significantly aided, as most academic writers are, by research assistance at the university. I would especially like to thank Rebecca Matveyev, Paul Klanderud, David Vernikov, Dan Ungurianu, David Polet, Keith Meyer-Blasing, and Andrew Swenson. Several sections of *Western Law, Russian Justice* are significantly modified versions of previously published journal articles: "The Imprisonment of the Law: Dostoevskij and the Kroneberg Case," *Slavic and East European Journal* 36 (1992): 415–34; "Western Law vs. Russian Justice: Dostoevsky and the Jury Trial, Round One," *Graven Images* 1 (1994): 117–35; "Death and Resurrection at the Russian Bar: Dostoevsky and the Kornilova Case," *Canadian-American Slavic Studies* 31 (1997): 1–32; "Crime and Redemption, Russian and American Style: Dostoevsky, Buckley, Mailer, and Styron," *Slavic and East European Journal* 42.4 (1998): 677–709.

Most of all I would like to thank my wife, Jill, whose love, enthusiasm, and editorial assistance were essential to the maturation and completion of this project. It is to her that the book is dedicated.

# Western Law,
# Russian Justice

# Introduction

## Western Law, Russian Justice

A man, let us say, has committed a crime; he does not know the law; he is ready to confess, but then the advocate appears and proves to him that not only is he, the criminal, innocent but that he is a saint.
—*Diary of a Writer*

The tribunes of our new courts are unquestionably an ethical school for our society and our people. Indeed, the people learn in this school truth and morality.
—*Diary of a Writer*

Yes, the bar is an excellent institution but, somehow, a sad one.
—*Diary of a Writer*

It's not I who say that, it's the Gospel.
—Summation of Fetyukovich, Dmitry Karamazov's lawyer,
*The Brothers Karamazov*

In his introduction to his poem "The Grand Inquisitor," in which he questions Christian theodicy, Ivan Karamazov tells his brother Alyosha that he must have justice or he will kill himself:

With my pitiful, earthly, Euclidian understanding, all I know is that there is suffering and that there are none guilty; that cause follows effect, simply and directly; that everything flows and finds its level—but that's only Euclidian nonsense, I know that, and I can't consent to live by it! What comfort is it to me that there are none guilty and that cause follows effect simply and directly, and that I know it?—I must have justice,

or I will destroy myself. And not justice in some remote infinite time
and space, but here on earth, and that I could see myself.

The existentialist Russian philosopher Nicholas Berdyaev had precisely
this maximalist Ivan Karamazov in mind when he pilloried the Russian intelligentsia for abandoning the quest for religious, philosophical,
and spiritual truth in favor of a universal justice based on equality
and material need. In *The Brothers Karamazov* Dostoevsky responds to
Ivan's demand for justice by incorporating him, as well as his brothers
Dmitry and Alyosha, into a justice narrative that is situated not in a
remote time and place (Spain of the sixteenth century) but in contemporary Russia. Ivan's brother Dmitry is on trial for a murder he did not
commit, but he is convicted nevertheless and sentenced to twenty years
of hard labor in Siberia. The concrete implementation of justice in the
real world mocks the ideal, even the tainted ideal that Ivan offers in
his poem as a practical replacement for the "impossible" ideal of Christ.

The jury trial in *The Brothers Karamazov* has received scant attention
in comparison to "The Grand Inquisitor," which is frequently excerpted
from the novel and appropriated as an independent, autonomous text
by philosophers, theologians, psychologists, anthropologists, and political scientists. Almost all discussion of justice in Dostoevsky's works
starts—and often ends—with an analysis of "The Grand Inquisitor." The
great philosophical interpretations of Dostoevsky by Vasily Rozanov
and Berdyaev flow directly out of "The Grand Inquisitor," from which
they derive diametrically opposite conclusions about truth and justice.
"The Grand Inquisitor" is "maximalist" Dostoevsky. Christ comes back
to Earth, in Seville of the sixteenth century, to visit his suffering flock.
He is greeted with adoration by the common people and performs
miracles, raising a child from the dead. He meets with a different reception from the church. He is apprehended by the head of the Inqui-
sition, the Grand Inquisitor, who explains to him why he should not
have returned—he is interfering with the good works of the church—
and threatens him with a second execution (not crucifixion but the
stake) if he does not leave immediately or if he returns again. Christ
is silent throughout. He makes just one gesture: he kisses the Grand
Inquisitor on the forehead and leaves.

Because "The Grand Inquisitor" occurs relatively early in the novel,
about a quarter of the way through, not only the trial but much of *The
Brothers Karamazov* may seem anticlimactic. Dostoevsky was concerned

about the section because he feared that he would not be able to counter what he called its logically irrefutable arguments. But any narrative, not to speak of a refutation of Ivan's arguments, was bound to be artistically problematic after "The Grand Inquisitor." Dostoevsky would have to let the reader down from the heights of "The Grand Inquisitor" to a far more prosaic reality. The jury trial is the ultimate prosaics; it is long and lawyerly.

In *Crime and Punishment* Dostoevsky delegates only two pages (in the first chapter of the epilogue) to Raskolnikov's trial, which covers much the same legal ground as the trial in *The Brothers Karamazov*. But in *The Brothers Karamazov* he devotes to the trial the last and longest "book" in the novel, far exceeding in length the chapter that contains the "The Grand Inquisitor." Each lawyer's summation alone, which the narrator says he has abbreviated and summarized to save space, is longer than "The Grand Inquisitor." Most of Dostoevsky's conclave scenes build up gradually before they explode in a sensational event. The trial in *The Brothers Karamazov,* however, concludes with relatively undramatic summations, which the novel continually undercuts or ridicules. Yet for all that, the trial is a fitting companion piece to "The Grand Inquisitor"—a sort of "Grand Inquisitor Redux"—and culmination of the novel. When we view the novel more from the point of view of the trial, we are bound to see a very different *Brothers Karamazov,* for the trial, not "The Grand Inquisitor," represents Dostoevsky's last and perhaps most important statement on the possibilities of justice in the modern world, a world ruled not by terror, intimidation, and violence ("The Grand Inquisitor") but by law.

The jury trial in *The Brothers Karamazov* also represents the culmination of Dostoevsky's passionate engagement with the legal reforms of 1864, which introduced into Russia, among other things, the Western-based jury trial. Dostoevsky became interested in the jury trial as a journalist in the early 1860s when the reforms were being debated in the Russian press. And he briefly incorporated some aspects of the trial process in the epilogue of *Crime and Punishment* (1866).[1] In the 1870s Dostoevsky began to write articles on some of the most famous cases of the day. He even became involved in an actual trial, the Kornilova case, and wrote extensively about the effects of his own interventions. In hindsight the trial in *The Brothers Karamazov* can be seen as the final chapter of still another narrative, related to but independent of *The Brothers Karamazov,* comprising the Kroneberg, Kairova, and

Kornilova cases, in which Dostoevsky utters his final word on the significance of Western judicial reforms for Russian society. Because the notion of responsibility is behind Dostoevsky's presentation of each case, by following the jury trials in his journalism and fiction, we can see the writer gradually working out his mystical notion of responsibility and its relation to salvation. The jury trial brings Dostoevsky's fiction and journalism—the major novels and *Diary of a Writer*—together at the end of his career.

There is still another important reason for studying the jury trial in Dostoevsky's work. For Dostoevsky the Western court was more than a parlous judicial experiment, it was a quintessential institution of the modern world; it had the potential to transform Russia even more radically than Peter the Great had done a century and a half earlier. Dostoevsky probably feared that the court more accurately presaged Russia's future than either the "The Grand Inquisitor" (the negative ideal) or "The Russian Monk" (the positive ideal). However much he hoped Russia could avoid following the path of the West, in the trial scene he explores the consequence for Russia, and for modern society, of the transformation of human beings into legal agents, defined not by their relation to Christ but by their relation to law. Dostoevsky incorporated into the jury trial almost all his essential concerns and passions. In every jury trial he writes about, but of course most prominently in the trial in *The Brothers Karamazov,* the question of Russia and the West is paramount. But so are the Dostoevskian oppositions of Western law and Russian justice, good and evil, responsibility and moral relativism, compassion and egoism, even good and bad art. As Dostoevsky becomes involved in each court case, he increasingly finds himself face to face with the question of his own narrative authority. The book *A Judicial Error* presents Dostoevsky's final—perhaps desperate—attempt to establish the authority of his own artistic word in a world that he fears will be dominated not by the Word but by the word of the law, specifically, the word of contending lawyers and the legal institutions that determine their roles. Ultimately, because *A Judicial Error* is a metanarrative about the artistic word, it represents Dostoevsky's most significant confrontation in his fiction with the role of art and the artist in the modern world. The jury trial is key to understanding not only Dostoevsky's greatest novel but the preoccupations of all his fiction and journalism.

In his excellent study of law in literature, Theodore Ziolkowski argues that in the vast majority of literary works dealing with the law, the existing legal system is generally accepted, not challenged. The focus is on the determination of the facts, which will lead to a more just resolution of the case, that is, to a concordant coincidence of law and justice, or at least of legal procedure and ethical standards. But in the literary masterpieces about the law, it is usually not the facts that are at issue but the law itself, especially "when the law and morality fall out of phase," when there is a division between the law and the ethical standards of the community. "It is at these moments when the tension between law and morality is increased to the breaking point that the law is changed and its evolution lurches forward again. And it is precisely those epoch-making moments that great literature reflects."[2] Ziolkowski makes only two very brief and passing references to Dostoevsky. After performing the by-now necessary analyses of the canonic works for law-in-literature—*The Eumenides, Antigone,* and *The Merchant of Venice*—he devotes almost all his attention to German examples, his field of specialization.

Yet Ziolkowski's idea that great literature that reflects the evolutionary or revolutionary changes in the history of judicial codes or systems is based on questionable assumptions about law and literature. Whether the judicial system in Athens in the fifth-century B.C.E. or in London in the late sixteenth century was really undergoing such critical transformations is not at all certain. It is quite another thing to maintain that the authors he treats *interpreted* the conflict between the law and morality as critical, although such a view again depends on one's interpretation of Aeschylus, Sophocles, and Shakespeare. Most interpretations of *The Merchant of Venice,* for example, do not see the legal issues in the play as particularly problematic, although we may want to see them as problematic today, especially in the way the law is cavalierly used to deal with outsiders who resort to law to advance their own interests. It is difficult to say whether the introduction of the jury system in Russia in 1864 reflected a national crisis comparable to the enormity of serfdom, but almost all educated Russians of the 1860s were aware of the glaring disparity between justice and the law in the pre-reform system. Most would have argued that the critical disjunction between law and ethics in terms of the judicial system was far greater before 1864 than it was after the reforms, when Dostoevsky worked on *The Brothers Karamazov*. Dostoevsky, however, situated the great legal crisis, the absolute bifurcation of morality and law, after

1864. Like Kafka, according to Ziolkowski, Dostoevsky was witnessing, in his own mind, the frightening division of morality and law that scholars see in almost all legal systems in the latest phase of their development.[3] For Dostoevsky this was the most profound crisis of Western civilization, a crisis that threatened everything he cherished. This crisis is what Dostoevsky so brilliantly, and often exasperatingly, portrays in his last journalistic and fictional works on the jury trial.

## Law and Literature

Before giving a brief account of the legal reforms of 20 November 1864, of which the jury trial is the centerpiece, I would like to address in some detail the issues raised by the interdisciplinary work done on the relationship between law and literature that is relevant for a work about Dostoevsky and the jury trial. The situation is complex. Before *The Brothers Karamazov* Dostoevsky used many ideas that we now associate with the law and literature movement, especially those relating to the incorporation of empathy and narrative in the judicial process. But after the Kornilova trial, in which Dostoevsky empathetically interceded in the legal process itself, and the Zasulich trial, at which he was a guest observer, Dostoevsky obviously became more skeptical, one might say, of his own practice. *The Brothers Karamazov* seems like a critique, avant la lettre, of many of the hermeneutic strategies and recommendations of the law and literature movement in the United States, including, among other things, the use of "literature" and literary criticism to advance progressive social and political agendas through the legal system.

It is generally held that the law and literature movement became "a distinct, self-conscious field" only with the publication of James Boyd White's *The Legal Imagination* (1973).[4] The movement has since developed apace, with an increasing number of articles and books published in the area every year. Despite significant overlap, law and literature has two main foci of interest and practice, usually designated as law-in-literature and law-as-literature.[5] *Law-in-literature* attempts to illuminate legal themes or issues in literature (novels, short stories, and plays), often focusing on the depiction of lawyers, courts, and trials. Of the classics, Aeschylus's *The Eumenides,* Shakespeare's *The Merchant of Venice,* Melville's *Billy Budd,* and Kafka's *The Trial* have received the most attention. *Law-as-literature* uses literature and literary criticism as means of informing the practice of law and delving into the intricacies and problems of legal interpretation. Because it focuses on law as text, law-as-literature raises the same questions as literary analysis regarding intention and interpretation. Law-as-literature attempts to illuminate "statutes, constitutions, judicial opinions, and certain scholarly treatises as if they were literary works," that is, as if coterminous with the texts that literary scholars analyze.[6] Those who concentrate on law-as-literature have become particularly interested in issues of narrative, storytelling, and rhetoric in court settings: the arguments of lawyers, the testimony of witnesses, the decisions of judges—that is, law-as-narrative.[7] J. M. Balkin and Sanford Levinson have argued that we should probably discard the law and literature analogy entirely and "replace the study of law as literature with the more general study of law as a performing art."[8] Both the law-in-literature and law-as-literature movements view literature not as an end but as a means. Despite what Richard Posner avers, the law-in-literature enterprise aims primarily to illuminate literary works not for their own sake but to discover insights into the practical, moral, political, and theoretical aspects of law that cannot be properly appreciated or understood through legal analysis alone.[9]

Although jury trials obviously do not figure prominently in literature before the nineteenth century, important examples exist in classic literature, and of course issues of justice are at the center of many of the greatest Greek tragedies. A jury trial, not significantly different from a twentieth-century version, occurs as early as Aeschylus's great fifth-century B.C.E. masterpiece *The Eumenides*. But jury trials start appearing frequently in literary texts only after many European states and principalities, influenced by the French legal system, adopted the jury trial in the nineteenth century. The jury trial that was introduced into Russia in 1864 is patterned after the French model. Thousands of twentieth-century stories, plays, novels, and films feature lawyers and trials. But one must be especially cautious about analyzing trials in literary works as though they were real legal cases. Fictional trials are imaginative recreations filtered through the perspective of often highly biased narrators, who carefully abbreviate, select, and manipulate case material (testimony, evidence, verdicts) for their own aesthetic purposes; such "trials" often reveal more about their creators than about the judicial system that they purport to simulate.[10]

Legal scholars—and even some literary scholars—often argue that
we may achieve in literary texts insight into the law unattainable by
other means.[11] But even if this were so, are legal scholars, by virtue of
their knowledge of the law, more able than literary critics to discover
in literary texts things of importance regarding the larger issues of
justice and the law? It seems not. The numerous articles written by
legal scholars about the trial and the law in Melville's *Billy Budd* are
no more insightful than those written by literary scholars with no legal
training.[12] Indeed, for lawyers to write insightfully about the trial in
*Billy Budd,* they must rely less on their knowledge of the law and perform more like literary critics. Furthermore, the average reader is in
little need of legal expertise to explicate jurisprudential issues in literary texts. Richard Posner is justifiably skeptical about the ability of
experts on the law to shed light on literary works in which lawyers and
trials are prominent, arguing that the intricacies of the law or the
specific strategies of the lawyer are rarely at issue in such works:

> By its very nature, literature—especially great literature—deals with the
> permanent and general aspects of human nature and institutions. Law
> in a general sense is one of those aspects, but in that sense it is not the
> lawyer's law, any more than the private justice system known as revenge
> is lawyer's law. Moreover, law as depicted in literature . . . the legal
> system of Elizabethan England, and even of Periclean Athens are readily
> accessible to a modern understanding. Between, on one hand, the Austro-
> Hungarian procedures reflected in Kafka's *Trial* or the nineteenth-
> century Russian criminal procedures reflected in *Crime and Punishment*
> and *The Brothers Karamazov,* and, on the other hand, modern European
> and even American criminal procedures, the differences, while impor-
> tant to lawyers, would seem small to most lay people.[13]

Posner correctly asserts that both the criminal investigation and trial
in *Crime and Punishment* and *The Brothers Karamazov* pose no significant barriers of understanding to anyone in the least familiar with
Western criminal trial practice. The trials that Dostoevsky describes
and creates differ only in insignificant ways from the typical American
criminal trial, whether in real life, fiction, or film.

Furthermore, the significant differences between the Russian and
American jury trial need to be treated in a literary as well as a judicial context. For example, although Russian juries were encouraged to

reach unanimous decisions, conviction required only a simple majority, with a tie being decided in the favor of the defendant. Thus in *The
Brothers Karamazov* Dmitry Karamazov faced a much tougher jury
than he would have confronted in an American trial: He needed six
votes rather than just one for acquittal. The unanimous decision against
him, given the well-known leniency of Russian juries (*nerepressivnost'*),
emphasizes the decisiveness of the verdict.

The portrayal of legal matters in *The Brothers Karamazov* diverges
from actual Russian practice in other, minor ways, but these too can
be dealt with in the appropriate context. Dmitry, for instance, receives
twenty years for a premeditated parricide. In real life he certainly would
have received a much harsher sentence. But, as we shall see, Dostoevsky
needed a maximum twenty-year sentence so that Dmitry would have
the possibility of rejoining the Russian community after his rehabilitation in prison, an important detail adumbrated in the notebook
plans for the novel. Because Dostoevsky often asked legal experts about
trial details, he obviously knew that in real life a parricide with Dmitry's
profile would have received a more severe sentence. In 1875 a person
convicted of parricide in Staraia Russa, where Dostoevsky had a summer home, was sentenced to life imprisonment. But Dostoevsky needed
Dmitry to be convicted of parricide and to serve a sentence of twenty
years. Dostoevsky had to sacrifice legal accuracy for novelistic truth.[14]

I intend to provide only a brief summary of the major elements of
the judicial reforms of 1864 here.[15] I will deal with specific aspects of
the reform and its effects and provide "thick description" (the creation
of a bar, the social complexion and behavior of Russian juries, expert
testimony, the testimony of close relatives, the Zasulich assassination
attempt, the sensationalization of murder trials in the press, among
other things) when doing so is relevant for illuminating the political,
moral, social, and aesthetic issues at hand. Dostoevsky uses the jury
trial as a means to an end; it is always a symptom of larger forces working themselves out in Russian society.

While it is doubtful that legal scholars either as legal experts or
literary critics can illuminate the issues of law and the jury trial in
Dostoevsky any better than literary critics untrained in the law, the
issue of lawyers interpreting literature is of the utmost importance for
Dostoevsky, especially in *The Brothers Karamazov,* where the lawyers
for the defense and the prosecution resort to literary criticism, in the
Russian progressive tradition, to advance their cases before the jury

and the Russian public. At the cornerstone of each lawyer's summation is a critique of Gogol's *Dead Souls* and an attempt to rewrite the ending of the novel in a more progressive fashion. Here literary criticism functions in the courtroom much as it did in many Russian contemporary "thick" journals, as a means of advancing social or political ends. As the boundary between law-in-literature and law-as-literature blurs, a more important distinction arises: that between law-for-literature (the analysis of literary texts) and literature-for-law (the exploitation of literature in real legal contexts). For legal studies the literary analysis of legal issues in fiction is almost always an instance of literature-for-law rather than law-for-literature. When literary analysis goes beyond explication de texte, beyond the discussion of explicitly legal issues, and, even more important, when it approaches the understanding of legal issues in literary texts as a means of informing legal practice and effecting legal reform, then we are obviously dealing more with literature-for-law than with law-for-literature. Because at different times Dostoevsky both exploited (the Kornilova case) and excoriated (*The Brothers Karamazov*) literature-for-law, outlining the specific forms that literature-for-law takes in the literature and law movement is worthwhile.

For many years James Boyd White has advocated that lawyers study literature not so much for the insight it may provide into the law but because it expands lawyers' intellectual and moral capacities as human beings and thus makes them potentially better lawyers.[16] Richard Weisberg writes: "My suggestion, speaking from within, is to emphasize from now on the central place of the literary text—more than literary theory—in the debates. . . . Novels about law, as I have suggested, and particularly 'procedural novels,' are the path to human understanding."[17] In supporting her earlier work with literature, Robin West writes: "Literature helps us understand others. Literature helps us empathize with their pain, it helps us to share their sorrow, and it helps us celebrate their joy. It makes us more moral. It makes us better people"—and thus, presumably again, better lawyers.[18] In almost all his fiction, starting with *The Insulted and the Injured* (1861), Dostoevsky expresses serious doubts about the Schillerian idea of sentimental education—that literature makes us moral and better individuals. Many of Dostoevsky's criminals are well educated and conversant with the monuments of world literature. Dmitry Karamazov argues, using himself as a prime example, that man is as at home with the beauty of Sodom and Gomorrah as with the beauty of the Madonna. In *The Brothers*

*Karamazov* literary knowledge certainly does not make lawyers better people; it just gives them an additional weapon to exploit in an adversarial system that emphasizes verbal combat among attorneys.

When literature and law—in fact, all cultural life—constitute interpretable texts to which the same hermeneutic strategies can be applied, the lawyer will have no qualms about treating law—even life—as though it were literature and literature as though it were law.[19] Both law and literature concern themselves "with matters of ambiguity, interpretation, abstraction, and humanistic judgment."[20] This erasure of boundaries between law and literature has different implications for the interpretation of literature than it does for the practice of law. With regard to the interpretation of literature, it opens the doors for lawyers to do literary criticism under the guise of doing law. One need not even confine oneself to works that focus on trials or legal procedures. Viewing law as an essential part of a cultural web that embraces the social and the political, many legal scholars tackle works in which the legal system figures only as an implicit subject.[21] One could never guess, for example, that White's analysis of Jane Austen's *Mansfield Park* was written by someone with legal expertise; it has almost nothing to do with law. But if all culture constitutes a superstructure suspended over deep legal structures, White's literary criticism, even though unrelated to any specific legal issues, can be about and for the law in a higher sense—to borrow a phrase from Dostoevsky. Because law is, like language, the means by which we see and relate to the world, all life must be as much about law as it is about language, for nothing represented in literature can lie outside the law. Kevin Crotty does not see his discussion of legal theory, which is centered on Aeschylus's *Oresteia*, St. Augustine's *Confessions*, and the poetry of Wallace Stevens, as an interdisciplinary approach at all:

> The term apparently presupposes that the law is a well-bounded "discipline." That is in fact just what I want to dispute; I want to situate law within the social amalgam of which it is such a vital and pervasive part. . . . The *jurisprudential* point of studying law through literature is to emphasize these multiple and intricate connections between law and the world around and within it. . . . Law and literature makes the assertion that literature is essential to our understanding of the law.[22]

Indeed, many analyses that go under the guise of law and literature are

primarily cultural studies that require no legal training and might be
done no less perceptively by sociologists, political scientists, psychologists, or philosophers.

For Dostoevsky the dangerous aspect of the idea of law and literature as virtually indistinguishable cultural practices was not for literary criticism. Dostoevsky would probably have been amused by the
idea that legal scholars would want to occupy themselves with literary
criticism for the sake of either moral self-improvement or a disinter-
ested study of literature itself. He was more concerned with lawyers'
exploitation of art and literature in the courtroom. If all law is literature, why should lawyers not use the methods of literature and literary criticism to advance their cases, especially in Russia, where literary
criticism was already being exploited to promote social and political
causes? Prominent Russian lawyers came to view and publish their
summations as literary creations. As Robert M. Cover states: "No set
of legal institutions or prescriptions exists apart from the narratives
that locate it and give it meaning. For every constitution there is an
epic, for every decalogue, a scripture."[23] And thus for every legal case,
there exists an appropriate exploitable narrative: whether it be, as in
*The Brothers Karamazov*, a "novel" of the lawyer's own invention or
the adaptation of a biblical text.[24] It is important to emphasize that
Dostoevsky presents the prosecuting and defense lawyers not just as
rhetoricians but as literary creators and critics who use the devices of
the psychological novel and the methods of progressive Russian literary criticism to advance their cases. One might facetiously rename "A
Judicial Error," the title of the last book of *The Brothers Karamazov*, as
"An Error of Novelistic Imagination or Literary Criticism," for neither
of the lawyers' forays in literature and literary criticism succeeds at
influencing the jury. But that is because Dostoevsky packs the court
with like-thinking peasant jurors, not because lawyers in other famous
trials were unsuccessful at exploiting art to achieve acquittals. On the
contrary, their success is precisely what Dostoevsky is reacting to. The
quality of the art, Dostoevsky understood, was not always commensurate with its success. After all, the literary criticism and fiction of the
radical critic Nikolai Chernyshevsky were always more popular and
influential than Dostoevsky's, despite Dostoevsky's efforts in *Notes from
the Underground* and *Crime and Punishment* to make Chernyshevsky's
work seem naive and ridiculous.[25] Although Vladimir Lenin was overwhelmed by *Crime and Punishment*, it did not at all prevent him from

adopting the title of Dostoevsky's bête noire *What Is to Be Done* for the dictator's most important work on the Communist Party. To some extent *The Brothers Karamazov* represents another attempt by Dostoevsky to get even with the radical critics by taking their literary fiction and criticism to court. Further, by portraying the lawyers as artists, he is much better able to alert his readers to the danger that lawyers present and to compete with them artistically for the hearts and minds of the Russian people.

Dostoevsky flirted with (even exploited) and then turned against another prominent focus of the law and literature movement: using literary techniques and strategies rather than traditional rhetorical ones to influence the emotions, sensitivities, and sensibilities of the jury. In the critical legal studies movement, lawyers and legal scholars have been drawn to literature partly out of frustration with what they perceive to be the structural limitations of the law.[26] The law is too formal and impersonal, lacking in empathy and vision, and insensitive to the ethical and moral contexts of real life.[27] Why could not literature provide a corrective? Peter Goodrich expresses his dissatisfaction with the deification of the law in the legal profession and declares his desire to go beyond the rule of law to achieve a new vision of law, in which literature may have to play an indispensable role:

> It has long been my belief that law is the most disabling or estranged of professions. Such at least is its most radical danger: it inculcates a fear which finds its most prominent expression in the closure of the legal mind, in the lawyer's belief in a norm or rule which speaks as 'the law'. In place of that faith I have tried to argue for a series of minor jurisprudences and specifically for a right to a life—to a literature, a poetry, an ethics, an intimacy of imagination—within law. . . . It has been my experience, time and again, that the faith or dogma of law, its distance from its subject, person or emotion, is precisely what precludes the dialogue or the attention to singularity which justice or ethics requires.[28]

Once justice and ethics are brought up, we are not far from going from a deeper understanding of the law, achieved through literature, to a more practical approach to the daily business of law informed by literary methods, especially narrative empathy.[29]

But literature, especially in the courtroom, can be a two-edged sword. Those with a nonmajoritarian social agenda should be especially wary of urging lawyers to hone their rhetorical prowess in the courtroom. Superior rhetorical skills will more often be used against their causes than for them. Dostoevsky recognizes that the best lawyers are often great artists, and their potential to perpetrate evil in the courtroom is directly related to their talent. In *The Brothers Karamazov,* where the lawyers are equally matched rhetoricians, they fight to a draw, but in other instances, as in the Kroneberg case, Dostoevsky shows the harm that can occur whenever the rhetorical abilities of the lawyers are unequal.

Dostoevsky is equally suspicious of using narratives of "literary empathy" in the courtroom. At the end of the 1980s lawyers and legal scholars called for law to be more inclusive, to restore the voices of minorities and outsiders, by paying more attention to context ("back to context"), by becoming more empathetic, and by using narrative (storytelling) in legal proceedings.[30] The proponents of this view, Toni M. Massaro writes, fear that the law "may lead to a disregard for individuals, and may exalt logical consistency and predictability over compassion and substantive justice. Therefore, the writers urge, lawyers, judges, and scholars should not suppress emotions and experiential understanding. Empathy, human stories, and different voices should be woven into the tapestry of legal scholarship, legal training, law formulation, legal counseling and advocacy, and law application and enforcement."[31] Michael Ryan argues that "power is exercised through narrative," and "alternative narrative can disrupt that power either by undermining narrative itself or by generating new visions and alternate world constructions."[32] But as Massaro pointed out in 1988, advocates of narrative empowerment in judicial settings can hold these views only when empathy and narrative support their political agendas. "When pared to its roots, the 'empathy' theme therefore seems not to call for more empathy, but for a different ordering of our empathetic responses. . . . Adherence to 'law for law's sake' therefore poses a problem *only* if one deems that particular law or its application to be foolish, cruel, narrow, or shortsighted."[33] Because most judges represent majoritarian points of view, they tend to empathize with insiders and be less receptive to the stories of outsiders.[34] If anything, one of the main criticisms traditionally lodged against American or English common law, as opposed to Roman civil law (which is more formal, structured, rational, and rule bound), is that it is too arbitrary and leaves too much discretion to judges.[35]

The trial scene in *The Brothers Karamazov* directly addresses the

abuse of empathy and narrative in the courtroom. The lawyers for the
prosecution and defense devise elaborate psychological narratives (novels) aimed at eliciting the jury's sympathies for or against the defendant. Each lawyer accuses his opponent of writing a psychological
novel about the defendant. But the use of narrative is done less in the
interest of the state or the defendant than in the interest of the lawyers
themselves, who wish to display their talents in the courtroom to a
national audience. In the end, empathy, storytelling, orality, and emotion become tools for personal and professional self-aggrandizement.

Among those with strong social and political agendas, as with some
in the critical legal studies movement, literature can progress from
being an empathetic and moral force to a subversive body of texts and
procedures that can influence social action and public policy, often
through the exploitation of postmodern hermeneutic strategies such
as deconstruction. Ian Ward states, "If law and literature is to maxi-
mize its potential as an educative and perhaps as a socio-political
force, then it must acknowledge the functionalist author-text-reader
relationship."[36] Expanding on this idea, Robert Weisberg outlines his
vision of what social and political form the law and literature enterprise should take:

> I would argue that as with the implication of an organic view of cul-
> ture, the unity of discourse argument is a potentially subversive one, and
> that law-literature writers accomplish little if they do not address this
> potential subversion. . . . The revelation of a connection between dis-
> parate forms of discourse is really illuminating only when discomfiting,
> or, better yet, subversive, because subversion of the *apparent* structure
> of a culture is precisely what this sort of "social text" approach can con-
> tribute. . . . Little may be accomplished by the law-literature connec-
> tion—or at least the law-*as*-literature connection—unless one is willing
> to commit us to some of the political or critical consequences of the
> connection.[37]

The use of literature to advance one's progressive political agenda
has a long history in Russia. Under the Soviets the exploitation of literature to promote political and social goals became state policy. They
formulated a literary method, socialist realism, to better realize those
goals.[38] But the Soviets were merely taking to their conclusions the
notions and practices of progressive and radical thinkers and literary

critics of Dostoevsky's time. In *The Brothers Karamazov* Dostoevsky
exposes the lawyers' use of narrative, empathy, and even the analysis
of literary and religious texts for advancing their political views in
court. Dostoevsky's representation of the lawyers in *The Brothers Karamazov* stands in stark opposition to White's and Dworkin's view of the
artist-lawyer or artist-judge, who, perfectly combining aesthetics and
morality, becomes a star of the community, a true political artist.[39]

The question of what literature is suitable for law and how it should
be used is certainly complex. Many of the "canonic" classics present
considerable problems for the activists and progressives of the law
and literature movement, for the classics rarely give or even attempt
answers or solutions. They invariably become unfinalizably interpretable. Robin West wishes to see Kafka's *The Trial* as a critique of Western law and legal institutions, especially the effects that they have on
the psyche of the average citizen, but others of a more conservative
bent can just as easily interpret Kafka's ambiguities to support the
opposite—conservative—conclusions. Pace Richard Weisberg, Dostoevsky is hardly exploitable material for law and literature, especially
because *The Brothers Karamazov* explicitly presents a critique of many
main ideas of the movement.[40] Second, the conservative moral, social,
and political underpinnings of *Diary of a Writer, Crime and Punishment,*
and *The Brothers Karamazov* are, as we shall see, not easily amenable
to radical appropriation. The aim of radical critical studies critique is
to expose ideology, to reveal the discourse of power beneath the veneer
of seemingly liberal—not openly conservative—rhetoric.

And as a conservative becoming disenchanted with the 1864 legal
reforms, which granted Russians greater participation in the judicial
process, Dostoevsky subjected to a blistering critique one of the few
Russian laws enfranchising previously excluded groups of citizens
(peasants, merchants, and intelligentsia). It is not only that Dostoevsky
is poor grist for political exploitation on the left but that he sometimes
uses the same deconstructionist techniques of the legal studies movement for conservative ends. *The Brothers Karamazov* implicitly questions
statutes and decisions promoting inclusion.[41] What is more, Dostoevsky often gives the same reasons for his attacks on the system as do
the representatives of the critical legal studies movement, namely, that
the liberal legal system substitutes reason for spirit, form for substance, and rule for context. The ends meet.

But as Dostoevsky shows, the incommensurability of literary material does not constitute an insuperable barrier to the exploitation of literature in the courtroom. In *The Brothers Karamazov* the liberal lawyers misappropriate and rewrite a conservative writer, Gogol, for their own ends. Also, Fetyukovich, Dmitry Karamazov's defense lawyer, quotes from Dostoevsky's own work to support the legal position that Dmitry should be acquitted of parricide. In *The Brothers Karamazov* Dostoevsky subverts the idea of exploiting both the content and methods of literature and literary analysis for high moral purposes in legal settings, although, as we shall see, he may also subvert his own literary methods in so doing.

Nor it is easy for legal activists to deconstruct Dostoevsky, especially the trial scene in *The Brothers Karamazov,* that is, to use him against his ostensible intentions, to show that his articles and novels about the jury trial support interpretations that are diametrically opposed to their rhetoric. In any case, a deconstruction that would present the jury in *The Brothers Karamazov* in a much more positive light than Dostoevsky portrays it would prove counterproductive for those with a radical judicial agenda, because Dostoevsky is attacking the post-reform system precisely because it gives minority points of view an empathetic forum from which to publicly express views that minorities could not express elsewhere.

## The 1864 Reform

The new jury trial introduced into Russia on 20 November 1864 marked the end of a fourteen-year period of debates, proposals, study, and political maneuvering regarding the reorganization of the entire judicial system. The new courts, primarily modeled after the French and German, replaced an antiquated, inefficient, inept, and most of all corrupt system based on closed hearings, written proceedings, inquisitorial investigatory style, and a presumption of guilt.[42] Judges were often illiterate, lawyers untrained; cases dragged on for generations, and bribery was accepted practice everywhere.[43] It is perhaps even misleading to call what existed before 1864 a judicial system. Richard Pipes, though a severe critic of all aspects of the tsarist government, has with some justice compared pre-reform Russia, which had no real law code, to ancient Asian monarchies in which royal officials dispensed justice as part of their administrative duties: "Russia knew nothing of independent justice. Justice was a branch of the administration, and as such its foremost concern was enforcing the government's will and protecting its interest. . . . Indeed, most of the fundamental laws affecting Russia's system of government and the status of its citizens were never at all promulgated in any formal way."[44]

As a result of the 1864 reforms, jury trials were opened to the public (*glasnost'*). The judicial system attained autonomy. The court relied much less on recorded documentation and more on oral testimony and argument (*ustnost'*). Investigations were still carried out by an organ of the administration (and thus were inquisitorial in nature),[45] but through the incorporation of adversarial (*sostiazatel'nye*) principles—sometimes referred to as accusatorial or controversial styles—jury trials gave increased representation and rights to the defendant.[46] Jury justice replaced emperor's justice (*koronnyi sud*). Juries became the most representative of all Russian institutions, with jurors recruited from all sectors of the population. An independent judiciary became well established; bribery was effectively eliminated; more and more lawyers became trained and rose to distinction; and Russian juries on the whole acted responsibly, turning out to be far less lenient than feared by some reform detractors.[47]

To understand Dostoevsky's position regarding the judicial reforms, we must see it in the context of their reception—as well as the assessment of the pre-reform system—among Dostoevsky's contemporaries. Dostoevsky's struggle was not only with what he believed was actually going on in the new courts but with how the general public perceived the reforms and how the media portrayed them. As time went on, the battle for the courts became increasingly ideological, and Dostoevsky's articles in *Diary of a Writer* and the last book of *The Brothers Karamazov* mark his full engagement in this foray. Dostoevsky was not attacking an easy target; the new judicial system was frequently eulogized, occasionally even by conservatives.

In any case, almost all were in agreement about the defects of the old system. Alexander Herzen was obviously resorting to hyperbole in characterizing the pre-reform court experience as worse than the punishment itself, but he nevertheless was accurately singling out one of greatest abuses of the pre-reform courts. "So great are the disorder, brutality, arbitrariness, and corruption of the Russian court and the Russian police, that a man brought to trial fears not the punishment of the court, but the trial. He looks forward to being sent to Siberia.

His martyrdom ends with the beginning of the punishment."[48] Focusing on other abuses of the pre-reform court, A. F. Koni, the most
famous jurist of the second half of the nineteenth century, who began
his career at the time of the reforms, recalled the rampant illiteracy
among court officials, from the lowest clerks to the highest judges:

> The law itself sanctioned the composition of courts (magistrate and
> aulic) in which all the judges were illiterate, prescribing that in these
> cases the decision of the judges must be written down by the secretary.
> In district courts, in which the majority of the justices were also illiter-
> ate, the cases were almost never reported to the bench. . . . In the early
> forties, among all the members of the seven Departments of the Senate
> in Petersburg, only six senators had received a university education.[49]

Even I. S. Aksakov, a prominent spokesman of the Slavophiles, a conservative group that looked askance at importing Western institutions,
recoiled at the memory of the judicial system's endemic ineptitude and
corruption: "Through what torments, what anguish our soul had to
pass, realizing how impossible it was to further justice because of the
fetters and nets of the judicial procedure of that time!"[50]

Initially, the elite held some skepticism about whether the jury system could work in a country as backward as Russia. Some conservatives and progressive thinkers agreed with the English philosopher
Herbert Spencer, who, writing in 1850, scouted the possibility of a successful jury system in Russia:

> That justice can be well administered only in proportion as man be-
> comes just, is a fact too generally overlooked. "If they had but trial by
> jury!" says some one, moralizing on the Russians. But they can't have it.
> It could not exist among them. Even if established it would not work.
> They lack that substratum of honesty and truthfulness on which alone
> it can stand. To be of use, this, like any other institution, must be born
> of the popular character. It is not trial by jury that produces justice, but
> it is sentiment of justice that produces trial by jury, as the organ through
> which it is to act; and the organ will be inert unless the sentiment is
> there.[51]

After the implementation of the reforms, most commentators agreed
that the doubts, both foreign and Russian, about the viability of the

upcoming reforms, were misplaced. Although the trial by jury could never measure up to the rhetoric with which it was at first advocated, it continued to enjoy widespread support among the population and was generally viewed, especially by liberals, as perhaps the only Russian institution that could draw favorable comparison with Western practice.[52] In the 1880s, when the reforms came under sharp attack from the right, Aksakov wrote a brilliant and controversial article reminding detractors of the enormous progress that the legal system had made in just two decades:

> Our Russian public has a strikingly short memory. . . . Are we really so forgetful that we completely lost the memory of what the old court was, less than a quarter of a century ago? . . . There was no light in the darkness of injustice! . . . Court and injustice were synonyms in the mind of the people. . . . Injustice was a kind of inescapable feature in our life. . . . Our boldest dreams did not go so far as to assume that a court completely without bribes—ah, but for a court without bribes!—could exist in our fatherland. And such a court became possible. What a miracle! . . . And not only possible—it exists in reality! This is not an assumption, not a dream. It is our reality, which is understood by the *entire* people! The fact that the contemporary judges do not accept bribes, that one can approach them without presents, that poverty is not a vice in the eyes of the court, that there is equal justice for the poor and oppressed and for the rich and the noble—this fact at the present time is known in all corners of Russia, to every peasant on the immeasurable expanse of our country. The young generations of a hundred million people are now being brought up in this spirit. And we, we ourselves, are suddenly shouting at, spitting on, abusing and trampling upon the tool of our resurrection—as though we were possessed—the very institution which dragged us out of the malodorous mire where we were stuck almost up to our heads . . . this "new court" which in only twenty years has already succeeded in pushing the old, godless iniquity into the background of our memory and even knocking it out of there. . . . Yes, our memory is short![53]

The conservative Aksakov's rhetoric may give some indication of the rhetorical challenge facing Dostoevsky, for Aksakov speaks in Dostoevskian populist and religious terms. The old court was not only a travesty of justice, it was a godless mire of sin and corruption. By contrast, the new court is educating the people in a new spirit. It has outpaced Russia's "boldest dreams." It can be described as nothing but a miracle. But most important, of course, especially in light of Dostoevsky's attack in *The Brothers Karamazov,* Aksakov views the court as the most important tool in the nation's spiritual resurrection. The Western court is, as it were, essential to the "Russian soul."

Most scholarship on the 1864 judicial reforms has focused on their origins: the particular political and social situation that gave rise to them, the provenance of specific aspects of the final laws, and the ideological debates surrounding them. After the reforms were enacted, Dostoevsky, like most Russians, was obviously more concerned with their implementation in Russia life. Therefore in the chapters that follow, I will be incorporating important insights of Girish Bhat's work on the 1864 reforms, which focuses on actual trials from the introduction of the jury trial in 1866 to Alexander the Second's death in 1881.[54] Questioning whether "the judicial statutes of 1864" constitute a "reliable guide to the actual operation of the new judicial system thereafter," he deals with the actual or experienced law (what actually happens to defendants in the system) rather than with normative law (what is supposed to happen according to the codified statutes), revealing more of what Dostoevsky must have observed in court as a daily reality, that is, the actual operations of the court and the peculiarly Russian implementation of its new laws, "the procedural realities of daily ordinary adjudication."[55] Because Dostoevsky deals with actual trials in *Diary of a Writer* and the transformations of those trials in *The Brothers Karamazov,* it will be necessary at times to focus on the discrepancies between normative and experienced law that bear on Dostoevsky's portrayal, both positive and negative, of the jury trial system. Dostoevsky does not give an unbiased view of court reform; on the other hand, there were in reality serious differences between the letter and spirit of the law and its implementation under Alexander II that accounted for at least some of Dostoevsky's disillusionment with the direction that the jury trial had taken in the late 1870s.

## Dostoevsky and the 1864 Reform

It is also interesting to view Dostoevsky's portrayal of the reforms in *Diary of a Writer* and *The Brothers Karamazov* against what he wrote in the early 1860s and what he expressed in his private correspondence. Because Dostoevsky was under strict observation of the secret police when the legal reforms were being hotly debated in the early 1860s, it is not surprising that we have no direct pronouncements on the reforms under his signature from that time. But because he was the de facto editor of several journals (*Vremia* and *Epokha*), we can probably assume that their cautious, but basically favorable, attitude toward the legal reforms reflected Dostoevsky's own views. Nor would such views be in any way unusual because, as we have seen, most opinion, and not only on the left, generally favored the proposed system.[56] We do have an important notebook entry from September 1864, in which Dostoevsky argues that Russia need not wait until it has everything in place to implement the legal reforms; in practice, the reforms will create the needed foundations. But Russia needs to stop talking or nothing will ever get done: something needs to be done right away. In any case, whatever is created will not be as bad as the old courts (*vo vsiakom sluchae khuzhe prezhnikh sudov ne budet*).[57]

In the first years after the reforms, Dostoevsky occasionally spoke favorably of the jury trial. On 16 August 1867, for example, he writes his friend Apollon Maykov:

> It is extraordinary how much strength and maturity the people have shown in receiving all our reforms (even if one takes only the judicial ones). . . . By God, our age, with regard to great changes and reforms, is hardly less important than that of Peter the Great. And what about the railroads? We must get down to the south quickly, as quickly as possible; the whole thing hinges on that. By that time we will have *just courts* everywhere. What a great regeneration that will be. Over here, I keep thinking and dreaming of all these things, and my heart beats faster over it. (28.2:206)

A few months later, on 9 October 1867, he again writes Maykov, reiterating his faith in the people and their role in the new courts:

> I so long to return to Russia. I would particularly like to have my say in print about the Umetsky case. As soon as I arrive in Russia, I'll immediately go to the trials and so on. Our juries are the very best; but regarding our judges, one would like to see more education and experience; and in addition, higher moral principles. Without that kind of

foundation, nothing will become firmly established. But thank God, it
is still going well. (28.2:228)

Dostoevsky's wife, Anna Grigoryevna, recalled that Dostoevsky "would
often be both enraptured and touched by the just and intelligent
sentences" of the Russian juries and "would always relate to me the
important information about the courts which he had read in the
newspapers."[58]

In *The Idiot* Dostoevsky makes several references to the practices of
unscrupulous lawyers, one of whom, Lebedev, is a central character.[59]
But the few references to the newly established courts are quite positive. Prince Myshkin, on returning to Russia, says that he has heard
many good things about Russian courts (8:19). And later in the novel
Prince S. refers to a conversation he had with Myshkin, who spoke
positively about the new law courts: "'My dear prince,' continued
Prince S. 'Remember what we discussed two or three months ago: we
remarked that in our newly opened courts one could already find so
many remarkable and talented lawyers! And there have been so many
wise verdicts from our juries! You were so pleased, and how happy I
was to see your joy. We said that it was something we could be proud
of [*My govorili, chto gordit'sia mozhem*]'" (8:279).

But, as *The Brothers Karamazov* and his articles on the Kairova and
Kroneberg cases clearly show, in the 1870s Dostoevsky grew more skeptical about the value of the jury trial for Russia—and the new judicial
system of which it was the showpiece. He never, however, explicitly
advocated a return to the pre-reform judicial system. If pressed, he
would probably have begrudgingly acknowledged that the new court
system was preferable to the one it replaced.

The vitriol that Dostoevsky displays toward the jury trial in *The
Brothers Karamazov* almost certainly derives from his outrage at the
result of the Zasulich case, the most famous Russian trial of the nineteenth century, in which a young woman who tried to kill the munic-
ipal governor of St. Petersburg, a Gen. F. F. Trepov, was, to the surprise
of most observers, found not guilty of a crime to which she had virtually confessed. The Zasulich affair probably gave Dostoevsky the idea
of incorporating a jury trial in *The Brothers Karamazov*, using it as a
means of filtering all his ideas about art, justice, good and evil, salvation, Russia, and the West. *The Brothers Karamazov* marks the point at
which the attack directed against the Western evils infiltrating Russia

and jeopardizing the Russian people moves from his journalism back into his fiction. The site chosen for the attack is the courtroom.

## The Cases

In the first chapter of my study, which is devoted to Dostoevsky's articles on the Kroneberg case, I show how Dostoevsky presents the jury trial, the centerpiece of the new legal reforms, as a corrupter of native Russian values. The first part of the Kroneberg chapter is devoted to two of the most important issues related to the reform of 1864: the court as a forum for educating the Russian public, and the creation of a professional bar based on an adversarial system. As I have noted, some original detractors of the judicial reforms argued that the jury trial could not be successful in Russia because the Russian public was insufficiently prepared. The supporters of the reform, however, saw the new judicial system as the best way of spiritually, intellectually, and morally educating the Russian people; it would become the nation's premier educational system, turning subjects into citizens. Instead of reinforcing the moral underpinnings of Russian society and providing a moral education for the Russian public, Dostoevsky attempted to show how the new system undermined Russian values by subordinating the questions of good and evil to questions of law. When defendants who have committed crimes are acquitted because of technicalities in the law or the prowess of their attorneys, the courts only confuse the Russian public by calling into question their moral standards. To Dostoevsky, for the courts to be effective in educating Russian society, they must first be able at least to distinguish between good and evil and call crimes by their rightful names; only then should they consider the extenuating circumstances that may alleviate sentences.

Dostoevsky in large part attributes the moral failure of the reformed court to the professionalization of the Russian bar and the introduction of the adversarial system. Usually, those on the left are more critical of institutions and those on the right more critical of individuals. A traditional conservative, Gogol attributes the failure of Russian institutions not to inherent defects in the institutions themselves but to the fallible human beings who run them. Dostoevsky surprisingly directs his strongest criticism not at the legal actors but at the legal institutions. For thousands of years writers have excoriated the instrumental tactics and utilitarian ethics of lawyers. Dostoevsky is no exception. But curiously, he places far greater blame on the bar than on the lawyers who make up the bar; he sees lawyers as prisoners of the system, bound, as champions of their clients and abusers of hostile witnesses, to act contrary to their conscience and therefore contrary to the interests of society. But it is not only the lawyers who are the prisoners of the system. I show Dostoevsky's attempt to portray the deleterious effect of the jury trial on all those who participate in the legal process, helplessly playing out their roles in a system over which they have no control and in which the institution, to the detriment of all Russian society, emerges as the only victor.

The second half of the chapter on the Kroneberg case is devoted to the role of art in the courtroom, one of the central issues of the trial scene in *The Brothers Karamazov*. Dostoevsky does mean art as rhetoric, the science cultivated since the ancient Greeks as a tool for lawyers arguing their cases in the courts. He sees lawyers as artists, not rhetoricians, and in his articles in *Diary of a Writer* he sets himself up as a rival artist in order to undo the damage that the lawyers have done in the courtroom as artists. In any case, what may be construed as a metaphor in *Diary of a Writer* is realized in *The Brothers Karamazov*, where each lawyer creates (*sochiniaet*) a novel based on Dmitry's character and the murder of Fedor Karamazov. Nothing seems to upset Dostoevsky more than the presence of artist-lawyers in the new reform courts. Because lawyers will exploit any device to advance their client's interest, the best of them—the artist-lawyers—are bound to abuse their artistic talent. Avant la lettre, Dostoevsky subjects art in the courtroom to a Tolstoyan analysis. He has no doubt that the art of the lawyer is art because it is unquestionably infectious. But it is bad—morally defective—art in the Tolstoyan sense because it undermines important Russian moral values. In combination with the formalistic procedures of the jury trial and the professionalization of the bar ushered in by the 1864 legal reforms, artistry in the courtroom becomes a subtle tool in the hands of lawyers, willy-nilly furthering a Western legalist, rational, and formalistic agenda against the spiritual, moral, and religious ideals of the Russian people.

Although no mention is made in the Kroneberg articles of the central issue of Dostoevsky's fiction, salvation, it is implicit throughout. If the salvation of the world depends on its acceptance of the faith of the Russian people, the only people who have kept in their hearts the image of the true Christ, anything that undermines their faith jeopardizes not only the salvation of Russia but all European civilization. While the article on Kroneberg constitutes a catalogue of the dangers threatening the sole remaining bastion of faith in Christendom, the Russian people, the four articles that Dostoevsky wrote on the Kornilova jury trial, the focus of the second chapter, directly address the salvific possibilities for Russia that Dostoevsky explores at great length in *The Brothers Karamazov*. The Kornilova articles seem at first to undercut some of Dostoevsky's most strongly argued positions in the Kroneberg case. In the Kroneberg case Dostoevsky excoriated Kroneberg's lawyer for vigorously defending a child beater; in the Kornilova case Dostoevsky defends a woman who threw her stepdaughter out of a fourth-story window. When Dostoevsky read about Kornilova's case, he envisioned the defendant as a monster whose crime was far more heinous than Kroneberg's; however, the more he became acquainted with the details of Kornilova's crime, the more he began to redirect his attention from the crime to the rehabilitation—the resurrection from the dead—of the penitent criminal. Whereas in the Kroneberg case the jury trial represented in microcosm all the ills of Western civilization that were endangering the Russian people, the Kornilova trial became the site for a communal religious experience in which all the trial actors came together, despite their adversarial roles and functions, to make possible the moral regeneration of a Christian soul. Dostoevsky views what happened at the Kornilova trial as a miracle, that is, as an event that took place despite the court rather than because of it. But that does not diminish the community that was achieved in the Western courtroom. If in the Kroneberg case Dostoevsky exploits the jury trial to advance his anti-Western agenda, in the Kornilova case he no less exploits the jury trial to convey his vision of Christian salvation. I show that Dostoevsky was able to achieve this vision of community in the courtroom because the fashioners of the 1864 reforms deliberately incorporated Russian customs and religious ideas into the jury trial procedures as a means of naturalizing them, making the system more acceptable to the majority of the population—a point that Dostoevsky invariably conceals. I also hope to demonstrate that despite Dostoevsky's specific intentions, it is quite possible to read his articles on Kornilova deconstructively, that is, to show that Kornilova was saved not in spite of but because of the Western court and that salvation could not have been achieved otherwise.

The Kornilova case differed radically from the Kroneberg case in still another way: Dostoevsky became personally involved with the defendant and her cause. His article in *Diary of a Writer* played a crucial role in Kornilova's retrial and acquittal, and he visited Kornilova in prison and in her home after her release. The problems that the artist faces as he becomes an actor in the judicial process make the Kornilova case much more complicated than the Kroneberg case. But Dostoevsky was not the only famous writer to champion a criminal and succeed in gaining the person's acquittal or release from prison. In chapter 3, I compare and contrast the relationships of William Styron, William Buckley, and Normal Mailer to their client-wards and Dostoevsky's relationship with Kornilova to illuminate Dostoevsky's peculiar understanding of the relationship between responsibility and salvation. Dostoevsky's mysticism comes with a strong dose of consequence ethics.

The chapters devoted to the Kroneberg and Kornilova cases show that the court could have been interpreted as a site of perdition (Western law) or salvation (Russian justice) to Dostoevsky when he imagined Dmitry's fate in his last novel. It is nevertheless surprising to see the sharpness of the turn that occurred between the Kornilova case and *The Brothers Karamazov,* in which we find Dostoevsky's most scathing representation of the jury trial and the Western legal system. It takes to their extreme conclusions all the criticisms that he lodged against the jury trial in Kroneberg. In chapter 4, I examine the methods that Dostoevsky uses to undermine all the actors of the jury trial, including the judge, expert witnesses, spectators, and lawyers for both the prosecution and defense. Because the prosecutor and defense attorney are both functionaries of the same system, Dostoevsky can pursue his anti-Western agenda just as vigorously with one as with the other. Sensing the possibility of interpreting his articles on Kornilova as paeans to the Western jury trial—which is exactly what Fetyukovich, Dmitry's lawyer, figures out—Dostoevsky attempts to make his demolition of the jury trial in *The Brothers Karamazov* "deconstruction-proof" by eliminating the possibility of reinterpreting the rhetoric of the novel against itself. In chapter 4, I try to illuminate Dostoevsky's radical turn against the jury trial by presenting it in the political and social context of the time, especially the Vera Zasulich trial, which probably confirmed all Dostoevsky's fears about the Western trial by jury. Dostoevsky reworked the speeches of the lawyers (especially the defense lawyer) and the instructions of the judge at the Zasulich trial into the trial of Dmitry Karamazov.

The Brothers Karamazov differs from Dostoevsky's earlier novels in that it attempts to develop in some detail alternatives to the evil that it portrays.[60] Not only do Dmitry's brothers, and the women Dmitry loved, Katerina Ivanovna and Grushenka, propose salvation plots for Dmitry but so does Dmitry's lawyer, the modern grand inquisitor, who uses many of the same strategies and metaphors that Dostoevsky used in imagining his salvation agenda for Kornilova. In chapter 5, I examine Dostoevsky's salvation "counterplot" for Dmitry, advanced by the jury's decision to reject the arguments of Dmitry's defense counsel: twenty years of suffering in prison for a crime he did not commit. I examine not only Dostoevsky's vision of salvation but also his mystical notion of responsibility, which first asserts itself in full force in the Kornilova case. I trace the evolution of Dostoevsky's views of responsibility through the jury trials of Raskolnikov in Crime and Punishment, Kornilova, and Dmitry Karamazov, showing how The Brothers Karamazov realizes the idea of responsibility first worked out in the Kornilova trial, where the defendant, in contrast to Raskolnikov, must acknowledge responsibility for a crime for which she was technically not responsible. In addition, I take a critical look at the novel's vision of an alternative to the Western judicial system for Russia, one based on an imagined ecclesiastical court. The novel does not advocate a return to the pre-reform court; rather, it champions a more ancient theocratic ideal, in which church and state become one, or more, properly, where the state is subsumed by the church. The Brothers Karamazov counters "The Grand Inquisitor" with "The Russian Monk," and "A Judicial Error" with "So Be It! So Be It!"—that is, secular Western law with ecclesiastic Russian justice.

The conclusion explores the question of the artist and the word. The real struggle that occurs in the jury trial is not so much about Dmitry's guilt or innocence but about the authority of the word: Who possesses the authority of the word in the modern world? For Dostoevsky the judicial system is actively attempting to usurp the Logos, to supplant the authoritative Word of God with the relative word of the court. But how under this onslaught can the implied author (not the narrator, who represents only a limited, internal point of view in the novel) discredit the word of the lawyer even as he establishes the authority of his own word? Dostoevsky makes a concerted attempt to dissociate his word from that of the lawyer—and the ironic and infinitely interpretable word of novel tradition—by composing a modern-day hagiography in "The Russian Monk," that is, by aligning his word with the Word of the Gospel as against the word of the law. It is a bold move but one that may aggravate the problem that it attempts to solve, especially for the resisting reader or the reader prone to read otherwise. The struggle between the lawyer and the novelist about the word and the Word also gets personal. Dmitry's lawyer misappropriates the Gospels in his summation, but he no less opportunistically and instrumentally exploits Dostoevsky's own words and strategies from the Kornilova case, inherently challenging the novelist's word and implicitly making the antinomian case for all discourse—in or out of court, in or out of the novel.

It is said that in the end, at least in fiction, art trumps logic. In the conclusion I address the question of the aesthetic effectiveness of Dostoevsky's counterattacks and counterplots. Dostoevsky understood from the beginning that he could not establish the authority of his word over that of his ideological opponents' through the superiority of argument. His hagiography of Father Zosima was created to deal precisely with this kind of problem. But, aside from hagiography, we need to look closely at the effectiveness of Dostoevsky's counterattacks against the word to see whether in the end they may be counterproductive, undercutting the author's word by using many of the same tactics as his opponents. Do his alternative counternarratives regarding salvation, the word, and the judicial system successfully create an image, an icon, of Russian justice that can counter the threat of Western law and the modern world, keeping the Western devils at the gate for however long? *The Brothers Karamazov* is often considered the first great modern novel. I hope to show that it may also be the last great attempt to forestall—at least aesthetically—the inevitable entry of the modern world, the world of the law, into Russia. If one reads "otherwise," especially in terms of the court, *The Brothers Karamazov*, which most consider to be Dostoevsky's most optimistic novel, may rival *The Idiot* in its dark vision of the future.

CHAPTER 1

# The Imprisonment
# of the Law

## Dostoevsky and the Kroneberg Case

---

In 1876–77, in his *Diary of a Writer,* Dostoevsky wrote impassioned articles about three of the most famous court trials of his time: the Kroneberg, Kairova, and Kornilova cases.[1] In retrospect, each can be seen as a preliminary study for the culminating jury trial scene in *The Brothers Karamazov.* However, they stand on their own as conservative critiques of the great 1864 legal reforms. In the Kroneberg case, the focus of this chapter, Dostoevsky takes direct aim at the bar as a legal institution and at the abuse of art in the courtroom. But he also broadens his assault by suggesting that the reforms have widened the breach between the law and ethical standards of the nation, thus precipitating a legal crisis greater than the one that the reforms were designed to correct. The Russian public was being subjected to both an immoral and amoral education. Western law was standing in the way of Russian justice, not of course of a Russian justice already in place but one that could arise more organically from the needs and ideals of the Russian people.

Like the jury trials in the Kornilova case and in *The Brothers Karamazov,* the Kroneberg case, when viewed in the context of Dostoevsky's writings, comes as somewhat of a surprise. As we have seen, Dostoevsky not only loved to attend trials, initially he seemed positively disposed to the new court reforms. He stated that the judicial reforms were no less important for Russia than the reforms of the Peter the Great and that their immediate spread throughout the entire empire was essential not only to Russia's economic well-being but also to its moral regeneration. "What a great regeneration [*chto za velikoe obnovlenie*] that will be. Over here, I keep thinking and dreaming of all these things, and my heart beats faster over it" (28.2:206). If Dostoevsky saw a legal crisis facing Russia in the 1860s, its solution lay in the implementation and dissemination of the legal reforms, not in their limitation or curtailment.

By 1876, the date of the Kroneberg trial, Dostoevsky's romance with the jury trial had soured considerably. Some disappointment and disillusionment with the legal reforms was bound to set in after their implementation, for no judicial system could have measured up to the inflated hopes for national transformation and regeneration that they initially raised. At first, the nobility and intelligentsia flocked to serve on juries. But jury duty in most cases proved to be dull and even onerous, especially for the peasants, and soon Russians began thinking more about how to avoid serving on juries than about performing their civic duty. But Dostoevsky's disillusionment has more profound roots. He began to fear that the legal reforms could bring about the opposite of the moral renewal that he had envisioned. Further, when he returned to Russia (while still working on *The Possessed*), he had already become much more conservative—undoubtedly in reaction to the political activities of the radical intelligentsia. He soon became a frequent visitor of prominent conservative figures in the tsarist administration, and in 1873 he become the editor, for a year, of a prominent reactionary newspaper (the *Citizen*).

## Moral Education Versus Moral Confusion

As we have seen, the proponents of judicial reform argued that the jury trial could uplift and educate the Russian public. Dostoevsky is especially concerned about the kind of education that the public was receiving from the new courts. In his article on the Kairova case he writes that "the tribunes of the new courts are, after all, unquestionably an ethical school for our society and people. Indeed, the people learn in this school truth and morality; how then can we possibly remain indifferent to things which sometimes are uttered from those tribunes?" (329; 23:19). Dostoevsky still maintains that the new courts, whatever their intentions, are a school for the Russian people. But what if the reformed courts are becoming disseminators of morally unsound ideas, serving as a conduit for alien relativistic notions of sin, crime, and responsibility—corrupters from within? Dostoevsky can think of nothing more destructive for a society in transformation than the blurring of distinctions between good and evil, which, in his eyes, can lead only to the legal decriminalization of crime.

Dostoevsky had first addressed the issue of the decriminalization of crime in 1866 in the epilogue of *Crime and Punishment,* which was published only two years after the enactment of the reforms but before the first courts were set up in St. Petersburg to conduct trials under the new system. He obviously thought that pernicious ideas had already taken hold in the precursors of the new reform courts. The magistrates and judges at Raskolnikov's trial interpret the facts to fit their fashionable psychological theories of diminished capacity. The novel focuses on Raskolnikov's calculation of the murder, but the lawyers summarily dismiss the hard work of the novelist, substituting extenuating explanations relating to psychological determinants of criminal behavior. If Raskolnikov did even not count the stolen money, he must have committed the murder in a fit of temporary insanity, they argued:

> They spent a long time attempting to find out why the accused should be lying precisely in this one particular [of course Raskolnikov was telling the truth—G.R.], when in everything else he had so willingly and accurately confessed. In the end, some of them (especially the psychologists) admitted even the possibility that he really hadn't looked into the purse and therefore didn't know what was in it; and not knowing, simply placed it under a stone; but it was precisely from this that they concluded that the crime itself could have been committed only in a state of temporary insanity, that is to say, in a state of morbid monomania manifesting itself in murder and robbery, without any other goals and without any consideration of gain. Here, by the way, the latest fashionable theory of temporary insanity came to the rescue, which is so often employed nowadays for various criminals. (6:410–11)[2]

From Dostoevsky's point of view, at Raskolnikov's trial the court lost sight of the crime that had been committed; the duty of the court, first and foremost, was to proclaim officially that a crime had been committed. The court should be a forum for sound ideas that clearly distinguishes good and evil. The actual sentence, by comparison, is a minor issue.

By 1876 Dostoevsky begins to explicitly deliver his message about crime and the courts from the pages of the *Diary of a Writer.* In his article on the Kairova case—in which the defendant attempted to slit her rival's throat with a razor—Dostoevsky comments: "I merely venture to remark that evil nevertheless should be called evil, and that it should not be extolled almost as an heroic deed, notwithstanding any humaneness" (326; 23:16). And so in Kroneberg the verdict of acquittal "should not have been applauded" (212; 22:51). Again, a crime should be proclaimed a crime. This passage from Dostoevsky's article on the Kairova trial seems to take up where *Crime and Punishment* leaves off:

> There appeared [in the court] either false sentimentality or the lack of understanding of the principle itself of the court—lack of understanding of the fact that in court the first thing, the major principle, consists of defining evil, of specifying it, if possible, of calling it evil, publicly. Afterwards, the mitigation of the criminal's lot, care for his correction, etc.—all those are entirely different problems, very profound and great problems, but altogether different from the task of the court, and belonging rather to other departments of public life. . . . It develops that a crime is not recognized as crime at all. On the contrary, it is, as it were, proclaimed to society—and this by the court itself—that there is no such thing as crime, that crime, don't you see, is merely sickness caused by the abnormal condition of society. (460; 23:137)[3]

Like the Kairova article, Dostoevsky's article on the Kroneberg case makes clear his displeasure with what he considers the court's abdication of its moral responsibility; it also is the first place that he lays out in detail his views about other important aspects of the legal reforms of 1864, warning the public, among other things, about the potential danger that the new jury trial presents for Russian society.

The defendant in the Kroneberg case, Stanislav Leopoldovich Kronenberg, was on trial for severely beating his little daughter.[4] For want of a statute in the legal code dealing with child abuse, Kroneberg was charged with torture. His defense lawyer was perhaps the greatest of all trial lawyers in nineteenth-century Russia, V. D. Spasovich (1829–1906), a former professor of law at St. Petersburg University and a prominent cultural figure. The case involved an issue that was becoming increasingly central to Dostoevsky's theodicial vision: the suffering and abuse of young children. In *The Brothers Karamazov* the suffering of children motivates both Ivan Karamazov's rebellion against God's world and Dmitry Karamazov's dream of universal responsibility.

Dostoevsky had written earlier about the suffering of little children—
in *Poor Folk* and *Crime and Punishment* in particular—but the issue
first arose in a legal context only with the Umetsky case (*delo Umet-
skikh*), which was tried in September 1867, when Dostoevsky was living abroad in Geneva. Olga Umetskaya was a child repeatedly beaten
by her parents, once for giving honey to a workman. No longer able
to bear her suffering, she tried, on four separate occasions, to set fire
to her parents' house and its adjacent buildings. Before her last attempt
at arson she had even tried to take her own life. Olga Umetskaya is one
of the earliest prototypes of Nastasya Filippovna, the heroine of *The
Idiot*—although little of her remains in the final version of the novel.
Dostoevsky's wife, Anna Grigoryevna, recalls:

> I remember that in the winter of 1867 he took great interest in the details
> of the Umetsky trial, which had caused quite a sensation at that time.
> His interest was so great that he intended to make Olga Umetskaya, the
> chief figure in the trial, the heroine (in the first plan) of his new novel.
> Her last name is taken down this way in his notebook. He very much
> regretted that we weren't in Petersburg, otherwise he would certainly
> have had his say about this trial. (Dostoevskaia, 169–70)

In other words, Dostoevsky wanted to say something about a case
of child abuse, even before he had linked the suffering of little children
with the issue of court reforms. It would seem that when the Kroneberg case came up, although it dealt with a less extreme form of
abuse, Dostoevsky could not but avail himself of the opportunity to
write about the trial in the *Diary of a Writer*. The two themes that were
to engage his fictional energies for the next four years had come
together in one place. But he needed one element before he could even
conceive an article: a miscarriage of justice, an egregious acquittal. It
seemed to Dostoevsky, as it did to others who were later to comment
on the trial, that there could hardly be a more clear-cut case for the
courts to decide in favor of the victim and against the "perpetrator,"
that is, for the courts to act as a proper forum for the education of the
public, by declaring that a crime had been committed, thereby reinforcing the crucial distinction between good and evil. But the court in
the Kroneberg case had, in Dostoevsky's eyes, decided that no crime
had been committed.

## There Was No Crime

In *The Brothers Karamazov* Dmitry Karamazov's defense attorney, Fetyukovich—modeled after Spasovich, Kroneberg's attorney—argues that his client should not be convicted of murder because no crime occurred: no reasonable, thinking person can consider the killing of a bad father murder. In the Kroneberg case Dostoevsky presents Spasovich as using a similar casuistic strategy. The defense attorney argued that because his client's action did not conform to the definition of torture as laid down in the statute, he was not guilty of the crime for which he had been charged. But according to Dostoevsky, Spasovich went even further: he argued that not only did his client's actions not constitute torture, they were not criminal in any sense. There was, in fact, no crime and therefore no case:

> "There was no torture, there was no offense inflicted upon the child!" He denied everything: "spitzrutens," bruises, blows, blood, integrity of the witnesses of the opposing side, everything, everything—an extraordinarily bold device, an onslaught, so to speak, against the jurors' conscience. . . . But Mr. Spasovich does not wish to yield anything; he wants to prove that there has been no torture at all, neither lawful nor unlawful, and also no suffering—not a bit of it! But for goodness' sake, what is it to us that the torture and racking of this girl did not comply with the letter of the legal definition of torture? (229; 22:57, 65)[5]

Confronted with the task of rectifying the egregious harm done by the court in the acquittal of Kroneberg, Dostoevsky had to demonstrate that a crime had indeed been committed and that the court had not only gone astray but was in danger of leading the Russian people astray. The case was already lost, but Dostoevsky could at least use the *Diary of a Writer* as a forum for doing what should have been done in court. Dostoevsky "retries" the case, transferring the venue from the St. Petersburg circuit to the *Diary of a Writer*—a higher court, as it were—where he can take over from the prosecuting attorney, who turned out to be no match for the talented Spasovich.

By taking the case out of the court, where it is amorally enmeshed, Dostoevsky is able to subject it to a different mode of aesthetic and moral perception and suasion. He does not conceal what he is doing;

he repeatedly insists that he is not a jurist. In the *Diary of a Writer,* in contrast to the court, passion and compassion are not only not out of place or "irrelevant," they are essential. Dostoevsky attempts to overwhelm his readers, infecting them with compassion for the beaten little girl, the compassion that Spasovich needed to destroy in order to achieve an acquittal for his client. The famous Russian prerevolutionary defense attorney O. O. Gruzenberg (he was the main defense lawyer for Beilis in the famous Kishinev blood-libel case of 1912), wrote that Dostoevsky's artistry and passion were what gained him the "moral" victory in the *Diary of a Writer.* Dostoevsky did not persuade him, Gruzenberg notes, but overwhelmed him by the "fit of compassion that he expressed for the child."[6] Gruzenberg characterizes Spasovich's speech as passionless and speculates that it might be explained by his decision to remain unmarried all his life and have no children— Spasovich did not know much about children and, apparently, did not like them. Dostoevsky attempts to restore the true image of the child, tarnished on the stand by Spasovich, by imaginatively re-creating the child's experience of torture, by substituting the Lebenswelt for the artificial system of the courtroom. Dostoevsky does not treat his readers as jurors who need to weigh evidence; rather, he transforms them into observers of the actual torture.

In counteracting Spasovich's claim that what happened was not torture, Dostoevsky recalls the brutal beatings that he personally witnessed when he was serving at hard labor in a Siberian prison camp. Before corporal punishment was abolished, his fellow prisoners—hardened criminals capable of withstanding incredible suffering—were regularly beaten with the same "sticks" that Kroneberg used on his seven-year-old daughter.

> I would like to inform Mr. Spasovich that in Siberia, in the convicts'
> wards in the hospital, I chanced to see the backs of prison inmates
> immediately after they had been subjected to flogging with spitzrutens
> (driven through the ranks) after five hundred, one thousand and two
> thousand blows inflicted at a time. This I saw several dozens of times.
> Would you believe me, Mr. Spasovich, that some backs literally swelled
> almost two inches thick, and yet think how little flesh there is on the
> back! These backs were of a dark purple color, with a few gashes from
> which blood would be oozing. You can be assured, not a single one of
> our present-day medical experts has ever observed anything like this;

(besides where could we, in our times, observe such things!). . . . And here is a fact: these punished men got discharged from the hospital on the sixth—at most, on the seventh—day after the punishment, because during that period *the back would almost completely heal up*, save for some minor—comparatively speaking—remnants; however, after ten days, for example, everything would have disappeared without leaving any traces. . . . Now, I will ask you, Mr. Defense-Lawyer, I will ask you this question: even though these sticks did not threaten her life and caused her not the slightest injury, isn't such a punishment cruel and doesn't it constitute torture? For heaven's sake, didn't the little girl suffer for a quarter of an hour under the dreadful rods, which lay on the table in court as an exhibit, screaming: "Papa! Papa!" Why then are you denying her suffering, her torture? (227–28; 22:64–65)

A duel is being fought here between definitions and perception, between legal codes and existential experience, between the language of the law and the language of Russian literature. Dostoevsky insists on the primacy of experience, Spasovich, in Dostoevsky's representation, on statutory definitions. Spasovich bases his case on a loophole in the definition of torture: "On this ground the Ruling Senate has held, in those very decisions upon which the prosecution is relying, that, on the other hand, by torture and racking should be meant such infringements upon the person and personal inviolability of a person as are accompanied by suffering and cruelty" (228–29; 22:65). And again: "They say that this punishment exceeds the scope of ordinary ones. This definition might have been excellent if we could determine what an ordinary punishment is; *but so long as there is no such definition,* anyone would be at a loss to state whether it exceeded the scope of ordinary punishments" (231; 22:67). Even at the conclusion of his speech Spasovich argues for acquittal on the basis of the incorrect formulation of the charges: "In conclusion, I take the liberty of stating that, in my opinion, the entire prosecution of Kroneberg has been framed altogether incorrectly—namely, that the questions, with which you are about to be presented, can in no way be resolved" (236; 22:72). In Dostoevsky's courtroom Spasovich cuts a sorry figure.

The writer refuses to take the position of a detached observer—a juror required by law to follow the letter of the law[7]—but calls on his harrowing experience in the Siberian labor camps to demonstrate that the absence of permanent harm or nasty scars in no way proves the absence of torture. Moreover, his authority in this matter—at least in the eyes of his readers—is virtually unassailable. Because Dostoevsky had suffered ten years of penal servitude and exile in Siberia, many saw him as a political martyr. His image and aura were further enhanced by his imaginative re-creation of his prison experiences in the semi-autobiographical *Notes from the House of the Dead,* a sacred part of the Dostoevskian canon that includes numerous graphic descriptions of brutal beatings, some lethal. Because corporal punishment had long been abolished by 1876, few members of Dostoevsky's class, the intelligentsia, could testify as authoritatively to the effect of the beatings as he. Moreover, Dostoevsky's readers were hardly going to privilege the legal definitions of torture of a lawyer who did not even see the girl after she had been beaten over the "first-hand account" of their beloved author, who lay side by side in a prison hospital with dozens of convicts severely beaten with the very same instruments of torture used on the child.

If *Notes from the House of the Dead* showed even the hardest of Russian criminals were human beings, and thus deserving of compassion, and that corporal punishment was inhumane—and few denied that Dostoevsky had succeeded remarkably in dramatizing this—what reader would not be shocked upon realizing that this tiny seven-year-old child (*mladenets*) was tortured with instruments similar to those used on hardened criminals and that the perpetrator of the torture was acquitted because no crime had been committed.[8] The readers of the *Diary of a Writer* would certainly remember the callous, inhuman beaters of the prisoners and the prisoners' cries for mercy in *Notes from the House of the Dead.* How much more painful for the reader must have been the blows dealt the little girl, and how much more terrible her cries of "Papa! Papa!" "Now, I will ask you, Mr. Defense-Lawyer, I will ask you this question: even though these sticks did not threaten her life and caused her not the slightest injury, isn't such a punishment cruel and doesn't it constitute torture?" Dostoevsky counteracts Spasovich's dry definition of torture—"Such infringements upon the person and personal inviolability of a person as are accompanied by suffering and cruelty"—with the helpless cry of "Papa! Papa" from a seven-year-old who is pleading for mercy from her enraged father, who had retained more control of himself than some of the beaters that Dostoevsky had seen in prison. Dostoevsky turns the case into a narrative in which he can empathetically introduce the child's story and her pain.

Throughout the article Dostoyevsky repeats the child's cry, "Papa! Papa!" using it to echo as a refrain, as it did during the actual beating, and refuting Spasovich's charge that no torture occurred—and therefore no crime.

Clearly, Dostoevsky has little patience with statutory definitions when the issue at hand is clearly the revelation and proclamation of the truth. Dostoevsky's strategy is to take advantage of his position, using all the literary means and cultural capital at his disposal. How can any reader believe that Spasovich can arrive at truth by using legal jargon that is alien to the spirit of the Russian language itself? Further, it is not a question here of Spasovich's representing a lesser and Dostoevsky a higher truth. Any court that has no place for registering the helpless cry of "Papa" from an innocent cannot be anything but the site of untruth and injustice.

But just as important as Dostoevsky's implied assault on the impersonality of the court is his attack on the language of the law. If the definitions of the law have nothing to do with the truth, then the impersonality of the court has, in Dostoevsky's mind, little to do with justice. In speaking about Russian justice—justice in the highest sense —Dostoevsky advocates the position of the Russian Slavophiles, who assailed formal laws and guarantees and preached in their stead inner law or justice based on mutual trust.[9] After presenting the legal arguments and hair-splitting definitions of Spasovich as bloodless and devoid of compassion, Dostoevsky personalizes his own narrative and establishes a bond of trust between himself and his readers, providing them with the only basis on which true Russian justice can be enacted, a trust based not on the letter of the law but on the letter of literature, not on impartial and rational distinction but on feeling (compassion), soul, heart, and spirit, on existential experience, on suffering.

One may argue that Dostoevsky is just a better rhetorician than Spasovich, but this would be to see the matter, as Lotman and Uspensky might argue, with the eyes of an outsider, someone outside the Russian semiotic system. Dostoevsky is using a semiotic code, intuitively and profoundly understood by his Russian audience, in which truth and justice lie not with the logician Spasovich but with the suffering child and her maligned defenders, the Russian peasant women who came to her aid.

To accomplish his mission of providing a totally different—and more just—point of view, Dostoevsky takes us more deeply into the perception of the child, the victim, and thus even further from the rational point of view of the bachelor-lawyer. A master of transcribing the consciousness and perception of children under duress, Dostoevsky effectively uses his obvious out-of-court advantage over Spasovich. In a previously quoted passage Dostoevsky tries to persuade his reader, on the basis of his personal experience, that a crime was indeed committed and to demonstrate that compassion for the insulted child is the only appropriate response. In the following passage Dostoevsky answers the even more heinous charge that the child, not the father, was guilty. This defense move prefigures the tactics of the defense attorney in *The Brothers Karamazov,* who argues that Dmitry would not be guilty of his father's death, even if he had killed him intentionally. Dostoevsky seems momentarily to lose patience here. But it seems artistically appropriate for him to do so. Dostoevsky's indignation and outrage here seem to be an integral part of his moral aesthetic. The situation demands as much passion from the author as it demands compassion from the reader. Dostoevsky asks what kind of criminal this abused little seven-year-old child could be:

> Is she a dangerous criminal? This little girl, this criminal, will run to play "robbers" with some little boys. Here we are dealing with the age of seven —only seven years; this must be constantly remembered in this case. Indeed, all that you are saying is a mirage! And do you know what it means to insult a child? Children's hearts are full of innocent, almost unconscious, love, and such blows evoke in them a scornful astonishment and tears which God sees and will reckon. For their intellect is never capable of grasping their full guilt. Have you ever seen, or heard about, tortured little children—say, little orphans in some strange, cruel families? Have you ever seen a child hiding in a corner, so that he may not be seen, and weeping there, wringing his little hands (yes, wringing his hands —I have seen it myself) and *striking his chest with his tiny fist [udariaia sebia kroshechnym kulachonkom v grud'* (22:69)] not knowing himself what he was doing, not fully understanding his guilt and the reason why he was being tortured, but sensing only too clearly that he was not loved? . . . Only then do these creatures penetrate our souls and take hold of our hearts when we, having begotten them, are watching *over* them from their childhood, never parting with them from the time of their first smile, and thereafter continuing spiritually to be mutually drawn closer to each other, day after day, hour after hour, throughout our lives. (233–34; 22:69)

In what sounds like a preamble to *The Brothers Karamazov*, Dosto-evsky again brings his central moral concerns to the fore: the suffer-ings of little children. He starts by warning Spasovich that he will have to pay in the next world—Dostoevsky is doing his best to make him pay in this one as well—for the moral and psychological trauma he has inflicted upon "the babe": God sees such insults, and they will figure in the ultimate reckoning. But the writer soon abandons threats for another, more empathetic, narrative strategy, presenting the percep-tion of both the child and a hypothetical father who observes his child's suffering. Dostoevsky casts himself in the role that Spasovich could not possibly fill, an ideal father, a compassionate participant, not a dispas-sionate observer. "And do you know what it means to insult a child?" Of course, Spasovich does not. How then can he be permitted to per-secute a child in the name of justice?

In the previous passage Dostoevsky cited the brutal prison world of a more barbaric age in order to find the proper analogies for the suffer-ing of a seven-year-old girl. It was a world he could vouch for and for which his authority was unchallengeable. He could also offer himself as a privileged observer of the world of suffering children, relying on his readers' knowledge of his previous works, *Poor Folk* and *Crime and Punishment*, among others. "Have you ever seen a child hiding in a corner, so that he may not be seen, and weeping there, wringing his little hands (yes, wringing his hands—I have seen it myself)." Dosto-evsky then takes the reader more deeply into the child's world as the child strikes himself with his tiny twisted fists, venting his humiliation and anger against himself. Dostoevsky presents the child's bewilder-ment: he does not know why he is being tortured; and his pain: he feels that he is unloved. A century ago, in what was intended as uncom-plimentary criticism, N. K. Mikhaylovsky wrote that Dostoevsky pos-sessed the unique ability to make us feel how a lamb feels as it is being devoured by a wolf.[10]

If Spasovich did everything he could to extirpate compassion in the jurors, Dostoevsky needs to reinstate that compassion in his readers and make them feel, as Russian citizens, responsible for the torture suf-fered by the child.[11] Everyone is responsible for the suffering of that child. Rather than writing a pure diatribe against the lawyer and the court, Dostoevsky resorts to a psychological narrative with one central powerful image: a little child striking himself with his twisted little fist. This bewildered and humiliated child directing aggression against himself (Dostoevsky uses two emotional diminutives here: *udariaia sebia kroshechnym kulachonkom v grud'*) is set against the image of the aggressive defense attorney (Mr. Defense-Attorney)—but more like a prosecutor or inquisitor—as he bears down on a helpless, innocent child.[12]

## The Real Crime

Dostoevsky was disturbed by Kroneberg's acquittal, not because Kroneberg went unpunished but because the writer wanted the court to speak the truth, to arrive at a verdict (truth telling), to proclaim that a crime had been committed, rather than a correct decision within the parameters of the legal code. He would not even have written the *Diary* article on the Kroneberg case had the defendant been found guilty and given a suspended sentence, in which case, the court, tempering real justice with mercy, could have remained a forum for public morality. Dostoevsky was even more upset by the behavior of the lawyer as an officer of the court and a representative of the bar. From Dostoevsky's perspective the psychological torture that Spasovich perpetrated in the courtroom was a more serious crime than the physical beating inflicted by Kroneberg on his daughter. Kroneberg could, after all, have been convicted, had he had a less talented lawyer, but nothing could ever have happened to Spasovich; in fact, Spasovich, a court-appointed lawyer, was just doing his job. It soon becomes clear that the real defendant in the Kroneberg article is not Kroneberg but Spasovich. Dostoevsky puts the lawyer on trial in his own court, the *Diary of a Writer*. If the great failure of the Kroneberg case was the failure to show that a crime had been committed, then the success of Dostoevsky's article in the *Diary of a Writer* had to rest on Dostoevsky's ability to reveal not only Kroneberg's crime but all the other "crimes" committed in and sanctioned by the nation's most prestigious courts.

Dostoevsky finds especially reprehensible Spasovich's use of the common trial practice of discrediting "dangerous" witnesses. Spasovich saw that undermining the credibility of the beaten little girl was in his client's interest. This, of course, has always been a tactic of trial attorneys, but Russian juries placed special weight on the moral character of victims as well as defendants in the jurors' determinations, often acquitting defendants for whom they had sympathy and convicting defendants who offended their moral or religious sensibilities. "The judicial relevance of the *crime victim's* personal qualities, although difficult to assess precisely, was by no means an atypical feature of Russian jury trials. Indeed, evidence of strongly unattractive traits in the *victim* (drunkenness, vulgarity, bad temper, perceived 'shrewishness' in women) sometimes made jurors more sympathetic to the defendant" (emphasis added).[13] The real horror of the defense attorney's attempt to humiliate and torment a child morally and psychologically in the interest of his client is that it is accepted court procedure, if not "sanctioned" by the court. It is, Dostoevsky protests, our responsibility before God to protect children, to "watch over them," to become spiritually drawn to them, to become closer to them, hour after hour, throughout our lives. Therefore the responsibility of court is to protect child-victims, not open them up to further exploitation in what should be "an ethical school for our society and people."

What Dostoevsky implicitly presents as Spasovich's "crimes" can be better understood in the maximalist context of *The Brothers Karamazov*, in which both Ivan and Alyosha refuse to build the future happiness of the world on the tears of even one innocent child:

> "Tell me straight out, I call on you—answer me: imagine that you yourself are building the edifice of human destiny with the object of making people happy in the finale, of giving them peace and rest at last, but for that you must inevitably and unavoidably torture just one tiny creature, that same *child who was beating her chest with her little fist* [bivshevii sebia kulachonkom v grud'], and raise your edifice on the foundation of her unrequited tears—would you agree to be the architect on such conditions? Tell me the truth."
>
> "No, I would not agree," Alyosha said softly. (14:223–24; emphasis added)[14]

The Kroneberg case, of course, anticipates *The Brothers Karamazov*, but *The Brothers Karamazov* consciously adapts and even directly quotes from Dostoevsky's article about the Kroneberg case. Ivan uses virtually the same words about the child beating himself against the chest with his little fist as Dostoevsky does in his *Diary of a Writer* article. The reference becomes even more striking in one of Ivan's examples of children tortured by adults, often by their own parents. In citing a case in which a child was beaten by her father with a birch, Ivan imagines the child crying, "Papa, papa." The case goes to court where a lawyer, a hired gun, claims no crime has been committed. The jury acquits the defendant. Ivan, outraged no less than the author of the *Diary of a Writer*, sarcastically calls for a statue to be erected in honor of the torturer:

> And so, an intelligent, educated, gentleman and his lady flog their own daughter, a child of seven, with a birch—I have written it down in detail. The papa is glad that the birch is covered with little twigs, "it will smart more," he says, and so he starts "smarting" his own daughter. . . . The child is crying, the child finally cannot cry, she has no breath left: "*Papa, papa, dear papa!*" The case, through some devilishly improper accident, comes to court. A lawyer is hired. Among the Russian people, lawyers have long been called "hired consciences." The lawyer shouts in his client's defense. "The case," he says, "is quite simple, domestic, and ordinary: a father flogged his daughter, and, to the shame of our times, it has come to court!" The convinced jury retires and brings in a verdict of "not guilty." The public roars with delight that the torturer has been acquitted. Ah, if I'd been there, I'd have yelled out a suggestion that they establish a scholarship in honor of the torturer . . . ! . . . *Can you understand that a small creature who cannot even comprehend what is being done to her, in a vile place, in the dark and the cold, beats herself on her strained little chest with her tiny fists and weeps with her anguished, gentle, meek tears for "dear God" to protect her?* (241–42; 14:219–20; emphasis added)

For Dostoevsky the psychological and moral scars that Kroneberg's daughter will take from the courtroom will long outlive the welts and even psychological trauma of the beatings.

> The secret vices of this little child (of only seven years!) were revealed aloud before the whole public by grown-up, serious, and even humane people.—What a monstrosity! Mais il en reste toujours quelque chose, for one's whole life—do understand this! And this will remain not only in her soul but, perhaps, will even be reflected in her fate. Something foul and bad has touched her in that courtroom, leaving something that will never be erased. And who knows?—Maybe twenty years hence someone will say to her: "Even as a child you appeared in a criminal court." (212; 22:51)

In order to show that the beatings were in some way justified, Spasovich attempted to expose the little girl's "secret vices" to the entire
court. The horror ("What a monstrosity") of this strategy was exacerbated by its cool calculation. Spasovich becomes that "foul and bad"
thing "that touched her in that courtroom," the one who left an indeli-
ble mark on her soul, the violator of childhood innocence, the true
child molester.

But Spasovich's attempt to discredit the victim harbors an even
more heinous crime: his direct assault on compassion, for Dostoevsky,
the quintessence of Christian love and the special gift of the Russian
common people. Spasovich tried "to root out of the hearts of his lis-
teners" any compassion for the victim of crime (219; 22:57). What is to
be made of a person, and the system that supports that person, for
whom compassion represents a mortal danger? In order to win his
case Spasovich feels compelled to turn a little angel of seven years old
into "a liar, a thief . . . with a filthy vice":

> Instead of a seven-year-old child, instead of an angel, there will appear
> before you a "mischievous" girl, a cunning, obstreperous girl with a bad
> disposition, who cries even when she is ordered into the corner; who is
> "great at screaming" (what a Russicism!); a liar, a thief, untidy with a
> filthy secret vice. The whole trick comes to this: in some way to destroy
> your sympathy for the child. Such is human nature: you will not pity
> anyone whom you dislike or to whom you feel an aversion, and, it is
> precisely your compassion that Mr. Spasovich fears most of all; other-
> wise, if you should start pitying the child, you might find her father
> guilty. (223; 22:60–61)

> He fears the child's suffering might—who knows—evoke in you humane
> feelings. And it is precisely these feelings that are dangerous to him.
> (230; 22:66)

> But at least leave us our pity for the babe: do not judge her with such
> a serious air, as if you were convinced of her guilt. This pity is our treas-
> ure, and it is dangerous to exterminate it in society. If society should
> stop pitying the weak and oppressed, it would itself be greatly harmed;
> it would become callous and wither; it would become dissolute and
> sterile. (236; 22:71)

Moreover, the damage done each time such an assault on compassion occurs spreads far beyond the child in the courtroom; it has the potential of undermining Russian society. A society in which compassion—Russia's national "treasure"—has been extirpated, a society which has stopped "pitying the weak and oppressed," is un-Christian and fated to wither and die morally. Dostoevsky elevates the Kroneberg case involving the relationship between a father and a daughter to a matter of national and universal importance. Not only Russian society, but any society from which compassion is rooted out, is no longer viable. The court is being assailed both for crimes of omission—it did not proclaim that a crime had been committed—and commission—it encouraged a direct attack on compassion, the greatest treasure of the Russian people.

But Dostoevsky's most effective tactic for transforming the issue of compassion into a national concern is his portrayal of the women who testified in court on behalf of the beaten child. Overcome by compassion, two simple peasant women courageously reported the beating to the police. Dostoevsky asks his readers to "please consider the aversion of our common folk to courts and their fear in getting mixed up in them, when one himself is not dragged into court. Yet she did go to plead and complain on behalf of a stranger—a child—knowing that, in any event, she would receive no other reward than bother and disappointments" (225; 12:62). Instead of lauding their courageous action, the court victimizes these exemplars of compassion from the Russian people. Their truth—their compassion—is trampled upon.

We have seen Dostoevsky implicitly cast himself in the role of the compassionate father who comes to the aid of the abused child (that is, as the symbolic protector in his own narrative), but he is anything but a hero in comparison to these simple women of the common people, antitheses to the sophisticated and artful Spasovich, the representative of Western rationalism and legalism. Spasovich also attempts to discredit these women, who not only did nothing wrong but even sacrificed their own interests out of compassion for the child. All the fears of the women—of the Russian people—are realized in court. They came to the aid of a victim, and they become victims themselves. It is as though they, not the true perpetrator of the crime, were on trial. Given such treatment, how could the common people, Dostoevsky implies, place any more faith in the new courts than in the old?

Though the abused child may represent the universal side of Dostoevsky's argument, a symbol of innocence outside time or place, the

governess and the porter's wife fit more closely into Dostoevsky's ideologically populist agenda (*pochvennichestvo*). They become the vehicles
by which the trial is transformed into a battle between rationalism and
moral feeling, West and East, Catholicism and Russian Orthodoxy,
between the mind of the Enlightenment and the Russian soul. By using
Western legal instrumentalism to discredit the simple Russian women,
Spasovich launches, according to Dostoevsky's logic, an attack on the
very soul—the truth and sense of justice—of the Russian people:

> Agrafyevna Titova is Kroneberg's former housemaid. It was precisely she,
> together with the porter's wife, Ulyiana Bibina, at the summer cottage
> in Lesnoe which Mr. Kroneberg was then renting, who was the first to
> bring charges of torturing the child. As for me, I may remark in passing
> that, in my opinion, Titova and, particularly, Bibina, are nearly the most
> attractive personalities in the whole case. They both love the child. . . .
> One senses in their words not only profound sympathy, but also evident
> in them is the keen glance of an observer—a glance permeated with
> inner compassion for the sufferings of an insulted tiny creature of
> God. It is only natural that the little girl came to love the servants from
> whom alone she received love and affection, and at times she used to
> run down to visit the porter's wife. For this Mr. Spasovich indicts the
> child, attributing her vices "to the corrupting influence of the servants."
> Please note that the little girl spoke nothing but French, and Ulyiana
> Bibina, the porter's wife, could not understand her well; therefore, she
> must have grown to love her purely from pity, from compassion for the
> child, which is so characteristic of our common people. (224; 22:61–62)

Dostoevsky artfully introduces his heroines: he must mention "in
passing . . . nearly the most attractive personalities in the whole case."
But, more important, the action of these women is not idiosyncratic;
it constitutes a collective response deeply rooted in the common people. Furthermore, linking their compassion with the perception of the
artist, Dostoevsky provides himself with a moral-aesthetic model for
his own article. "One senses in their words," Dostoevsky writes, "not
only profound sympathy, but also evident in them is the keen glance
of an observer—a glance permeated with inner compassion for the
sufferings of an insulted tiny creature of God." The insight of the people is special in that it is unlike the detached insight of the artist, who
must distance himself from life to observe it accurately and who must

pay for his perception by his alienation from the life he observes.[15] The insight of the women is inseparable from their love and compassion. Theirs is the perception of engagement, not detachment, an engagement followed almost immediately by action. In the Kroneberg article Dostoevsky attempts to create a work in imitation of the simple women of the people that can produce the same moral effect, that itself can constitute a form of moral symbolic action. Moved by their compassion and deeds, Dostoevsky, the Russian intellectual, pays obeisance to their superior wisdom, attempting to instill in us the feelings that guided these women.

By having Spasovich convert the women's compassion, the truth of the people, into "a corrupting influence" on the child, Dostoevsky is able to cast Spasovich in the same role as he does Dmitry's defense lawyer, Fetyukovich, in *The Brothers Karamazov*: a corrupter of thought. Dostoevsky writes that it was "only natural that the little girl came to love the servants from whom alone she received love and affection, and at times she used to run down to visit the porter's wife." Spasovich's art emplots child and servants in what might be called a conspiracy of compassion, organized against the father and against the law itself. Casting aspersions on Russian compassion and, by extension, the mission of the Russian people in and for the world, Spasovich utters the ultimate calumny, the ultimate blasphemy: "Just what, after all this, is their testimony worth?" (226; 22:63). The court has become, for Dostoevsky, a forum for the dissemination of the lie (*fal'sh'*). By castigating Russian truth from the position of Western law, Spasovich commits his greatest transgression: He uses the court as a means of extirpating Russian truth, the only truth still capable of saving not only Russia but all European civilization.

In *The Possessed* Ivan Shatov, who expresses several of Dostoevsky's pet ideas, underscores the relationship between the Russian people and their faith in the truth of their word. His formulation is the prototype of many similar passages in the *Diary of a Writer*: "If a great people does not believe that the truth exists in itself alone (in itself alone and in itself exclusively); if it does not believe that it alone is capable of and destined to resurrect and save the world by its truth, then it would immediately cease being a great nation, and would immediately be transformed into ethnographical material, and not a great people. . . . There is only one 'god-bearing' people and that is the Russian people" (10:199–200). The Christian love by which the Russian people will save the world reveals itself most clearly in the compassion of the simple Russian women whom Dostoevsky eulogizes in Kroneberg. Spasovich is thus not only victimizing two innocent, compassionate Russian women, he is discrediting Russian truth and justice (*pravda*) in the eyes of the Russian people, who must believe in their truth in order to perform their salvific world mission. The Western court has become the site of an insidious attack against the Russian people's truth that jeopardizes their potential role in the divine plan. Dostoevsky thus doubly casts Spasovich into Fetyukovich's role in *The Brothers Karamazov*, not only as a corrupter of thought but as a petty inquisitor who directly questions the truth of Christ in the name of the new legal order.

### Who or What Is to Blame?

One would think, given Dostoevsky's blistering criticism of Spasovich and all the crimes that he implicitly ascribes to him, that the lawyer would stand out as the arch villain of the piece and that Dostoevsky's article might just constitute another in the long litany of diatribes against lawyers—consciences for hire—dating to the ancient Greeks. But no matter how much Dostoevsky dislikes Spasovich and his methods, he does not present him as the main culprit. The lawyer is not primarily responsible for the assault against the babe, the rooting out of compassion, and the questioning of Russian truth; the responsible party is the new legal institution ushered in by the reforms of 1864, in particular, the crown jewel of that system: the jury trial.

Spasovich is certainly presented as a supreme manipulator of the legal system, who uses the law to attain ends that appear to be diametrically opposed to the law's intentions. But when seeking causes of the lawyer's actions in the Kroneberg case and what occurred to the babe and the peasant witnesses, Dostoevsky finds the institution to be the primary culprit. Spasovich did not derive pleasure from discrediting the little girl or the Russian peasant women, but he believed he could not do otherwise in fulfilling his responsibility to his client; he thought he was doing his duty. What is worse, Spasovich is not unique. Dostoevsky often presents lawyers more as prisoners than masters of the legal system—poor players whose defined roles commit them morally and legally to defend immoral positions—that is, to act amorally. The lawyers' sense of self-esteem, their reputation, professionalism, and financial well-being are all determined by the system. The lawyer is not a usurper of the system but its inevitable product. The judicial system exists not for the plaintiff or the defendant, but neither does it exist for the lawyer, who is really its servant and prisoner.

> Whatever you may say, there is in this institution, in addition to that which is undeniably beautiful, something sad. Truly, one can hear: "Plotters! Ticks!"—and also the popular saying: "Advocate—hired conscience." But the principal point is that one seems to be haunted with the most absurd paradox that a lawyer is never able even to act in accord with his conscience; that he cannot but play with it, *even if he wished not to do so*; that he is a man simply doomed to dishonesty, and finally, that—and this is the most important and most serious point in the whole matter—this sad state of affairs has been, as it were, *legalized* by somebody and something, so that it is regarded not as a deviation at all but, on the contrary, as a most *normal state of affairs*. (215; 22:53–54; emphasis added)

So the reform court and not Spasovich—or lawyers in general—turns out to be the main reason for the dire state of Russian justice. Dostoevsky does not go so far as to present the torturer of the child as a victim, but, given his larger view of the law as a potentially pernicious institution, Spasovich emerges as a much lesser and more passive figure than he at first appears. Dostoevsky insists that "the blame should be laid at the door of the falsehood of the circumstances which, in this case, grouped themselves around Mr. Spasovich; from this falsehood he was completely unable to extricate himself, owing to the very force of things" (218; 22:56–57). "But then the thought occurs to you that he is deliberately defending and acquitting a guilty person; and what is more—that he is unable to act differently, even if he wanted to. . . . It seems to me that, generally speaking, it is as difficult for a lawyer to avoid falsehood and to preserve honesty and conscience as for any man to attain a paradisiacal state" (214; 22:53). Regarding the defense lawyer in the Kairova case, Dostoevsky comments: "As regards attorney-at-law Utan, he 'commended the crime' because, probably, he imagined that he could not have acted differently. Thus, clever men are being led astray, and the results are by no means clever" (317; 23:8). The lawyers turn out not to be dishonest human beings but prisoners of the system, of law as an institution: they cannot act otherwise.[16] Spasovich, Dostoevsky says, does not enjoy humiliating a seven-year-old, but he is compelled to do so, for it is only by discrediting witnesses hostile to their clients that lawyers can win their cases. The little girl must be proved to be depraved so as to show that the severe beatings she received from her father, though excessive, were nevertheless justified. To Dostoevsky lawyers are trained, even "morally" obliged, to sacrifice their consciences to their clients. The moral yardstick of the profession becomes the defense of the client, not the truth.[17] Spasovich was in no sense vouching for his client—asserting his private belief in his client's innocence; he was a court-appointed lawyer who had little to gain from his defense of Kroneberg, and he was seriously risking his reputation for defending someone whom conservatives, liberals, and radicals alike thought guilty of a serious crime.[18] In fact, Spasovich, who was a respected liberal professor and lawyer, was ostracized by his former sympathizers for his defense of Kroneberg.

What is worse, Dostoevsky can see the situation only deteriorating, for already the bar, as he points out at the end of the article, is becoming increasingly institutionalized, professionalized, and hardened. It is a school that corrupts its pupils, priding itself on its instrumental function, which it has raised to a principle.

> However, willy-nilly, I must exclaim: yes, the bar is a remarkable institution, but, somehow, also a sad one. This I have stated in the beginning, and I repeat it again. So it does seem to me, and unquestionably only because I am not a lawyer—therein is my whole trouble. I keep visualizing a certain young school turning out shrewd minds and dry hearts—a school perverting every healthy feeling whenever occasion calls for such distortion; a school of all sorts of challenges, fearless and irresponsible; a continual and incessant training, based on need and demand, raised to the level of some principle, and because of our want of habit—to the level of prowess, which is applauded by everybody. (237; 22:73)

At the heart of Dostoevsky's critique of the jury trial is his fear that the growing professionalization of the bar and formalism of legal procedures would sow moral confusion in society by institutionalizing the separation of ethics from legal practice. It was not so much that immorality was been preached in the courts but that the whole issue of ethics was being subordinated to procedure, to the letter of the law, and that such a subordination was being elevated to a principle above all others. Dostoevsky's consternation was probably compounded by the position taken by some of his ideological rivals, who, though sharing his distrust of lawyers, welcomed the dissociation of ethics from the law.[19] M. E. Saltykov-Shchedrin, who also wrote critically of the performance of the defense in the Kroneberg trial, nevertheless strongly argued in favor of a professionalism that would encourage lawyers to operate amorally, as it were, as "hired guns" for their client. He maintained that it was best if lawyers did not meddle in areas—ethics and politics—in which they were unqualified. Lawyers once performed a moral, social, and political function similar to that of writers and critics, but they had long since limited their concern to the minutiae of the law. It was now best for them to remain narrowly professional. "As the bar so quickly expressed its intention to dissociate itself from general intellectual and moral interests [which it once shared with literature—G.R.], it is necessary to take advantage of this inclination and not force on it a liaison with literature; it is necessary to assign to the bar the place that it should occupy among various other professions."[20] Saltykov was advocating, in effect, a course that would further institutionalize the separation of ethics and law that Dostoevsky saw precisely to be the main problem. According to Saltykov: "Literature serves society; the bar serves its clients [*Literatura sluzhit obshchestvu, advokatura—klientu*]" (15.2:228).[21] Dostoevsky was fighting not only a specific court decision but the views of prominent public figures advocating the very divorce of ethics from the law that he saw jeopardizing the moral foundations of Russian society. Dostoevsky exposes the real source of the problem in the institution, not in the lawyers. Saltykov even agrees with Dostoevsky that the bar has become more important than the individual lawyers comprising it but thinks that it is not a problem at all but a good thing: Saltykov does not want lawyers meddling in political and ethical questions, areas beyond their competence.

Dostoevsky emphasizes that the lawyers are not the only prisoners of the legal system, so are the jurors. Their freedom to express their conscience—permissible by Russian law—is, in actual practice, effectively shackled by judicial procedures.[22] The legalistic formulation of the question to be decided in the Kroneberg case ruled out the possibility of returning with a guilty verdict, that is, it prevented the jury from performing what Dostoevsky thinks is its greatest responsibility: determining on the basis of both a reasoned and emotional understanding of the evidence, a understanding in which compassion must play a principal role, whether an act was or was not a crime. It should be up to the judge, and other legal organs, to temper justice with mercy.[23] The most important element in any jury trial, according to Dostoevsky, is "the jurors' conscience" (319; 23:10), but the jury did not convict Kroneberg, just as it did not convict Kairova, "because they were unable to modify their verdict in any other way" (318; 23:9).[24]

> I believe that had the jurors been in a different position, that is, had they the possibility of rendering a different verdict, they would have grown indignant over such an exaggeration on Mr. Utan's [the defense lawyer's] part, and thus he could have harmed his client. But the whole point was that they literally could not have brought in a different verdict. In the press, some have commended them for this verdict, while others—it is rumored—have censured them. I *believe that here there is no place for either praise or censure: they rendered this verdict because of the absolute impossibility of uttering anything different.* Please judge for yourselves. (317; 23:8–9; emphasis added)

Dostoevsky shows that the role of compassion in the jury's decision is both seriously complicated and compromised by the formalism of legal procedures. He would like compassion (and other nonrational elements) to enter the determination of the jury's duty—after all, criminal trials involve the emotional behavior of human beings—yet he does not want compassion to interfere unduly with the jurors' desire and need to do what is right and just.[25] Jurors, moved by compassion, for example, might vote acquittal for a man whom they thought was guilty if a guilty verdict entailed a disproportionately harsh sentence. The adversarial system of lawyers, then, not only may lead to attempts to root out compassion in the jury, but the formalism of the legal process turns the positive manifestations of compassion to an evil end—the seeming vindication of criminality.

Equally devastating—and understandably the most personal element in the article—is Dostoevsky's attack on the legal system's imprisonment of art. There could hardly be anything so distressing to Dostoevsky as the misuse of art—art in the service of immoral ends. But this is most certainly to Dostoevsky the fate of art in the courtroom, especially in the hands of artistically talented lawyers. Art is in danger of being transformed into a tool of practical law, becoming, in the end, no less institutionalized, no less part of the system, than the lawyers and prosecutors who use it. Dostoevsky always recognized the potential of art for evil, and the Kroneberg case must have justified his worst fear.

Because the lawyers are tools of the institution that they seem to command, the art they use serves not the lawyer but the law itself; the lawyer must subordinate his artistic talent to his institutional function—the defense of the client—regardless of the client's guilt or innocence:

> There arises an insoluble question: does talent possess man, or does man possess his talent?—As far as I am able to observe men of talent, both living and dead, it does seem to me that in the rarest of cases only is a man capable of mastering his gift; and that, contrariwise, talent almost always enslaves its owner—grabbing him, so to speak, by his neck (quite so—oftentimes in this humiliating manner), carrying him very far away from the right road. . . . Thus, *not money alone is to be feared* by a lawyer as a temptation . . . but his own power of talent. (215; 22:54/218; 22:56)

When Dostoevsky stresses that artistic talent has a dynamic of its own, that as the law dominates the lawyer so can art easily possess its master, he is not saying that art operates under its own laws, completely free of constraints imposed by the lawyer or the judicial system but that art that is in control may help the lawyer win his case—as in Kroneberg—and thus serve the institution of the law as well or better than almost any other device at the lawyer's disposal. Thus the damage that is done in the courts is exacerbated by talented lawyers who get carried away by their own rhetoric and are transformed, as it were, into lawyer-performers, playing for the approval of the jury as though it were an audience at a drama.[26] The court is a breeding ground for the exploitation of art, for bad art in the Tolstoyan sense, art that infects its audience with negative emotions.[27]

For Dostoevsky, Spasovich is a perfect example of the imprisoned artist, a man both possessing and being possessed by talent. Spasovich's general talent is as troubling as his talent as an artist of the word. Dostoevsky repeatedly emphasizes that lawyers can be artists and that art is at the very foundation of their talent.[28] "Poetry is, so to speak, the inner fire of every talent. And if even a carpenter may be a poet, so certainly may a lawyer be a poet, too, if he is endowed with talent. . . . Mr. Spasovich, too, is a remarkably gifted lawyer. To my way of thinking, his speech in this case is a climax in art" (216, 218; 22:55, 56).[29] Dostoevsky goes over every one of Spasovich's devices to expose the lawyer's exploitation of art. At every step of the way Dostoevsky catches the lawyer, the "extraordinary talent," using another strategy to lead astray, to confuse, to deceive. Dostoevsky devotes an entire section to "Mr. Spasovich's Speech: Adroit Devices." "Mr. Spasovich has adroitly confiscated age as a thing most dangerous to him" (219; 22:57). "This is very clever" (219; 22:57). "By this device Mr. Spasovich at once breaks the ice of distrust and through this one little drop he infiltrates your heart" (219–20; 22:58). "However, in these little, subtle, as it were, fleeting, but incessant innuendoes, Mr. Spasovich is the greatest master, with no rival, of which you will become convinced later on" (222; 22:59–60).[30] And most important: "But the height of art [*verkh isskusstva*] was reached when Mr. Spasovich completely confiscated [*konfiskoval*] the age of the child!" (229; 22:66).

What is the purpose of all this talent, this mastery, this rhetoric, this art in the service of one's client? Is it not bad enough that Spasovich leads us astray, attacks the sanctity of childhood, and attempts to root out compassion and pity?[31] At the artistic climax, in a complete inversion of values, the defense lawyer not only "confiscates" the innocence of childhood but extols the child abuser as the foundation of the family, of the state itself:

> "When this bad habit in the girl had been revealed"—says Mr. Spaso-
> vich—(that is, the habit of lying)—"added to all her other deficiencies;
> when the father learned that she had been *stealing*, he really flew into
> a rage. I believe *each one of you would have flown* into the same type of
> rage, and I believe that to prosecute a father because of the fact that
> he has severely, but *deservedly*, punished his child, is poor service to the
> family, poor service to the state, because the state is solid only when the
> family is strong. . . . If the father grew indignant, he was fully within his
> rights." (232; 22:68)

In the defense of his client Spasovich maintains that the very welfare of the state must at times countenance, even require, the beating of innocent children. Spasovich, the attorney for the defense, suddenly assumes the role of prosecuting attorney; the seven-year-old innocent becomes the defendant and the father the unjustly accused, persecuted for exerting his rights, for exacting just punishment for the welfare of the state itself. The Kroneberg case, argues Spasovich, is not about child abuse at all but the righteous indignation, the "just wrath, of the father." Spasovich situates the law not outside the government, an institution that would protect individuals from arbitrary state power, but as the main support of the state. Dostoevsky recasts the liberal Spasovich as a conservative, if not a reactionary. Spasovich was led by the force of his own rhetoric to a position diametrically opposed to his private sympathies and allegiances, in effect, turning a prominent liberal into a defender of the autocracy. When Dostoevsky writes of Spasovich's losing control or being carried away, he does not mean that Spasovich hurt his own cause by losing control. Quite the opposite: the apparent loss of control should be seen as the institution exerting its power over the lawyer, usurping the lawyer's art for its own purposes. One is reminded of Dostoevsky's description of Raskolnikov's rational casuistry, which provided the justification for the murder of the pawnbroker and later led him "blindly" and "mechanically" to the perpetration of the deed:

> However, the last day, which had arrived so unexpectedly and which had decided everything all at once, had an almost completely mechanical effect on him. It was as though someone had taken him by the hand and drew him along irresistibly, blindly, with unnatural strength, without objections. It was as though a piece of his clothing had been caught in the wheel of a machine and he was being pulled into it. (6:58)

Raskolnikov thinks he is in complete control. It is the nature of "his casuistry with the cutting edge of a razor" to encourage the feeling that everything has been properly and systematically worked out and ordered (6:58). But rather than being the master of his faculties, he is led like an unprotesting slave to his undoing. Moreover, the force that overcomes him is an impersonal mechanistic one—"a huge machine of the most modern invention" (8:339)—as Ippolit Terent'ev might say (*The Idiot*)—which catches its apparent master in its wheels and uses its victim for its own purposes, not unlike the way the law has made that master of lawyers, Spasovich, a prisoner of its own impersonal logic—at least according to Dostoevsky.

Narrative Empathy

Dostoevsky's approach to the injustices he observed in the Kroneberg case in the *Diary of a Writer* has much in common with the agenda of lawyers and scholars in the critical legal studies movement. In the Kroneberg case Dostoevsky attempts to use narrative as an emotional and empathetic force in subverting the rigid, formal, and rational constraints of the legal system, especially when it privileges the forces of authority, here represented by the state (the legal system) and the father. Of course, Dostoevsky is not using narrative directly in the courtroom. What he has done, as we have seen, is to transfer the case, after the fact, to another venue, a narrative venue, the *Diary of a Writer*. Here, unconstricted by the legal formalism of the court, he can rectify the miscarriage of justice in Kroneberg by playing both prosecutor and defense attorney. He can retry Kroneberg, put Kroneberg's lawyer, Spasovich, on trial, and act as a more effective, passionate, and compassionate defense attorney for the real victims in the case, the little girl and the peasant women who came to her defense. And here art again becomes the issue. In Tolstoyan aesthetic terms, Dostoevsky must use his own artistic powers in the cause of the good to overcome the bad art of Spasovich.

Dostoevsky must restore in his audience, the Russian public, the compassion destroyed by the lawyer. We have seen how Dostoevsky used his personal experience in Siberia and his authority as a master child psychologist to proclaim that a crime had been committed and to elicit compassion from his audience. Dostoevsky goes beyond personal commitment; he implies that all who do not follow his example, who remain silent (including, as we shall see, Dostoevsky himself in the past), are complicit in the crimes that are being perpetrated by the court. In the passage that follows, Spasovich is cast in the role of torturer, the little girl as a helpless chick, the peasant women as mother hens, and Dostoevsky as complicit in the crime, a protector, however unwilling, not of the chicks but of the torturer:

Can you visualize that hen—that brood-hen—shielding her chicks, spreading out her wings to protect them? These pitiful hens, when defending their chicks, sometimes become almost dreadful. During my childhood, in the country, I used to know a boy [*mal'chishka*] from among the house servants, who was terribly fond of torturing animals and particularly of slaughtering chickens with his own hands, whenever they had to be cooked for the master's dinner.[32] I remember he used to climb on the straw roof of the barn in search of sparrows' nests: upon finding one, he would immediately start wringing their heads. Now, just imagine this same torturer being awfully afraid of a hen, when, in a fury, with its wings spread out, it stood in front of him, defending its chicks. On such occasions he used to hide behind me. So then, about three days later, unable to bear it any longer, this pitiful hen, after all, actually went to the authorities to lodge a complaint, taking along with her that bundle of rods with which the little girl had been flogged, as well as her blood-stained underwear. (225; 22:62)

This passage combines, in even sharper contrast than the previous ones, the virtuous common women of the people and the nefarious Spasovich. The hen risks her life to save her chicks. The servant women, however, are making the sacrifice not for their own chicks but for someone else's child, that is, not merely from maternal instinct but out of Christian love, compassion for the soul of an insulted innocent. The last stroke comes with Dostoevsky's implicit comparison of Spasovich and the boy who wrings the necks of little birds.

The differences are as striking as the similarities. Spasovich does not derive the same satisfaction from discrediting the testimony of the peasant women as the boy does from twisting off the necks of fledglings. He is also no boy, backing off in terror as the hen sacrifices herself for her brood. On the contrary, he is in his element in the court, he is the cock of the court. In the court of law the Russian peasant women become more like chicks than hens, more like the little girl whom they hoped to defend. They are victimized by a system they cannot understand and against which they have little protection. Dostoevsky's role as defender, but not defense *attorney,* becomes both morally and politically imperative. He makes us feel that detached narrative—like observation—would, on his part, be no less a crime against the child and her compassionate protectors than Spasovich's.

Dostoevsky, as a boy, that is, as the original detached observer, did nothing to curtail the activities of the servant boy, whom he watched torturing the helpless chicks. He stood by, passively shielding the boy from the fury of the terrifying mother hen. By contrast, Dostoevsky, as narrator, takes up the role of defending not only the little girl but the entire Russian people and its truth, which are being attacked by the cold, unfeeling forces of legalism and rationalism embodied by the "king of the Russian bar," as Spasovich was called by his admirers. It is not the mother hen but Dostoevsky himself—no longer the detached observer of his youth—who, dreadful but compassionate, spreads his wings to protect his helpless people against the abuses of this dangerous incursion from the West: the jury trial. Just as the peasant women could not stand idly by as detached observers, he too must intercede—now through narrative—to defend the bearers of the Russian word.

## Western Law, Russian Justice

It is not difficult to understand why Dostoevsky wrote so critically of the jury trial in *The Brothers Karamazov*, the subject of a later chapter. It is a little more difficult to assess the motivation for his harsh assessment of the Russian legal reforms in the Kroneberg article. Dostoevsky had been critical of lawyers (but who has ever not been?) ever since the courts started to operate. But he had faith in Russian juries. The political trials of 1877 and 1878 (the Trial of Fifty, the Trial of 193, and the Zasulich case), which were so important for *The Brothers Karamazov*, had occurred some time after the Kroneberg case, which had few political implications. The defendant was not a young terrorist intent on overthrowing the autocracy but a fairly well-educated man trying to make a career in St. Petersburg. His liberal attorney was defending some rather conservative positions: the strict interpretation of statute law, the rights of parents, and the noninterference of the state in family affairs. Nor was Spasovich trying to achieve jury nullification—in contrast to Fetyukovich in *The Brothers Karamazov*—but to make the jury decide the case on the law. Much of Dostoevsky's animus, of course, can be explained by his growing conservatism. Because Dostoevsky viewed the court as a school from which the Russian public was being morally educated, he could not help but be concerned about its potential deleterious influence on the moral fabric of the common people, the ultimate hope for the spiritual and social transformation of the nation. His dissatisfaction with the court was undoubtedly exacerbated by the former high hopes he held for the court's role in the country's moral renewal. Much can be explained by disillusionment.

But perhaps an even more important determinant of Dostoevsky's animus toward the jury trial was his growing distrust of Western law and institutions, of which the jury trial was the most celebrated instantiation in Russia of the 1870s.

A maximalist who abhors the middle ground, the customary locus of the law, Dostoevsky does not even consider the possibility that the problem in Kroneberg may indeed have been the specific law under which he was tried and that the solution to the problem lay not in rejecting the system but in amending the law to make brutal beatings a criminal offense. Nothing in the Russian legal system would have made it impossible to change the law. In fact, it is specific cases like these, in which gross disparities between law and ethics arise, that lead to changes in the law. But for Dostoevsky the defect in the law is symptomatic of something much deeper, something structural and uncorrectable.

## Laodicean Ethics

The Russian legal scholar Bogdan Kistyakovsky would probably have attributed Dostoevsky's reasoning in Kroneberg to a larger Russian cultural phenomenon: the woefully low level of legal consciousness among Russia's educated classes. Kistyakovsky argued that in "other civilized" countries like France, England, and Germany, where legal ideas have always been central to public intellectual and social discourse, legal consciousness could, through a long evolutionary period, become a part of an almost unconscious heritage. In Russia, because of "the totality of ideas out of which our intelligentsia's world-view takes shape, the idea of law has no place at all."[33] Even after the reforms of 1864, Russian legal consciousness did not develop in the manner of other Western nations.

> It would be impossible to point out anything of an analogous nature in the development of our intelligentsia. Law faculties have been formed at all our universities, some of which have been in existence for more than one hundred years; and we have five specialized institutions of higher education in law. All this amounts to about 150 law chairs for all of Russia. But not one of the holders of these chairs has ever produced even a legal study, to say nothing of a book that had broad *public* significance

and that would have influenced our intelligentsia's legal consciousness. In our juridical literature, you could not point to a single simple essay that has advanced even one vital, original legal idea, not necessarily profound but at least essentially true, like Jhering's *The Fight for Law.* Neither Chicherin nor Solovyov ever created anything of particular significance in the realm of legal ideas.[34]

But equally as important as Kistyakovsky's accusation regarding the dire state of Russian legal consciousness is his assessment of its cause, which he found not only, as others did, in Russia's autocratic past but in a worldview held by the most prominent members of the intelligentsia, both on the left and the right: antipathy to compromise.[35] Russian intellectuals refused intellectually and morally to accept a middle ground, to be satisfied with anything but a total solution. In fact, they celebrated the absence of the middle ground in Russia as a comparative virtue. Socialists like A. I. Herzen and radicals like N. K. Mikhaylovsky, seeing legal systems inextricably bound to the social orders in which they operated, championed the absence of legal systems in Russia as an opportunity to bypass a whole stage of historical development and to pass directly on to socialism.[36] For the social democrat G. V. Plekhanov, it was simply salus revolutia suprema lex.[37] The intellectuals on the right, especially the Slavophiles, and here at least we must count Dostoevsky among them, saw this absence of legal forms as a reflection of the most positive aspects of the Russian national character, to which formalism and the instrumental rationalism of the West were inherently alien. The relation between people should be guided by inner justice and trust, not by laws and guarantees. Kistyakovsky quotes the prominent Slavophile Konstantin Aksakov, who maintains that "'guarantees are evil. Where guarantees are needed there is no good; it would be better for life without good to be destroyed than for it to stand with the help of evil.'"[38] The Russian maximalist consciousness makes little room for the legal order; worse, it sees the legal order as antithetic to justice itself, nothing less than a contract with the devil: ethics and the law are fundamentally irreconcilable.

Ziolkowski has argued that the greatest art about the law occurs in crisis periods in which artists perceive a growing rift between ethics and the law. But Dostoevsky has gone much beyond the idea of crisis. For Ziolkowski art not only dramatizes the rift between law and justice, it envisions a solution, even if only implicitly, in which the rift can be healed. But if law and ethics are seen as inherently incompatible, if justice lies outside the law, then justice can never occur in the courtroom, especially in a Western court. Russian justice can take place at a trial only through a miracle, a suspension of natural law: that is exactly how Dostoevsky portrays the achievement of justice in the Kornilova case. Kistyakovsky, by contrast, argues that the legal system lies at the heart of every society and that the court is the most important institution for the establishment of the rule of law. Every nation that has "a developed legal consciousness must concern itself with, and must value, its own court as the guardian and organ of its legal system."[39]

Kistyakovsky's analysis of the crisis of Russian legal consciousness is indirectly supported by Yury Lotman and Boris Uspensky's semiotic analysis of Russian medieval culture, which they argue had a profound effect on the so-called Europeanized periods of Russian cultural development. The West, Lotman and Uspensky argue, always set aside a middle ground, a place in which the extremes of space, behavior, and ideology could be mediated. Purgatory was a middle place, a neutral zone, where eternal salvation could be won "after some sort of purgative trial. In the real life of the medieval West a wide area of neutral behavior became possible, as did neutral societal institutions, which were neither 'holy' nor 'sinful,' neither 'pro-state' nor 'anti-state,' neither good nor bad. This neutral space became a structural reserve, out of which the succeeding system developed."[40] Russian culture, on the contrary, was characterized by a bipolar field "divided by a sharp boundary without an axiologically neutral zone."[41] Russian culture had no notion of purgatory, because "intermediate neutral spheres were not envisioned. Behavior in earthly life could be correspondingly either sinful or holy. This situation spread into extra-ecclesiastical conceptions: thus secular power could be interpreted as divine or diabolical, but never as neutral."[42]

Though Lotman and Uspensky limit their study to the end of the eighteenth century, they imply that the bipolar model is equally relevant for an understanding of nineteenth-century Russian cultural consciousness and precisely those spheres of neutral space most perfectly embodied by the law. Lotman comes even closer to the crux of the legal problem in his study of the different attitudes toward agreement and contracts in Russian and Western culture. Almost from the very beginning, Western religious culture validated the language and practice of agreements and contracts. By contrast, in Russian Orthodoxy the sense of agreement was invariably associated with that which was pagan. In the West agreements were essentially neutral: They could be made with the devil, but they also could all be made with "the forces of holiness and goodness."[43] But in Russia an agreement could be made only with a satanic power or its pagan counterpart: It could only be sinful to honor such a contract and salvific to break it.[44] In the West a contract is a sign, a construction of convention; in Russia it is a symbol and achieves validity only by the authority sanctioning it. One makes contracts with one's equals; one does not make deals with God; one gives oneself to God unconditionally. Lotman does not see Russian culture as entirely uniform or monolithic. He views the eighteenth century as a Russian attempt to transform itself into a society based on Western ideas of conventional, contractual relationships, both in government and social life. Lotman implies, however, that the efforts of the eighteenth century in this direction were largely reversed in the nineteenth century, an age of symbolism, in which the sign and the conventional were again demoted, and the idea of self-surrender to the absolute—equally for those on the left and the right—became the order of the day. Neither side would have trucked with a compromised middle ground.

Thus it would be mistaken to see Dostoevsky's position on the issue of mediated middle-ground truths as maximalist or anomalous.[45] The later Tolstoy, to whom swearing an oath in court was tantamount to selling one's soul, saw the whole legal system (scathingly presented in his last novel, *Resurrection*) mired in a nether region of untruth, even lower than the one described by Dostoevsky in Kroneberg. Tolstoy's view of the truth is aptly capsulized by the "subtitle" of his most famous play, *The Power of Darkness*: "Once its claw is caught, the whole bird is lost."[46] Even Chekhov, a liberal and in many ways the antithesis of Dostoevsky and Tolstoy, seems either to share their view of truth and justice, or at least presents the view as representative of the Russian people. Crutch, a common worker, and one of the more positively presented characters in *My Life* (to be sure, a first-person narrative), offers his view of truth: "The way I understand it, if a common man or a nobleman takes even the very smallest interest, he's a villain. Truth [*pravda*] can't exist in such a person. . . . Lice eats grass, rust eats iron, and a lie, the soul. Lord, save us sinners."[47] After presenting in great and graphic detail many of the negative sides of the Russian peasant, the narrator of *My Life* finds something essential and substantial in the peasant that he does not see in the members of the educated classes, namely, the peasant's "belief that truth [*pravda*] is the most important thing on earth, that his salvation and that of all people is in that truth [*pravda*] alone; and that is why it is justice [*spravedlivost'*] that he loves more than everything else in the world."[48] It is clear from the context that the justice mentioned is not one associated with any legal system but an inner and, ultimately, a transcendental justice. We see the same attitude deeply ingrained in the consciousness of Russian liberals under communism, like Vasily Grossman. In his long suppressed *Life and Fate* Grossman envisions as the most desirable alternative to fascist and communist totalitarianism not a middle ground, not a social contract, but Russian truth and Russian justice, for, as he writes: "There is only one truth. There cannot be two truths. It's hard to live with no truth, with scraps of the truth, with a partial truth, a lopped-off truth, cropped truth. A partial truth is no truth at all."[49] Evidently, God hates partial truths. When the liberal Stepan Trofimovich Verkhovensky, one of the main characters in Dostoevsky's *The Possessed*, is on his deathbed and requests that the woman caring for him read from the Bible, the first passage to which she opens is, not inappropriately, Revelation: the end of time, where the law is at long last suspended and the truth is finally revealed; it is the passage about the Laodiceans, those, like Stepan Trofimovich, lukewarm in religion, those who occupy the worst of all places—the middle ground.

> And unto the angel of the church of the Laodiceans write; These things saith the Amen, the faithful and the true witness, the beginning of the creation of God; I know thy works, that thou art neither cold nor hot: I would thou wert cold or hot. So then because thou art lukewarm, and neither cold nor hot, I will spue thee out of my mouth. (Rv 3:14–16)

## Problems

Admittedly, in light of Dostoevsky's portrayal of the jury trial in *The Brothers Karamazov*, it is tempting to see Dostoevsky's position in the Kroneberg case as a rejection of the middle ground and thus to see *The Brothers Karamazov* as a logical conclusion of the earlier trial. As we have seen, there are many direct references to *The Brothers Karamazov* in the Kroneberg trial. But there are direct references in *The Brothers Karamazov* to an even more interesting later trial, the Kornilova trial, which does not at all lead directly to *The Brothers Karamazov* but represents, by contrast, a grudging and uncharacteristic acceptance by Dostoevsky of the judicial process. Dostoevsky became personally involved in the Kornilova case, the middle ground, and felt compelled to take positions that he had denounced, or seemed to denounce, in the Kroneberg case. In the Kornilova case Dostoevsky defended a woman convicted of child abuse, thus placing himself in the minds of his critics in exactly the same position that he had placed Spasovich. The vindication-salvation of Kornilova in the Western court that Dostoevsky celebrates in the *Diary of a Writer*, despite what he says explicitly, may make his summary rejection of the legal system in Kroneberg seem in varying degrees inconsistent, eclectic, impulsive, and opportunistic.

Just as problematic, especially in light of *The Brothers Karamazov*, is Dostoevsky's empathetic approach in the Kornilova case, an approach which represents a continuation and intensification of the approach that he took in the Kroneberg case. As though following the counsel of the more liberal wing of new critical studies, in the Kroneberg case Dostoevsky came to the aid of the disenfranchised and marginalized, a young girl and her peasant women defenders, exposing the legalistic, formalistic arguments of the defense attorney while exploiting his mastery of empathetic narrative to elicit compassion in his audience. He would use the very same method in the Kornilova trial but with the perpetrator of the crime, not the victim. Did empathy and compassion compel him to make a deal with the devil, the Western court?

CHAPTER 2

# Dostoevsky and
# the Kornilova Case

## The Realization of Russian Justice

Dostoevsky's article on Kroneberg little prepares us for the extraordinary series of articles that he wrote about the Kornilova case, which preoccupied him more than any other trial of the post-reform period.[1] *Novoe vremia* reported on 13 May 1876 that two days earlier a recently married twenty-year-old woman, Ekaterina Kornilova, had thrown her six-year-old stepdaughter out of a fourth-story window. The child sustained no serious physical injuries. When Dostoevsky learned of the Kornilova case, he immediately began to imagine that it would become another egregious example of Western justice, one that would outdo the earlier cases in miseducating the Russian people and blurring the distinction in the public mind between good and evil. Toward the end of his article on the Kairova case (*Diary of a Writer,* May 1876), Dostoevsky interjects a few comments about Kornilova's crime. He imagines that the defense of Kornilova will closely resemble those of Kroneberg and Kairova. The lawyer will undoubtedly show that Kornilova committed no crime; even worse, that she was justified in defenestrating the child, for the child was in fact the one at fault. Dostoevsky acknowledges that he is drawing a caricature, but given the examples of the Kroneberg and Kairova cases, the caricature cannot, he implies, be far from the truth:

> By the way, I imagine how advocates will be defending that stepmother: we shall hear about the helplessness of her situation, and about the fact that she is a recent bride of a widower whom she married under compulsion or force, or by mistake. We shall have pictures drawn portraying the miserable existence of destitute people, their never-ending work.

She, the naive, the innocent, believed when she married, an inexperienced little girl (particularly under our system of upbringing!), that married life brings nothing but joys—and here instead of them—washing of dirty linen, cooking, bathing the child: "Gentlemen of the jury, it is only natural that she started hating the child (who knows, maybe there will appear a 'defense lawyer' who will begin to smear the child and will find in a six-year-old girl some bad and hideous qualities!)— in a moment of despair, in a state of madness, almost without remembering herself, seized the girl, and . . . Gentlemen of the jury, who among you wouldn't have done the same thing? Who among you wouldn't have thrown the child out of the window?" (329; 23:19)

At her trial, which took place on 15 October 1876, it was revealed that no one had seen what Kornilova had done; nevertheless she went immediately to the police and confessed. She was tried, convicted, and sentenced to two-and-a-half years of hard labor in Siberia. Although Dostoevsky originally saw the Kornilova case in the context of Kroneberg—that is, as another example of child abuse bound to vindicate the perpetrator and victimize the victim—the articles he wrote about Ekaterina Kornilova differ radically from his earlier articles on the reform court. He wrote his first article about Kornilova after she was found guilty. The court proclaimed that a crime had been committed. But just as significant, even before Kornilova's trial, Dostoevsky sensed something about Kornilova that made her situation seem different from Kroneberg's. In the same article about the Kairova case that I just quoted, Dostoevsky remarks that something is fantastic (*fantastichno*) about Kornilova's act, something, in fact, that might constitute extenuating circumstances bearing on the sentence, if not on the crime itself. "The act of this monster stepmother, is, indeed, too queer, and perhaps it warrants a subtle and profound analysis which might even tend to alleviate the lot of the delinquent woman" (329; 23:19).

After her conviction, to the surprise of many readers of the *Diary of a Writer,* and also to many of his ideological opponents, Dostoevsky wrote a series of articles defending Kornilova, using the techniques of empathetic narrative that he had worked out in the defense of the peasant women who had reported the beating of Kroneberg's daughter to the police. Dostoevsky ran the risk of becoming the social pariah that Spasovich had become after defending Kroneberg. Spasovich did not seek out the Kroneberg case; he was a court-appointed lawyer. By contrast, Dostoevsky chose to defend Kornilova, knowing in advance how his ideological opponents would react to his defense of a child abuser, especially given his position in the Kroneberg case.

By the time Dostoevsky had finished the last of his four articles about Kornilova in December 1877, he had thoroughly incorporated the Kornilova trial into his religious and ideological agenda. In his first three articles about the case, Dostoevsky, by gradually shifting the focus from Kornilova's crime to her potential for spiritual regeneration, despite his intentions, transforms the Western court into an instrument for realizing, through faith and community, the highest form of Russian religious justice. In the fourth article, devoted to Kornilova's actual spiritual progress, Dostoevsky turns Kornilova's moral regeneration into a parable of the Russian people's potential for redemption and turns the decision of the jury, as well as the behavior of all members of the court, into a blueprint for the salvation, through mercy and compassionate understanding, of all Russian society. In conclusion, Dostoevsky attempts to present that double miracle as occurring despite the Western court from which it emerged. But, as I hope to show, he may have unwillingly made a good case for the opposite conclusions, portraying the jury trial as playing an essential, perhaps even indispensable, role in bringing about Russian justice, community (*sobornost'*), and resurrection from the dead.

### For a Moment the Court Becomes the Site of Russian Justice

In the October 1876 issue of the *Diary of a Writer,* Dostoevsky severely criticized the sentencing of Kornilova to two-and-a-half years of hard labor, arguing that she should have been acquitted because of temporary insanity ("madness without madness" [*sumasshestvie bez sumasshestviia*]; 534; 24:43) resulting from her pregnancy. Dostoevsky was well aware that taking the side of a woman who threw her stepdaughter out a window might cause the same societal confusion about crime that he had so recently decried in the Kroneberg and Kairova cases. Despite the problematic nature of this position, Dostoevsky took the risk, he said, out of love and compassion, relying on the faith of his readers that he could hardly be defending crimes against innocent children:

I fully understood that I was writing an unsympathetic article; that I was raising my voice in defense of the torturer, and against whom?—Against a little child. I foresaw that *certain people* would accuse me of insensibility, self-conceit, even of sickliness: "He is defending a stepmother, the murderess of a child!" I clearly foresaw this inflexibility of accusation on the part of some judges—for instance, on yours, Mr. Observer—so that, for a while, I hesitated, but in the end, I made up my mind: "If I believe that here is the truth, is it worth while to serve deceit for the sake of gaining popularity?"—that is what I finally said to myself. (933; 26:108)

But how could Dostoevsky argue in the Kroneberg case that the father should be convicted for severely beating his child and in the Kornilova case that the stepmother who pushed a child out a fourth-story window be acquitted? Only recently, he had fulminated against several similar acquittals of female defendants. How could the acquittal of Kroneberg be a miscarriage of justice while the conviction of Kornilova was a judicial mistake (*sudebnaia oshibka*)? Further, how could he present the later acquittal of Kornilova (at her second trial) as the highest form of justice?[2]

Dostoevsky wrote the four pieces about the Kornilova trial during a fourteen-month period. The first was so successful that it resulted in the rescinding of Kornilova's conviction and a retrial. The prosecutor and the presiding justice announced publicly at the retrial that, as Dostoevsky states, "the first verdict was quashed precisely because of my suggestion in the *Diary* that 'the act of the criminal woman may have been prompted by her pregnant state'" (914; 26:92). Further, Dostoevsky started to visit Kornilova in prison about once a month after her conviction, and he visited Kornilova and her husband at their home after her acquittal. The four pieces are not entirely consistent, nor are they written—nor could they be, considering the course of events—from exactly the same point of view. Each time Dostoevsky integrates a slightly amended summary of events, his arguments for acquittal, and the consequences of acquittal for both Kornilova and her family, including her stepdaughter.

To justify his call for acquittal by reason of what might be called "prepartum depression," Dostoevsky briefly outlines Kornilova's situation at home and her actions directly after the crime. Her relationship with her husband had become especially strained right before the crime. He

had beaten her in front of her relatives two days earlier for not having
returned one night from a family gathering. They had not talked for
two days. When her husband went out to work on the third day, she
fed and dressed her stepdaughter. Then, in a sudden vindictive impulse, she told the child to go to the window to look for something
and pushed her out. Kornilova did not even look out the window to
see what happened to the girl but immediately went to the police station to confess the crime. She told the police that she had contem-
plated committing the crime the night before because of her malice
toward her husband. She pleaded guilty and made no attempt to defend herself.

As Dostoevsky emphasizes, Kornilova could easily have gotten away
with the crime had she wanted to. She was conscious of what she was
doing, but she was herself amazed by what she had done. As she later
explained to Dostoevsky during one of his visits, it was as if she were
two women: "I wanted to do that evil thing, but it was as though it
were not my will to do so, but someone else's," and "I didn't want to
go to the police station at all, but somehow I arrived there, I don't
know why, and then I confessed to everything" (531; 24:39). Dostoevsky's explanation of Kornilova's strange behavior was that Kornilova,
who was in the fourth month of her pregnancy, was subject to an
admittedly rare pathological compulsion, "an insanity without insanity" (*sumasshestvie bez sumasshestviia*; 534; 24:43), caused by her pregnancy.[3] Even had she not experienced these pathological inclinations,
she might, to be sure, have thought about doing harm to the child to
get back at her husband, but she certainly would not have thrown the
child from the window. Dostoevsky does not insist that Kornilova experienced this pregnancy-induced pathological state when she committed the crime but that she may have. He does say that if she did,
the jury should have given her the benefit of the doubt and—despite
her crime—acquitted her out of mercy:

> It is well known that during pregnancy a woman (especially with her
> first child) is subject to strange influences and impressions which
> strangely and fantastically affect her mind and spirit. The influences, at
> times—however, in rare cases only—assume extraordinary, abnormal,
> almost absurd, forms. But what does it matter if this occurs rarely (i.e.,
> as exceptional phenomena)? In the present case, to those who had to

decide upon the fate of a human being, it should have been sufficient that such phenomena do occur, and even only that they may occur. (461; 23:138)

Dostoevsky brings up Kornilova's pregnancy only because Kornilova confessed to the crime. In the Kroneberg and Kairova cases, in Dostoevsky's view, evil was not only not proclaimed as evil, it was almost praised as virtue; however, Kornilova in no way tried to defend her action; she confessed to the crime and sincerely believed herself to be a criminal.[4] Although she continued to see her action as something alien to her, she nevertheless understood that she alone had to take complete responsibility for her sins before God and the community. The time, Dostoevsky argues, was therefore ripe for mercy. "Of two possible errors, it is far better to err on the side of mercy" (463; 23:140).

> What if in the present case, too, there was an affect of pregnancy? This is something to be considered. At least, in such a case, mercy would have been intelligible to everybody and would not have produced mental vacillation. And what if there should have been an error?—Better an error in mercy than in castigation—all the more so since in a case such as this nothing could have been verified. The delinquent woman is the first to consider herself guilty: she confessed immediately after having committed the crime; she also confessed six months later in court. (462–63; 23:139)[5]

Kornilova's pregnancy—the theoretical cause of the crime—interests Dostoevsky far less than the regeneration of the criminal, for Kornilova fits into a much different agenda than do Kroneberg and Kairova, the defendants in the two previous cases about which Dostoevsky wrote in the *Diary of a Writer*. Once she confesses her crime, Kornilova becomes part of a larger concern, something that the narrator in *Crime and Punishment* opined could be a sequel to the novel: the story of a criminal's regeneration and resurrection from the dead. Once the social issue has been satisfactorily resolved by the confession, the duty of the court is to deal with the equally, if not more, important religious duty of sowing the seeds of mercy essential to the salvation of an errant soul. Dostoevsky presents Kornilova as not in control of herself—that is, temporarily insane—when she committed the crime, not to prove her not responsible but rather to show that her act was an aberration and that it will never be repeated. Kornilova's crime was committed not by a hardened criminal but by a woman who has the potential for spiritual and moral regeneration.

Likewise, Dostoevsky is concerned about the punishment not because it is excessive in terms of Kornilova's crime but because it is excessive for Kornilova's character and situation. It is counterproductive for everyone concerned: for Kornilova herself, her stepdaughter, her infant child, her husband, and, as Dostoevsky will later imply, even for Russian society. Hard labor in Siberia will lead Kornilova to almost certain ruin; it will destroy the possibility of her resurrection from the dead. What will happen to the stepchild and to Kornilova's newborn? How will she support the infant? Will she not have to resort to prostitution? Will the child not have to follow her mother's path?

> Thus, perhaps, she will go to Siberia, sincerely and profoundly deeming herself guilty; thus she might also die, repenting in her last hour, and considering herself a murderess. And it will never occur to her or to anyone in the world that there is such a thing as a pathological affect [*affekt*] which occurs in the condition of pregnancy, which precisely may have been the cause of everything, and that, had she not been pregnant, nothing would have happened. . . . Nay, of two errors it is better to select the error of mercy. One will sleep more peacefully. (463; 23:139–40)

Dostoevsky stresses less the dire consequences of the verdict (the past) than the possibilities of redemption (the present and future). He imagines a farewell scene between husband, wife, and stepdaughter in which the family comes together in mutual forgiveness. It is a scene that deserves the attention of the public; it is an undramatic, unromantic story that Russian novelists should really be writing about. "And imagine—I was about to write: 'and nothing would come of it [this theme],' whereas, perhaps, it might come out better than all our poems and novels, with their heroes, 'full of sublime foresight, whose lives are torn asunder.' You know, I really cannot understand what our novelists are looking for. Here is a theme for them, and let them describe it step by step—the whole truth!" (464; 23:141). But obviously only Dostoevsky can see the importance of this subject. "Oh, the eye is all-important: what to one eye appears to be a poem, to another will be merely dross" (465; 23:141).

Indeed, look: this Kornilov is again a widower; his marriage is dissolved by the exile of his wife to Siberia. And now his wife—no longer his wife —in a few days will bear him a son [she actually gave birth to a daughter] (because she will certainly be permitted to deliver the child before she starts on her journey), and while she recovers she will be kept in the prison hospital or wherever she may be sent for that period. I'll bet you that Kornilov will visit her in a most prosaic fashion and—who knows —perhaps with that same little girl who flew out the window. They will get together and they will be speaking about the simplest, everyday things—say, about some miserable cloth, or warm shoes and felt boots for her journey. Who knows if they will not, perhaps, come together in the heartiest manner, when they have been divorced? And formerly they used to quarrel. Perhaps there will not be a single word of mutual re-proach—just a bit of sighing about fate and, compassionately, one about the other. And this little girl who flew out the window, I repeat, every day will, without fail, be running errands—from her father to "mama dear," bringing her "kalaches." "Here, mama dear, papa is sending you a kalach, together with tea and sugar; tomorrow he will come to you him-self." Perhaps the most tragic thing that is going to happen will be when, bidding each other farewell at the railroad station, at the last moment, between the second bell and the third, they start howling at the top of their voices. Following their example, the little girl will start howling, too, with her mouth wide open. Without fail, husband and wife, one after the other, will make low bows to each other: "Forgive me, *matushka* Katerina Prokof'evna; don't nourish a grudge against me!" And she, in turn: "Forgive me, too, *batiushka* Vasilii Ivanovich (or whatever his name might be). I'm guilty before you. My guilt is great . . . " At this juncture the nursling—who most certainly will be there—will start vociferating, no matter whether she [Kornilova] takes him [the nursling] with her or whether he be left with the father. (463–64; 23:140–41)

Dostoevsky imagines another miracle occurring, one even greater than the unharmed child. While the Kornilovs were husband and wife, they quarreled bitterly; the last quarrel precipitated the crime against the step-daughter. Now at their parting Dostoevsky sees a simple but moving reconciliation, one perhaps that could only have come about this way among the simple Russian people. The reconciliation, moreover, is one not only between former wife and husband but also, and perhaps most important, between criminal and victim, between the stepmother and the stepdaughter. The little girl seems to bear her stepmother no ill will; she even has become more attached to her "mama dear" than ever before, serving in effect as the main line of communication between her stepmother and father. Dostoevsky does not tell us what the little girl might know about what actually happened—and even in the later pieces he never does—but he clearly presents the young girl as feeling compassion for her "mama," forgiving her for any crime she may have committed. Dostoevsky emblematizes their complete reconciliation, at the time of permanent separation, with a collective peasant howl, the howl of former husband and wife, a howl joined first by the stepdaughter and then by the newborn herself. In a scene prefiguring many of the thematic and religious concerns of *The Brothers Karamazov*, Dostoevsky focuses on three crucial aspects of the Kornilovs' reconciliation, especially that between husband and wife: compassion, mutual forgiveness, and the acceptance of responsibility, which in the second piece he refers to as "the living truth" (*zhiznennaia pravda*; 529; 24:37). The time has passed for bitterness, for mutual recrimination; former husband and wife come closer together than they ever have—or perhaps ever will—by looking compassionately on each other's fate and asking for forgiveness, thus acknowledging their possible guilt before each other.

The asking of forgiveness takes the form of a deep Russian bow, a bow similar to the one that Father Zosima makes before Dmitry Karamazov's future suffering. It is the same profound exchange of bows that concludes the interpolated story, "Akulka's Husband," in *Notes from the House of the Dead*, when the peasant hero and heroine, taking leave of each other forever, must not part without asking for mutual forgiveness. Dostoevsky can hardly imagine a more perfect representation of his Russian Christian ideal, embodied in a simple, idealized peasant family. After witnessing such a scene—transformed through the creative imagination—one can only wonder along with Dostoevsky whether this verdict against Kornilova "could not be mitigated? Is it altogether impossible? Verily, here there might have been an error. . . . I keep thinking that it was an error [*oshibka*]" (465; 23:141).

Dostoevsky throws down the gauntlet to the new Russian court. For the court to dissolve this family—when reconciliation, on the soundest Christian principle, is still possible—would constitute more than a judicial error; it would be a great miscarriage of justice. Why cannot a Russian court bring the same ideals of compassion, forgiveness, and reconciliation to its decision that Dostoevsky imagined? Or must the jury trial follow, as in the Kroneberg case, only the strict rules of Western formalist jurisprudence? But, on the other hand, can a court that shows mercy, compassion, and forgiveness still send the requisite message about crime and good and evil to the Russian public, which is being educated by the new judicial system?

Dostoevsky wrote the first article on the Kornilova case to express his dismay that the jury did not err on the side of mercy. Like his articles on the Kroneberg and Kairova trials, he wrote it after the verdict had already been rendered. Dostoevsky wrote the second article about Kornilova after he learned that her conviction had been vacated "because of the violation of Section 693 of the Code of Criminal Procedure" and that the case would be retried "by a jury in another division of the court" (532; 24:41–42).[6] He wrote with renewed hope but also with grave forebodings. The Russian jury system had another chance to prove that it could not only maintain the distinction between good and evil, calling crime by its rightful name, but also temper justice with mercy, achieving what Dostoevsky would surely have called Russian justice in its highest manifestation. The second trial, then, was more than a retrial of Kornilova; it was a retrial—judged by Dostoevskian standards—of the entire judicial reform of 1864.

Moreover, Dostoevsky himself elevated the consequences of the court's decision by becoming personally involved in Kornilova's fate. His first article had brought about a retrial. He visited Kornilova several times in prison, first after she had given birth and was awaiting deportation and then about once a month after the invalidation of the conviction, when she was preparing for the second trial. Dostoevsky made the first visit to confirm the conjectures of his first article about the nature of Kornilova's crime, on which he based his "risky" decision to come out in favor of Kornilova's acquittal.[7]

Having finished that article and having brought out the issue of *The Diary*—and being still under the impression of all that I had imagined—I made up my mind, by all means, to interview Kornilova while she was still in the local jail. I confess that I was very curious to verify whether there was any truth in my conjectures about Kornilova and in my subsequent dreams concerning the case. It so happened that there soon occurred a circumstance which enabled me to visit Kornilova and make her acquaintance. (529; 24:38)

Dostoevsky needs to know whether Kornilova is the woman he imagined her to be, for only if she is can he justify advocating her cause.
She must be the good soil on which the proverbial seed falls, a woman
whose acknowledged crime and guilt make her ripe for spiritual rebirth. If she is such a woman, a conviction can only be the antithesis
of Christian justice, for it will deprive her of the chance to change her
life radically, to be reborn for herself and her family. Here Dostoevsky
seems to become even more personally involved, imagining a scenario
from his own life, when he had faced an irrevocable sentence but was
miraculously pardoned. He writes:

> God grant that this youthful soul, which has already endured so much,
> be not crushed forever by a new "guilty" verdict. It is terribly hard for a
> human soul to endure such shocks: they are akin to a situation where a
> man condemned to die before a firing squad would suddenly be untied
> from the post; hope would be restored to him; the bandage would be re-
> moved from his eyes; once more he would see the sunlight—but five min-
> utes later he would again be led back to be tied to the post. (533; 24:42)

A twenty-year-old peasant woman with a newborn can hardly be expected to survive such a harsh sentence, let alone be reborn. "Will she
derive much from hard labor? Will not her soul harden? Will it not be
depraved and exasperated forever? When had hard labor ever reformed
anyone?" (534; 24:43).[8] A second conviction would thus deal Kornilova
an even more devastating blow than the first one, and it would quash
Dostoevsky's hopes for Kornilova, which were further ele-vated by his
visits. Dostoevsky is exultant in announcing the accuracy of his conjectures: "I myself was even surprised. Can you imagine that at least three-
quarters of my meditations proved to be true: my guesses were as
correct as if I had been present at what actually happened" (529; 24:38).
As for the remaining quarter or less, these were only the most accidental things. "Indeed, in certain things I was mistaken, but not in the
essential ones" (529; 24:38). Kornilova's husband was a peasant (*krest'-
ianin*) but wore German clothes; he was younger than Dostoevsky
imagined him to be and had a good job in the Government Printing
Office. Kornilova was also gainfully employed as a seamstress. In other
words, they were better off and somewhat more sophisticated than
Dostoevsky had imagined them. When Dostoevsky imagines poor people, he often gives rein to his maximalist tendencies.[9]

But these differences from his imaginings, Dostoevsky repeats, are "insignificant disparities," whereas "in the most important matters, in the essential there was no mistake at all" (530; 24:38). And here Dostoevsky uses the word *oshibka* for error or mistake, as though to contrast his minor errors in imagining the Kornilovs with the judicial mistake, *oshibka*, made by the jury in Kornilova's conviction. Dostoevsky had guessed that Kornilova's husband would come to visit her and that "the two" would be "bidding farewell—one to the other—and they" would "be forgiving" (530; 24:38). The little girl did not actually come because she was attending a school where the girls were not let out, but, according to Kornilova, the little girl would have come to see her if she could have. Dostoevsky reports that he was pleased with the impression that Kornilova made on him. She turned out to be a simple woman (*prostodushnaia*), good-looking, and with an intelligent face. Although during the first visit she was still enervated by her recent childbirth and shaken by the guilty verdict, she answered all of Dostoevsky's questions about the crime forthrightly. "She fully confessed that she was a criminal guilty of everything of which she had been accused" (531; 24:39) and showed no bitterness toward her husband. She did not at all take offense at Dostoevsky's interest in her but rather expressed gratitude for his sympathy. On a subsequent visit, when she learned from Dostoevsky that a murderess by the name of Kirilova had been acquitted, Kornilova again showed no bitterness or envy.[10] She seemed sincerely to regret that she had taken out her anger at her husband on the child. But Dostoevsky was equally impressed by the testimony of the prison guards and the assistant warden. The assistant warden, in whom Kornilova had aroused considerable sympathy, confided to Dostoevsky that a dramatic change had taken place in Kornilova after she had been in prison for two weeks: she had become an altogether different creature. Whereas on arrival she had been coarse, rude, spiteful, and wicked tongued, she soon became kindhearted, open, and meek. Kornilova's dramatic change played an important role in her acquittal at the second trial. But even more relevant for Dostoevsky's project was the testimony from those who had been with Kornilova every day for a long time, testimony not about the person who committed the crime (the other Kornilova, as it were) but the real Kornilova, the real self who returned after the temporary aberration induced by pregnancy. The real Kornilova, as Dostoevsky had hoped, proved worthy of vindication because she demonstrated the potential for moral and spiritual regeneration; the real Kornilova was not the malicious woman who had entered prison but a good, kindhearted, and meek woman who merited a second chance. Thus Dostoevsky can state at the end of the second piece:

> Acquit the unfortunate and, perhaps, a young soul will not perish—a soul which, maybe, has so much life in the future and in which there are so many good potentialities for life. In prison all this will unfailingly be ruined, since the soul will be depraved, whereas now the terrible lesson, already endured by her, will guard her, perhaps, for her whole life, against an evil deed; and what is most important—it will help to develop and ripen those seeds and beginnings of good which apparently and unquestionably are present in this youthful soul. And were her heart truly hard and spiteful, mercy would unfailingly soften it. But I assure you, it is far from being hard and spiteful and I am not the only one to bear witness to this. Is it not possible to acquit her—to *risk* acquitting her? (534–35; 24:43)

At the end of chapter 2, section 5, of the *Diary of a Writer* for April 1877 (right after the end of the story called "Dream of a Ridiculous Man"), Dostoevsky included a three-page note entitled "Discharge of Defendant Kornilova," in which he informed his readers that Kornilova, who had been tried for a second time, had been acquitted. Dostoevsky writes that this time he was present in the courtroom, and he tells his readers that he regrets being unable to convey all his impressions but that he must limit himself to a few words. But he needs now only to report the outcome of the case, the acquittal of Kornilova.[11] Dostoevsky's prayers have been answered.

On 22 April there occurred not only the possibility of a resurrection from the dead but the triumph of Russian justice in a form that even Dostoevsky could not have imagined beforehand, in which compassion, forgiveness, and mercy all come together, and, even more important, in which defendant, jury, prosecutor, counsel for the defense, public—even author and reader—come together, as a collective in an emblematic *sobornost'*, in celebration of the renewal of a new soul.

Although Dostoevsky wrote the Kornilova pieces in 1876–77, they take on added significance when seen through the prism of Dmitry's trial in *The Brothers Karamazov*, written about three years later. The Kroneberg and Kairova articles present lawyers and expert witnesses quite negatively, but in *The Brothers Karamazov* Dostoevsky goes much further, excoriating almost every aspect of court proceedings, including attorneys, witnesses, the public, and the press. The participants are not evil nor even ill-intentioned, but the whole procedure suffers irreparably from an absence of collective spirit (*sobornost'*). Every participant has his or her own agenda, siding with or against Dmitry for the wrong reasons. The lawyers are equally matched, as are the medical experts for both prosecution and defense. Now Katerina Ivanovna makes a dramatic display in Dmitry's defense, only to follow it with an even more dramatic display to incriminate him for the sake of his brother Ivan. The Kornilova piece radically subverts our expectations, whether derived from the Kroneberg and Kairova cases or from our reading of *The Brothers Karamazov*, for Dostoevsky presents everything about the second Kornilova trial as truly remarkable (*zamechatel'no*), a word that he uses almost as a refrain.

The mistress of the women's division of the prison, a new witness, obviously gave "remarkable" testimony in favor of the defendant and so did the defendant's husband, the very husband who had tormented his young wife with reproaches and whose child she had thrown from the window. In other words, as Dostoevsky imagined—and perhaps even as he imagines again—the husband had completely forgiven his wife and they had been reconciled. The husband's justifying testimony —in court—becomes the site and the means of their final reconciliation, for the husband is now defending his wife publicly, in front of the jury, that is, the people, the Russian Orthodox collective.

Perhaps nowhere in Kornilova does Dostoevsky promote his utopic agenda more energetically than in the presentation of the expert testimony, especially that of the doctors and the psychologists. Dostoevsky usually subjects medical and psychiatric testimony to the most sardonic irony. In *Crime and Punishment* he impugns the latest psychological theory of temporary insanity, presenting it as a harmful novelty that sows unsound ideas in the Russian public. "But it was precisely from this that they concluded that the crime itself could have been committed only in a state of temporary insanity, that is to say, in a state of morbid monomania manifesting itself in murder and robbery, without any other goals and without any consideration of gain. Here, by the way, the latest fashionable theory of temporary insanity came to the rescue, which is so often employed nowadays for various criminals" (6:410–11). The testimony of almost all expert witnesses is further compromised by the adversarial process itself; the medical experts are no less hired hands than the lawyers themselves. In places, as in *The Brothers Karamazov,* their testimony borders on farce.

But in the Kornilova articles Dostoevsky has almost unadulterated praise for the testimony of the doctors and psychiatrists.

> Furthermore, the selection of expert witnesses was also remarkable. Altogether, six experts were summoned—all men of repute and celebrities in medical science. Five of them took the stand. Three experts unhesitatingly testified that a pathological condition peculiar to a pregnant woman *could have* caused the commission of the crime in this case. Only one—Dr. Florinsky—dissented from this opinion, but fortunately, he is not a psychiatrist, and his opinion proved of no consequence. The last man to testify was our noted psychiatrist Dukov. He spoke for almost an hour answering the questions propounded to him by the prosecutor and the presiding justice. It is difficult to conceive a more refined understanding of the human soul and its pathological states. I was also amazed by the wealth and variety of extremely curious observations gathered by him over a long period of years. As for myself, decidedly, I listened to certain statements of this expert with admiration. (691–92; 25:120)

In contrast to *Crime and Punishment,* Dostoevsky not only praises the psychologists in the Kornilova trial but trots out, of all things, the theory of temporary "insanity without insanity" (*sumasshestvie bez sumasshestviia*) as a mitigating circumstance.[12] Obviously aware that he is opening himself up to the same charge of which he has accused others, Dostoevsky implicitly argues that Kornilova constitutes that rare case in which the explanation of temporary insanity is entirely justifiable. Dostoevsky was dismayed by the Kornilova conviction precisely because the temporary insanity defense, which had been used with great success to acquit murderers, was not used, it would seem, in the sole case where it was perfectly appropriate.

All Dostoevsky's customary reservations about expert testimony, the temporary insanity defense, and contemporary sociological theories posing as psychology are swept aside in the Kornilova case because of Dostoevsky's need to turn the trial into a process entirely antithetical to the Kroneberg trial. The greatest praise of all is afforded to the psychiatrist, who argued not that Kornilova's pregnancy could have contributed to the crime but "that *positively* and *conclusively* . . . the defendant, at the time of the perpetration by her of the dreadful crime, was in a pathological psychic state" (692; 25:120). In other words, the psychiatrist had gone even further than Dostoevsky had allowed himself. Further, in contrast to the Kroneberg case, in which Dostoevsky fulminated against Spasovich as a rival artist—moreover an artist who was abusing his talent and could not help doing so because of the position in which he had been placed by the judicial system itself—Dostoevsky treats the psychiatrist in the Kornilova case as a great man who, like Dostoevsky himself, is using his profound psychological knowledge for advancing Russian justice. He is presented as a sort of colleague of Dostoevsky's in the profession of understanding the human soul and psyche, a man from whom even Dostoevsky could learn. "It was difficult to conceive a more refined understanding of the human soul and its pathological states" (692; 15:120).

But Dostoevsky is actually praising less the correctness, even the brilliance, of the expert testimony than its miraculous unanimity. (Dostoevsky discounts the testimony of Dr. Florinsky because he is only an accoucheur and not a psychiatrist). Here experts who can hardly ever agree on anything, often merely out of professional pride and vanity, put aside their professional and personal agendas to achieve complete intellectual and spiritual accord. The "miraculous" in the last sentence of the piece refers to the acquittal itself, but given Dostoevsky's animus toward expert testimony, it seems equally applicable to the unanimity of the expert witnesses. Dostoevsky needs a collective Russian judgment that he can juxtapose to such miscarriages of justice as occurred in the Kroneberg and Kairova decisions fostered by Western adversarial procedures.[13]

Dostoevsky is overwhelmed by a still greater miracle, the concord of the lawyers, who rise above their narcissism, Western education, and adversarial relationship.[14] The prosecutor, Dostoevsky says, did a rather good job. Considering the seriousness of the crime, Dostoevsky would not have had it any other way. But despite his formidable speech (*groznaia rech'*), the prosecutor agrees to withdraw the most important weapon in his case, premeditation.[15] Fortunately, this time the defense lawyer is competent. Whereas the great skill of the defense attorney Spasovich in the Kroneberg case provoked Dostoevsky into an attack against the entire adversarial system, the defense lawyer's extremely adroit handling of the accusations against Kornilova now receives unqualified approval. At the second trial the defense attorney no longer needs Dostoevsky to disprove the accusations lodged against his client. In Dostoevsky's reconstruction of the trial, the customary Western adversarial relationship of the lawyers is replaced with a sort of partnership: lawyers working together in the interest of the victims, the accused, and society in general.

The decision goes far beyond the courtroom and legal procedures; it involves the public both within and outside the courtroom and, perhaps most important of all, Dostoevsky's readers. Dostoevsky understands that the decision itself will affect Russian society far less than the disseminated report of the decision. After telling us about the remarkable judge and jury, Dostoevsky praises the public audience at the trial itself.

> After a long charge by the presiding judge, the jurors retired to the jurors' room, and in less than fifteen minutes they rendered a verdict of acquittal which produced very near rapture amongst the numerous public. Many people crossed themselves, others congratulated and shook hands with each other. The husband of the acquitted that same evening, after ten o'clock, took her home, and she, in a happy mood, returned to her home after an absence of almost one year, with the impression of a lesson learned for all her life and of manifest divine fate in this whole case—beginning with (to mention but one fact) the miraculous salvation of the child. (692; 25:120–21)

At the Kornilova trial, in contrast to the Kroneberg and Kairova cases, the conscience of the jury was not shackled by administrative procedures. The swift decision, facilitated by the presiding judge, showed unwavering unanimity, despite the most thorough investigation and the most relentless and weighty arguments of the prosecutor (914; 26:92).[16] The jurors seemed to listen with the same ears as Dostoevsky; they were equally impressed by the expert medical witnesses, with the exception, of course, of Dr. Florinsky, the accoucheur. In fact, the present jury took no longer to acquit than the previous jury took to convict.[17]

The public (*publika*) plays a special role in Dostoevsky's reconstruction of the Kornilova trial. In *The Brothers Karamazov* Dostoevsky casts the public in as negative a light as he casts the lawyers, reporters, and medical experts. He represents the public as possessing the very lowest Platonic form of knowledge: opinion, something resembling that fantastic insubstantiality of rumor in Gogol's *Dead Souls,* to which

*The Brothers Karamazov* is probably alluding. The public wants Dmitry to have killed his father; it is so much better theater. In the Kornilova case, however, the public is at one with the jury and with all the other participants of the judicial process, in which Russian justice emerges triumphant. Dostoevsky uses the word *vostorg,* rapture or ecstasy, to describe the reaction of the public to the acquittal of Kornilova. *Vostorg* is a word he often reserves for the most profound religious experiences of joy, for describing, for example, the mystical experience of Alyosha Karamazov and the mystical theology of Father Zosima in *The Brothers Karamazov.* The collective harmony that Dostoevsky sees as essential to Russian justice extends to all the participants, so that jury and public are not separated by judicial procedure but have become one in their mutual desire to bring about the salvation of a soul. The second trial took place around Easter. At the trial the diverse members of the public not only agreed with the decision, they became closer to one another as they shared in the miracle of compassion and forgiveness. Dostoevsky's portrayal of what occurred in the courtroom is not unlike a Russian Easter celebration. There is joy and rapture (*vostorg*) in celebration of resurrection and its promise of future resurrections from the dead, not the least of which may very well be Kornilova's. When leaving the court-church—in Dostoevsky's re-creation—one can easily imagine all the congregants at least wanting to congratulate each other with the greeting "Christ has risen. Yes, truly, he has risen."

The third article on the Kornilova case ends on a religious note. The defendant does not leave as a "free" woman but a woman who takes with her a lesson for life, who understands that the whole affair bears the divine mark. The affair began with the miraculous salvation of her step-daughter and continued with the birth of her own child, and with the miraculous decision of the jury, which grants her the possibility of re-birth. The coming together of the people at Kornilova's trial in the interest of one of their own is presented as an epiphany, a manifestation of the divine presence, a communion between God and his people.

## The Court and the Russian People

In April 1877, after Kornilova's acquittal, Dostoevsky thought he had finished with the Kornilova case. But just one month later an article appeared in the *Northern Messenger* (*Severnyi vestnik*), which, among

other things, attacked the decision of the court and questioned Dostoevsky's personal role in the case, specifically his articles of October
and December 1876 and his visits to the defendant from the time after
her conviction to the night before her retrial on 22 April 1877. Dostoevsky wanted to respond immediately, but, as he later stated, at the
time he did not have all the information necessary to refute the charges
leveled against him and the decision of the court. By December 1877,
that is, seven months later, the necessary evidence was in. Dostoevsky's
refutation, which occupied the entire first chapter of the December issue
of the *Diary of a Writer* for 1877, turned out to be about 50 percent
longer than all his previous pieces on the Kornilova case combined. But
this last article went far beyond refutation. Dostoevsky not only used
it to further promote his idea of personal justice, but he also incorporated the reborn Kornilova—and the court that showed her so much
mercy—into a vision of social justice based on class reconciliation.

As we have seen, Dostoevsky feared from the beginning that the
public might misunderstand the acquittal of the defendant, as he himself had done, as another case bound to sow the seeds of confusion
about the nature of crime and the difference between good and evil.

> Even so, at the time, that very day, the thought occurred to me that in so
> important a case involving the highest motives of civic and spiritual life,
> it is very desirable that everything be explained in all the minutest de-
> tails so that in society and in the souls of the jurors, who have rendered
> a verdict of acquittal, there no longer remain any doubts, vacillations,
> regrets that an indubitably criminal woman was left unpunished. . . .
> After the verdict had been announced, suddenly doubt began to torment
> me: Didn't the verdict leave a residue of discontent, perplexity, distrust
> of justice, even indignation in society? . . . Personally I should have not
> answered the author, but in that article I perceived exactly the same
> thing I was afraid to encounter in a certain portion of our society, viz.,
> confused impression, perplexity and indignation against the verdict.
> (914–15; 26:92–93)

He was especially hurt by the *Northern Messenger's* personal attack on
his participation in the case, and he was ready to counterattack. He
caustically notes that by vilifying the court's decision, without any knowledge of the actual proceedings, the critic of the *Northern Messenger*
reveals himself far more responsible than Dostoevsky for adversely

influencing "society, the courts, and public opinion" (916; 26:94). Dostoevsky cites the information he was awaiting in order to defend Kornilova, the facts regarding Kornilova's spiritual and moral rebirth that confirmed his hopes after the acquittal. In the April 1877 piece Dostoevsky compares the mercy, forgiveness, and compassion of the court's decision to a seed that had fallen on good soil. But in April Kornilova's regenerative turn was still only a hope. His conjectures and imaginative re-creations had proved correct before, as Dostoevsky himself reported in his December 1876 article on Kornilova, but now he needs more extensive and substantial proof. If he could show that the seed had really fallen on good soil, he could put to rest all society's fears about the evil ramifications of such a decision for the prosecution of crimes against children. Six months' time showed Dostoevsky that Kornilova was not a murderess; that her crime resulted from an aberration of her pregnancy; that the state in which she committed the crime had not returned and could never return; and, most important, that Kornilova had proved to be a good and humble soul (*dobraia i krotkaia dusha*), really worthy of compassion and mercy (*deistvitel'no byla dostoina sozhaleniia i miloserdiia*). In his novels Dostoevsky presents resurrection from the dead, though miraculous in essence, as a process, a lifelong travail accompanied by great suffering. In most cases Dostoevsky just shows the beginning of the process. Likewise, in Kornilova's case, six months would have to do.

Dostoevsky begins his rebuttal, as he attempted to do in the previous articles, with mistaken notions about Kornilova's behavior toward her stepdaughter directly before and after the crime. Dostoevsky shows that, despite her occasional severity, Kornilova was "a very good stepmother; she cared for the child and was attentive to her" (919; 26:97). However, Dostoevsky understandably finds more troublesome, especially when seen against the child-abuse charges of the Kroneberg case, Kornilova's very severe beating of her stepdaughter for bed-wetting. Even her severe husband regarded this beating as excessive. Dostoevsky states that the court positively established that Kornilova's severe beating of the child, however cruel, was a single isolated incident. The older and more educated Kroneberg was far more responsible for child abuse than the peasant woman Kornilova. Dostoevsky had focused more on Kroneberg's beating of his child precisely because the defense of Kroneberg was based on the contention that the beating was not cruel and thus not a criminal act; he therefore needed to establish the commission of a crime.[18] In the Kornilova case the defendant conceded the criminality of her act: She confessed to the crime. The focus of the case shifted onto the cause: Could her crime be attributable to temporary insanity?

Dostoevsky visited Kornilova in prison about once a month after the first trial—including a visit on the eve of the second trial—and three times after the second trial. He visited again, once, three days after the acquittal, once perhaps at the end of June, and once again during the Christmas season.[19] Dostoevsky writes only of the first and last visits, starting with the last visit at Christmas. In the Christmas visit he focuses on the relationship between stepmother and child. The Kornilovs placed the child in an orphanage because they could not take care of her by themselves, but during the holiday season they frequently took her home. Despite how busy she was with her own work and the care of her newborn, Kornilova often visits her stepdaughter at the orphanage, bringing her presents. Kornilova's reconciliation with her stepdaughter, against whom she committed such a horrendous crime and before whom she still felt enormous guilt, remained her overriding concern. According to Dostoevsky, Kornilova dreamed, even while in prison, of somehow making "the little girl forget the incident." And these fantasies, Dostoevsky reports, actually come true: "Right before Christmas, about a month ago, not having seen the Kornilovs for about six months, I stopped at their apartment, and Kornilova, before anything else, told me that the girl 'jumps with joy and always embraces her whenever she, Kornilova, calls on her at the children's home.' And when I was leaving them, suddenly she told me: 'She will forget . . .'" (927; 26:103).

Dostoevsky, however, emphasizes the reconciliation between husband and wife far more than that between mother and stepdaughter. Because the reconciliation of the spouses must overcome even greater difficulties, it becomes a truer measure, at least for Dostoevsky, of the distance that Kornilova has come spiritually and morally and of her worthiness of the court's act of faith. To prove his point Dostoevsky directs all his attention to one crucial episode that occurred on the night after the acquittal. The husband and wife related the episode to Dostoevsky when he visited them three days later.

Dostoevsky was impressed by the husband. He was a man of the old traditional ways, quite stern and unexpressive, a "puritan," in fact, but at the same time very honest, pious, and unmistakably kind and magnanimous. He looked upon marriage as a sacrament: "He is one of those husbands who can still be found in Russia, and who, abiding by the ancient Russian custom and tradition, upon returning home from the wedding and retiring to the bedroom with his newly wed wife, first of all, throws himself upon his knees before a holy image and prays long, asking God that He bless their future life" (928:26:104). And that is exactly what happened. The husband related that when they came home at five o'clock in the morning from court, they sat down at the table and he began to read the Gospels to her. Just as with Kornilova's behavior toward the child, Dostoevsky realizes that his readers will think that Kornilov's behavior toward his wife was rather harsh and inappropriate given the physical and emotional exhaustion caused by her long ordeal and arduous trial.[20] He should have let her rest from the trauma of recent events; it certainly did not seem the time to read her lectures about virtuous behavior.

> His act seemed to me almost awkward—all too inflexible, because it could actually have worked against achieving his purpose. A very guilty soul—especially if it painfully feels its own guilt and has already en-dured from it much torment—should not be too obviously and *hastily* reproached for its guilt, lest a reverse effect be produced, especially when it repents anyway. In circumstances such as these, the man upon whom the woman depends, exalting himself over her in the aureole of a judge, appears to her as something merciless, too autocratically invading her soul, and sternly repulsing her repentance and the good sentiments regenerated in her: "Not rest, not food, nor drink, are needed for one such as you. Sit down and listen to how one has to live." (928; 26:104)

But Kornilova's reaction to her husband's sermon pleasantly surprises Dostoevsky, emphatically confirming his assessment of her character and his hopes for her future. Dostoevsky's depiction of how a woman in Kornilova's situation might have reacted to the overbearing ap-proach of her husband seems to come right out of his novels. But Kornilova is not a high-strung, proud, and educated Dunya (Raskol-nikov's sister), Nastasya Filippovna, or Katerina Ivanovna.[21] Kornilova responds positively to her husband's lecture; she does not perceive his attitude as condescending or overbearing; she does not think: "Why doesn't he at least show me some pity?" (930; 26:106). She, in fact, encourages her husband in his sentiments and tries to fit in with his tone—not only because she wants to please her husband but because, as a great sinner, she thought the reading of the Gospels entirely consonant with her own desire to live honestly and righteously. This is the kind of psychological evidence that Dostoevsky needs to justify his hope in Kornilova's resurrection. He writes: "I don't know, but it all seems clear to me. Readers will understand why I am recording this. At present it may be at least hoped that the great mercy of the court did not spoil the delinquent woman more, but that, on the contrary, it struck good soil" (930; 26:106). Dostoevsky applies the biblical parable not only to the merciful decision of the court but also to the husband reading his wife the Gospels.[22]

The Word is often a stumbling block to Dostoevsky's characters, and it could easily have been one for Kornilova here, precisely because of its form (her husband's lecture); but Kornilova not only recognized the Word but received it with an honest and good heart.[23] The jury and public can now feel at ease with their merciful decision. Dostoevsky does not say that the larger question regarding Kornilova's salvation (for which the jury is still out, just as it is still out for any of us) is resolved, but mercy is not granted on the basis of certainty. The jury performed its duty well by taking a risk on mercy, by giving a young soul the chance for moral and spiritual rebirth.

The Kornilova article is not only a story about personal redemption, it is an allegory about the fate of the Russian people. The good ground or soil (*pochva*) on which the seeds of resurrection are sown relates directly to Kornilova's fate, but it also is a key concept of Dostoevsky's political populist ideology (*pochvennichestvo*), which held that Russia's greatest problem was the rift dividing the common people, the *narod,* from the educated classes, which had been cut off from Mother Russia and their roots in the native soil. The common people, however great their failings, never lost contact with the truth of the soil, with Russian Orthodoxy (and its strong ties with the earth), and the true Christ. From the writing of *Notes from the House of the Dead* (1862), Dostoevsky came to see his own spiritual and moral rebirth, and that of his class, as being intimately linked with that of a morally regenerated common people. No one in Russia can be saved individually, all must be saved together. Dostoevsky uses Kornilova as a symbol of Russia's potential for regeneration. She is a great sinner, but she is still young and her soil is deep and rich. By treating her with compassion and forgiving her trespasses, the court makes possible the spiritual rebirth of all that Kornilova symbolizes. Further, the Kornilova case provides the law with an opportunity to work, as a collective, in Russia's defense. Dostoevsky writes of Kornilova: "At present, however, believing herself a criminal and considering herself as such, but suddenly forgiven by men, overwhelmed with benefits and pardoned, how can she fail to feel a regeneration and rebirth into a new life superior to the former? It was not some single person that pardoned her, but everybody: the court, the jurors, which means society as a whole, bestowed mercy upon her" (935; 26:110). All society participated in granting Kornilova new life, and by so doing it created the same possibility for itself: its own salvation is prefigured in Kornilova's. The seed fallen on good ground will be fruitful for all.

But to fully understand the concluding section of the December 1877 article, we need to push the allegory still a little further. The article ends curiously with an explanation of the word *happy* (*schastlivaia*), a section ridiculed by the critic of the *Northern Messenger*. Dostoevsky takes the critic to task for quoting the passage out of context but admits that his statement may have been unclear: "That same evening, after ten o'clock, the husband took her home, and she, in a happy mood [*schastlivaia*] again returned to her home after an absence of almost one year, with the impression of an enormous lesson derived by her for her whole life and of manifest divine providence in the whole case, beginning with the miraculous salvation of the child" (933; 26:110). Dostoevsky does not equate happiness—or good fortune—with the acquittal. Kornilova's good fortune, conceived in religious terms, was the lesson she learned from her harrowing experience and the realization that the whole affair bore the guiding mark of Providence. Dostoevsky writes that there can be no greater happiness than to be convinced of human mercy and of people's love for each other, and he implies that there can be no greater hell than the loss of faith in people's goodness, ideals, and divine origin.[24] Thus for Kornilova happiness was a gift of faith, love, and compassion, entailing a lifelong obligation (*dolg*). "After that how could she have failed to bear in her soul a feeling of an immense indebtedness [*dolg*]—for her whole life— to those who had taken pity on her, that is, to all men on earth?" (935; 26:110). The acquittal restored Kornilova to the human community by restoring her faith in all other human beings and in the possibility of her own salvation. Kornilova feels her debt not only to the jury that acquitted her but to all people for the rest of her life.

Kornilova's restored faith in other people directly bears on the tragic rift, mentioned earlier, between the common people, the *narod,* represented by Kornilova, and the educated classes, represented, among others, by the officials of the court, by Dostoevsky, and perhaps, most important, by Dostoevsky's readers, the public at large (*vse liudi*). The rift was exacerbated, in Dostoevsky's mind, by the educated classes' contemptuous treatment of the common people and by the hatred and distrust that the common people harbored for the educated classes. In the semiautobiographical *Notes from the House of the Dead,* Dostoevsky writes that the worst torment he had to bear in prison was the common people's hatred of the prisoners from the nobility. He considered his greatest success in prison to be his ability to overcome —at least in some of the prisoners—the people's hatred of him as a member, and thus a representative, of a class of bloodsucking oppressors. The salvation of Russian society depended on the elimination of this rift.

In the Kornilova case not only the jury and the court officials but all society, as an organic unity, took an enormous step in fulfilling their obligation to the people, exhibiting their faith in the people's potential for spiritual and moral renewal. Dostoevsky attempts to show that Kornilova justified that faith; the seed fell on receptive soil. Thus Kornilova represents not only a soul for whom resurrection becomes a possibility but a hope that the rent in the Russian social fabric will be repaired, permitting Russia to fulfill its national and international salvific agenda. In the second trial the court broke down the greatest barrier of all, the hatred and enmity between classes. Kornilova now looks not just upon the jurors but upon all people—even those of the educated classes—as brothers and sisters bound together in mercy and love for each other. She has come to see the educated classes, represented especially by Dostoevsky himself—the man most responsible for her acquittal—not as her oppressors but as her saviors.

Dostoevsky wished to bring about a radical change in the educated classes' attitude toward the people, but he also wanted to break down the people's distrust for the educated classes. Dostoevsky presents the Kornilova trial as an essential first step in his vision of class reconciliation and mutual salvation. It is indeed ironic that this first step was taken in a Western court. On the other hand, this step certainly conformed to Dostoevsky's original hopes for the court as the site of Russia's moral and spiritual renewal.

## Against Dostoevsky, for the Court

I have given a reading of the Kornilova articles based on their rhetoric and Dostoevsky's imputable intentions. But we need to look at the Kornilova article through different eyes. Although his interpretation of the jury trial in the Kornilova case differs dramatically from his interpretation of the Kroneberg and Kairova trials, Dostoevsky's monophonic approach is quite similar. In the Kroneberg and Kairova articles, Dostoevsky is on the offensive, striking out at the court at every opportunity, relenting only when he needs to show empathy and compassion for the little girl and the women who came to her defense. In the Kornilova case Dostoevsky operates just as monophonically, but he is working in a utopic mode—much as he does in the last few sections of his famous article on the Jewish question in the *Diary of a Writer*, where he even more imaginatively paints a picture of reconciliation, not of Russians among themselves but among all peoples (Russian, Polish, Jewish, and German) and all religions (Jewish, Protestant, Catholic, Russian Orthodox).[25] We do not know whether, in fact, Kornilova justified Dostoevsky's hopes and the mercy of the court that acquitted her, but clearly Dostoevsky needed Kornilova as much as she needed him. It is impossible to know what the real Kornilova was like because Dostoevsky creatively transforms everyone and everything connected with the trial in his imagination. But for the reader to accept the second trial as an exemplum of *sobornost'*—that is, as an affirmation of Dostoevsky's political, religious, and social agenda—requires a predisposition to see this really not very extraordinary trial as something much more than an acquittal on the basis of temporary insanity. What is more, Dostoevsky himself provides the model for a counterreading of the trial. It was not only the author of the article in the *Northern Messenger* who suspected Dostoevsky's imaginative reconstructions about Kornilova: Dostoevsky himself suspected them. He had to visit Kornilova several times to see whether his portrayal of her conformed to reality: Was she really, he asked himself, the person he imagined her to be?

But even on the basis of the facts that Dostoevsky himself adduces, his imaginative transformations—if not distortions—of the actual trial are evident. Dostoevsky rarely treats acquittals so positively. He often expresses his outrage about acquittals of female defendants, especially when temporary insanity was used as a defense (the Kairova case). But one may find just as troublesome and surprising Dostoevsky's summary dismissal of the testimony of the accoucheur in favor of the medical doctors and psychiatrists. The accoucheur represents traditional, practical, native Russian medicine, based on years of experience devoted exclusively to the problems of pregnancy, unencumbered by Western theories of temporary insanity or diminished capacity. The medical experts that Dostoevsky cites, and whose wisdom, sanity, and balance he so praises, are all Western-trained professionals of the Russian intelligentsia, whose expertise he had always severely criticized.

Dostoevsky also seems overly appreciative of the reaction of the public, which seem to serve almost as a surrogate for the readers of the *Diary of a Writer*. He reports that those who did not cross themselves, obviously the more liberal element in the courtroom, applauded. Interpreting this applause positively, Dostoevsky presents it as though it were tantamount, among the less formally religious, to making the cross: the applause showed that the public had all come together as a result of the merciful decision. This is a most unusual treatment of applause in Dostoevsky's courtroom accounts. Dostoevsky was outraged by the applause that greeted the decision of acquittal in the Kroneberg case (22:51). He also was well acquainted with the case of Anna Kirilova, whose acquittal on charges of shooting and murdering her lover was greeted by the public with such loud applause that the judge had to clear the courtroom (24:394). To forward his agenda Dostoevsky interprets otherwise many of the same elements of previous jury trials that had infuriated him. In one case applause epitomizes a shocking decline in public morality, in the next, the highest manifestation of *sobornost'*. Dostoevsky obviously never intended to give an objective representation of the trial proceedings in the Kornilova case —after all, he openly presents himself as a direct participant in the trial—but he goes much further when he exploits and reshapes the trial to present his utopic vision of Russian justice and social revolution along Orthodox principles.

Dostoevsky's portrayal of Kornilova's trial also tantalizingly leaves open to interpretation the means by which Russian justice was, and can be, achieved in a Western court, an institution supposedly alien to the Russian spirit and to Russian and Orthodox ideas of justice (*pravda*), which, as Berdyaev argues, combines our notions of moral truth, justice, and law.[26] Dostoevsky probably wanted the decision site and process to be regarded as much a part of the miraculous event that ended in the granting of forgiveness and mercy as the acquittal itself. In other

words, he presents the decision as something that was reached not because of the court but despite the court. Something happened in the
courtroom that is not rationally explainable, something that overtook
the members of the jury—and all the others associated with the judicial system—such that for a few moments there existed a place, a sort
of heaven on Earth, where the laws of reality were miraculously suspended. For once, just as in Dostoevsky's utopic visions in other pieces
—again, the reconciliation sections of his article called "The Jewish
Question" come to mind—the participants in the human drama behave
in accordance with neither their own character nor their own social
and professional roles. The public does not take sides, the prosecuting
lawyer agrees not to use certain types of evidence, the judge gives the
proper instructions to the jury, and the experts all testify to the same
truth. From Dostoevsky's point of view, one could more easily believe
in the miracle of the child thrown unharmed from a fourth-story window than in such a wise and just decision arrived at in the new Western court. The miraculous decision, reached despite Western judicial
procedures, fits in perfectly with the article's leitmotif of the miraculous, which accompanies the stepdaughter's miraculous escape from
death, the birth of Kornilova's little girl, and the rebirth of the repen-
tant Kornilova herself.

But one can argue that Dostoevsky makes just as good a case for
exactly the opposite interpretation of the court's decision. First of all,
one can easily see the court's decision as something other than a miracle, but, even more significant, the decision came down not despite the
Western jury but because of it. Kornilova's acquittal could hardly have
occurred under the old corrupt "legal system," an arm of the tsarist
administration that even prominent conservatives acknowledged was
disgracefully inefficient, inept, and corrupt.[27] Under the old system
Dostoevsky would hardly have heard about Kornilova, not to speak of
being able to intercede for her and gain her a retrial. Kornilova was
spared because the institution of the law, through its hypostasis, the
court, came to her defense against the forces of the state. However
Dostoevsky may animadvert on defense attorneys—of course, with
the exception of the defense attorney in the Kornilova case—the institutional practice of defense counsel, not Kornilova's specific defense
attorney, led to her acquittal. The testimony of Western-trained expert
witnesses from the medical profession was what helped convince the
jury that Kornilova was incapacitated by her pregnancy. Kornilova's

"peers," the community of jurors who judged her case with mercy and compassion, constitute an essential part of this Western legal institution, initiated as a means of protecting the individual against the overwhelming and arbitrary power of the state. Dostoevsky berates the system as a system when, in his opinion, it reaches bad decisions, and he presents the good decisions as miracles reached despite the system. He certainly may take such a view, but few members of the public in the courtroom would have viewed the proceedings that way. Moreover, Dostoevsky runs the risk—as he often does in his fiction—of taking the implications of his own presentation to ambiguous conclusions. True Russian justice and class reconciliation may have occurred in the Western courtroom because the court, better than any other venue, permitted this "miracle" to take place. To borrow Dostoevsky's own metaphor, the Western courtroom provided the receptive soil from which the miraculous decision arose. Certainly, few such examples of true justice take place within the courts. But perhaps when they do occur, they occur in and through the court, whose proceedings, as we have seen, Dostoevsky likens almost to a religious experience.

And why should the miracle have not occurred in the Western court? It was not obligatory, even for Slavophile conservatives, to see the Western court as intrinsically antagonistic to the Russian national spirit. The prominent Slavophile Ivan Aksakov defended the jury trial and the new Western system as an enormous improvement over the old system and as something of which all Russians should be proud.[28] Moreover, what happened in the courtroom—at least the way Dostoevsky recounts it—conforms exactly to the vision that Dostoevsky had in the late 1860s of a judicial system that would lead to a moral renewal of the Russian people. Other conservatives—Aksakov, for example— not only nurtured the same hopes as Dostoevsky, they even saw their hopes realized in the new legal system, despite its shortcomings; the Western courts had become for them the site of Russian justice. And they did not have to betray their conservatism to view the courts in this way, nor did they have to overcome anxieties about embracing and celebrating an alien institution. Instead of interpreting the Kornilova verdict as a miracle, something that occurred despite the court, the resistant reader could just as easily see the verdict as a validation of the Western jury system's potential for achieving Russian justice. Moreover, the justification for such a view of Western justice exists in the specifically Russian adaptation of legal reform itself.

From the very beginning of the debates about the reform of the legal system, the reformers were intent on adapting Western legal procedures to Russian conditions. That was why so many different systems were carefully examined before enacting the new law. Many supporters of the reform knew that the reform could succeed only if it was in conformity with the moral, religious, and cultural values of the Russian people. In fact, much was done to satisfy the different Russian estates and classes regarding jury etiquette and procedures. In his description of the trials in the *Diary of a Writer,* Dostoevsky generally passes over these Russian adaptations, and when he does include some, as in the Kornilova trial, he presents them as aberrant, unique, or miraculous.

Although some theorists may have argued that ethics and law should be separate, as Salytkov-Shchedrin did in his remarks on the Kornilova case, the intention of the government and many reformers was to make the new court the site of Russian moral and religious justice. The religious character of the judicial oath, which Dostoevsky does not mention in his trial accounts and which he treats dismissively in *The Brothers Karamazov,* is a case in point. Article 666 of the statutes of criminal procedure stipulates the swearing-in of the jury.

The priest, in imparting to the jurors the sacredness of the oath, reads out before them the following sworn promise:

> *I promise and swear to almighty God, before the Holy Gospel and the life-giving Lord's Cross,* that in this case for which I have been selected as juror, I shall devote the full force of my mind to a diligent examination of the circumstances both incriminating the defendant, and vindicating him. I shall cast a decisive vote on the basis of what I see and hear in court, according to the plain truth and the conviction of my conscience. I shall neither acquit the guilty nor convict the innocent, *remembering throughout that I must give answer before the law and before God on the Day of Judgment* [na strashnom sude Ego]. *In affirmation thereof, I kiss the word and cross of my Savior. Amen.*
>
> *Each juror, putting his lips to the cross and the Gospel, pronounces aloud: I swear.* (emphasis added)[29]

For witnesses the procedure was quite similar:

> *I promise and vow to almighty God, before the Holy Gospel and the life-giving Lord's Cross,* that being swayed neither by friendship, kinship,

expectation of advantage or any other such motives, I shall, according to my conscience, reveal the plain truth on all aspects of this case, and shall not conceal anything unknown to me. *I shall bear in mind that in all this I will have to give answer before the law and before God on the Day of Judgment. In affirmation of the said oath, I kiss the word and cross of my Savior. Amen.* (emphasis added)[30]

Kissing the cross had gradually established itself as the distinctive feature of the various types of oaths used throughout imperial Russia.[31] The jury trial procedure of 1864 maintained the tradition of cross kissing and even expanded the religious component in the court rituals by stipulating that jurors kiss the "Gospel" and that witnesses kiss the "word" (*slovo*) of their savior. The very structure of the procedure, then, with a priest solemnly intoning the oath and the assembled jurors or summoned witnesses assenting to it by word and gesture, imparted to the trial setting a definite sense of routine and ritual.[32]

The Russian oath was much more religious than those administered in Western European courtrooms, where the oath emphasized the social responsibility of the jury. "God was invoked briefly, and then only in an assisting capacity," notes Girish Narayan Bhat.

> You shall well and truly try and true deliverance make between the sovereign lord the king and the prisoner at the bar, whom you shall have in charge and true verdict give according to the evidence, so help you God.
>
> Do you swear and promise before God and before man to examine with the most scrupulous attention? (England)

The Russian oath grounds the court proceeding in the Orthodox religious tradition, linking the word of testimony to the word of the Gospels, specifically to Christ's resurrection and humanity's salvation (the cross). What is done in the court (*sud*) not only has legal consequences ("before the law"), it bears directly on salvation. False testimony will follow the perjurer to the final court (*strashnyi sud*), where judgment will be far harsher than in any court of law.

Whether Russians lied less under oath than other Europeans is impossible to determine. But witnesses and other court actors took the oath seriously. "Our simple folk [*prostoliudiny*] give honest testimony only on being administered the oath and do not consider it a sin to give false unsworn testimony."[33] The symbolic gesture of kissing both the Gospels and the cross had a profound effect on average Russians. The serious attitude toward the judicial oath is substantiated by the inordinate time spent in court proceedings regarding who would and would not testify under oath. In American courtrooms then and today, spouses are spared having to testify against each other under oath. The Russian system excluded almost all family members from compulsion to testify. Even if they volunteered their testimony, they could not give it under oath: "The husband or wife of the accused, his relatives by direct ascending or descending lineage, and his own brothers and sisters as well, may remove themselves from testimony. If they do not wish to avail themselves of this right, they should be cross-examined without having to take the oath."[34] As Bhat points out, the 1864 reformers' exclusion of sworn testimony for close relatives reveals the reformers' desire to adapt the legal reform to Russian cultural and moral practices. They viewed any system that compelled close relatives to give testimony under oath as tantamount to suborning perjury:

> Given the need to safeguard the inviolability of the family unit, which is the foundation of every human community, it would be improper to require testimony both from persons related to the defendant through matrimony or direct kinship, or from the defendant's own brothers and sisters. Such individuals may be permitted to testify, however, if they do not disqualify themselves from testimony voluntarily. But even if no legal challenge is subsequently brought against them, they shall not be permitted to take the oath before being admitted as witnesses. For no matter how great their determination to give impartial testimony, the sentiment of love binding them to the accused can suppress the demands of conscience against their will. . . . The law should not place anyone in a position that carries with it the clear and threatening danger of perjury.[35]

The reformers, sensitive to the social significance and sacral nature of the Russian family, were not about to institute a legal code that required witnesses to betray family ties. Although the statute did not forbid the testimony of close relatives, it implied that such testimony could not be validated by an oath and therefore would have to be corroborated by other purely evidentiary standards—actually, the accepted practice in the West, where the oath was considered an additional means to support testimony but not the most important. By contrast, Russian courts consistently devalued testimony not given under oath. And juries often disregarded it. Because of the status of the oath in the Russian legal system, frequent wrangling occurred in court regarding who was and who was not to testify under oath. "Indeed, it would not be an exaggeration to say that the justification for administering the oath was one of the most important procedural issues in any given trial," notes Bhat.[36]

The issue for the Kornilova case is not whether witnesses told the truth under oath or even told the truth under oath more frequently than witnesses in English or French courts. The oath shows that the reformers did everything they could to frame the proceedings within Russian cultural and religious practice. Perhaps that is one of the reasons, at least in the first years of the court's existence, why some conservatives, including Dostoevsky himself, could see the court as essential to Russian renewal. Dostoevsky could have easily presented the acquittal of Kornilova as not a miracle or, if a miracle, a miracle made possible by an institution that had been successfully adapted to forward a nationalistic and religious agenda. Because before testimony a Russian priest would rise and administer the oath, and all witnesses would swear by the Word of the Gospels and the life-giving cross, kissing the Gospels and the cross to aver that their testimony was true, the heavenly final judgment (*strashnyi sud*) was continually evoked in the courtroom, impressing upon witnesses that their testimony had a higher religious significance and that they were by virtue of the oath on trial themselves, not only legally but morally and religiously. The reformers intended the court to be the site, to use Dostoevsky's own words, of sound and salutary ideas and practices. In order to present Kornilova's acquittal as a miracle, Dostoevsky must implicitly dismiss the oath taking as an empty formula used to disguise the anti-Russian and anti-Christian agenda being prosecuted, even though the legislation on oath taking was consistent with Dostoevsky's own views about the sanctity of the family and the need to preserve it at almost any cost—views that Dostoevsky emphasized in both the Kroneberg and Kornilova cases.

Since Dostoevsky had come to see the court as the epitome of Western adversarialism, the antithesis of the Russian Orthodox ideal of community (*sobornost'*), he was compelled, by the force of his own logic, to present the unanimity of the court actors in the Kornilova case as a miracle. But if we look at actual practice in the reform courts, of which Dostoevsky was a direct observer, he seems to present as aberrant, extraordinary, even miraculous, adjudicatory procedures that actually conform to indigenous Russian cultural styles of conflict resolution. Here again Bhat throws the most light on the issue by showing that in contrast to the West, where adversarialism was characteristic of both legal code and practice, Russian court actors attempted as much as possible to achieve unanimity, a practice that Bhat calls consensualism. For Dostoevsky the defense lawyer epitomizes the new adversarialism; he is an unprincipled advocate of his client, and his role is almost completely determined by his institutional function. But Dostoevsky greatly exaggerates the power of the defense lawyer. In reality, the office of the Russian district attorney held enormous advantages over the defense. A minority of scholars of the reform do not even see a sharp break between the inquisitorial (investigatory) system of the pre-reform and post-reform courts. The defense attorney could do nothing for his client until the trial began.[37] At trial he was compelled to exploit all his oratorical skills to overcome the overwhelming advantage gained by the prosecution in the pretrial investigation and proceedings. Bhat argues that the Russian administration as well as court actors were never completely comfortable with adversarialism and in practice leaned toward a form of consensual adjudication, in which justice is "negotiated, agreed, and worked out rather than gained, rendered or meted out."[38]

The object of the jury trial was conceived not in terms of conviction or acquittal but in the attainment of the truth. Prosecutors were enjoined not to exaggerate the evidence or present it one-sidedly and, if convinced of the innocence of the defendant, to cease the indictment against him:

> The prosecution attorney, instead of functioning as an adversarial actor in a legal drama driven by the clash of competing interests, should in fact conceive of himself as a vital, influential part of an adjudicative system whose highest priority was to arrive at justice, not merely determine it. Thus, even the state's defender and principal legal opponent of the accused had a significant burden to bear in this collective process of judicial truth-inquiry. . . . It would seem that the post-Reform version of *sostiazatel'nost'* in fact encouraged the judicial consensus in all aspects of a trial. The path to this end did not lie in a rigorously adversarial, "binary" clash of legal counsel; rather, it entailed dissent, dispute, confrontation,

and resolution of issues through the more or less unfettered participation of all those present, except of course the spectating public. The judge, in his capacity as the presiding member of the court, consistently viewed the realization of such judicial ideals as his central responsibility. . . . A consensus on guilt, even if turbulently attained, was consistently regarded as the principle aim of a meaningful trial. The process of justice in such cases thus took on the qualities of a group-negotiated and collectively arbitrated courtroom pronouncement on guilt or innocence.[39]

For Bhat the tendency toward collective judgment was founded in the Russian tradition of "collectively structured decision making." So although there is little question that adversarialism played a significant role in the post-reform court, it was tempered by a deeply ingrained native tradition of collective decision making that strove for unanimity. Dostoevsky implies that in the Kornilova case he is describing a miraculous unanimity, but one could just as easily see this unanimity as a natural outgrowth of the Russian cultural and religious tradition that found a perfectly appropriate home in the Western court.

Dostoevsky's analysis is also highly idiosyncratic concerning the restraints placed on Russian jurors, of whom he was usually quite proud. In the Kroneberg verdict Dostoevsky does not blame the jury because he sees it hemmed in by the law, unable to express its conscience, to say its moral, salvific word. For Dostoevsky the Kornilova case was in a sense the exception that proved the rule. But, in fact, quite the opposite was probably true. There were no overly legal constraints placed on Russian jurors. Russian juries often did not decide on the basis of statutory law and did not generally consider themselves bound by the law. Russian juries were mainly "law-finding" (lawmaking) rather than "fact-finding" bodies, that is, they placed less emphasis on the facts and how they were supposed to interpret them according to law; they placed more emphasis on moral and circumstantial issues, such as the moral character of the defendant, the defendant's past behavior, evidence of contrition, and the commensurability of the sentence and the indicted behavior. Even though jurors might believe that the defendant committed the crime for which she or he was charged, if they were sympathetic to the defendant's plight, interpreted the circumstances of the crime extenuatingly, or believed that the punishment did not fit the crime, they might engage in jury nullification, that is, find a defendant not guilty for crimes they knew she or he did in fact commit. Ironically, the law-finding (moral) decisions of Russian juries actually reflected the law itself. Just as in the French system, from which the Russian reformers extensively borrowed, jurors were supposed to carefully weigh the evidence and deliver a decision in accord with conscience (*po sovesti*). In other words, moral considerations were meant to be as important as facts in the verdict, truth telling. In his closing remarks to the jury at the Zasulich trial, the presiding judge, A. F. Koni, exhorted the jurors to pronounce a verdict that was "according to your deepest conviction, based on all that you have seen and heard, and constrained by nothing beyond the voice of conscience [*krome golosa vashei sovesti*]."[40] From this point of view the Kroneberg trial seems to be the aberration, a case in which, contrary to practice, the Russian jurors—to many observers' surprise, not only Dostoevsky's—paid too much attention to the letter of the law or were too easily persuaded by the brilliant defense attorney. The Kornilova decision was far more typical of the verdicts of Russian juries. In her first trial Kornilova received a relatively light sentence for the crime she committed. Even Dostoevsky understood that it would have been difficult for the jury to have decided otherwise, especially because the reason he gives for why they should have acquitted her (temporary insanity) was something that he himself had invariably rejected and criticized as a reason for acquittal. In the second trial the jurors acted the way they typically did, taking into consideration the turn for the better in the defendant since her crime, the circumstances of her pregnancy, and consequences of a two-and-a-half-year sentence in Siberia for the defendant with a newborn in tow. It was a typical moral, law-finding verdict. It may have been an exception, a miracle, in Dostoevsky's eyes and in the eyes of readers of the *Diary of a Writer* whom Dostoevsky was able to persuade to his point of view but probably in the eyes of few others.

Dostoevsky could have interpreted Kornilova's acquittal as an understandable phenomenon—not a miracle—if he had not needed to see the post-reform court as an alien transplant. He was only too ready to pounce on the atypical decision, as in the Kroneberg case, that could justify his anti-Western agenda. He was set against seeing the court as an institution that had incorporated Russian cultural practices and therefore could provide a site for precisely the kind of consensual, moral justice he himself advocated and envisioned. In reading the responses to his articles about Kornilova, Dostoevsky realized that not

everyone saw the case way he did. He suspected that his articles could
be read otherwise, especially by unsympathetic and resisting readers.
He probably came to suspect that it might actually be read, to use the
modern term, "deconstructively": that is, as a possible vindication of
the Western court after his Kroneberg and Kairova articles and a portrayal of the court as the site for the achievement of Russian justice.
This suspicion certainly seems justified if we read the Kornilova articles in the context of *The Brothers Karamazov,* for in his last novel Dostoevsky attacks the places where he left himself most vulnerable in
the Kornilova articles: the exploitation of empathetic narrative and the
portrayal of the jury trial as a peculiarly Russian site for achieving
justice and truth. Through empathetic narrative Dostoevsky turned
the defendant, Kornilova, into the heroine of a utopic narrative. He
would not permit the defense attorney in *The Brothers Karamazov* to
make the defendant, Dmitry Karamazov, into a hero of a similar novel
of rebirth and resurrection—no matter how much the defense attorney's novel borrowed from Dostoevsky's own article on Kornilova—
and he would attempt to leave absolutely no opening for the jury trial
to emerge as anything other than the site of injustice and untruth. No
one escapes unscathed from the judicial process in the last book of *The
Brothers Karamazov,* entitled "A Judicial Error" or "A Miscarriage of Justice" (*Sudebnaia oshibka*): there is no acquittal, no redeeming decision,
no honest, well-meaning lawyers, no public *sobornost'*, no applause,
no redemption, and no intervening guardian angel by the name of Dostoevsky. Russian justice would not be attained in court; it would have to
be attained elsewhere and otherwise.

# CHAPTER 3

# The Perils of
# Narrative Empathy

## Dostoevsky, Buckley, Mailer, Styron, and Their Wards

---

In both the Kroneberg and Kornilova trials, Dostoevsky calls upon one of his most effective weapons, narrative empathy, to retry errant cases out of court and to advance his moral interests. In the Kroneberg case he attempted to elicit compassion for the victims, not only the little girl beaten by her father but also the peasant women victimized by Kroneberg's defense attorney, Spasovich. The prominent prerevolutionary trial attorney O. O. Gruzenberg wrote that he did not accept Dostoevsky's arguments against Spasovich, but Gruzenberg was overwhelmed by Dostoevsky's compassionate narrative in the *Diary*. If empathy could have won the Kroneberg case, Dostoevsky should certainly have been the prosecutor. But he was not, the case was lost, and Dostoevsky's only hope was that his empathetic article could repair some of the damage that had already been done to Russia's moral compass.

In the Kornilova case Dostoevsky was more fortunate. Although he came to see the conviction as a mistake, at least the crime had been publicly proclaimed. Further, his empathetic approach was far more effective than he could have ever imagined. His *Diary* article became the impetus for a new trial at which Kornilova was acquitted. But Dostoevsky went much beyond empathetic narrative: he visited Kornilova in prison before her second trial and at her home several times after her acquittal. He incorporated her into his salvific agenda, seeing her almost as an alter ego, a variation on his own life of error, forgiveness, and resurrection from the dead. By 1876 Dostoevsky had written several salvation narratives (*Notes from the House of the Dead* and *Crime and Punishment*), but they were more or less projections of his own fate. With Kornilova, Dostoevsky became directly involved with the fate of a woman "of the people," someone who was culturally and intellectually different from Dostoevsky but essential to his vision of personal and national salvation. Empathetic narrative and symbolic action had real life consequences: Dostoevsky found himself person-ally responsible not only for the retrial and acquittal but also for the fate of Kornilova for the rest of her life and his. What if she committed another crime? How could he be sure that his empathetic article would bear good fruit? Could the article be judged entirely by its author's in-tentions? Or would the empathy that occasioned his personal involve-ment lead down a parlous path, and would it ultimately be judged in terms of consequences over which he could have no control? Dostoev-sky's personal and ideological involvement with Kornilova constitutes almost a test case for narrative empathy in a legal situation. Indeed, at times in the article he seems to sense the dangers of empathy, the possibility that he may have indeed gone too far. He feels compelled (and is under pressure from his ideological opponents) to justify what he increasingly comes to see as a risk for salvation. Dostoevsky never had to experience any real danger with Kornilova, for she died just more than a year after her acquittal. He did not have to worry over her. He not only never mentioned her again, he parodies his own approach to her trial in *The Brothers Karamazov*.[1]

To better understand Dostoevsky's arguments and anxieties about empathy and risk in the context of the legal system, it is useful to com-pare his relationship with Kornilova with the experience of several prom-inent twentieth-century American literary and journalistic figures whose empathetic narratives and intense personal involvement, often involv-ing significant risks to their reputations (and in some cases to their persons), led to the release of prisoners whom they had championed and incorporated into their salvific agendas. Certainly, the most famous and hermeneutically illuminating for Dostoevsky's intercession are William F. Buckley's defense of Edgar Smith, Norman Mailer's defense of Jack Abbott, and William Styron's defense of Benjamin Reid. In each case the risk that each writer took was inseparably linked to his re-demptive agenda.

Dostoevsky may have been one of the few writers and journalists in the nineteenth century to work for the release of a convicted felon, but by the second half of the twentieth century such intercessions in Western

Europe and the United States were far from uncommon, receiving considerable publicity and, in some cases, notoriety. The conservative columnist James J. Kilpatrick interceded for Joseph Giarratano, who confessed to raping and strangling fifteen-year-old Michelle Kline and stabbing to death her forty-four-year-old mother. The governor of Virginia, L. Douglas Wilder, eventually commuted Giarratano's death sentence to life imprisonment. Joyce Carol Oates, E. L. Doctorow, Norman Mailer, William Styron, and Salman Rushdie spoke out in defense of Mumia Abu-Jamal, a journalist convicted of murdering a Philadelphia police officer.[2] Bob Dylan interceded on behalf of the prizefighter Rubin "Hurricane" Carter, for whom he even wrote a song. Carter was fighting a conviction and a life sentence for a 1966 triple murder in Paterson, New Jersey. He was freed by the New Jersey Supreme Court, which had ordered a new trial.

In Europe the Austrian murderer Jack Unterweger, who wrote a best-selling book while in prison, became a cause célèbre for intellectuals who petitioned for his release. The French writer Roger Knobelspiess, who also wrote books in prison, received a pardon from President François Mitterrand after he had served part of a five-year sentence for several 1977 robberies. His cause was championed by, among others, Michel Foucault. Jean Genet, who was jailed for theft and male prostitution, was granted a presidential pardon, thanks to pleas from André Gide, Jean Cocteau, Paul Claudel, and Jean-Paul Sartre.

The unfortunate outcomes of several of these intercessions underline the considerable risks that the champions of criminals have taken for redemption. In 1976, while awaiting trial, Rubin Carter severely beat the woman who was coordinating his defense fund. His retrial ended in a second conviction. After Unterweger was released, he went on to kill thirteen women. In 1983 Knobelspiess was arrested for armed robbery. In all three of the American cases that I analyze here, the prisoners, once released, went on to commit serious crimes for which they were returned to prison.

Dostoevsky's articles about the Kornilova case show that, contrary to the stereotypes of Russians who privilege intentions (the movements of the heart) over consequences and Americans the opposite, Dostoevsky was far more concerned about the consequences of his actions than any of his American counterparts. Although Dostoevsky is an intentionalist, he rarely de-emphasizes consequences; he just presents them as arising from intentions. Raskolnikov's murder of the pawnbroker in

*Crime and Punishment* is a case in point. In *The Idiot,* however, there is indeed a greater separation of intentions and consequences in the portrayal of the hero, Prince Myshkin. The terrible fate of Rogozhin and Nastasya Filippovna, especially in recent criticism of the novel, has been ascribed to Myshkin's passivity or inaction (a consequence interpretation), but these casualties are presented as the unintended consequences of Myshkin's behavior or his good heart, and the novel does not judge him harshly for that. Besides, Rogozhin and Nastasya Filippovna, who are constantly courting destruction, hardly need Myshkin to take them to their doom. So some may be surprised that Dostoevsky is so preoccupied with the consequences of the jury's risk for salvation in the Kornilova case.

To cope with the formidable task of comparing four cases and writers, I will first describe an American case in some detail (these cases need to be fleshed out if they are to serve as bases of comparison), and then I will compare the American case and the Kornilova case in terms of the issues of risk, consequences, redemption, and the law. Although this chapter is meant to discover what light the American examples can shed on Dostoevsky, it implicitly raises the question of the worth of studying Dostoevsky for examining the idea of redemption and rehabilitation—or lack thereof—in contemporary American culture. Since the late 1970s increasing demands for public safety and concerns for victims of crime have resulted in the construction of more American prisons, whose purpose is not to rehabilitate and reform errant souls but to punish and sequester dangerous offenders. Our interest in deterrence, punishment, and even retribution have certainly outweighed our perhaps romantic concern for criminals and the possibility of their redemption.[3] In fact, at least in regard to the legal system, not only the idea of redemption but even the word itself has gone out of fashion.[4]

## Buckley/Smith

In 1971 William F. Buckley's intercession on behalf of Edgar Smith led to Smith's release from prison, where he had served fourteen years on death row for murder. Smith was twenty-three when he severely beat a fifteen-year-old high school cheerleader, Victoria Zielinski, with a baseball bat and then crushed her skull with a forty-pound rock, leaving her to die in the town's gravel pit. He was sentenced to die in the electric chair in 1957. The jury deliberated for less than two and a half hours.

During his fourteen years on death row, where he became an expert jailhouse lawyer, Smith unsuccessfully appealed his conviction eighteen times and wrote *Brief Against Death*, a book proclaiming his innocence that eventually became a best-seller.[5] While in prison he began to read Buckley's magazine, the *National Review*; soon afterward they began a correspondence. Buckley, who visited Smith in prison, wrote an influential article in *Esquire*, outlining his doubts about Smith's guilt and the implausibility of the evidence against him.[6] Buckley donated his fee from the article to Smith and became the main organizer as well as a substantial financial supporter of Smith's defense fund.[7] In *Getting Out*, Smith's 1972 book about how he got out of prison the year before, he gratefully acknowledges his debt to Buckley:

> One event took place in 1962 which was to alter irrevocably the course of my life and which would prove decisive in my fight to remain alive and regain my freedom. William F. Buckley entered my life. . . . There was never a time when he was needed that he did not make himself available. . . . The man literally kept me alive. He picked me up when I was down, knocked me down when I got too cocky. . . . Even above the fact that he did keep me alive, he taught me what true friendship is all about. For that, for everything, I love him dearly.[8]

Smith's defense fund eventually grew large enough and his book sales brisk enough that he could hire the prestigious Washington law firm of Edward Bennett Williams to challenge his conviction. In 1971 the U.S. Supreme Court ordered a hearing to determine whether an incriminating statement that Smith made to police had been illegally obtained. A trial court judge in New Jersey ruled that Smith had not been advised of his legal rights and that his statement had been obtained by coercion. The judge ordered that Smith be retried or released. He was retried. Carefully rehearsed for days by his lawyers, Smith gave a tour de force performance on the stand at his retrial.

By 1971 Smith had become a celebrity (almost a star) and cause célèbre, with two popular books to his credit; the New Jersey court decided to make the best deal it could under the circumstances. In return for a full confession, it counted Smith's fourteen years served as partial fulfillment of a new eighteen-year second-degree murder sentence (without the original confession, the state could not obtain a conviction on premeditated murder), and it placed Smith on parole for the remaining four years of his sentence.

When Buckley became involved in the Smith affair, he had long enjoyed the reputation of being the most prominent conservative journalist in the United States. Although some of Smith's views on prison reform and on the Attica riots remained poles apart from Buckley's, they shared basic conservative positions. Further, while he was in jail Smith, a high school dropout, became a member of Mensa and an excellent lawyer and writer: the two books he wrote in prison protesting his innocence, *Brief Against Death* and *A Reasonable Doubt*, received considerable critical praise.

Buckley's review of the evidence and Smith's perseverance, intelligence, and talent convinced Buckley not only that Smith may not have killed Victoria Zielinski but that his was a soul worth saving, in fact, someone who could even make a significant contribution to society. In other words, Smith fully justified the risk that Buckley was prepared to take. In the 21 January 1977 issue of the *National Review*, Buckley noted that even the judge at the retrial, who "was profoundly convinced that Smith had in fact . . . killed the girl," asserted that "if he had seen a rehabilitated man, here he was."[9] After being released from prison and picked up in a limousine, Smith appeared on Buckley's television show, *Firing Line*, where he recanted his confession, asserting that his admission of guilt was merely a way to placate New Jersey authorities and expedite his release from prison. Smith spent his first night out of prison in a suite at the St. Regis Hotel in New York City. By this time (1971) Buckley had gone far beyond his influential article about Smith in *Esquire* magazine (October 1965) and his organization of Smith's high-powered defense: he had helped free Smith and, in effect, made him a celebrity. The retrial, which had become a tremendous media event, had the same circus atmosphere—mutatis mutandis—as Dmitry's trial in *The Brothers Karamazov* and the criminal trial of O. J. Simpson in 1995. Smith writes in *Getting Out*: "I think it was then that I realized for the first time that I had become a sort of antihero, a 'celebrity' of some kind. The street outside the courthouse was filled with photographers and TV cameramen, and everywhere I looked someone was sticking a microphone in my face and asking how it felt to be a free man."[10] Upon Smith's release from prison, Buckley organized a celebration in New York, capped by a string of interviews, shows, and parties that lasted more than a week.

During the next few years Smith took financial advantage of his identity as a wrongfully convicted man. He appeared on hundreds of radio and television talk shows and lectured at colleges, collecting $1,000 speaking fees. Smith remarried in 1974 and moved to San Diego, where he found work for a while as a security guard for an exclusive apartment building in La Jolla. But marriage and work did not go well. In the fall of 1976 (four years and ten months after his release from prison), he was convicted of the kidnapping and the attempted murder of Lefteria Lisa Ozbun, a thirty-three-year-old San Diegan who worked as a seamstress at a Chula Vista garment factory. Ozbun managed to escape death at Smith's hands by jumping from his moving car with a butcher knife lodged in her back.

During the San Diego trial Smith changed his story (probably for tactical reasons) about the Zielinski murder, confessing not only that he had killed the girl but also that he had molested an eleven-year-old girl when he was a teenager.[11] He was sentenced to life without possibility of parole. But a year later, as a result of new legislation, Smith became eligible for parole in 1982. His biennial requests for parole, however, were repeatedly turned down. His former wife Paige Hiemer dismissed Smith's statements about his crimes as self-serving ploys to secure his release: "Edgar is a master at manipulating the system. . . . He manipulated his way out off Death Row in New Jersey. He conned Bill Buckley. And now he's doing in California what he's always done. He's working the system, until the odds are in his favor for parole. But people should realize that his last victim is very lucky to be alive today. The next woman he goes after may not be so lucky."[12] When Buckley learned that Smith, who was at large after committing his second crime, had contacted the offices of the *National Review*, Buckley promptly called the FBI, whose agents picked Smith up within five minutes of the call. Buckley later wrote:

> Why, I believe now that he was guilty of the first crime. There is no mechanism as yet perfected that will establish beyond question a person's guilt or innocence. There will be guilty people freed this year and every year. But for those who believe that the case of Edgar Smith warrants a vow to accept the ruling of a court as always definitive, it is only necessary to remind ourselves that, this year and every year, an innocent man will be convicted. Edgar Smith has done enough damage in his lifetime without underwriting the doctrine that the verdict of a court is infallible.[13]

A judicial mistake had occurred. Buckley, of course, regretted that he had championed Smith's cause, but he implies that, given the perspective of the events of 1962–67, what he did was right. As long as innocent men are sent to prison every year, it must be our duty to help those whom we believe have been erroneously convicted; the benefits to our system of justice far outweigh the risks. Better to free one hundred guilty people than to convict one innocent one.[14] Putting the best —albeit a very different—spin on Buckley's involvement in the Smith affair, Mark Royden Winchell writes: "To his credit, Buckley does not apologize for his behavior in the Smith case. . . . What is also sadly fallible is one's faith in the redemption of any given individual. At worst, William Buckley loved not wisely but too well."[15] In other words, according to Winchell, Buckley took on Smith not so much because he wished to keep our justice system honest—as he said—but because he believed that this man of considerable talent, who had already been sufficiently punished, and who entirely rehabilitated himself in prison, should be given another chance, both for his own good and that of society, because society in the end has as much a stake in redemption as it has in justice.

## Dostoevsky and Buckley: Redemption and the Law

Dostoevsky's and Buckley's journal articles played crucial roles in securing new trials for their charges. But Buckley's intercession was an active, protracted nine-year process—almost a campaign—to secure a new trial for Smith. Dostoevsky, by contrast, did not even imagine that his article would influence Kornilova's fate. He wrote the first Kornilova article, just as he had written the Kroneberg and Kairova articles, after the verdict. He could lament the decision, instruct his readers about it, but he did not think he could alter it. Dostoevsky was both surprised and proud that his article influenced an official in the Ministry of Justice to reverse Kornilova's conviction, but, as we have seen, he did not actively campaign for Kornilova's release, nor did he initiate his visits to Kornilova in prison.[16] Because they had few hopes that a legal appeal could succeed, Kornilova's defense attorney and Dostoevsky thought that Kornilova's only hope was to appeal directly to the tsar for clemency. The case was not a cause célèbre; few people became as actively involved in the Kornilova case as Dostoevsky did. Further,

Dostoevsky did not organize a defense for Kornilova, and he did not hire the best lawyers; in fact, she had a state-appointed lawyer.

But more important, Dostoevsky, in contrast to Buckley, took Kornilova's part primarily because she confessed to her crime and recognized it as a terrible sin before both society and God—for Dostoevsky, the precondition of spiritual resurrection. In the Smith case Buckley and the lawyers focused primarily on securing Smith's release from prison, which they hoped to do by appealing the original decision. They attempted not to prove that Smith was not guilty—or innocent—but to show that the state had violated their client's constitutional rights. The focus in the Smith case was entirely on matters of law. Smith confessed to the crime only because it was a condition of his immediate release.

What happened in the Smith case, therefore, is exactly what Dostoevsky decried in cases like Kroneberg's, where the letter of the law, he argued, was exploited in the interests of the client. The court acquitted a murderer; the criminal neither confessed his guilt nor maintained his innocence. Punishment did not make Edgar Smith contrite but prouder, harder, and more determined. Had Smith's case occurred in Dostoevsky's time, it would have confirmed the Russian's greatest fears about the jury trial and the legal system. A proud psychopathic murderer becomes a first-rate lawyer in prison, earns enough money from his fabrications to hire even better lawyers, and then convinces the highest court in the land to reverse his conviction and order a new trial. Dostoevsky would have been the first to advocate the release of a prisoner who had greatly suffered and repented of his crime so that he could rejoin the human community and seek his personal salvation through others. But Smith transformed his trial into a vehicle not for justice and redemption but for con artistry and pride. He had pitted himself against the system and he had come out victorious, a conquering hero, wined and dined by intellectuals and the press. Society celebrated the acquittal as a victory of justice. Given Dostoevsky's populism and his negative portrayals of intellectuals, Smith's transformation into a writer and intellectual could hardly have influenced Dostoevsky the way it did Buckley. Dostoevsky, in fact, also received letters from a prisoner, A. Kovner, a journalist who was serving a sentence for embezzlement. He asked Dostoevsky to help him forward his literary career. Although Dostoevsky was not unsympathetic to Kovner's situation, he was disturbed by Kovner's pride and lack of repentance for his crime. Kovner's leftist journalism did not help matters.[17]

Dostoevsky took far less of a "personal" risk for redemption than Buckley took for Smith. The twenty-year-old Kornilova had never done anything resembling her criminal act before; she confessed to the crime and begged for forgiveness. Nevertheless, Dostoevsky was still quite wary. After the reversal of Kornilova's conviction Dostoevsky became even more tentative, in striking contrast to Buckley. While Buckley drew closer to his charge and victoriously whisked him away after his release from prison, Dostoevsky withdrew to maintain a protective distance. He seemed more concerned about what evil Kornilova might still do than he was proud of his role in her acquittal.[18] He understood that the process of regeneration and renewal was lifelong, and thus his six-month revisit did not constitute a guarantee.[19] A defender of children against their abusive parents in the Kroneberg case, as well as in his literary works, he felt uncomfortable, especially before her conviction, in defending an attempted child murderer, especially one whom he himself had branded, in print, as a monster before her conviction.

But most of all, Dostoevsky was wary because of his larger ideological concerns. In coming to Smith's defense, Buckley wrote that he was defending the entire system of justice of which Smith's case was a touchstone. For Dostoevsky, Kornilova represented the Russian people, on whom the salvation of all Russians depended. However committed Dostoevsky was to his faith in the people, he needed to be certain that Kornilova justified the faith that he had invested in her. Another crime might jeopardize in the minds of his readers and political opponents his entire populist ideology. There was little likelihood that Kornilova would commit another crime, but if she did, the ideological stakes, in Dostoevsky's mind, were enormous.

Buckley was thus taking a greater personal risk and a much smaller ideological risk. When Smith committed another heinous crime, that is, when he proved unworthy of redemption, the justification for defending him had to be found elsewhere. Because Buckley could no longer (retrospectively) defend the risks in terms of redemption, he fell back on the law: better that a hundred guilty go free than one innocent be convicted. For Buckley, Smith started out as a person (a soul to be redeemed) and turned into an abstraction (a legal issue).

Despite Dostoevsky's reservations about the court reforms of 1864, he invests the Kornilova jury trial—and the law—with greater social and redemptive significance than does Buckley. Both Smith and Buckley opportunistically looked upon Smith's retrial solely as a means of obtaining Smith's freedom, his confession being a mere ploy to expedite his release. The jury trial served a moral purpose neither for the defendant nor for the public. For Smith release from prison was the end; for Kornilova it was only a beginning. Dostoevsky, in effect, presents the trial as essential to Kornilova's spiritual rebirth, for it permits her to confess her guilt before all the Russian people, and it permits the Russian people to witness her contrition. This court's community of compassion and forgiveness restored Kornilova's faith in all people, the essential prerequisite, as Dostoevsky presents it, for any resurrection from the dead. In contrast to Buckley, Dostoevsky started out with a criminal, an abstraction, a moral monster who should be put away, and ended with an individual for whom the law and the court—now representing justice tempered by mercy—gave hope of personal salvation and reconciliation with the Russian community.

Had Dostoevsky witnessed a Russian trial similar to Smith's, Dostoevsky would certainly have been confirmed in his fears about the post-reform court. In the Smith case the court became a mere instrument beyond moral control. Smith manipulated the system perfectly: he exploited his lawyers and his supporters; he performed brilliantly in court; and he confessed only as a ploy to gain his release. No party really viewed the trial as a site of justice. The government had, as it were, to plea bargain with a defendant whose case had become a cause célèbre. Given that the entire focus of Smith supporters was his release from prison, it is not surprising that they came to see the trial as a means to an end, a case in which they had to out-lawyer the opposition. Buckley also played the game. Because he thought Smith innocent, he gave tacit support to Smith's decision to make a false confession (which, of course, later turned out to be the truth) as expedient to gain Smith's release from prison. For Dostoevsky, whatever the court was in practice, it still had to be judged in terms of the ideal. It had to serve justice and truth not only for the actors but for the Russian people, whose moral education was being conducted through it. In the Smith trial Dostoevsky would certainly have argued that it was bad enough that the court had perpetrated an injustice—as was bound to occur with any human institution—but even worse was that society seemed no longer to believe in the court as the site of justice. It had either lost its faith in the moral basis of its own legal system or did not even care. It celebrated the release of the confessed murderer as though it was the return of a conquering hero. And what happened after the trial did not seem to concern Buckley. A celebration also followed Kornilova's acquittal, but for Dostoevsky it was the beginning, not the end, of her story. The hardest part was to yet to come. At any moment she could prove unworthy soil for the seeds of salvation—unworthy of the risk taken by the court, the nation, and Dostoevsky himself.

### Mailer/Abbott

On 18 June 1981 Jack Abbott murdered a waiter during an argument about the restaurant's bathroom; this occurred about two weeks after Abbott was released from prison on parole and about five years after Edgar Smith abducted and stabbed Lefteria Lisa Ozbun. Jack Abbott was a very different kind of criminal from Edgar Smith, who had no criminal record before the Zielinski case and had been a model prisoner. Abbott had been a violent criminal from the age of twelve and was reputed to be one of the most dangerous prisoners in the entire federal penal system.[20] But like Smith, Abbott took up writing in prison and impressed influential people with his intelligence and his prose. As Mailer said: "The man's brilliant. . . . He's read twenty times more books than I've ever read. He's spent his life reading."[21] Abbott's violent character and his literary brilliance not only attracted Mailer to Abbott but made him a perfect candidate for Mailer's ideas about personal and social redemption.

Mailer ties his redemptive ideas, which Jean Malaquais has called "romantic idealism," not to rehabilitation and reintegration into the community but to an anarchistic, anticommunal ethos of individual violence that he presents most explicitly in his book *The White Negro*.[22] For Mailer the evil that exists in the world comes not from individual violence but from state-condoned and -sponsored violence against individuals. Although Mailer does not see the United States as Nazi Germany or Stalinist Russia, it nevertheless represents a totalitarian society of conformity, which saps the creative energy from all but its most alienated citizens, the hipsters, those oppressed individuals living on society's fringe who will engage in personal violence rather than be regimented, desexed, and robbed of their vital energies. If personal violence represents a reaction against social and state-condoned oppression, it must be seen as healthy or at least superior to the violence perpetrated every day by the state.[23] In such a society the psychopath, the truly antisocial individual, must be our ideal.

But Mailer also argues that personal violence can be creative as well as destructive and that it is liberating not only for the individual perpetrator but for society as a whole. The psychopath's care only for himself, in the end, proves beneficial for all, for he shows us all the way to be more creative, to attain the apocalyptic orgasm, "the paradise of limitless energy." By some redemptive magic violence, by expending itself, leads to its own destruction and transforms itself into its opposite: creativity.

Jack Abbott, a creative individual crushed by society and compelled to express his creativity through violence, becomes an exemplum of Mailer's ideas about personal and social redemption.[24] Yet, however much Mailer romanticized violence, he was not unaware of the tenuousness of his optimistic view of its potential. He understood that his view required great faith, because his archetype violent hipster was not far from the brutal storm trooper: "It takes literal faith in the creative possibilities of the human being to envisage acts of violence as the catharsis which prepares growth."[25] But as Mailer said about Jack Abbott: "Culture is worth a little risk."[26]

Of course, many would characterize Mailer's championing of Abbott not as faith but blindness or, at the very least, a willful misreading both of Abbott's deeds and writings. Mailer knew that Abbott was not just a violent criminal but one of the most violent criminals in the prison system and well known as the most recalcitrant.[27] Abbott admitted to Mailer that he was emotionally immature, that he probably could not be rehabilitated, and that he found murder to be the ultimate self-defining act—and not only in prison. "There are periods in our history when a man was given high honors only through acts of what we today call murders or suicides. A man who killed his father was looked upon with awe at one time, for example," Abbott writes.[28] His idols, Lenin, Stalin, and Mao, "teach the highest principles of human society."[29] Did Mailer really think that these are the principles that Jack Abbott would use to make us free?

In 1977, having learned that Norman Mailer was writing *The Executioner's Song*, a book about Gary Gilmore, Abbott wrote to Mailer, volunteering to provide Mailer with information about prison violence and its effect on inmates. Mailer, who called Abbott's writing "as good as any convict's prose that I had read since Eldridge Cleaver," began to correspond regularly with Abbott.[30] In 1980, when the question of Abbott's parole was at issue, Mailer wrote to the federal parole board, assuring them that Abbott was a major literary talent and that if he were paroled Mailer would hire him as a research assistant at $15,000 a year. Because Mailer had promised Abbott a job, the parole board was able to make a more favorable decision about his parole.[31]

On 5 June 1981 Mailer met the newly paroled Abbott at a New York airport. Abbott frequently visited and had dinner with writers and publishers; his book was about to appear with an introduction by Mailer. He also appeared with Mailer on *Good Morning America* and gave interviews to magazines, including *Rolling Stone*. Approximately two weeks after being paroled, Abbott fatally stabbed Richard Adan, an aspiring actor and playwright, who worked as a waiter in his father-in-law's restaurant to make ends meet.

Abbott was eventually captured in Louisiana and returned for trial. He seemed far more concerned about the fate of his book than about his victim.[32] He was convicted of first-degree manslaughter. During the trial, in a room adjoining the court, the defendant joined with his mentor, Norman Mailer, and others to celebrate his birthday with chocolate cake.

Although Mailer did expedite the procedure, he was not solely responsible for Abbott's parole.[33] In fact, had Abbott—contrary to his wont—continued to behave himself, he would probably have been released, though somewhat later. Mailer read and responded to Abbott's letters, in which Abbott held as little back verbally as he had physically; only later did Mailer confess that he should have stuck "close to him." Mailer's "little risk for culture" sounds disingenuous because Abbott bragged openly to Mailer about how dangerous he was, how little capable he was of forgiveness (which Abbott viewed as a weakness), and how murder spoke louder than words. Had Mailer simply misread Abbott, or had he assumed that on the outside—which Mailer, however, likened to a large prison—Abbott's aggression would be transformed into pure art?

After Abbott killed Adan, Mailer was sincerely contrite. He admitted he made a mistake, and he understood, perhaps a little more clearly, the difference between writing about murder and committing it. Mailer was harshly criticized for his role in the Abbott affair; some even suggested that Mailer be tried along with Abbott.[34] This criticism made Mailer defensive and more sympathetic to Abbott. Mailer may no longer have harbored the same hopes for the mystical transformation of physical violence into socially beneficial art as he had before Adan's murder, but Mailer still saw Abbott's sentence as a waste of artistic potential. "Abbott should not be punished too harshly for this murder. It is true that he is not in any condition just now to walk around loose, but he is a talented writer. Being put away in prison for too long, says Mailer, might stifle Abbott's creativity."[35]

Eight years later, in a civil suit filed against Abbott by Adan's widow and father-in-law, the six-member jury awarded Ricci Adan $5.57 million for the lost lifetime earnings of her husband, the actor Richard Adan, and an additional $2 million for his conscious pain and suffering. Abbott seemed no less uncontrite and arrogant at the civil trial, where he represented himself, than at the criminal trial.

> Abbott repeatedly suggested his victim, an aspiring actor, was responsible for his own death, accused his widow of feigning tears to win the jury's sympathy, and proclaimed that the efforts to lay claim to royalties from Abbott's best-selling book about prison life, "In the Belly of the Beast," and film rights, were an attempt to prevent him from publishing his writings. . . . Repeatedly, Abbott described what he considered his place in the field of literature. "I've become a writer," Abbott told the jury. "As good as any other writer in this country, or even in Europe. This was something told to me, and I was encouraged to write. It was told to me by some of the top publishers and editors in this country."[36]

At the civil trial, in contrast to the criminal trial, few writers or celebrities stood by Abbott. Nor did Mailer, though he did comment that he thought the award granted the plaintiffs was too high. Mailer had obviously modified his redemptive agenda: Abbott was no longer in the vanguard of a new dispensation. On 10 February 2002 Abbott hanged himself in his cell in an upstate New York prison. He was fifty-eight.

### Dostoevsky and Mailer: Redemption and Repentance

Buckley thought he was dealing, at worst, with a completely rehabilitated man. If he viewed his intercession for Smith as a part of a much larger issue—the defense of an individual's legal rights—that seemed to occur to him only after Smith had committed his second crime. Mailer, on the other hand, was dealing with an unrehabilitated and unrepentant criminal from the very beginning and therefore could intercede for Abbott because he had projected onto him a much larger redemptive project. Mailer could take a greater risk only because in the long run there was far more to gain. In comparison with both Buckley's and Dostoevsky's intercessions, Mailer's seems reckless. But Mailer could argue that he was following in the path of Dostoevsky. Like Dostoevsky, Mailer conceived his redemptive project in the broadest social and ideological terms from the beginning. He may even have borrowed directly from Dostoevsky some of the rhetoric relating to the redemption of criminals, buttressing his sponsorship of Abbott—and the downtrodden in general—by framing it in a Dostoevskian progression from crime, imprisonment, and punishment to redemption. In his introduction to Abbott's *In the Belly of the Beast,* Mailer writes:

> There is a paradox at the core of penology, and from it derives the thousand ills and afflictions of the prison system. It is that not only the worst of the young are sent to prison, but the best—that is, the proudest, the bravest, the most daring, the most enterprising, and the most undefeated of the poor.[37]

Mailer's words here echo those of the narrator from the last page of Dostoevsky's *Notes from the House of the Dead,* decrying the loss of so much human potential in prison:

> And how much youth was uselessly interred within those walls, what great powers perished here in vain! One really has to tell the whole truth; the people [*narod*] here were exceptional. Why, they might have been the most talented, the strongest of our people. But their tremendous strength was spent in vain, abnormally, unjustly, irrevocably. But who was to blame? (4:231)

Dostoevsky's statement is in complete accord with his populist, social, and political ideas. If the salvation of Russia depends directly on the regeneration of the Russian common people and their reconciliation with the educated classes, then the wasting away in prison of "the most talented, the strongest of all our people" clearly constitutes not only a terrible paradox, to use Mailer's term, but a national tragedy with international implications. Dostoevsky, however, comes to radically different conclusions about this "wasted" potential.

Although in *Notes from the House of the Dead* Dostoevsky finds the prisoners of the common people stronger, more talented, more resourceful, and more educated than the common people on the outside, he never romanticizes their violence, only their potential. Dostoevsky is writing about a time when serfdom still existed, the early 1850s, and he attributes much of the violence of peasant life to Russia's many centuries under foreign domination and domestic slavery (serfdom). The convicts of the people often do not take responsibility for the crimes they commit against the nobility because they see such "crimes" as the inevitable consequences of unfortunate circumstances. But Dostoevsky does not translate this explanation, as Mailer does with Abbott, into a justification for releasing violent offenders, however talented. The narrator emphasizes that many of the most talented prisoners are dangerous criminals who probably can never be rehabilitated:

> Of course the criminal who has revolted against society hates it, and almost always considers himself in the right and society in the wrong. Moreover, since he has already been punished by society, he almost considers himself cleansed and his debt to society paid. From such a point of view, one might conclude that one must justify the criminal. But in spite of all views on this matter, everyone will agree that there are crimes which always and everywhere, from the beginning of the world, under all legal systems, have been considered indisputable crimes, and will be considered such as long as man remains human. (4:15)

And some of the convicts whom Dostoevsky encountered in prison had committed terrible crimes for which they experienced no guilt whatsoever. Moreover, these crimes had no ready social explanation. Mailer seems to have misread Dostoevsky as well as Abbott. Dostoevsky never shows artistic talent and criminality as mutually exclusive. When the two coexist, criminality far more often exploits talent than talent sublimates criminality. The most artistically talented prisoner in *Notes from the House of the Dead*, Baklushin, is morally clueless. He understands that the state puts people away for murder, but he cannot fathom why killing a German is a crime.

Dostoevsky also understands the danger of releasing a violent prisoner who blames society for his actions and who does not even consider what he has done to be a crime. The unrepentant criminal will always remain dangerous. He can neither save himself nor liberate others, for to save himself he must rejoin and ask forgiveness of the community against which he has sinned. The more intelligent and proud the criminal, the greater the danger he poses to others. Under no circumstances would Dostoevsky have let the highly intelligent self-willed Petrov (*Notes from the House of the Dead*) out of prison, nor would he have helped expedite Abbott's parole. What is more, for Dostoevsky violence among intellectuals never leads to liberation or enlightenment; rather, it is the inevitable consequence of aberrant ideas such as Mailer's.

Mailer turns the Dostoevskian paradigm completely upside down, valorizing Abbott's unrepentant criminality and turning it into the means by which Abbott and the West will be reenergized and redeemed. No great gain will occur without great risk, notwithstanding his disingenuous remarks about the need to take a "little risk for culture."[38] Knowing that the criminality of Abbott could be as easily appropriated for Hitler as it could for redemption, Mailer was taking more than "a little risk for culture." Nothing could be more different than Mailer's and Dostoevsky's ideas about the individual and the collective in terms of redemption. Mailer openly champions Abbott's unrepentant individualism. Dostoevsky too is interested in the salvation of the individual, but he emphasizes that salvation must also be communal and collective: separation from the community, fostered by a cult of extreme individualism—which Dostoevsky tended to see as the ideal of the West—can lead only to alienation and destructive behavior. Mailer misread Dostoevsky's *Notes from the House of the Dead* to support his notion of redemption, only to see it destroyed when Abbott killed again.

The almost dismissive, insouciant attitude that Mailer and Abbott showed toward the jury trial again contrasts sharply with the existential and metaphysical significance that Dostoevsky attached to all aspects of the trial process. Though Mailer's and Abbott's attitude toward the jury trial and the entire judicial system certainly differed from Buckley's and Smith's, both attitudes would have seemed equally dangerous to Dostoevsky. Dostoevsky would have been disturbed by Smith's manipulation and exploitation of the judicial process and his subsequent lionization by the media and the literary world. By contrast, for both Abbott and Mailer, who in different degrees saw crime as a justifiable protest against the legal system, the trial could be nothing but an insignificant sideshow. It is not difficult to imagine the article that Dostoevsky would have written in the *Diary of a Writer* after Mailer and other Abbott supporters celebrated the defendant's birthday in a separate room at the courthouse during the criminal trial. In the civil trial, which took place eight years later—Mailer by this time had effectively distanced himself from his former ward—Abbott, who represented himself, turned his defense into a farce, arguing that the murdered man was responsible for his own death. Dmitry Karamazov's defense lawyer, Fetyukovich, argued that Fedor Karamazov was responsible for his own murder. Dostoevsky raged against the court because it diverged from his ideal, from his vision of the court's great potential to renew Russian life. His hostility arose from an idealist's disillusionment, not from indifference or disrespect, even when later in *The Brothers Karamazov* he turned his satiric gaze on the proceedings of Dmitry Karamazov's trial. The instrumentalism of the Buckley-Smith team and the contemptuous dismissiveness of Abbott and Mailer would have struck Dostoevsky as equally unpardonable.

## Styron/Reid

William Styron once confessed in an interview that he too had a Jack Abbott in his life—a convicted murderer and rapist by the name of Benjamin Reid. In January 1957 Ben Reid, a nineteen-year-old African American, beat a woman to death with a hammer during an attempted robbery. He was convicted of premeditated murder and sentenced to death by electrocution. Styron, who had once accepted and even argued for capital punishment, eventually became convinced of the barbarity of state-sanctioned killing, and in 1962 he wrote a spirited attack against capital punishment in general and against the imminent execution of Ben Reid in particular.[39] Styron did not know Ben Reid personally, but he was told years later by George Will that his article had galvanized many people to take up Reid's cause. "So, I suppose it may be inferred that had I not written the original essay, Ben Reid would most likely have gone to his doom."[40] But Styron came to see life imprisonment without parole as a death in life and thus worse than execution itself: "It is of course important that Reid's life was saved. It is more important that he will not be left to rot," that he not be deprived of the possibility of salvation and redemption.[41] "A majority of criminals, however—including those whose deeds have been quite as ugly as Ben Reid's—are amenable to correction, and many of them can be, and have been, returned to society."[42] Styron took equal pride in the effects of a second article he wrote for *Esquire* in November 1962, in which he advocated amending the Connecticut criminal code, which prescribed mandatory execution or life imprisonment without parole for all first-degree murderers. He wrote that such a law assumes all murderers "to be a species of uncontrollable brute."[43] A legislator who read Styron's article, Robert Satter, "introduced legislation that eventually brought about a more equitable procedure regarding capital offenders [it permitted parole]. So I felt that my initial ventures into journalism had hardly been wasted time."[44]

Styron's plea for clemency and argument for risk (the possibility of parole) is, to be sure, partly motivated by guilt. Like Mailer, he suffers from the guilt of good fortune, seeing the character of those who grow up in wretched conditions as largely socially determined.[45] Reid's life was one of unrelieved deprivation, neglect, and poverty. Styron agrees with the view of Neva Jones, a nurse at the home where Reid spent eight years: "It's society's fault, really. I mean, all of us. People should know more about this situation, where these poor abandoned children are taken in for a while, and then sent back just at the wrong age to that awful environment."[46] Styron argues that had Reid not been a poor black male, he would not have been sentenced to death.

Styron focuses far more on redemption than on the crime because his essential concern is with the potential salvation of every sinner. To deny the great sinner, however great the sin, the possibility of redemption entails the rejection of that possibility for ourselves. To justify his argument concerning redemption and risk—the consequences of granting parole to a potentially dangerous criminal—Styron turns to the inmate's exemplary behavior in prison and, equally important, to his moral growth, characterized in Reid's case by his recognition of, and contrition for, his crime: "I just merely want a chance to show everyone that I have reformed and repented of my wrong that was done thoughtlessly, senselessly."[47] Reid also impresses Styron with his quest for enlightenment. Styron could hardly have imagined a better candidate for his ideal of redemption:

> How sweet it was to see this candidate for redemption come alive from his benighted dungeon in a way that would quicken the heart of any Christian salvationist. How beautiful it was to witness this outcast victim flower and grow, once rescued and given that chance for which these honest Quakers had prayed on their knees. For the simple fact is that

Ben Reid—now that he was snatched from the electric chair and released into the general prison population—demonstrated qualities of
character, of will, and above all, of intelligence that defied everyone's
imagination. . . . Reid, it turned out, was quite bright, in certain ways
even brilliant, and the metamorphosis he underwent in prison was
something to marvel at. He became a star baseball player, a leader
among the inmates; he secured his high school equivalency diploma,
began to take college work. A model prisoner he was—in every sense of
that worn and risky description. A triumph of faith over adversity.
Maybe someday a winner.[48]

Except for one occasion, Styron did not visit his protégé in prison, but
like Buckley and Mailer he "corresponded" with Reid "quite a few times
over the years since his commutation."[49] Anticipating Reid's parole in
April 1970 (thirteen years after his crime), and wanting to enroll him
as a special student, Trinity College approached Styron, asking whether
he would permit Reid to stay at his house for a few weeks until Trinity could receive him. "The idea of my studio in Roxbury becoming
Ben Reid's halfway house filled me with pleasure, and I understood the
blessings of redemption."[50] Like Dostoevsky, Styron implicitly sees his
own redemption marvelously tied to Reid's. Mailer repented for not
having paid closer attention to Abbott when he was released to a
halfway house. But Styron was later to admit that he was perhaps lucky
to have been personally spared these "blessings of redemption," for
before Reid could take up Styron's offer, just a few days before his
parole, Reid senselessly escaped from prison, abducted a woman and
her two children, and raped the woman before letting her and her children go. He was caught and sentenced to ten to fifteen years in state
prison.

Styron had been partly responsible for the commutation of the
death sentence and later the rescission of the sentence of life imprisonment without parole. After Reid had committed the second crime,
Styron understood the risk more personally. If Reid had stayed in his
house, his own daughter, he admits, could have been one of Reid's victims. Twelve years after Reid's second crime, Styron was still anguish-
ing over the question of risk and redemption. Writing his third piece
on Ben Reid in 1982, he faced an even more difficult dilemma than
twelve years before, when he had offered his house to foster the miracle of redemption. After Reid's second violent crime, Styron, as well

as others who had helped Ben Reid, experienced a sense of betrayal. Styron had to decide again between Reid's potential victims and his idea of redemption. He argues that it would have been easier to play it safe, to disengage himself personally from Ben Reid's story, but to do so was morally unacceptable; it also meant rejecting the possibility of our own redemption, for we are all potentially Ben Reid. For "he is also human, and subject to the same laws and the same forces which determine the desires of every one of us."

> It is tempting to treat him as something utterly foreign from ourselves and so avoid looking into our own depths. . . . But finally, do we abandon Jack Abbott and Ben Reid? . . . My own sense of betrayal has been strong, but not so complete that I have been able to turn my back on Reid's destiny. . . . His conduct in the Massachusetts prison system has been once more, I say, exemplary. . . . But hope persists. I have talked to Ben Reid several times; he speaks of his remorse and his repentance, and of his conviction that he will make good on the outside, and I cannot explain why I believe him.[51]

Styron must believe in him; not to believe is to lose his faith in redemption.[52]

There could have been no better test of Styron's faith than Ben Reid, for Reid's most recent exemplary behavior, remorse, and repentance had to be less reassuring than they had been before he escaped from prison and terrorized a mother and her child thirteen years earlier. Styron suggests that his Presbyterian upbringing, which may have fashioned his views on Christian redemption, influenced him to believe that greater risks must be undertaken when the salvation of a soul is at stake. For Styron the mysteries of grace must take precedence over categories of risk and consequence.

> Rereading the two pieces I wrote on this case, possibly I became aware of how important to my argument against the death penalty was the Christian doctrine of redemption. This interests me now, because I thought that by the time I was past thirty-five—at the very least agnostic and surely swept by the bleak winds of existentialism—I had abandoned the Presbyterian precepts of my childhood.[53] But I can see that the Gospels were as much a mediating force in my attempt to save Reid's life as were Camus and Heidegger.

## Dostoevsky and Styron:
## Faith and Redemption

Whereas the Abbott-Mailer and Kornilova-Dostoevsky cases show redemptive concerns taking writers in diametrically different directions,
Styron's defense of Ben Reid seems like a faithful adaptation of salvific
ideas from the *Diary of a Writer*—as though Styron were actually waiting for the proper criminal to whom he could apply Dostoevsky's
paradigm of Christian redemption.[54] Despite Styron's crusade for the
abolishment of capital punishment and of life sentences without possibility of parole, his main concern in the Ben Reid case—in contrast
to Buckley's concern for the law after Edgar Smith committed his second crime—is almost entirely rehabilitation and redemption. He argues
not only for the potential salvation of every soul—"all men must be
given at least the possibility of redemption"—but "the potential res-
toration of every soul to the community."[55]

Although Styron seems to share Dostoevsky's views of redemption,
on the question of risk he not only radically diverges from Dostoevsky,
he also actually goes much beyond either Buckley or Mailer. Because
Kornilova died less than a year after she was acquitted at her second
trial, Dostoevsky did not have to deal with the second crime that Buckley, Mailer, and Styron all had to face.[56] After Smith's second crime
Buckley immediately distanced himself from his ward. Mailer distanced himself from Abbott, but because he was put on the defensive
by his critics, he did so more slowly. Styron, on the other hand, stood
up for Reid just as vigorously after the second crime as after the first.

Dostoevsky is, of course, no less interested in redemption than
Styron; it is the dominant concern of his fiction. But because of his
populist ideology—his interest in collective redemption—Dostoevsky
must place far greater weight on consequences and risk. He must balance his impassioned personal plea for Kornilova's redemption against
the effect a reversion to crime might have on the educated classes' faith
in the common people's potential for moral and spiritual reform and
regeneration. For Styron the focus remains on the individual as a universal: everyone in potentia. The greatest risk is not to take a risk; it is
to lose faith in the grace of God, for whom no one is completely beyond redemption. Dostoevsky might have been persuaded to let Reid out
of prison on the basis of his genuine repentance and good behavior.
But only the first time. After the second crime Dostoevsky's attention

would have turned not only to the potential victims but to the damage that another crime might do to his redemptive agenda—if Reid had been part of it. For Styron, Reid was a test of his own faith. Dostoevsky had to be particularly concerned about the political and social consequences of recidivism.

In 1990 Styron seemed to see his faith justified. In his introduction to Judge Robert Satter's book about life as a trial lawyer, Styron wrote: "Now these many years later, having paid his debt to society, Reid is free and has become a peaceful and productive citizen—certainly living testimony to Robert Satter's invincible belief in redemption and fairness, concepts poorly apprehended in a culture that is unfairly arranged and, in matters of justice, often vindictive."[57]

In fact, Ben Reid was released from prison in 1982 after completing his second term. Until December 1996 he lived as a free man. But in January 1997 he was returned to prison for violating his parole, having been charged with threatening a woman minister. His parole violation was appealed. Redemption, as Dostoevsky understood it, is a lifelong project. For Styron so is faith in redemption, which Reid has now tested for the last forty-one years.

Both Dostoevsky and Styron argue the same redemptive points. They do not deny that a serious crime has been committed; they protest only the sentences. Dostoevsky argues that the court did not take into consideration Kornilova's psychological condition, Styron that the court did not consider Reid's history of deprivation and abuse. But most of all, they believe that the sentences would deprive their wards of the possibility of redemption. Although the jury trial plays almost no role in Styron's discussion of his relationship with Ben Reid, Styron was actually much more involved in confronting the legal system than was Dostoevsky. Dostoevsky never thought that his article would have any effect on the Kornilova case. It did, but it affected only one case, and Dostoevsky viewed the acquittal at the second trial as a miracle, an exception to the rule. Styron was reacting to a systematic legal injustice—capital punishment and life imprisonment without parole —and his articles were aimed at changing the law. His interest in the law, therefore, was not so much to free only Ben Reid—as Buckley's interest was to free Edgar Smith—but to give everyone the possibility of redemption. Kornilova is acquitted almost despite the law, Reid because of the law.

Individual Versus Collective Redemption: American and Russian Justice

Dostoevsky's intercession for Kornilova had important things in common with the intercessions of Buckley, Mailer, and Styron for their wards. In defending Kornilova, Dostoevsky became involved in the intricacies of the law, just as Buckley and Styron did. Dostoevsky's intercession was as ideologically motivated as Mailer's. The Russian's concern for redemption did not differ significantly from Styron's. All the writers understood—though to different degrees—the risks that they were taking by interceding for convicted felons. Gender does not account for all the differences here. Kornilova may have been less violent than the male wards of the American writers. But Dostoevsky was especially critical of earlier juries that acquitted women who had committed what were, in his view, serious crimes. He came out in defense of Kornilova not because she was a woman but because he thought she was temporarily insane when she committed the crime.

But as we have seen, the differences between Dostoevsky's redemptive agenda and those of the American writers are significant. Dostoevsky is much more concerned with consequences, especially those that might adversely affect the general perception of the Russian common people and their potential for renewal. By contrast, Buckley's ideological position—the defense of the law—takes on even greater importance after Smith's second crime. Mailer acknowledged from the beginning that the psychotic personality that he had advanced could bring forth storm troopers as easily as brilliant artists but averred that it was worth the risk. Ben Reid seemingly could not commit another crime that would compromise Styron's faith in redemption.

But perhaps what most differentiates Dostoevsky from his American counterparts is his focus on the communal nature of redemption. Despite the great differences dividing the American writers, they are, in comparison with Dostoevsky, devoted to the cause of individuals. Buckley takes on the whole legal establishment. Whether Smith wins or loses, whether Smith committed the original crime or even commits another crime, at least in retrospect he becomes less important than the fight for individual rights. In Abbott, Mailer champions the pathological individual. Society cannot save the individual. It is society that needs to be redeemed, and only the individual, perhaps only the pathological individual, can save it. For Styron the salvation of the individual soul, the soul of Ben Reid, seems to eclipse all other concerns because of its symbolic significance. Society benefits from its enduring faith in the redemption of all who have sinned, but redemption quintessentially concerns individuals. Because the American writers place so much emphasis on the individual, they seem to downplay the possible consequences of their intercessions for others, that is, risk. Only a second crime brought home to Buckley and Mailer the reality of risk, and for Styron the consequences never seemed to overcome the hope for eventual redemption.

Throughout his articles on the Kornilova case, as well as on similar cases about which he wrote in the *Diary of a Writer*, Dostoevsky focuses on the effect that court decisions have on the Russian community. He also sees redemption not as the private affair of individuals in their struggle against larger social and legal forces but as a reciprocal process in which society and the individual come together in their mutual desire for reconciliation. Kornilova needs to asks forgiveness not only of the child and her husband but of the entire Russian community against which she has sinned, and the Russian community needs to prepare itself to take her back into its bosom.[58] For the American writers the trial becomes a means for freeing the individual from the society that has oppressed him. For Dostoevsky, at least in the Kornilova trial, it becomes the vehicle for bringing together the individual and society, erasing the lines of division. Kornilova's resurrection from the dead is as much a communal as a private affair. For the American writers the court succeeded or failed in terms of how it worked for or against their wards. The court did not represent justice. More often than not, justice resided outside the court. For Dostoevsky the jury trial and the court seem far more important because he sees the court as a communal institution that sets the standards for truth and justice for the entire society. Its main purpose is less to decide the fate of individuals than to forge a moral body politic. Kornilova is especially important because her fate is inextricably tied not only to the actors in the courtroom but to all Russians. That is why, when Kornilova is acquitted at her second trial, the courtroom takes on the aura of a Russian Orthodox service, in which not only Kornilova but all see the possibility of salvation. Dostoevsky's animus toward the court in the 1870s, with, of course, the possible exception of the Kornilova trial, is a direct reflection of how much capital Dostoevsky had invested in it and how bitter was the disillusionment when it fell so far short of his expectations and hopes.

# CHAPTER 4

# *The Brothers Karamazov*

## Prosecuting the Jury Trial

Given the almost religious celebration of Kornilova's acquittal in the *Diary of a Writer*—despite Dostoevsky's intention to portray what oc-curred in court as a miracle—the vilification of the jury trial in *The Brothers Karamazov* comes as another surprise. Two months *before* the last of the Kornilova articles, in the October issue of the *Diary*, which Dostoevsky devoted to the Hartung case, he maintains that truth and trial by jury are inherently incompatible and that the coincidence of the two could come only under a new dispensation, when "we grow wings and all people are converted into angels." At that time "on the stage there will be no spectacle, no game, but a lesson, an example, edification" (870; 26:54).[1] Dostoevsky immediately recognizes the con-tradiction, for when we grow wings and all become angels "there will be no courts."[2]

But it could be argued that Dostoevsky's articles about the Kornil-ova case present the answer to his own riddle. For what is the Kornilova trial in the *Diary of a Writer* if not "a lesson, an example, edification," an approximation of Utopia that has come to pass, that is, a coming together of legal procedure and truth. The comments quoted from the Hartung case in the first paragraph seem almost out of character—and not only in the context of the Kornilova case. After the October 1876 issue of *Diary of a Writer* carried his first article on the Kornilova case, Dostoevsky began to tone down his criticism of the jury trial. So in his article about the Dzhunkovsky trial (July–August 1877), Dosto-evsky seems to focus less on child abuse than on what fathers need to do to provide positive examples for their children. He cites the entire indictment as printed in the *New Times*. The parents were charged with neglecting, mistreating, and frequently beating their three children "with anything that happened to be around—even with fists, rods, switches, with a whip intended for horses—with such cruelty that it was frightful to behold and (according to the testimony of the boy Alexander) so that the child's back ached five days after one of the castigations" (764; 25:182). The parents were acquitted.

Dostoevsky takes a different tack than in Kroneberg, arguing that the defendants should not have even been charged in the first place. Given the criminal code (and here Dostoevsky cites Kroneberg), the mistreatment could not have reached the level of "cruel and inhuman torture," according to the law. If the charge is negligent, incompetent, and heartless parenting, "it would be necessary to condemn half of Russia—nay, far more than that!" (766; 25:183). With regard to flogging with rods, Dostoevsky writes sarcastically: "Well, who doesn't flog children with rods? Nine-tenths of Russia practices this. By no means can this be subject to the provisions of the law" (766: 25:184). One cannot send the majority of the population to prison.

But because the Dzhunkovskys were brought to trial, Dostoevsky feels compelled to offer his own resolution of the case: he writes a speech that the presiding judge should have made to the defendants, really an admonishment, reminding the parents of their sacred responsibility toward their children not only not to mistreat them but to provide them with a positive model.[3] Dostoevsky here is restating his conviction that the jury should be an institution of moral instruction for Russia, a forum for correct ideas. He understands, however, that the court is of this world; it cannot do everything that we would like it to do, and he agrees that it did the best it could under the circumstances. Such a concession, however reluctant, seems like a shift away from his position in the Kroneberg case.

In the only other trial that he wrote about in the *Diary of a Writer,* the trial of Gen. L. N. Hartung that I mentioned earlier, Dostoevsky expresses his anxiety about the ease with which Russians accept the limitations of the new legal system. But he again is understanding: the court exists in the real world. Rather than face his sentence, Hartung committed suicide, leaving a statement that he was innocent of all the charges made against him. Dostoevsky probably thought the judgment was harsh but inevitable, given the evidence. He does not fault the jury alone. "Briefly, Hartung dies convinced of his complete innocence. Even so, strictly speaking, there was no error . . . no judicial error at all [*no i oshibki . . . sudebnoi oshibki, v strogom smysle, ne bylo*]. This was fate, a tragedy occurred" (866; 26:50). He argues that all of Russian society is ultimately responsible for what happened.

Dostoevsky is far more critical of the adversarial system's attitude toward truth. In the October 1877 issue of the *Diary of a Writer,* in a section sarcastically entitled "Deceit Is Necessary to Truth. Deceit Multiplied by Deceit Produces Truth. Is This So?" Dostoevsky takes aim at the exaggerations (the distortions of the truth) of the prosecution and defense. What disturbs Dostoevsky most about this practice is that he sees it as alien to the Russian character, something "that we have borrowed with such a felicitous lightness from Europe and that has implanted itself in our representatives of both defense and prosecution" (869; 26:53). The trial is turned into a public entertainment, a contest between gladiators. The public knows that each side is not only exaggerating but lying, but it enjoys the competition, the rhetorical battle. If the sides are not equal, if the lawyer on one side is an artist with talent and the lawyer on the other is incompetent, a great injustice can occur. Though Dostoevsky expresses dissatisfaction with the mechanical and alien method by which decisions are reached in Russia's Europeanized courts, he realizes that nothing better is available to take their place. He can only hope that the situation will improve, but he does not expect a cure: as in all such matters, humanity must wait for the next dispensation. Again, we have a criticism of the court but not a vilification, and a begrudged acceptance of an imperfect institution in an imperfect world.

Dostoevsky's judicial "turn," which most probably occurred just a few months after he wrote his last article on Kornilova, which strongly defended the court's acquittal, coincided with the Zasulich trial, the most famous Russian trial of the nineteenth century.[4] Vera Zasulich was a twenty-eight-year-old revolutionary, who, on 24 January 1878, tried to kill the military governor of St. Petersburg, Gen. Fedor F. Trepov, because she believed that he had illegally ordered the flogging of a Populist political prisoner for a minor offense.[5] Trepov sustained a serious but not life-threatening gunshot wound. Because the government believed Zasulich's motivation to be political, the 1864 judicial code required that she be tried in an "exceptional" court of the Senate rather than by a jury of her peers. But this time the government preferred a jury, thinking it could win an easy conviction. Just as important, having Zasulich convicted by a jury of her peers would take the onus off the government and, as Count C. I. Pahlen, the minister of justice, assured the tsar: "The jurors would deliver a guilty verdict and thereby teach a sobering lesson to the insane, small coterie of revolutionaries; they would show all the Russian and foreign admirers of Vera Zasulich's 'heroic exploit' that the Russian people bow before the Tsar, revere him, and are always ready to defend his faithful servants."[6] But the trial, which took place on 31 March 1878, turned into a disaster for the administration. Many conservatives later remarked that the testimony about corporal punishment allowed by the presiding judge, A. F. Koni, the president of the Petersburg circuit court, put the government on trial rather than the defendant. Zasulich was acquitted. Loud applause broke out in the courtroom, and Zasulich's supporters carried her away triumphantly on their shoulders. In his memoirs Koni recalled the reaction of the public at the trial:

> It is impossible for one who was not present to imagine the outbursts that drowned out the foreman's voice and the movement that like an electric shock sped through the entire room. The cries of unrestrained joy, hysterical sobbing, desperate applause, the tread of feet, cries of "Bravo! Hurrah! Good Girl [*molodtsy*]! Vera! Verochka! Verochka!" merged in one roar both moan and howl. Many crossed themselves; in the upper, more democratic sections for the public people embraced; even in the places for the judges there was enthusiastic applause [*userdneishim obrazom khlopali*].[7]

Almost immediately after the acquittal, the government tried to re-arrest Zasulich, but she eluded police and went into hiding. Because the trial was an international sensation, Zasulich became an instant heroine for almost every European with leftist sympathies. Many European papers wrote enthusiastically about her acquittal. The tsar fired Pahlen for mishandling the case.[8]

In May 1878, after the government vacated Zasulich's acquittal and ordered a retrial, she decided that it was too dangerous to remain in Russia and escaped abroad. But her acquittal gave political radicals encouragement and justification to engage in a series of terrorist attacks against highly placed government officials, which, in March 1881, a month after Dostoevsky's death, culminated in the assassination of the tsar. Michael T. Florinsky expresses the received interpretation of the political consequences of the acquittal: "The Zasulich case gave a powerful impetus to political terror; the verdict, interpreted as public endorsement of terroristic methods, swayed many populists who had formerly opposed political murders. Attempts on the lives of high officials and police officers became increasingly frequent."[9]

During the trial Koni was under tremendous pressure from Pahlen and even the tsar himself to get a conviction at any cost. But the judge refused to make any concessions. His impartiality was not the only factor in Zasulich's acquittal. Most commentators agree that even more crucial was the prowess of Zasulich's defense attorney, P. A. Aleksandrov, one of Russia's most talented defense lawyers and a brilliant orator. He proved, not unexpectedly, to be far more effective than the prosecutor, K. I. Kissel. Kissel was actually the third choice of the administration, whose first two choices turned the position down.[10] As Dostoevsky feared, the verdict was determined less by truth than by talent, a theme that runs through all his *Diary* articles about the jury trial.

The trial occurred after Dostoevsky had halted publication of the *Diary of a Writer*, so he never wrote about the Zasulich case. He attended the trial himself, so he most certainly would have written about it. He used his connections to procure a ticket to the trial, to which he was admitted as a member of the press (*v kachestve predstavitelia pechati*). On the basis of the few statements that friends recall that he made during and after the trial, Dostoevsky seems to have feared equally an acquittal—which would virtually sanction political assassination—and a conviction—which would transform the attempted murderer into a martyr. But he did not think that Zasulich should have been found guilty. She did not resist arrest, she confessed to the crime, and she understood that what she had done was wrong.

Because we have only a few brief reports about what Dostoevsky said about the case, and only one statement from his pen (in his working diaries), one can only speculate why he thought that Zasulich should have been acquitted. He probably saw similarities between Zasulich and Kornilova, women who were sorry for what they had done and who had lost control of themselves. They were both in their twenties. He would have liked the court to assume the position in the Zasulich case that he spelled out in his article about the Dzhunkovsky trial, in which, taking over the role of the presiding judge, he let the defendant go home with a lecture. Friends recall that he said, "You have sinned, you wished to kill a man, but you have already atoned for it. Go, and do not transgress again. . . . Sin no more."[11] But as in the Dzhunkovsky case, Dostoevsky realized that the court was incapable of doing that.

Zasulich's acquittal was not the only thing that must have disturbed Dostoevsky about the case. He could not have been pleased by the revelations regarding the government's abuse—physical and mental—of political prisoners (Dostoevsky, after all, had been a political prisoner himself); the enthusiastic reaction to the acquittal; the political violence that ensued directly thereafter; and the role that lawyerly talent played in swaying the jury. But what must have especially concerned him was the use of the jury as a forum for advancing political ideology. The radicals were winning the propaganda war, and they were using the courts to do it. Although the Zasulich trial may have marked the beginning of a period of terroristic assassinations of government officials, Dostoevsky probably interpreted it as the culmination of the propaganda war waged through the jury trial. Richard Pipes, who, like many other scholars, views the judicial reforms of 1864 as the most successful of the Great Reforms, places most of the blame for "sabotaging" the legal reforms on the "radical intelligentsia and its sympathizers among the well-meaning, enlightened and liberal public." Pipes, no lover of the tsarist autocracy, concludes:

> Defendants in political trials realized quickly what a superb opportunity had been handed to them to broadcast nationwide their views from the privileged tribune of the court and rather than defend themselves often used the trials as an occasion to make political speeches attacking the system. These speeches were duly reported the following day in the *Government Messenger*. Sometimes, as for instance, in the so-called Trial of Fifty (1877), the defendants refused to recognize the competence of the court; at other times (e.g. the Trial of the 193 in 1877–8) they hurled insults at the judges.[12]

Even before the political trials of 1877 and 1878, Dostoevsky's articles and commentaries on the jury trial argued for the court as a forum for morally sound ideas. He could not have commented in the *Diary of a Writer* on the Trial of 193, which took place in January 1878. He could, however, have commented on the earlier trial, the Trial of Fifty, which took place in 1877, but evidently chose not to. Perhaps he did not want to write a scabrous article about the jury trial while he was portraying the court that acquitted Kornilova as the site of reconciliation and Russian justice.

After the Zasulich case there were no more political trials on which

Dostoevsky could comment, for the government removed all political crimes from the jurisdiction of the jury trial system in an attempt, among other things, to deprive the radicals of a public forum to air their views. But Dostoevsky's silence was obviously not related solely to contemporary legal developments. He would have his say on the jury trial in his new novel, *The Brothers Karamazov*. The radicals had used the jury trial as a consummate forum for their propaganda; Dostoevsky would use the jury trial for his own ideological and moral purposes in a forum—the social novel—where he could be even more effective and persuasive than in the *Diary of a Writer*. Dostoevsky takes the reader back to the roots of the contemporary moral morass, the legal reforms of 1864 and their implementation in 1866. But having his say about the Zasulich case was far from the main reason for using the jury trial as the conclusion of *The Brothers Karamazov*. Dostoevsky obviously saw the jury trial, and the entire Western legal system on which it was based, as the perfect vehicle for advancing his moral, religious, and political ideas.

The articles in the *Diary of a Writer* show Dostoevsky attempting more and more to take cases out of court in order to rewrite them. But the rewriting had limits. In the Kroneberg case he was responding to a fait accompli. Even in the Kornilova case, in which his *Diary* article led to a retrial, he became anxious about the consequences of his intercession, specifically about what might happen after Kornilova's acquittal. *The Brothers Karamazov* gave him the opportunity of taking complete control of the trial process. He could now leave nothing to chance, creating the participants as well as the witnesses (lay and expert), the lawyers (prosecution and defense), the jury, the judge, and the journalists. And by creating a personal narrator, he could to a certain extent re-create himself as an observer of the entire process.[13]

Dostoevsky's assault on the jury trial not only goes beyond Kroneberg, it implicitly takes issue with his own articles on the Kornilova case, striking hard at his own hopes—illusions, in retrospect—that the court by some miracle might be the site for reconciliation and regeneration. Many have seen the trial scene in *The Brothers Karamazov* as an extension of Dostoevsky's position in Kroneberg. But far more likely, it is an attack against narrative empathy, which Dostoevsky exploited in the Kornilova case when he became personally involved with the defendant. In Kroneberg the issue was the destruction of empathy for the victimized witnesses for the prosecution, the empathy that Dostoevsky

tried to restore in the *Diary of a Writer*. In the Kornilova trial—and of
course in the Zasulich trial—the issue, and the risk, were empathy for
the defendant.

In the Hartung trial Dostoevsky emphasized that there was no
*sudebnaia oshibka*, that is, no judicial error or miscarriage of justice,
although the defendant was probably innocent.[14] By contrast, Dostoevsky entitles the last book of *The Brothers Karamazov*, which is devoted entirely to Dmitry Karamazov's trial, "Sudebnaia oshibka," though
Dmitry did not commit the murder for which he is being tried. Apro-
pos the Hartung case, Dostoevsky called the jury trial an un-Russian
institution in which the truth is supposed to be attained through deceit
and theatrics. In *The Brothers Karamazov* if deceit and theatrics do not
bring about the judicial mistake, they compound its consequences in
Dmitry's sentence.

The scope and intensity of Dostoevsky's attack against the jury become especially clear when one compares his handling of the direct and
indirect jury participants—the judges, lawyers, jury, witnesses, defendants, spectators, press, and narrator—with their counterparts in the
Kornilova case. The jury trial in *The Brothers Karamazov* can easily be
interpreted as a deconstruction of Dostoevsky's article on Kornilova.


### The Judge


Dostoevsky says little about the judges in his articles on the Kroneberg
and Kornilova trials. In his piece about the Kornilova trial, he mentions the judge only once, noting that he took a long time reading out
the instructions to the jury (*posle dlinnoi rechi predsedatelia*; 25:120).
During the trial in *The Brothers Karamazov* the judge only occasionally attracts the narrator's attention, for example, when he threatens to
evict Dmitry from the courtroom because of his periodic outbursts.
The judge's function is to set the procedural tone, keep order, and ask
a preliminary set of factual questions of all the witnesses before turning the interrogation over to the prosecuting and defense attorneys. He
also gives instructions to the jury before they leave to deliberate—
about which the narrator notes: "At last the jury rose to retire for deliberation. The presiding judge was tired, which is why his instructions
to them were so weak: 'Be impartial,' he said, 'do not be impressed by
the eloquent words of the defense, and yet weigh carefully, remember

that a great obligation rests upon you,' and so on and so forth" (751; 15:176). The narrator seems to criticize the judge for his weak instructions, although he concedes that it is understandable under the circumstances: everyone is tired. But the narrator would in any case have dismissed the judge's remarks as pro forma, as an empty part of court procedure. Generally dismissive of all court procedure at Dmitry's trial, the narrator implies that it merely covers up the truth with a veneer of formalities. Koni, the presiding judge at the Zasulich trial, was Russia's most respected jurist and a good friend of Dostoevsky's. Dostoevsky is not directing his criticism at Koni through the judge at Dmitry's trial but merely emphasizing, as the writer did in the Kroneberg trial, that the institution, not the court participants, dictates trial procedure. Koni too was upset by the Zasulich verdict. Dostoevsky probably thought that Koni did the best he could under the circumstances. Koni tried to be objective, which is evident in his instructions to the jurors, but he did not imply that their decision was in any way mechanical, that is, a strict application of law to a particular instance. Rather, he emphasized at the end of his instructions that "only the voice of your conscience" should determine the verdict, leaving the door open, as was common in Russian trials, to jury nullification, that is, sanctioning the right of the jurors to take into consideration the nature and situation of the defendant in their verdict and rule against the strict interpretation of the law.

In the 1860s Dostoevsky, who then had great faith in Russian juries, expressed serious reservations about Russian judges, on whom, he wrote his best friend A. N. Maykov (9 October 1867), the success of the reform greatly depended. "Our juries are the very best; but regarding our judges, one would like to see more education and experience; and in addition, higher moral principles. Without that kind of foundation, nothing will become firmly established" (28.2:228). But obviously, his remarks here are relevant neither to the Zasulich case, over which his friend Koni presided, nor the Karamazov case, in which Dostoevsky presents the judge as a well-educated and decent man:

> As for our presiding judge, one can simply say of him that he was an educated and humane man, with a good practical knowledge of his work, and of the most modern ideas. He was rather vain, but not overly concerned with his career. His chief goal in life was to be a progressive man. Further, he had a fortune and connections. He took, as it turned out

later, a rather passionate view of the Karamazov case, but only in a general sense. He was concerned with the phenomenon, its classification, seeing it as a product of our social principles, as characteristic of the Russian element, and so on and so forth. But his attitude toward the personal aspect of the case, its tragedy, just as toward the personality of the participants, beginning with the defendant, was rather impersonal and abstract, as, by the way, it perhaps should have been. (658–59; 15:91–92)

We can best decode this passage with the help of the *Diary of a Writer*. An incompetent judge would undermine Dostoevsky's point here, for judicial incompetence was one of the major defects of the pre-reform courts. Dostoevsky is intent on undermining the seemingly more competent post-reform court. The judge is well educated, competent, decent, and independent (he is well-off and not overly ambitious). As a man of progressive ideas, he passionately believes in the legal system, which serves justice only when it acts dispassionately, impersonally, and, as Dostoevsky was wont to express it, mechanically, that is, when it works outside morality and emotion. Though the judge is constrained by legal procedures, he loves those constraints. The narrator adds in the last line that the judge has an impersonal attitude toward the personal aspect of the case, and, given the organization of the legal system, that is precisely the attitude that he is supposed to have. It is not the judge who is the problem (Dostoevsky had earlier hoped that the judges would be the main problem) but the system that defines his role. The judge cannot tell Dmitry, as Dostoevsky "told" the Dzhunkovskys, that Dmitry should go home and sin no more. It makes no difference that the judge is well educated, decent, and competent, if the system itself is defective and unresponsive to context. The judge's instructions are meaningless, for they ignore the most important point: the tragedy of the defendant. Just as bad, only one thing seems to trump judicial procedure in the judge's mind: talent. Although he is a stickler for order, contrary to his usual procedure he does not clear the court, as he had threatened, when applause breaks out during and after Fetyukovich's speech; the judge resorts only to ringing his bell. Art is at its most dangerous in the courtroom. The stolid judge is overcome by the orator.[15] The judge gets off lightly in *The Brothers Karamazov* because Dostoevsky needs to show him as competent in order to undercut the system that makes his competence irrelevant. This is not to say, of course, that the old system, in which judges exercised power arbitrarily and were often ill informed, was better but that the new system has not made a significant difference. Dostoevsky could make no more damning statement, given the incompetence and corruption of the old system.

## Expert Testimony

In the Kornilova case, contrary to his wont, Dostoevsky fulsomely praised the expert testimony, stressing both its psychological profundity and its unanimity. In *The Brothers Karamazov* he treats the testimony of the medical experts as farce, comically emphasizing the glaring disparities. The famous Moscow doctor, called in by Katerina Ivanovna to take care of the severely depressed and hallucinative Ivan Karamazov, testifies that Dmitry was suffering from temporary insanity at the time of crime:

> The Moscow doctor, questioned in his turn, sharply and emphatically confirmed that he considered the defendant's mental condition abnormal, "even in the highest degree." He spoke at length and cleverly about "mania" [*maniia*] and the "fit of passion" [*affekt*] and concluded from all the assembled data that the defendant, before the arrest, as much as several days before, was undoubtedly suffering from a morbid fit of passion [*affekt*], and if he did commit the crime, even consciously, it was also almost involuntarily [*nevol'no*], being totally unable to fight the morbid fixation that possessed him. (672; 15:104)

We can see Dostoevsky retreating here from his defense of Kornilova on the basis of temporary insanity and returning to his dismissal of the temporary insanity defense in *Crime and Punishment*. Dostoevsky is not summarily dismissing temporary insanity as a defense; rather, he is arguing against the exploitation of temporary insanity as a justification for murder. Dostoevsky goes much beyond *Crime and Punishment* here. Even Dmitry's defense attorney, Fetyukovich, does not take the temporary insanity defense seriously. Fetyukovich will eventually argue that if Dmitry really killed his father, he not only knew what he was doing but had a right to do it. The temporary insanity idea "was introduced solely at the insistence of Katerina Ivanovna" (671; 15:103). Even the narrator makes fun of it. Without even examining Dmitry, the Moscow doctor argues that Dmitry's inability to speak of the three thousand rubles (which he believed his father owed him) constituted the main indication of his temporary mania.

The local doctor, Herzenstube, agrees with the Moscow doctor, stating that the "mental abnormality of the defendant is self-evident" (671). But he bases his argument on the way that Dmitry walked into the courtroom, looking straight ahead rather than to the left, "where among the public, the ladies were sitting" (671: 15:103). Dmitry should have looked left because "he was a great admirer of the fair sex and ought to have thought very much about what the ladies would be saying of him" (671: 15:103). To make the situation appear even more ridiculous, the Moscow doctor agrees with his colleague—or, rather, rival—that Dmitry's looking straight ahead reflected his "abnormal psychological condition at the moment" (673; 15:105), but the Moscow doctors says that Dmitry should have looked to the right, where his attorney, "in whose help all his hopes lie, and on whose defense his entire fate now depends," was seated (673; 15:105).

It would be too pat—and contrary to Dostoevsky's point here—for all the experts to agree about the same wrong idea. Dostoevsky does not want unanimity here even if it is false unanimity. The third doctor, Dr. Varvinsky, therefore argues for Dmitry's sanity, but he partly bases his argument, as we might now expect, on Dmitry's looking straight ahead. "So that, by looking straight in front of him, he thereby precisely proved his perfectly normal state of mind at the present moment" (673; 15:105). The privileged reader knows that Dr. Varvinsky is far closer to the truth—that Dmitry is sane—not because of Dmitry's cry of "Precisely so" (673; 15:105) but because of the cumulative evidence in the preceding eleven books. But that is not even the point. Varvinsky bases his argument for asserting Dmitry's sanity on a ridiculous proposition—that he looks straight ahead rather than to the side.

Dostoevsky shows that the testimony of the experts is compromised from the very beginning, albeit for different reasons. The Moscow doctor is a hired expert, Herzenstube is muddleheaded, and Dr. Varvinsky, like most experts, cannot resist the temptation of contradiction for its own sake. Further, when professionals come together, personal vanity, envy, and pride invariably prevail over truth. As soon as the Moscow doctor arrives in the town and sees some of Herzenstube's patients, he begins to make disparaging remarks about his colleague. The ensuing personal rivalry surfaces in court. So when at the trial Herzenstube interprets Dmitry's not looking to the left on his entrance into the court as an indication of his abnormal psychological condition, the doctor from Moscow is compelled to argue not only that Dmitry should have looked to the right but also that his not looking to the right constitutes the main proof of his condition.[16] Given the satiric mode in which the chapter is written, the reader doubts that Dr. Varvinsky, who argues for Dmitry's sanity, is closer to the truth because of his superior psychological acumen. As a professional who knows that all of Russia is attending every word of his statement, he must stake out his own independent position, agreeing with neither of the previous experts. The interpretation of Dmitry's innocuous entrance into the courtroom is one of the most brilliant intrusions of Gogolian aesthetics into the Russian psychological novel. Context is everything here. In the Kornilova case the experts were brilliantly unanimous about the defendant's temporary insanity because Dostoevsky needed their support and unanimity. In *The Brothers Karamazov,* where every part of the jury process must be undermined, the expert testimony appears ludicrous.[17]

But Dostoevsky has to be careful. He must not derogate the testimony of the experts solely because it is bought or subjective; he must make the case that such testimony is inherently defective because of the venue in which it is given. He does not want inadvertently to cast himself in the role in which, in the Kroneberg case, he cast Spasovich, who discredited testimony by undermining the character of "hostile" witnesses. Dostoevsky partly avoids this pitfall by adding depth to the characterization of one of the expert witnesses: Dr. Herzenstube, who, except for his "expert" testimony in court, is presented as an honest, good-hearted, generous, pious man who is respected and loved by the entire community to which he has selflessly devoted himself for many years. He once took pity on the young Dmitry, buying him a pound of nuts. Dmitry warmly recalls the doctor's kindness many years later. This is the kind of salvific memory that Dostoevsky presents as essential to all moral development and that Alyosha emphasizes in his "sermon" to the boys gathered around Ilyusha's stone in the epilogue. "You must know there is nothing higher, or stronger, or sounder, or more useful afterwards in life, than some good memory, especially a memory from childhood, from the parental home. . . . And even if only one good memory remains with us in our hearts, that alone may serve some day for our salvation" (774; 15:195).

Herzenstube's role as an incompetent expert witness is less important than his role as a victim of the judicial process. This becomes clear if we see him against his prototype, Dr. Hindenburg, in the *Diary of a Writer*. In March 1877 Dostoevsky devoted a chapter of the *Diary of a Writer* to the Jewish question in response to some of his Jewish readers' accusations that he was a Jew-hater. Dostoevsky attempts first to counter the charge and then to offer his own solution to the Jewish problem *(evreiskii vopros)* by portraying a self-sacrificing Protestant German doctor, who was able through his humanitarian works to reconcile— for a few hours—the heterogeneous religious and ethnic population of the Russian borderlands. When he died at eighty-four, he did not leave enough money to pay for his burial expenses.[18] Hindenburg often visited the poor in their hovels, treating them for nothing, giving them money. "On some occasions, he would leave with the poor as much as thirty or forty rubles; he also gave money to the poor peasant women in villages," Dostoevsky writes. He presents Hindenburg as much more than a solution to the Jewish problem; his significance is universal. "And it is not necessary to wait until everybody becomes as good as they or a great many: only very few of such men are needed to save the world—so strong are they. And if that is so, how can one fail to hope?" (659; 25:92). As in the article on Kornilova's acquittal, Dostoevsky ends his piece on the Jewish question on a Russian Orthodox note of reconciliation *(soedinenie)*: all people are united in love as though they were not only of one heart but also of one church: "Fifty-eight years of service to humanity in this town; fifty-eight years of unceasing love, united everybody, at least once, at his coffin in common ecstasy [*vostorg*] and tears" (659; 25:92). The rabbi sheds the same tears (*te zhe slezy*; 659; 25:92) as the Protestant pastor.

Dr. Herzenstube of *The Brothers Karamazov* closely resembles Dr. Hindenburg:

> He was an old man of seventy, gray-haired and balding, of medium height and sturdy build. Everyone in our town valued and respected him very much. He was a conscientious doctor, and excellent and pious man, some sort of Herrnhuter or "Moravian brother"—I am not sure which. *He had been with us for a very long time and behaved with the greatest dignity. He was kind and philanthropic, treated poor patients and peasants for nothing, visiting their hovels and cottages himself, and left them money for medications.* (671;15:103; emphasis added)

Although these German doctors are embedded in very different plots, much of Hindenburg shines through in Herzenstube. Herzenstube is being used less to ridicule expert testimony than to show the deleterious effects of the jury system on its participants. Herzenstube is a conscientious and selfless general practitioner; he is not a psychiatrist. Because he is called by the court to comment on Dmitry's psychological condition, Herzenstube seems to make a fool of himself, interpreting Dmitry's entrance into the courtroom as proof of psychological abnormality. But he does not make a fool of himself at all; the court makes him look like a fool, compelling him to take on a completely inappropriate role. The system—not the narrator—turns the saintly Hindenburg into the comic Herzenstube. Even an expert witness can be turned into a victim. The process consumes its actors.

In Herzenstube, Dostoevsky shows what would happen to the modern saint Hindenburg, were he enmeshed in the judicial process, just as Dostoevsky asked himself a decade earlier what would happen to another beautiful man, Prince Myshkin, were he to return to a Russia engulfed in chaos. Myshkin is frequently perceived as ridiculous, even mistaken for an idiot, precisely what Dostoevsky most feared.[19] But Dostoevsky makes amends with Herzenstube. He calls him back not as an expert but a character witness, a role in which the doctor can redeem himself in the eyes of spectators and readers alike, where instead of delivering an absurd assessment of Dmitry's mental state, he tells of his personal relationship with and compassion for Fedor Karamazov's eldest child.[20] Like the peasant women in the Kroneberg case, the doctor took pity on the babe. Had the doctor not done so many other deeds of love, the pound of nuts he gave Dmitry would certainly have served the same purpose as the onion of the legend: the deed that pulls the sinner from hell. When Dmitry hears Herzenstube tell the story, Dmitry cannot restrain himself, begins to weep, and calls the doctor a man of God (*bozhii ty chelovek*; 374; 15:107). By so doing, Dmitry pays Herzenstube back, restoring the good man that the court took away.


## Witnesses

Of the other witnesses, the most important in light of the post-reform jury trial are those for the defense: Katerina Ivanovna, Ivan Karamazov, and Alyosha Karamazov. Called on by the author to perform a simple function—to reveal the truth that is not believed or the lie that is—they become enmeshed, just as the author is, in a much more complex plot involving empathetic narrative and novel writing. The narrator may be criticized for using the same histrionic techniques with the defense witnesses that both lawyers use with Dmitry Karamazov. Again, Dostoevsky is playing a dangerous narrative game.

In the portrayal of the defense witnesses, Dostoevsky relies on conventional nineteenth-century omniscient narration to create the requisite dramatic irony. The reader has privileged knowledge denied to all the characters: who committed the murder and all the details of what happened on the night of the murder. Only the reader knows that Alyosha's testimony confirms the most contentious piece of evidence in the whole trial: what happened to the three thousand rubles that Dmitry received from Katerina Ivanovna and failed to return to her. It is important for the prosecution that Dmitry spent all the money in his first fling with Grushenka; it is important to the defense that he saved half of it. Alyosha remembers Dmitry's pointing to the money two days before the murder. No one believes Alyosha. Both the novelist and his narrator are implying that had this been a real trial and had they been jurors, they would probably not have believed Alyosha either. As an institution, the jury trial will never be able to distinguish truth from lie—and Dostoevsky sets up the testimony so that indeed the truth is not deemed credible.[21] By measuring the jury trial in terms of ascertainment of truth, Dostoevsky is, of course, imposing on it an impossibly high standard. The jury is supposed to adjudicate between the claims of contesting parties as best it can on the basis of the evidence. It seeks to do justice in the broadest sense, but it rarely attains "truth," even in the face of the queen of proofs, confession. Zasulich confessed that she attempted to kill Trepov, but she still was acquitted. In *Crime and Punishment* a peasant who wants to take suffering upon himself confesses to the murder committed by the hero, Raskolnikov.

The day before the trial Ivan Karamazov learns that Smerdyakov committed the murder. Ivan believes that he is at least as responsible for his father's death as Smerdyakov himself, for Ivan not only wished his father dead but became a tacit collaborator. He confesses in court. But because he is delirious, no one believes that he is telling the truth—and understandably so. No one would trust the ravings of a madman and acquit a defendant against whom there is so much circumstantial evidence. Dostoevsky would have been the first to have written an article attacking the court, had a jury relied on such testimony rather than the preponderance of all the other evidence. The novel revels in the irony that the only ones who possess the truth, the two brothers, are not believed and could never be believed in a court of law. If Father Zosima were judge and jury in an ecclesiastical court, he would immediately have understood that Alyosha and Ivan were telling the truth. Whether he would have released Dmitry and told him "to go home and sin no more" is something for which the novel can give no clear answer, at least not the kind of answers that Dostoevsky himself gave in the *Diary of a Writer* in his article on the Dzhunkovsky case.

Also, significant facts about the testimony of relatives are not evident to contemporary readers but would have been so to readers in Dostoevsky's time. We have seen that Russian law, in an attempt to respect the sacredness of family ties, did not permit close relatives to give testimony under oath. Russian juries generally viewed all testimony not given under oath as unreliable and defective. That is why lawyers spent so much time before the actual trial proceedings on who was or was not going to testify under oath. One could, in effect, discredit a witness's testimony if the judge ruled that the witness could testify but not under oath. Juries would have considered testimony of close relatives against their loved ones as unnatural and testimony in support of their loved ones as not creditable—oaths or no. Dostoevsky's readers and the knowledgeable members of the courtroom audience know beforehand that anything that Alyosha and Ivan say in favor of their brother will not be believed.[22] That is why neither lawyer is particularly concerned about the testimony of Dmitry's brothers. The testimony is not given under oath (it could not be given under oath), and no one would give it much credence. Dostoevsky places his readers in a position that they could never be in the real world, party to the truth and aware beforehand that the truthful testimony given by Dmitry's brothers could never be believed in a court of law. The institution itself becomes a barrier to truth and justice.

Dostoevsky makes the court the site where the truth cannot be known, even when it is publicly revealed. He converts those revelations of truth into the most memorable moments of the trial for his readers, if not for the trial actors and observers. Their testimony not only reveals the limitations of the jury—its inability to perceive and accept the truth—it also marks an important turning point in the spiritual development of the brothers. In recalling the detail about Dmitry's pointing to something near his neck—the unspent money from Dmitry's first escapade with Grushenka—Alyosha becomes convinced of his brother's innocence. Alyosha has had his faith tested once again; he is happy that he may have played a crucial role in saving his brother. Ivan's testimony at the trial constitutes a necessary first step, a public confession of his guilt, essential to his potential recovery.[23] (All the reader knows is that he eventually recovers from this mental breakdown.) What occurs here with regard to truth and justice in Ivan's case happens again, probably against Dostoevsky's intentions, just as it did in the Kornilova case. Ivan's confession is not the same as Kornilova's, but the court again provides the site for the revelation of the truth. For Ivan it is not important that others believe the truth but that he say it before others. Ironically, the court provides a site of truth despite its attempts to deny its admissibility. Even when some good is performed in court, it comes about despite the court, not because of it.

### Dmitry as Post-reform Defendant

But in the context of the jury reforms of 1864, the most surprising and interesting "performance" in the fictional courtroom is that of Dmitry Karamazov himself. At best he is a passive, mostly silent, participant at his own trial. The reader may get the impression that Dmitry is not silent at the trial because of his periodic outbursts, which elicit the stern warnings of the presiding judge. But such outbursts were not exactly what the 1864 law had envisioned in terms of the defendant's right to actively participate in his own defense. The strong participatory role for defendants in Russian criminal trials closely resembled the French system. Because of the strong inquisitorial nature of the pre-trial investigation of the crime by the office of the prosecutor, during which the defense lawyer and defendant had very little access to information, the reform attempted to level the playing field somewhat by giving the defendant the right to confront every one of the witnesses against him, asking questions of them and responding to their testimony. Girish Narayan Bhat explains:

> As stipulated by the 1864 statutes, in the event of a "not guilty" plea by the defendant, the judge was directed to pose the following question to the defendant as every witness was about to leave the stand: "Do

you object to this witness's testimony?" The accused thus possessed an acknowledged and continuous right of rebuttal throughout the proceedings, which gave him or her an active and vocal role in the trial, equal in many respects to that of both the defense and prosecution counsel. Within the system of controversial advocacy by professionally partisan legal representatives, *the reform sought to foster a legally valid though informal "dialogue" between defendant and witnesses.*[24] (emphasis added)

Because most of "A Judicial Mistake" is devoted to the speeches of the attorneys, not much attention is given to jury mechanics. But the narrator on several occasions recalls that the judge asked Dmitry whether he had anything to say concerning the testimony he had just heard, for example, after the testimony of his father's servant Grigory (664–66; 15:96–98), who gives the most damaging testimony in the trial (about the open door); after the testimony of Rakitin (666–68; 15:99–101); and after Alyosha's testimony regarding Dmitry's pouch with the money (675–79; 15:107–10). We can thus presume that after the testimony of each witness the judge asked Dmitry whether he wanted to question the witness and challenge any testimony.

But practically speaking, as Bhat observes, the rights given to the defendant in court did not always help the defendant, even when he or she made use of them. In the American system defense lawyers often do not want their clients to speak, fearing that they will do irreparable harm to the case. The lawyers will put their clients on the stand only if they think that they are articulate and believable and will not be taken advantage of in cross-examination by the prosecuting attorney. Edgar Smith, who became a jailhouse lawyer and used his retrial to gain his release, would probably have taken good advantage of his rights as a defendant in the Russian system, in contrast to the untrained Jack Abbott, who insisted on being his own lawyer at his second trial and did much more harm than good.

The post-reform jury trial procedures that were supposed to help defendants actually work against Dmitry from the very beginning. The problem is Dmitry's Russian exuberance and honesty. The novel presents the court as a deracinated un-Russian institution that cannot abide Dmitry's quintessential earthy Russian character, which is too broad. (Even Dmitry thinks the Russian character may be too broad.) Whenever it rises up, it is immediately suppressed by the judge, who

warns Dmitry that he is ruining his case. Because Dostoevsky continually builds up reader sympathy for Dmitry—and the reader knows
the facts—Dmitry's outbursts appear to be the truth and the judge's
warnings seem to be attempts to suppress it. Again, poetics trumps
reason. Here, for example, is the exchange between the stolid Grigory,
the exuberant Dmitry, and the stern presiding judge:

> The judge, addressing the defendant, asked whether he had anything to
> say concerning the present testimony.
> "Except for the door, it's all true as he said," Mitya cried *loudly*. "For
> combing the lice out of my hair, I thank him; for forgiving me my blows,
> I thank him; the old man has been honest all his life, and was as faith-
> ful to my father as seven hundred poodles."
> "Watch your words, defendant," the judge said *sternly*.
> "I am not a poodle," Grigory also grumbled.
> "Then I am a poodle!" *cried* Mitya. "If he's offended, I take it upon
> myself and ask his forgiveness: I was a beast and cruel to him! I was cruel
> to Aesop, too."
> "What Aesop?" the judge again picked up *sternly*.
> "That Pierrot . . . my father, Fyodor Pavlovich."
> The presiding judge repeated once again to Mitya, imposingly and
> *most sternly* now, that he should watch his words more carefully.
> "You are harming yourself in the opinion of the judges." (666;
> 15:98–99; emphasis added)

After the testimony of Grigory, the first witness, the narrator does not
refer again to these cross-purpose exchanges between Dmitry and the
judge. We know that Dmitry reacts emotionally to much of the testimony and cries out on other occasions (twice during the testimony of
Dr. Herzenstube alone, for example) as he did after Grigory's testimony—to his legal detriment. This pattern was set in the preliminary
investigation, where at first Dmitry was forthcoming and then became
silent when he believed that the information he volunteered was being
used against him. There is no question that Fetyukovich, Dmitry's lawyer, would prefer that his client be silent, and he even views Dmitry's
outbursts as detrimental not only to Dmitry's case but to the more important case, Fetyukovich's. The lawyer, of course, is using his client to
advance his personal and political agenda. Dmitry's word, the Russian
word, is effectively silenced. As long as his word is not in conformity with

Western legal procedures, it is out of order. Once the cross-examination of the witnesses is concluded, Dmitry is thus represented solely by Fetyukovich's word. Dmitry controls himself during the speeches of both the prosecutor and the defense attorneys. By the time he is given the opportunity to speak again, four hours have gone by, and he is no less tired than the judge. Dispirited and defeated, he speaks for only a minute.

> *Then the defendant himself was given the opportunity to speak, but said little.* He was terribly tired in body and spirit. The look of strength and independence with which he appeared in court that morning had all but vanished. He seemed to have experienced something that day for the rest of his life, which had taught and brought home to him something very important, something that he had not understood before. His voice had grown weaker, *he no longer shouted as earlier.* Something new, resigned, defeated, and downcast could be heard in his words. (750; 15:175; emphasis added)

What happened to Dmitry at the trial is the complete opposite of what happened to Kornilova. Her voice was heard, and because it was heard, she was acquitted. The Russian communal word managed for a moment to emerge victorious over the adversarial word of the Western court. Dmitry is not Kornilova. Dostoevsky makes sure that the conclusion of the trial in *The Brothers Karamazov* will be the obverse of the Kornilova case. What the court did in Kornilova was to make a place for the Russian word. It suppressed that word in Dmitry's trial, although the statute itself had been devised to give the word to the defendant. The road to hell is paved with good intentions.

## Spectators

In a novel devoted to exploring the truth of the inner life, often revealed in dreams, hallucinations, and mystical experience, the opinions and impressions of spectators, who are easily swayed by interested testimony and the rhetorical powers of lawyers, can carry little sway. Dostoevsky would not even bother with the courtroom spectators if they did not represent a microcosm of the Russian public, on whom the jury trial was having a deleterious influence. Dostoevsky often expressed dissatisfaction with Russian courtroom spectators, especially when they applauded acquittals of clearly guilty defendants. In the Kornilova trial Dostoevsky found or imagined something rare: an ideal audience, that is, one that enthusiastically supported an acquittal for the right reasons. At the same time he understood that exploiting audience approbation for one's cause gives one's position a shaky foundation. The audience was much more likely to applaud a decision of which Dostoevsky disapproved than one he supported (the Kornilova case). *The Brothers Karamazov* represents a complete reversal of the Kornilova case vis-à-vis the treatment of the audience; it is one of most negative portrayals of a courtroom audience in imaginative literature.

The absurd division of opinion among the expert witnesses is multiplied in the opinions of the spectators. Whereas Dostoevsky undermines the testimony of the experts by reducing it to different explanations of why Dmitry looked straight ahead when he first walked into the courtroom, the author makes the spectators' opinions ridiculous by likening them to the differences between the male and female parties regarding the identity of Chichikov, the hero of Gogol's *Dead Souls*. The value of spectator opinion is further degraded by its complete indifference to Dmitry's crime. The men and women alike think that Dmitry committed the crime. But the women want him to be acquitted, not despite his guilt but because of it: guilt makes an acquittal so much more romantic and theatrical.

> I even think that the ladies, one and all, who yearned with such impatience for the acquittal of an interesting defendant, were at the same time fully convinced of his complete guilt. Moreover, I believe that they would have been upset if his guilt were not unquestionable, for in that case there would be no great effect at the denouement [*razviazka*] when the criminal was acquitted. And that he would be acquitted, all the ladies, strangely enough, remained utterly convinced almost to the very last moment. (663; 15:123)

Each lawyer accuses the other of concocting a psychological novel about the defendant, but the female part of the audience creates its own sentimental drama even before the trial begins. The women want Dmitry acquitted because he killed for love.

> Almost all the ladies, at least the majority of them, favored Mitya [*stoiali za Mitiu*]²⁵ and his acquittal. Mainly, perhaps, because an idea had been

formed of him as a conqueror of women's hearts. It was known that two women rivals were to appear. One of them—that is, Katerina Ivanovna —especially interested everyone; a great many remarkable things were told about her, astonishing tales were told of her passion for Mitya despite his crime. Special mention was made of her pride (she paid visits to almost no one in our town), her "aristocratic connections." It was said that she intended to ask the government for permission to accompany the criminal into penal servitude and to marry him somewhere in the mines, underground. (657; 15:90)

The scenario that envisions Katerina Ivanovna accompanying Dmitry to the mines in Siberia replicates the most romantic model of self-sacrifice in Russian culture: that of the wives of the Decembrists, who accompanied their husbands to prison in Siberia. Many Decembrists received long sentences of hard labor in Siberian mines for their participation in a failed attempt in 1825 to overthrow the Russian government.[26]

Katerina Ivanovna's double confession at the trial goes beyond even the ladies' expectations. "Yes, I suppose our lady spectators [*damy zritel'nitsy*] were left satisfied: the spectacle [*zrelishche*] had been a rich one" (693; 15:122). When the jury returns with a guilty verdict, the women are stunned. "But, my God, what came over our ladies! I thought they might start a riot [*bunt*]!" (753; 15:178).[27] The jury of peasants destroys the romantic denouement.

For obvious reasons the men want the parricide convicted: the narrator cites personal animosity (Dmitry was, after all, a bully) but also jealousy, vanity, and contrariness as the most important reasons for their desire for a conviction. "Many ladies quarreled with their husbands owing to a difference of opinion about this whole terrible affair, and naturally, after that, all the husbands of these ladies arrived in court feeling not only ill disposed toward the defendant but even resentful of him. . . . It was also true that Mitya had managed to insult many of them personally during his stay in town" (657; 15:90–91). Not surprisingly, then, when the verdict comes in, "many among the male public turned out to be very pleased. Some even rubbed their hands with unconcealed joy" (735; 15:178). For both the men and women Dmitry becomes a convenient locus of psychological projection. On the other hand, they seem completely indifferent to the issues of justice and truth. The men are happy not because Dmitry has been convicted but because their wives have been disappointed. The most significant consequence for the town—from the point of view of the spectators—will be that for a few days the women, including the wife of the prosecutor, will refuse to speak to their husbands. Dmitry's twenty-year sentence pales by comparison. So much for the opinions of the spectators.

*The Brothers Karamazov* is one of the earliest presentations of the jury trial as theater or circus, where the trial exists more for the spectators than for the direct participants—the state and the accused. The atmosphere during the trial in *The Brothers Karamazov* bears an uncanny resemblance to many famous, media-exploited American trials of the late twentieth century, including those of Edgar Smith, Jack Abbott, and O. J. Simpson. The trial in *The Brothers Karamazov* seems quite long, but it occupies only one day, albeit a very extended one: from ten in the morning to one-thirty in the morning of the next calendar day. But Dostoevsky presents the national press's long obsession with the case, since Dmitry's indictment several months earlier. Predictably, the press sensationally distorts the facts of the case, either to pander to its readership or to promote the political agenda of the publishers.[28]

In his comments on the Hartung case, Dostoevsky emphasized the danger of turning trials into mass entertainments, in which the public, having come mainly to watch the duel between attorneys, cares little about the issues of truth and justice:

> The public attending the trial, perhaps, will actually gather for the purpose of witnessing a show [*zrelishche*], for the contemplation of a mechanical and very shrewd device, and, listening with delight to, say, how ably the talented defense counsel lies against his conscience, they are ready to applaud him from their seats: "Why, how well the fellow lies!" But in the bulk of the public this generates cynicism and falsity which take root imperceptibly. Not truth is craved for but talent; let it only make people merry, let it amuse them! (869; 26:53–54)

And, in fact, this is exactly what happens at Dmitry's trial. The spectators have come not because of the terrible issues that will be weighed by the court or because of their interest in the defendant but because they, especially the men, wish to observe the gladiator-attorneys do battle. Not for nothing are tickets hard to come by. The spectators get what they came for. Fetyukovich brings the house down, even though he argues against the very conviction that the majority of the male spectators actually desire.

Here the orator [Fetyukovich] was interrupted by unrestrained, almost frenzied applause. Of course, the whole room did not applaud, but still about half the room applauded. Fathers and mothers applauded. From above, where the ladies were sitting, shrieks and cries could be heard. Handkerchiefs were waved. . . . Even the dignitaries, the old men with stars on their frock coats, who were sitting on special chairs behind the judges, were applauding and waving handkerchiefs to the orator. (746; 15:171)[29]

## Spectator-Lawyers and Readers

The narrator also pays particular attention to a special group of spectators: lawyers. The Karamazov case has gained such national prominence that prominent lawyers from all over the empire converge on the small town of Skotoprigonevsk to observe the trial. It was evidently insufficient for Dostoevsky to pillory the prosecution and defense lawyers—he had to go after as much of the legal profession as he could encompass.

The lawyers alone, who arrived from all over, turned out to be so numerous that no one knew where to put them, since the tickets had all been given out, begged, besought long ago. I myself saw a partition being temporarily and hastily set up at the end of the courtroom, behind the podium, where all these arriving lawyers were admitted, and they even considered themselves lucky to be able to stand there, because in order to make room, the chairs were removed from behind the partition, and the whole accumulated crowd stood through the whole "case" in a closely packed lump, shoulder to shoulder. (657; 15:90)

Because the lawyers are there as spectators and not as champions of their clients, Dostoevsky is able to reveal their real opinions about the trial. Just like the judge, they are indifferent to Dmitry and interested in the abstract legal issues of the case. Dmitry becomes a particular instance of a much more significant abstract legal question. They "cared not about the moral aspect of the case, but only, so to speak, about its contemporary legal aspect" (658; 15:91). No doubt, they are even more interested than the other spectators in the performance of the attorneys, especially the illustrious Fetyukovich, the king of the Russian bar (*korol' advokatury*).[30]

But if the trial is to have national—even universal—significance,

Dostoevsky must expand the audience. It is not only the lawyers who have come from all over Russia to observe the trial; everyone is following the trial, as though the fate of Russian society was to be decided by the verdict. Dostoevsky presents the Karamazov case as the trial of the century. "Everyone also knew that the case had been publicized all over Russia [*poluchilo vserossiiskuiu oglasku*] but even so they never imagined that it had shaken all and sundry to such a burning, such an intense degree, not only among us but everywhere, as became clear at the trial that day" (656; 15:89). For one day the little town becomes the center of attention of all Russia. Were the decision confined only to the courtroom, it could obviously do a limited amount of damage. But Dmitry's trial is being played both outside and inside the court. Knowing this, the lawyers address their speeches more to the larger public outside the courtroom than to the jury itself. Again, Dmitry gets lost as the court becomes a forum for other agendas.

Dostoevsky plays a double game here. When upset by the acquittal of the defendant in the Kroneberg case and the conviction of the defendant in the Kornilova case, he used the *Diary of a Writer* to reach and influence thousands of his readers. He could argue that he was not fanning the flames but only reacting to the abuses of the court in the Kroneberg case and responding to the accusations lodged against him in the Kornilova case. But now the Russian public, it seemed to him, was being more badly educated by the representations of trials in the Russian radical press than by the jury trials themselves. This is why the radical reporter Rakitin is presented so negatively in *The Brothers Karamazov*; he is not only an enemy of the Karamazov brothers and Grushenka, he is poisoning the body politic with his distorted reports of the trial and its significance for Russian society. Dmitry not only gets lost in the trial, his trial becomes a prime means for miseducating the public, irrespective of conviction or acquittal. Dostoevsky saw the Zasulich trial as unwinnable: once the main arena of the trial was transferred from the courtroom to the newspapers and journals, Zasulich's conviction or acquittal worked equally to the advantage of the radical intelligentsia.

## The Narrator

Dostoevsky also plays a double game with his narrator. He uses the narrator to subject the female and male parties—the lawyers, the judge, the expert witnesses, and the important visitors—to a blistering satire, but at the same time he presents the narrator in some ways as no less a prisoner of the judicial process than the other participants and spectators. The narrator is present as an observer at the trial, almost in the same capacity as a reporter—as was Dostoevsky at the Zasulich trial. Furthermore, the narrator's impressions of the trial in many respects do not differ significantly from the other spectators'. How, then, is his role different from that of other spectators and reporters? Here a few words need to be said about narration and narrators in the novel.

In *The Brothers Karamazov,* as in *The Possessed,* Dostoevsky uses two narrators.[31] The first is a mostly impersonal, omniscient narrator who recounts private conversations between the major characters as well as private thoughts, hallucinations, and nightmares. For example, he transcribes the three conversations between Smerdyakov and Ivan Karamazov. He also records Ivan Karamazov's hallucinations, Dmitry's dream of the starving babes, and Alyosha's mystical experience at the side of Father Zosima's decaying body.

The other narrator is an observer-chronicler situated in the world of the novel itself. Dostoevsky complicates the presentation of this narrator by including a double time perspective in the narrative voice, or persona. First there is the narrator's younger self, the narrator of 1866, who witnessed the actual trial and whom Dostoevsky uses to give the reader a sense of the immediacy and confusion surrounding the events. Then there is the older, presumably wiser, recollecting narrator, who has had thirteen years to check the facts and comment on his former confusion and misunderstandings. The older narrator thus recounts both how he perceived the events thirteen years earlier and how he interprets them now.[32] Degrees of conflation of the omniscient author and observer-chronicler exist as well. The most common is for the omniscient author to interject authoritatively to correct misinformation, primarily about the personal integrity of Alyosha and Father Zosima.

Although Dostoevsky did not work out a plan for the narration, we can retrospectively make out a general outline. In the beginning of the novel the observer-chronicler dominates. He is a highly opinionated narrator who openly reveals his love for his hero, Alyosha, and continually shows his contempt and disgust for Fedor Karamazov. This narrator in some ways resembles the narrator that Dostoevsky uses for large parts of *The Idiot,* where the narrator, with little privileged knowledge, reports all the scandals and rumors involving Myshkin,

Rogozhin, and Nastasya Filippovna. It is not surprising that Dostoevsky exploits this narrative method because he devotes the first two
books of *The Brothers Karamazov* to the scandal in the hermitage. After
book 2 the more objective, unobtrusive, omniscient narrator takes over
the novel until the trial scene, where a narrator similar to but not identical to the personalized narrator of the first two books dominates. The
omniscient narrator takes over once again in the epilogue.

At the trial the personalized observer-chronicler calls attention not
only to his presence at the events but also his confusion about what
actually happened:

> I will say beforehand, and say emphatically, that I am far from consid-
> ering myself capable of recounting all that took place in court, not only
> with the proper fullness, but even in the proper order. I keep thinking that
> if one were to recall everything and explain everything as one ought, it
> would fill a whole book, even quite a large one. Therefore, let no one
> grumble if I tell only that which struck me personally and which I have
> especially remembered. I may have taken secondary things for the most
> important, and even overlooked the most prominent and necessary fea-
> tures. . . . But anyway I see that it is better not to apologize, I shall do what
> I can, and my readers will see for themselves that I have done all I could.
>
> And first of all, before we enter the courtroom, I will mention some-
> thing that especially surprised me on that day. By the way, as it turned
> out later, it surprised not only me but everyone else as well. (656; 15:89)

The narrator, in other words, confesses to giving a highly subjective,
personal, and selective account of the trial, marred, in addition, both
by a less than perfect memory and a tendency to take what was secondary for what was most important. That he frequently was surprised
at what occurred must astonish the reader less than the narrator's
acknowledgment that he reacted much like all the other spectators at
the trial. No matter how sardonically the reminiscing narrator treats
the other spectators, he presents himself as having reacted no differently than the general public.

His rendition of Katerina Ivanovna's testimony in particular shows him
caught up in the same melodrama as the spectators in the courtroom:

> She magnanimously concealed it, and was not ashamed to present it as if
> she, she herself, had gone running to a young officer, on her own impulse,

hoping for something . . . to beg for money. *This was something tremendous! I had chills and trembled as I listened; the courtroom was dead silent, grasping at every word.* . . . And indeed the image of an officer giving away his last five thousand rubles—all he had left in the world—and respectfully bowing to the innocent girl, made a rather sympathetic and attractive picture . . . *how my heart ached!* (680–81; 15:112; emphasis added)

Dostoevsky is not attempting to compromise the impressions of his younger narrator; rather, he is underscoring that no trial observer can possibly obtain accurate information about the objective facts—what actually did happen—not to speak of what is in the heart and mind of the defendant. The narrator presents himself as though he is attending a drama that has captured the emotions of the entire audience. The public comes to erroneous conclusions about so many things, not only because of its own interests and predispositions but because the jury trial by its very nature cannot yield factual or moral knowledge. The formal, rational, legal procedures of the trial on one hand, and its histrionics on the other hand, compromise the evidence and the testimony from the start. Dostoevsky uses his narrator to show that even the most astute observer will become a prisoner of the procedure and rhetoric of the trial. Only after the passage of thirteen years does the narrator gain enough distance and perspective to reach a better, if still incomplete, understanding of what happened. But what is most astonishing about this passage is that it *erases,* not underscores, the distance between the experiencing and recounting narrators. As the narrator recalls how he was overwhelmed by the evidence and character of Katerina Ivanovna, he seems to be overtaken by the same emotions he felt then. His heart seems to ache as much in recalling the events as when he first observed them thirteen years earlier. The narrator will always be held captive by the trial, no matter how many years pass.

The problematic situation in which the narrator finds himself at the trial, as well as years after the trial, dramatizes Dostoevsky's reservations about the power that the jury trial wields over all those who become emotionally and intellectually involved with it. Just being present at the trial unsettles one's emotional and moral bearings. Here the narrative closely replicates Dostoevsky's personal experiences at trials. It is one thing to pontificate against the jury trial when one is not present at the trial itself and when one only reads about it from newspaper summaries; it is a very different thing to be personally present.

Dostoevsky himself was a spectator at the Zasulich trial. He knew that he was going to be dissatisfied with the decision, however it came out. But he also got caught up in the drama and emotion of the trial. He could not see how this young woman could be convicted, given all the emotional testimony, especially the testimony about corporal punishment, which Dostoevsky himself discussed at length in his article on the Kroneberg trial. Dostoevsky is not necessarily underscoring the narrator's limitations in the last book of *The Brothers Karamazov*. The narrator does his best. His position is completely comprehensible. When one is present at a trial, one can no longer really vouch for oneself, for one gets caught up emotionally and imaginatively in the psychological and moral drama of the proceedings. Anyone in the narrator's situation, even Dostoevsky himself, had he been there, would have been affected in a similar way.

### The Principal Attorneys: The Prosecutor

But it is the lawyers who dominate the last book of *The Brothers Karamazov*: Dostoevsky devotes eight of the book's fourteen chapters (chapters 6–13) just to their summations, of which the narrator says that he has transcribed only the major parts. Much of the preceding chapters (2–5) covers the lawyers' cross-examination of witnesses. The speech of the less prominent lawyer, the prosecutor, Ippolit Kirillovich, is longer than "The Grand Inquisitor."

We are introduced to Ippolit Kirillovich during the preliminary investigation (*predvaritel'noe sledstvie*) of Fedor Karamazov's murder. The background of secondary characters is usually related quite subjectively in *The Brothers Karamazov*, so it is difficult to establish the facts of the prosecutor's biography or career. We know that he is thirty-five and ailing. Passed over long ago, he nurtures a great deal of resentment. He had been known in Petersburg, but obviously not respected, for his passion for psychology and his oratorical delivery. The highest position he could attain was assistant prosecutor (*tovarishch prokurora*; 458; 14:413) in the small provincial town of Skotoprigonevsk (Cattle Pen). Ippolit Kirillovich looks upon the Karamazov case as his last chance to prove himself and to show up his detractors, including his old enemy Fetyukovich. Ippolit Kirillovich knows that he is in poor health and thinks that he may not have long to live. He actually dies nine months after the trial. But the narrator hears people saying that Ippolit Kirillovich "had been resurrected [*voskres*] in spirit by the Karamazov case and even dreamed of resurrecting [*voskresit'*] his flagging career through it" (658; 15:91). Obviously, both cannot be true. The narrator tries to defend Ippolit Kirillovich against some of the accusations of his detractors, implying that he is going to be a much more formidable opponent than others assume.

The prosecutor's speech combines the demon of psychology, which was only briefly addressed in Raskolnikov's trial in *Crime and Punishment*, with the demon of legal performance. To win Ippolit Kirillovich knows that he must be a better psychological novelist than Fetyukovich, but Ippolit Kirillovich almost must be a better performer, orator, and actor too. Now Ippolit Kirillovich's whole life, not to mention Dmitry's, hangs on his performance at the trial, that is, on his talent. "He considered his speech his chef d'oeuvre, the chef d'oeuvre of his whole life, his swan song" (693; 15:123). Ippolit Kirillovich puts everything he has into this speech; when it is over, he almost passes out. Dostoevsky elevates the importance of rhetoric in Ippolit Kirillovich's speech, persuasion for its own sake, far above Spasovich's speech in the Kroneberg case. Spasovich used all his strategies to convince the jurors that they were compelled by law to find his client not guilty. Ippolit Kirillovich directs his performance not at the ignorant jurors, who cannot understand psychology or appreciate a masterful novel, but at the public in and outside the courtroom, especially the lawyers who have ridiculed him and hindered his career. Ippolit Kirillovich must now persuade all Russia that his prodigious talents have been wasted in a provincial backwater, to the terrible detriment of the fatherland. He is not interested in winning on a technicality. His victory outside the court must be as magnificent as inside.

At times it seems that Ippolit Kirillovich is trying the case with the Zasulich trial in the back of his mind. The Karamazov trial takes place in 1866, but Dostoevsky is really backdating a contemporary trial that is directly responding to contemporary issues and legal precedents. It becomes completely understandable from the Russian context why Ippolit Kirillovich suspects that he cannot win on the facts alone, no matter how overwhelmingly in his favor the facts might be.[33] Zasulich confessed to shooting the governor of Petersburg and was still acquitted. Jury nullification was always possible in Russian criminal cases, as it was in the Simpson case in the United States, where the jury's focus

shifted from the defendant to the character and actions of the prosecution. In the Zasulich case the prosecutor Kissel did a competent job.
He methodically laid out the incriminating evidence. But the jury
turned out not to be a fact-finding jury; it paid greater heed to the
rhetoric of the defense attorney than to factual evidence from the prosecutor. Ippolit Kirillovich knows that the facts alone will not win the
case for him; he must outdo Fetyukovich at his own game.[34] He also
knows that the facts will not win the case for him outside the court,
his real audience. Ippolit Kirillovich's summation may resemble a theatrical performance, but it is a practical strategy designed to win the
case in the legal environment of the late 1870s.

But Ippolit Kirillovich also knows that psychology, rhetoric, and
mastery of the facts alone will not assure him of victory; his summation must have an ideological component: he must directly address the
burning moral, social, and political questions of the day. So Ippolit
Kirillovich begins immediately with Russia's moral and spiritual ills,
the responsibilities of Russian citizens, and the future direction of the
country. He maintains that the Karamazov case is not an isolated one,
arguing that it is much more important for what the defendant symbolizes than for any determination of guilt or innocence:

> "Gentlemen of the jury," the prosecutor began, "the present case has
> resounded throughout Russia. . . . But what is most important is that a
> great number of our Russian, our national, criminal cases bear witness
> to something universal, to some general malaise that has taken root
> among us, and with which, as with universal evil, it is very difficult to
> contend. . . . Yes, perhaps some day the foremost minds both here and
> in Europe will consider the psychology of Russian crime, for the subject
> is worthy of it. But this study will be taken up later on, at leisure, and
> when the whole tragic topsy-turveydom of our present moment has
> moved more to the background." (693–94; 15:123–24)

And, predictably, Ippolit Kirillovich concludes by emphasizing the
national significance of the jury's decision:

> Remember still that at this moment you are in the sanctuary of our jus-
> tice. Remember that you are the defenders of our truth, the defenders
> of our holy Russia, of her foundations, of her family, and all that is holy
> in her! Yes, here, at this moment, you represent Russia, and your verdict

will resound not only in this courtroom but for all of Russia, and all of Russia will listen to you as to her defenders and judges, and will be either heartened or discouraged by your verdict. (722; 15:150)

To put this kind of rhetoric in its proper context, it is important to understand the significance of attorney summations in the post-reform Russian criminal courts. Because the post-reform system gave a decided advantage to the prosecutor's office, especially in the preliminary investigation (Dmitry has no lawyer during the investigation and does not have one until Fetyukovich arrives several months later[35]), a tremendous burden was placed on the defense attorney, especially on his summation. If the defense attorney was to counteract the advantages of the prosecution, he had to make an especially effective speech and to use every tactic and strategy at his disposal.

As was the case in France, the basic structure of adjudication in Russia meant that these speeches inevitably possessed inordinate importance in establishing the basis for the jury's deliberations and verdict. The looseness and relative informality of the "mixed" criminal procedure . . . the jury's novelty and complexity . . . and the unprecedented spectacle of adversarial justice all served to place an especially heavy burden on the rhetorical skills of the procurator and the defense attorney. Furthermore, because the reform statutes and subsequent accepted practice imposed significant limits on the defense counsel's involvement in and access to the pre-trial investigation, the opportunity to summarize the case in the trial's final, openly partisan speech often became the crucial moment for the accused.[36]

Dostoevsky's almost exclusive focus on the summations may seem excessive, even strange, to a contemporary reader. In most twentieth-century courtroom dramas and trial novels, witness testimony and cross-examination are the main foci. Juries often make up their mind before the summations. But in the Russian courts the summation could be everything. Aside from the scandal, most of the audience in *The Brothers Karamazov* has come for the summations, on which they feel Dmitry's fate depends. Russian attorneys, who had great leeway in their summations, often used them to expatiate on character, morality, environment, and the universal significance of the jury's verdict. Because the jury was, in theory, supposed to vote its conscience, it was only natural that the lawyers would not stay with the facts or even with the law but do whatever was empathetically necessary to engage and win over the jurors. The speeches by both Ippolit Kirillovich and Fetyukovich resemble the summation of Johnnie Cochran in defense of O. J. Simpson: Cochran openly argued that it was more important to send a message to the nation than to convict his client. Ippolit Kirillovich asks that the jury convict the defendant in order to send a message not only to Russia but to all Europe.

Dostoevsky spends so much time on the summations and less on testimony because, among other things, he is attempting to re-create the general emphases of the Russian criminal trial. Besides, the reader already has privileged knowledge of the facts, and the attorneys will go over the testimony in detail again in their summations. The prosecutor's summation is so long because Ippolit Kirillovich knows the skill and experience of his opponent in similar cases—"and this was not the first time he [Fetyukovich] had come to the provinces to defend a celebrated criminal case" (658; 15:91)—therefore, he knows that he must make the summation of his life. He must create a brilliant narrative—anything less will result in ignominious defeat and an end to his rekindled hopes for career and fame.

But Dostoevsky hardly treats Ippolit Kirillovich's concluding speech as a swan song. Though the prosecutor's speech is at times psychologically insightful and rhetorically effective, Dostoevsky inserts dozens of traps, in which Ippolit Kirillovich consistently gets caught. The most treacherous is Ippolit Kirillovich's chapter-long proof of the incontrovertible innocence of the real murderer, Smerdyakov, whose crime the prosecutor correctly reconstructs, only to dismiss his own reconstruction as absolutely preposterous, concluding: "No, gentlemen, fantasy, too, must have its limits [*est' predel i fantaziiam*]" (711; 15:140). Psychology thus misleads the prosecutor into thinking that Dmitry is the killer; fantasy, which he completely rejects, uncovers the actual perpetrator, Smerdyakov. Or, again, regarding the amulet[37]—where in fact Dmitry kept the fifteen hundred rubles—Ippolit Kirillovich triumphantly concludes: "But as for the legend of the amulet—it is hard even to imagine anything more contrary to reality. One can suppose anything but that" (701; 15:131). So much for psychology.

Many of Ippolit Kirillovich's judgments and conclusions are wrongheaded and some even ridiculous. For example, he praises the flighty Madame Khokhlakova's compassion for Dmitry and her "reasonable advice" that Dmitry go and make his fortune in the gold mines in Siberia; Ippolit Kirillovich characterizes Smerdyakov as a highly honest young man by nature; the prosecutor views Fedor Karamazov as an innocent babe in comparison to most Russian sensualists; and Ippolit Kirillovich repeatedly characterizes what we know as the truth as absolutely unimaginable. He presents Dmitry as a man always capable at one and the same time of "devilish calculation" and unbelievable heedlessness but glosses over both the calculation and the rashness whenever it suits him. How can Dmitry, who carelessly throws the envelope containing the supposed stolen money on the floor next to the dead body, cunningly hide fifteen hundred rubles, which no one can find after two months of almost continuous searching?

The most damning aspect of Dostoevsky's presentation of the prosecutor's arguments is that the writer presents them as perfectly reasonable interpretations from imperfect knowledge. After all, on several occasions, in the presence of numerous witnesses, Dmitry threatened his father, and Dmitry once beat his father within an inch of his life in the presence of his other sons. Dmitry and Smerdyakov are the only possible suspects, and Smerdyakov did in fact suffer a real epileptic attack on the night of the murder. And then there is all that blood on Dmitry—without the possibility of refuting this evidence through DNA analysis.[38] Given the preponderance of circumstantial evidence against Dmitry, Ippolit Kirillovich argues a strong case. And that is precisely the problem.[39]

But there are still more important reservations that Dostoevsky has about the prosecutor, in particular, Ippolit Kirillovich's political, social, and religious ideas, which form the better part of his summation. For example, the prosecutor reproves Alyosha for holding Russian religious, populist views, in other words, beliefs similar to Dostoevsky's own. Ippolit Kirillovich interprets Alyosha's desire to become a monk as a childish gesture born of fear, and he hopes that the young man will not be led astray by the twin devils of mysticism and chauvinism. After books 6 ("The Russian Monk") and 7 ("Alyosha"), Ippolit Kirillovich's dismissal of Alyosha Karamazov's mystical and spiritual experiences subverts not only what he says about Alyosha but also what he says about Dmitry.

> He clung to the monastery you see, you see; he all but became a monk himself. In him, it seems to me, unconsciously, as it were, and so early

on, there betrayed itself that timid despair that leads so many in our poor society, fearing its cynicism and depravity, and mistakenly ascribing all evil to European enlightenment, to throw themselves, as they put it, to the "native soil," so to speak, into the motherly embrace of the native earth like children frightened by ghosts, who even at the dried-up breast of a paralyzed mother wish only to fall peacefully asleep and even to sleep for the rest of their lives, simply not to see the horrors that frighten them. For my part, I wish the good and gifted young man all the best. I hope that his youthful brightheartedness and yearning for popular foundation will not turn later, as so often happens, into dark mysticism on the moral side, and witless chauvinism on the civic side—two qualities that perhaps threaten more evil for the nation than the premature corruption owing to a falsely understood and gratuitously acquired enlightenment from which his elder brother suffers. (697; 15:127)

Ippolit Kirillovich defends enlightenment, castigating those who mistakenly ascribe to it all the evils of Russian life. Those who wish to establish the basis of Russian life on the common people and their ties to the soil are escapists, ignorant that the breasts of Mother Russia have already dried up. Thus Ippolit Kirillovich ridicules the image of the Russian women with dried-out breasts, the inspiration for Dmitry Karamazov's dream through which he attains an existential understanding of the underlying moral ideal of the novel: mutual responsibility. By having Ippolit Kirillovich warn Alyosha that he faces the terrible prospect of "dark mysticism," Dostoevsky sets his views against those of the "Cana of Galilee" chapter, in which Alyosha's "dark" mysticism culminates in an epiphany that stands as counterpoint to the rationalism and individualism of "The Grand Inquisitor." Ippolit Kirillovich's remarks about mysticism and chauvinism prompt two or three claps of approbation from the crowd, always a sign in Dostoevsky—excepting, of course, the Kornilova trial—of a cheap appeal to the latest fashionable liberal ideas.

Ippolit Kirillovich further compounds his problems—with the implied reader, if not with the spectators—by embedding his political and social views in imaginative flights of fancy. He appropriates the image of the Russian troika from Gogol's *Dead Souls* to conquer his opponent, but rather than getting out of the way of the Russian troika, which he advises others to do, he turns himself, as it were, into its first victim, by misusing the image of the troika to advance his liberal ideas regarding Russian's mission.

> A great writer of the previous epoch, in the finale of the greatest of his works, personifying all of Russia as a bold Russian troika galloping toward an unknown goal, exclaims: "Ah, troika, bird-troika, who invented you!"—and in proud rapture adds that all nations respectfully stand aside for this troika galloping by at breakneck speed. Let it be so, gentlemen, let them stand aside, respectfully or not, but in my sinful judgment the artistic genius ended like that either in a fit of innocent infantile sunnymindedness, or simply from fear of contemporary censorship. For if this troika were to be drawn by none but his own heroes . . . then no matter who is sitting in the coachman's box, it would be impossible to arrive at anything sensible with such horses! And those were still former horses, a far cry from our own, ours are no comparison. (694; 15:125)

What exactly the prosecutor's allusions to Gogol have to do with the Karamazov case is unclear. After calling Gogol an artistic genius and *Dead Souls* the greatest of his works, Ippolit Kirillovich criticizes the ending with its rushing troika as infantilely innocent and optimistic. He implies that the Europeans might indeed, especially now, want to get out the way of the Russian troika. It was bad enough when the Sobakeviches, Nozdrevs, and Chichikovs were driving the troika, but can Russia afford to have the Dmitry Karamazovs in control? Convicting Dmitry will send a message to Europe that Russia is ready to rein in the Russian troika and take its place among the civilized nations of Europe. Dmitry must be found guilty for Russia's salvation.[40] Ippolit Kirillovich tries to improve upon Gogol, by concluding his own masterpiece with a revised and corrected version of Gogol's finale. Dostoevsky entitles the concluding remarks of the prosecutor's summation "The Galloping Troika." It is not so much the Sobakeviches, or even the Dmitry Karamazovs, who are driving out of control but Ippolit Kirillovich. Ippolit Kirillovich concludes by denouncing Russia.

> Then do not torment Russia and her expectations, our fateful troika is racing headlong, perhaps to its ruin. And all over Russia hands have long been held out and voices have been calling to halt its wild, impudent

course. And if so far the other nations still stand aside from the troika galloping at breakneck speed, it is not at all, perhaps out of respect, as the poet would have it, but simply from horror—mark that—from horror, and perhaps from loathing for her. And still it is good they stand aside, but what if they should suddenly stop standing aside, and form into a solid wall before the spreading apparition, and themselves halt the mad course of our unbridledness, with a view to saving themselves, enlightenment, and civilization! We have heard already such anxious voices from Europe. They are already beginning to speak out. Do not tempt them, do not add to their ever-increasing hatred with a verdict justifying the murder of a father by his own son. (722; 15:150)

In likening Russia to an apparition from the East, Ippolit Kirillovich uses the Western perception of Russia as an Asiatic peril, as the source from which great plagues rush across the steppes of Euro-Asia to infect Europe. By referring to the troika's course as unbridled, Dmitry becomes the personification of the Russian scourge. The prosecutor in several short paragraphs transforms Gogol's *Dead Souls* from a Russian national epic into a vitriolic denunciation of Russia, though such a derogation does not prevent Ippolit Kirillovich from using the term *Holy Russia* when rhetorically convenient.

Dostoevsky entitles the last chapter devoted to Fetyukovich's summation "An Adulterer of Thought" (*Preliubodei mysli*), but, for the populist Dostoevsky, who sees the Russian people as the last hope for European Christian salvation, Ippolit Kirillovich is no less an adulterer of thought than his adversary. In the summation Dostoevsky uses Ippolit Kirillovich's warning to the world to equate the lawyers' speeches and their ideological positions. The prosecutor threatens Russia with the wrath of Europe, just as Fetyukovich threatens fathers with the wrath of their sons. Everything that Europe does to protect itself, including, one would presume, military intervention, is justified, given the nature of Russia's mad unbridled troika. If Russia does not behave like a good nation, other nations have the right to consider it a threat and take whatever action appropriate for their security. (Fetyukovich argues in a similar manner: if Fedor Karamazov is a bad father, his sons will not consider him their father but their enemy and take the necessary measures against him.) Any action that Europe might take against Russia can rightly be considered self-defense—and here Ippolit Kirillovich even gets ahead of Fetyukovich—which is essential to preserving and enhancing "enlightenment and civilization." Ippolit Kirillovich's troika has done far more damage than Gogol's troika could ever have done. Dostoevsky presents Ippolit Kirillovich's speech as the quintessence of Russian self-hatred. Once again, as in the article on Kroneberg in the *Diary of a Writer,* art in the service of the law in post-reform Russia can be dangerous for Russian society. Ippolit Kirillovich exploits art because Russian jury trial realities (the importance of summations) encourage it and thus he promotes art's misappropriation and abuse.

But Dostoevsky's critique goes deeper than the content and tactics of the prosecutor's summation. Ippolit Kirillovich's greatest "crime," like Fetyukovich's, is against the word, especially the authority of the word, the word that Dostoevsky himself uses to expose the words of Ippolit Kirillovich and Fetyukovich and to valorize the words of Alyosha and Father Zosima. And here we need, contrary to expectation, to look less at Ippolit Kirillovich's misstatements, liberal pronouncements, and attacks against Dostoevsky's cherished ideas, and more at the statements and views he expresses that are actually validated by the novel, in particular his rebuttal of Fetyukovich's justification of parricide. In some cases Dostoevsky shows that Ippolit Kirillovich derives erroneous conclusions from valid suppositions; in others Dostoevsky shows how Kirillovich's correct conclusions are meaningless because of the context—the courtroom—in which they are uttered.

In fact, Dostoevsky inserts into the prosecutor's speech many statements that occur in his own journalistic and fictional work, not an unusual practice for Dostoevsky, who frequently has negative characters express his most cherished ideas. Ippolit Kirillovich's statement about epilepsy could have come from Dostoevsky's own letters; the prosecutor's analysis of contemporary moral decay from numerous passages from the *Diary of a Writer*; his observations about criminals demanding punishment for their crimes, from *Notes from the House of the Dead*; his description of the feeling of a man about to be executed, from *The Idiot* and one of Dostoevsky's own letters to his brother Mikhail; and his extolling of the importance of childhood memories, from numerous places but most important, of course, from Alyosha's speech to the boys in the epilogue of *The Brothers Karamazov*. Like Fetyukovich, Ippolit Kirillovich is a man of considerable intelligence and rhetorical skills, who, because of his ideology, is bound to misuse, if not abuse, his insight and intelligence.

Ippolit Kirillovich reiterates Dmitry's words about the broadness of

Russians and their equal attraction to the beauty of Sodom and Gomorrah and the beauty of the Madonna: "Precisely because we are of a
broad Karamazovian nature—and this is what I am driving at—capable of containing all possible opposites and of contemplating both
abysses at once, the abyss above us, an abyss of lofty ideals, and the
abyss beneath us, an abyss of the lowest and foulest degradation" (699;
15:129). But Ippolit Kirillovich undercuts his own idea by arguing that
Dmitry could not have hidden any money in an amulet placed around
his neck. The prosecutor derives a completely false—some might say
completely illogical—conclusion from an insight into Dmitry's character.[41] If Dmitry contains all opposites, why could he have not killed
his father for the money and hidden some money around his neck?
Let's put aside for a moment the troublesome fact that Dmitry did not
kill his father and did sew the money into an amulet around his neck.

Ippolit Kirillovich narrates a marvelous scene describing the last
moments of a man condemned to death in order to describe how
Dmitry must have felt at Mokroe several hours after murdering his
father. "For I cannot imagine the horror and moral suffering of Karamazov when he discovered that she loved him, that for him she rejected her 'former' and 'indisputable' one, that she was calling him, him,
'Mitya' to renewed life, promising him happiness" (717; 15:145). But not
only did Dmitry not kill his father, the reader knows that Dmitry experiences the exact opposite of what the prosecutor describes. In fact, he
experiences a rebirth of hope when he realizes that Grushenka has
rejected her former lover and that she really loves Dmitry.

Ippolit Kirillovich uses one of Dostoevsky's most cherished ideas
about the importance of childhood memories, but he uses it to make the
opposite point made by Alyosha. We may recall that Alyosha states that
one good memory left from childhood may provide the basis for future
salvation: "some good memory, especially a memory from childhood,
from the parental home" (774; 15:195). The prosecutor states: "I am a
prosecutor, but also a defender. Yes, we, too, are human and are able
to weigh the influence on a man's character of the earliest impressions
of childhood and the parental nest" (698; 15:128). Ippolit Kirillovich
introduces this idea with reference to the testimony of Dr. Herzenstube,
but he uses it for a very different purpose. Whereas the text shows the
effect that the memory of Herzenstube's small act of kindness had on
the mature Dmitry, Ippolit Kirillovich uses the doctor's testimony to
show the lasting effect of bad childhood memories and impressions.

Dostoevsky handles Ippolit Kirillovich's rebuttal of Fetyukovich's speech differently. There are few of the psychological, aesthetic, and moral lapses of his summation. Ippolit Kirillovich effectively exposes all Fetyukovich's ploys and adulterated ideas. He accuses the defense attorney of creating a novel far more unrealistic than his own, of romanticizing Smerdyakov, of arguing that Dmitry both killed and did not kill his father at the same time, of demanding that the jury find parricide a mere prejudice, of playing fast and loose with evidence just to obtain an acquittal; and, most of all, of correcting the Gospels: preaching an eye for an eye rather than turning the other cheek, thereby substituting a Westernized liberal interpretation of Christ for the Christ of the Russian Orthodox Church. He, in effect, accuses Fetyukovich of being a corrupter of thought, immediately after Dostoevsky makes the case for such a charge in the chapter title.

> The Gospel and religion are corrected; it's all *mysticism,* he says, and ours is the only true Christianity, tested by the analysis of *reason and sensible ideas.* And so a false image of Christ is held up to us! "*With what measure ye mete, it shall be measured to you,*" the defense attorney exclaims and concludes then and there that Christ commanded to measure with the same measure as it is measured to us—and that from the tribune of truth and sensible ideas! We glance into the Gospel only on the eve of our speeches, in order to make a brilliant display of our familiarity with what is, after all, a *rather original work,* which may prove useful and serve for a certain effect, in good measure, all in good measure! (749; 15:174; emphasis added)

This response would constitute an almost perfect rebuttal (from the author's point of view) if the reader did not know its purpose and context. It is pure rhetoric. First of all, Ippolit Kirillovich is no less guilty of committing these errors than his opponent, and paradoxically he is no less an adulterer of thought, even when lodging this criticism against his opponent. After all, these remarks come from a lawyer who disparages Russian Orthodoxy as obscurantism (the antithesis of European Enlightenment) and ridicules Alyosha Karamazov's desire to become a monk as the beginning of a path to dark mysticism and witless chauvinism. Ippolit Kirillovich says that Fetyukovich makes "a brilliant display of our familiarity with what is, after all, a rather original work" (the Bible) to bolster the fortunes of his client, but Ippolit Kirillovich uses exactly the same ploy with *Dead Souls*—also a rather original work. Moreover, rather than rejecting the principle of an eye for an eye and adhering to Christ's precept of turning the other cheek, Ippolit Kirillovich calls for revenge.

Given Dostoevsky's contextual, but not situational, ethics, it makes no difference whatsoever what Ippolit Kirillovich says, however brilliant, however accurate, because his words are vitiated both by his intentions and the institutional parameters in which he operates: the jury trial. His excellent rebuttal underlines this point. Dostoevsky purposely makes the lawyers as different as possible—they are bitter opponents, with seemingly different intentions and goals, different styles and rhetoric, different personal agendas, backgrounds, and successes—to show that in the end they are only *irrelevantly* different, that is, fundamentally the same. Although Ippolit Kirillovich and Fetyukovich are engaged in what seems like a life or death agon, they actually hold identical views. They are Russian liberals who idealize Western institutions and social developments and condemn native Russian ones.[42] Presupposing, as it were, the identity of opposing counsel, Dostoevsky gives both attorneys virtually the same lines regarding the need to reject fantasy, to adhere to reason, and to defend the values of Western civilization. Each attorney demands that Russians not turn away from unpleasant realities like children but face the hard truths like responsible, enlightened citizens. Each attorney asks the jury not to be led astray by the other attorney's psychological novel and so on. The novel almost assumes that had Ippolit Kirillovich been Dmitry's attorney, and had he come up with Fetyukovich's idea that Dmitry could not have committed parricide because Fedor Karamazov was not a real father, Ippolit Kirillovich would certainly have had no compunction about exploiting it to the best of his ability. As we have seen, Ippolit Kirillovich makes exactly the same argument with regard to the relationship between Europe and Russia as Fetyukovich makes regarding the relationship between Fedor Karamazov and Dmitry.

The more Dostoevsky personalizes the agon between the lawyers, the more he is able to depersonalize the legal process and show that its procedures and conclusions are predetermined in its form. After observing the Zasulich trial, Dostoevsky had already imagined what the attorneys had to say in the Karamazov case. The lawyer, as champion of his client, will use any device to win his case, and it is not primarily his fault. He must do so, according to Dostoevsky, if he is to fulfill his professional mission in accord with the 1864 legal reforms and the professionalization of the Russian bar. Dostoevsky may have even been aware that the intent of the reform was to introduce a less antagonistic adversarial system than existed in West. We have seen that the Russian system worked hard to arrive at a consensus in its verdicts. In addition, the statutes of 1864 made quite explicit that the role of the prosecutor was not primarily to secure a victory for the state but to search for the truth and do justice. If it became clear that the defendant was innocent, the prosecutor was required by law not to press for conviction. But for Dostoevsky the intention of the reforms had become irrelevant. He had himself been a supporter of the reforms and had hopes that they would play a crucial role in Russia's moral regeneration. It was even more disillusioning and disheartening if in practice the institution was subverting the intentions of its creators and the hopes of its supporters.

For Dostoevsky, Ippolit Kirillovich's logical inconsistencies, overblown rhetoric, liberal political commonplaces, and literary inanities are much less parlous than his correct and insightful observations and remarks. The prosecutor might utter only pearls of wisdom, accurately cite maxims from the Gospels, but in the end his word is totally compromised by his intentions and the context (the law) in which his word is used. Such a word becomes far more insidious than all his other falsehoods, fabrications, and rampant psychology, for it passes itself off as—masquerades as—good Christian art, or as Fetyukovich will later say, "real Christian work" (*nastoiashchee khristianksoe delo*; 745; 15:170–71).

Because the word itself is imprisoned by the trial, the words (rumors, opinions, newspaper articles) about the trial—specifically, the spectators' comments about the summations—carry little weight, however interesting or correct they may seem. After Ippolit Kirillovich finishes speaking, the narrator eavesdrops on several conversations in which the participants share their impressions of the merits and weaknesses of the prosecutor's performance. The narrator records thirty brief comments made in four groups of observers. The concluding remark of each group, except for the last, concerns how Fetyukovich will respond to Ippolit Kirillovich's performance. The last group would have ended the same way had the bell signaling the beginning of Fetyukovich's speech not sounded. Here, for example, are the comments of the first group:

> "A serious speech!" a gentleman in one group observed, frowning.
> "Too wrapped up in psychology," another voice was heard.
> "Yes, but all true, irrefutably true!"
> "Yes, he is a master of it."
> "Summed it all up."
> "Us, too. He summed us up, too," a third voice joined in, "at the start of the speech, remember, that we're all the same as Fyodor Pavlovich?"
> "And at the end, too. But that was all rubbish."
> "There were some vague spots."
> "Got a bit carried away."
> "Unjust, sir, unjust."
> "No, but anyway it was clever. The man waited for a long time, and finally he said it, heh, heh."
> "*What will the defense attorney say?*" (723; 15:151; emphasis added)

The impressions of this group about Ippolit Kirillovich's speech (they are meant to be taken as representative) run the gamut, that is, from irrefutable truth to rubbish. Though again some of the judgments are correct ("Got a bit carried away"), they are impressions determined by personal bias and shaped, positively or negatively, by the prosecutor's rhetoric; they carry little authority. Dostoevsky "sums up" the significance of these comments in a sampling from the fourth group, the concluding group, which takes up the meaning of the troika metaphor in the summation's finale. The fourth group (and thus probably many in the audience) evidently not only perfectly understood the implications of Ippolit Kirillovich's warning about foreign intervention but took it seriously enough to speak about the prospects of and responses to an imminent invasion.[43]

> "But that was good about the troika, the part about the other nations."
> "And it's true, remember, where he said the other nations won't wait."
> "What do you mean?"
> "In the English Parliament just last week one member got up to speak about the nihilist issue, and asked the Ministry if it wasn't time to intervene in a barbarous nation, in order to educate us. It was him Ippolit meant, I know it was him. He talked about it last week.

"There's many a slip."

"Slip? Why many?"

"We'll close Kronstadt and not give them any grain. Where will they get it?"

"What about America? They can get it from America now."

"That's nonsense."

But the bell rang, all rushed to their places. Fetyukovich mounted the rostrum. (724; 15:12)

The resolution of Dmitry's case, in the opinion of some, will transform the economic and foreign policy of Russia, England, and America. Not only the text but the logic of *Dead Souls* and *The Inspector General* have entered *The Brothers Karamazov*.

### The Principal Attorneys: The Lawyer for the Defense

In Fetyukovich, Dmitry's defense attorney, Dostoevsky takes indirect aim again at Spasovich, the lawyer who outraged him with his successful defense of Kroneberg. *The Brothers Karamazov* gives Dostoevsky another opportunity to confront the great artist-lawyer but now with a distinct advantage. In the Kroneberg article Dostoevsky had to take Spasovich out of court, for Spasovich had already won the case. In *The Brothers Karamazov* Dostoevsky, as it were, returns him to the courtroom.

Though Dostoevsky skirts the boundaries of the grotesque in the last of the four chapters ("The Adulterer of Thought") devoted to Fetyukovich's summation, he does not gloss over the defense attorney's intelligence, flair, psychological acumen, and performance art. The first three chapters of "A Judicial Error" show Fetyukovich's superiority over Ippolit Kirillovich. Because of dramatic irony the reader views Fetyukovich differently than the spectators, who are far more impressed by his rhetoric in the fourth chapter than with his brilliant reconstructions of crime scenarios in the preceding three chapters. He conceives of his summation as a speech about a speech, that is, a critique of the summation of his "most talented" (*vysokotalantlivyi*) opponent. Despite the obligatory words of respect, Fetyukovich skillfully challenges the prosecutor's assumptions about every piece of evidence. He shows that psychology cuts both ways, and even though psychology is supposedly not his forte, he demonstrates that he is as least as good a psychologist as Ippolit Kirillovich. We must be fair to the prosecutor. Although Ippolit Kirillovich is dealt a strong hand regarding the available evidence, he is at a great disadvantage with the reader, who knows that the prosecutor is attempting to gain a murder conviction by proving that what did not happen actually happened: that Dmitry committed both a robbery and a murder, when in fact he did neither. Fetyukovich, on the other hand, needs to show that there is reasonable doubt about what in fact did not happen. The reader knows much better than Fetyukovich himself that the facts support his arguments for reasonable doubt.

In the first half of his summation, Fetyukovich attacks the novel that Ippolit Kirillovich has constructed on the basis of psychology, just as much as he attacks his psychology per se. He pokes holes in Ippolit Kirillovich's case and offers psychological explanations as plausible as his opponent's. And he uses his own psychological arguments to produce an equally verisimilar psychological novel. Fetyukovich taunts his opponent by using his opponent's weapons, disparaging his psychological approach and novelistic forays. The narrator characterizes the first half of Fetyukovich's speech as being in places malicious and sarcastic (*zloe i sarkastichekoe*; 725; 15:153).

As though alluding to Dostoevsky's article on Spasovich's talent in the Kroneberg case, Fetyukovich accuses Ippolit Kirillovich of letting his talent for psychology lead him astray into fiction. While careful to call his opponent the highly talented prosecutor (*vysokotalantlivyi obvinitel'*), he depreciates Ippolit Kirillovich's attempts to create an artistic work from psychological speculation. Fetyukovich, in effect, shows Ippolit Kirillovich how one can create a far more ambiguous—and thus convincing—novel from the very same evidence. But he emphasizes the danger of art in the courtroom and not because he wants the jury to accept his alternatives. Rather, he wants to undercut the novel as a way of ascertaining truth in real life.[44]

> But there are things that are even worse, even more ruinous in such cases than the most malicious preconceived attitude toward the matter. Namely, if we are, for example, possessed by a certain, so to speak, artistic play, by the need for artistic creativity, so to speak, the creation of a novel, especially seeing the wealth of psychological gifts with which God has endowed our abilities. (727; 15:154)

Because novels are not part of real life (as he later will also say of religion and mysticism), Fetyukovich argues that novels do not belong in the courtroom. He characterizes the prosecutor's suggestion that Dmitry's unspent money is hidden in Mokroe as a "fantastic . . . novelistic suggestion [*fantastichekoe . . . romanicheskoe predpolozhenie*]" (731; 15:158) and says that "such novels" can "ruin a human life" (721; 15:158). He accuses Ippolit Kirillovich of creating a Dmitry Karamazov to suit his interpretation of the evidence but implies that even as a novel it is unconvincing: "The court decided this afternoon to continue its session, but in the meantime, while waiting, I might incidentally make some remarks, for example, about the characterization of the late Smerdyakov, drawn with so much subtlety and so much talent by the prosecutor. For astonished as I am by such talent, I cannot quite agree with the essence of the characterization" (738; 15:164). After criticizing Ippolit Kirillovich's characterization of Smerdyakov, Fetyukovich provides his own analysis. His method is to undermine his opponent's constructions, improve upon them, and then disparage his own improvements, in effect, undermining the validity of using the techniques of the psychological novel in a jury trial. Fetyukovich is so confident of his powers that he is willing to throw away his gains so that he can achieve an acquittal, not as a talented psychological novelist but as a tribune of rational, sensible, and liberal ideas. The adulterer of thought, as it were, does not want a victory adulterated by cheap psychology and half-baked forays into the novel.[45]

That is why Fetyukovich almost throws away his reasonable doubt argument. Although he begins by professing his belief in his client's innocence—"I swear by all that's holy. I believe completely in the explanation of the murder I have just presented to you" (740; 15:166)—he eventually asks the jury to suppose that his client actually committed the murder. Fetyukovich needs an acquittal of a murderer, not an acquittal of an innocent man.[46] This tactic, which obviously failed, looks defective only from hindsight. Fetyukovich had obviously been successful with this procedure many times before in provincial trials. Had he not been so dismissive of the psychological approach and placed all his bets on justifying parricide to a peasant jury, he probably could have avoided the unanimous conviction without extenuating circumstances.

Dostoevsky implicitly compares Fetyukovich to the other legal actors at the trial. Like the judge, the other lawyers, and the prosecuting

attorney, Fetyukovich is not interested in Dmitry as a person; he
"vouches" for his client from purely technical and strategic considerations, just as he would attempt to discredit any witness whom he
found potentially dangerous. Fetyukovich admits to the jury from the
very beginning that he did not accept his position as defense counsel
because of Dmitry Karamazov but because of the intellectual challenge
and idiosyncrasies of the case.[47]

> In a word, I was interested first of all in a certain juridical fact, which
> appears often enough in legal practice, though never, it seems to me, so
> fully or with such characteristic peculiarities as in the present case. . . .
> It was in order to demolish this terrible totality of facts and show how
> undemonstrable and fantastic each separate accusing fact is, that I
> undertook the defense of this case. (725–26; 15:153)

Fetyukovich professes belief in his client only because he is required
to do so; he has, after all, been hired by Katerina Ivanovna. But his professional interest in the purely legal side of the case—which again links
him with the judge and the other lawyers—is also a ruse. What he
wants most is to transform the Karamazov "affair" into a major political and social event for all Russia, with himself at the very center. That
is why his performance in the first three chapters, however competent,
seems almost perfunctory, child's play, as though he were merely going
through his paces in discrediting the various witnesses.

   The Zasulich case undoubtedly influenced Dostoevsky's shaping of
Fetyukovich's summation. What disturbed Dostoevsky most about the
lawyers in the Kroneberg and other cases was the amoral position into
which the adversarial system cast them: they were virtually required,
he argued, to be the champions of their clients. In the Zasulich and
other cases Dostoevsky saw something far worse. In the Kroneberg
case Saltykov-Shchedrin had argued for the separation of ethics and
the law, the exact opposite of Dostoevsky's position. The writer continued to view the court as one of the most important institutions for
the moral education of the public. Saltykov-Shchedrin wanted the
lawyer to remain a technician and not to get involved in ethical and
political issues. However, *The Brothers Karamazov* shows Dostoevsky
moving away from his former position under the pressure of Russian political realities. The recent political trials had given defendants
the opportunity to use the court as a forum for expressing their case

against the government. But in the Zasulich trial it was becoming clearer that some lawyers were beginning to see their profession less instrumentally and more ethically and civilly: they continued to use the court for their own self-aggrandizement, but they also began to exploit it concomitantly as a tribune from which to influence the conscience and spiritual development of the nation. Dostoevsky's wish for a more ethical bar was being realized, but it was taking a direction diametrically opposite to the one he desired. Aleksandrov, Zasulich's attorney, consistently argued that the defense attorney should not merely be the champion of his client but should perform the role of a "citizen-lawyer," placing the interests of society at least on a par with the interest of the client. And that is the way he argued the Zasulich case. He admitted that his client committed the crime and was therefore legally guilty according to the statutes of 1864, but he implored the jury not to judge her according to the statute law but to apply a higher law, governed by overriding Russian moral, social, and political realities. Moral innocence should supersede legal guilt. Was he not arguing, like Dostoevsky, that Russian justice should take precedence over Western law? All of Dostoevsky's arguments about the court could easily be appropriated by his ideological opponents to forward their own agendas. Both sides agreed that Russian justice should take precedence over Western law—they just had diametrically opposite views of what constituted Russian justice.

Accordingly, Dostoevsky does not at all present Fetyukovich as a champion of his client, a gun for hire, but rather as someone who is willing to take the case for nothing, even to lose the battle—the case[48] —if he can win the war, that is, influence the course of Russian society through the molding of public opinion, replacing the Russian and Christian idea with the European and liberal idea. Dostoevsky transforms Dmitry's defense attorney into a lawyer-citizen and by so doing takes the Zasulich case in a more radical direction. As we have seen, the Zasulich trial was the last of several highly political trials in which politically radical defendants used the court as a forum for disseminating their ideas. The lawyers may have tried to present their clients as sympathetically as possible but the lawyers themselves were not advancing specific political and social ends. And this was true of Aleksandrov, Zasulich's lawyer, who argued not for the abolition of the autocracy but for the jury to take into consideration all the social, political, and moral factors that went into Zasulich's assassination attempt on the governor of Petersburg. Dostoevsky completely reverses the dispensation of forces. For most of his life Dmitry was a dissolute Russian officer and bully, not a political revolutionary. He expresses almost no specifically political views in the course of the novel, other than contempt for those, who, like Rakitin, are exploiting his case for their political agendas. Dmitry is accused of a purely personal crime with no overt political associations or connotations, and none is brought up in the course of the trial. In contrast to the Zasulich trial, it is the lawyers who politicize the trial, exploiting and transforming the unpolitical Dmitry into a pretext for their political ideas. Ippolit Kirillovich exploits politics to win his case; Fetyukovich uses the case to forward his politics.

In Kroneberg, Spasovich's main weapons were technicalities in the law and the discrediting of witnesses. In Dmitry's trial Fetyukovich is interested in neither. He assumes the role of the Russian novelist as a prophet, sage, and leader of public opinion. In the end, Fetyukovich misjudges the jury and loses the case. He might have won such a case in the real world, but Dostoevsky will not have it. In Dostoevsky's world, the world of the novel, Fetyukovich loses on all counts—with the jury and the reader. The jury does not even listen. The lawyers put their careers on the line for one great speech, but their speeches fall completely flat for the peasant jurors. They experience the ultimate novelistic deflation: their readers, the jurors, are bored.

Dostoevsky also cannot resist transforming Spasovich into a much larger figure than he was in Kroneberg, integrating him into the book's larger metaphysical, religious, and political concerns. Once he becomes a citizen-lawyer, an ideologue, it is easy to cast him in the role of a contemporary Grand Inquisitor, an updated hero of Ivan's narrative poem. The jury trial becomes the contemporary counterpart of the Spanish auto-da-fé, the premier spectacle of its day. The Grand Inquisitor tells Christ that because he has been a bad father to his children, because he has acted as though he were his children's enemy, his children have the right to rise up against him, both the ascetic elect (the Ivans) and the unbridled masses (the Dmitrys). Because he has not been a real father to his children, his burning at the next auto-da-fé cannot by definition be considered parricide (or deicide). Fetyukovich is cast in the role of the Russian Jesuit, the new corrupter of thought, ready to convince the people, all Russia, that parricide is a prejudice, just as the Grand Inquisitor attempts to convince the people that he has enslaved them out of love—and for their own good. The new church is the law court, at whose head stands the modern Grand Inquisitor, Fetyukovich.

Dostoevsky is not content to let Dmitry's case remain in the prosaic middle ground of the law; he raises the ante by making Fetyukovich a modern-day equivalent of the devil incarnate, posing as humanity's greatest benefactor. The new legal system is being used by a class of liberal professionals to destroy Russian civilization from within, to accomplish, in effect, what every foreign invasion had failed to do. The Grand Inquisitor has as little concern for the unbridled Dmitrys as Fetyukovich has. But Dostoevsky goes further with Fetyukovich than with the Grand Inquisitor. The Grand Inquisitor is a projection of Ivan's spiritual division—which Father Zosima noted in the meeting in the hermitage—between his love for Christ and his contempt for humanity, a division that will lead either to madness or suicide on the one hand or resurrection from the dead on the other. Fetyukovich, who cares little for Dmitry, is neither plagued by spiritual doubt nor torn between Christ and the devil; he can choose the devil and reason over religion and mysticism without the slightest travail of the spirit.

But the greatest danger that Fetyukovich poses to Russian society— and to Dostoevsky's novel—arises through his appropriation and usurpation of the Word, especially through his implicit challenge of the authority of his creator's word: the word of the novelist himself. We have seen that Fetyukovich "adopts" and adapts Dostoevsky's own rhetoric in the Kroneberg case by attacking the misuse of psychology and artistic talent in the courtroom. From the Kornilova articles he appropriates Dostoevsky's rhetoric of salvation, which he uses to persuade the jury to treat his client with mercy. The novel actually takes more seriously Fetyukovich's appropriation of Dostoevsky's own rhetoric of salvation from the Kornilova case than Fetyukovich's more egregious attempt to argue that parricide, in some situations, may be a prejudice, a strategy that not only the jury but many of the spectators see through right away.[49] If he can use the Gospels, why not the words of his real creator, Dostoevsky? One might imagine Fetyukovich's saying: "It is not only I who says this, but so does my creator. You can check the *Diary of a Writer*." Dostoevsky is obviously playing a dangerous game of metacriticism here, almost acknowledging that the spoken word has no validity in itself but depends for its real meaning and veracity solely on the authority of its source.

If we compare the end of Fetyukovich's summation with Dostoevsky's statements about Kornilova from the *Diary of a Writer,* we see that with a few exceptions almost everything that Fetyukovich says in Dmitry's defense was said by the real Dostoevsky in defense of Kornilova. Dostoevsky even bemoans the failure of Russian novelists to write about such crucial matters.

Fetyukovich tells the jurors that if they sentence Dmitry to hard labor, they will be sending him to his ruin, and they will be doing so on insufficient evidence. In the *Diary of a Writer* Dostoevsky says: "Will she derive much from hard labor? Will not her soul harden? Will it not be depraved and exasperated forever? Whom and when did hard labor ever reform? And the most important thing—all this in the presence of an utterly unexplained and not refuted doubt concerning the psychological affect of her pregnant condition at the time" (534; 24:43). But because Dmitry has a good heart, if you temper justice with mercy, if you overwhelm him with your love, you will restore his soul, rekindle his faith in other human beings, and resurrect him from the dead. He will remain eternally grateful for the rest of his life. How could he forget this act of kindness, if he still remembered the act of Dr. Herzenstube, who gave him a pound of nuts twenty-three years before? All this is said in the same language of the Kornilova case and the Father Zosima sections of *The Brothers Karamazov,* that is, in the language of salvation, love, mercy, repentance, resurrection, regeneration, tender emotion (*umilenie*), repentance, obligation, responsibility, tears, and Russian truth and justice.

But this is not all that Fetyukovich "borrows." Dostoevsky writes that Kornilova's crime was perhaps not a crime at all. "It was an involuntary instinctive sentiment that the perpetrated crime—so obvious and unquestionable to their simple way of thinking—essentially, *perhaps, is not a crime at all,* but something that has strangely occurred and has been strangely perpetrated, as if not by their will, but by God's judgment for the sins of both of them" (529; 24:37–38). And he had written earlier, "And what if there should have been an error?—Better an error in mercy than in castigation—all the more so since in a case such as this nothing could have been verified" (463; 23:139–40). Fetyukovich echoes: "Oh, it is so easy for you to do it, this act of mercy [*miloserdie*], for in the absence of any evidence even slightly resembling the truth, it will be too difficult for you to say: 'Yes, guilty [*Da, vinoven*].' "It is better to let ten who are guilty go, than to punish one who is innocent."[50]

In the *Diary of a Writer* Dostoevsky cautions about punishing Kornilova according to the letter of the law: "Tell me, what would have been the sense of ruining and corrupting a life which at present, it would seem, has returned to truth, in consequence of a severe purge and repentance, with a regenerated heart? Isn't it better to reform, discover and restore a human being than simply to chop off his head? It is easy, abiding by the letter of the law, to cut off one's head, but it is always far more difficult to examine a case in accordance with truth, humanely and paternally" (931; 26:106). Fetyukovich makes the same Christian argument. "Is it for me, insignificant as I am, to remind you that the Russian courts exist not only for punishment [*kara*] but also for the salvation of the ruined man [*spasenie cheloveka pogibshego*]! Let other nations have the letter and punishment [*bukva i kara*], we have the spirit and meaning [*dukh i smysl*], the salvation and the regeneration of the lost [*spasenie i vozrozhdenie pogibshikh*]" (747–48; 15:173). In other words, Europe lives by the dry letter of the law and the old ethic of punishment, but Russia has now come—principally through the courts—to represent a higher, Christian ethic, characterized by a salvific agenda inspired by love, mercy, and compassion—true Russian justice (*pravda russkaia*). Dostoevsky also writes about the criminal's being overwhelmed by the mercy of the court. "At present, however, believing herself to be a criminal and considering herself such, but suddenly forgiven by men, overwhelmed with benefits [*oblagodetel'stvovannaia*] and pardoned, how can she fail to feel a regeneration to a new life superior to the former?—It was not some single person that pardoned her, but *everybody*—the court, the jurors, which means society as a whole, bestowed mercy upon her" (935; 26:110). Here Dostoevsky speaks of the court as representative of society as a whole. Again, Fetyukovich might add: "It is not I who say this, but my creator." Fetyukovich continues: "But overwhelm such a soul with mercy [*miloserdie*], give it love, and it will curse what it has done, for there are so many germs of good in it. The soul will expand and behold how merciful [*miloserd*] God is, and how beautiful and just people are [*prekrasnye i spravedlivye*]. He will be horrified, he will be overwhelmed with repentance [*raskaianie*] and the countless debt [*dolg*] he must henceforth face" (747; 15:172–73).

Fetyukovich can even appropriate the ideas—and the tears—from Father Zosima. After all, in court all is permitted (*vse pozvoleno*). He can pretend to be the spokesman of both religious emotion and universal responsibility, the responsibility that arises from true Christian humility, expressed in the mystical experiences of Alyosha Karamazov, Father Zosima, and Father Zosima's brother, Markel. Fetyukovich argues that Dmitry will be the first to confess: "I am guilty before all people and am the least worthy of all people [*Ia vinovat pred vsemi liud'mi i vsekh liudei nedostoinee*]" (747; 15:173). Fetyukovich promises that "in tears of repentance [*v slezakh raskaianiia i zhguchego stradatel'skogo umileniia*] and burning suffering tenderness he will exclaim: 'People are better than I for they wished not to ruin but to save [*spasti*] me!'" (747; 15:173).

Readers may have the eerie feeling that they often have when reading Dostoevsky's early novel *The Double*: not knowing who is tracking whom or who is playing with whom. Fetyukovich, as part of Dostoevsky, seems aware of everything that Dostoevsky writes and thinks and feels no compunction whatsoever about using it all for his own ends, including placing the court at the very center of Russian justice (*pravda russkaia*) and Christian brotherly love. Does not Mr. Golyadkin in *The Double* feel betrayed when he confides in his insidious double, who then uses that confidential information to betray his creator? Dostoevsky perhaps overdoes, for satirical ends, Fetyukovich's reduction of parricide to an unfortunate prejudice, and the writer is unable to resist the temptation of painting the lawyer as devil, Jesuit, and liberal all at the same time.[51] But Dostoevsky also cannot resist the temptation of presenting Fetyukovich as an even more accomplished artist than Spasovich was in Kroneberg, making the defense lawyer talk to the jury in the much the same way that Dostoevsky addressed his readers in the Kornilova case. The bad can steal from the good.

> The devil can cite Scripture for his purpose.
> An evil soul producing holy witness
> Is like a villain with a smiling cheek,
> A goodly apple rotten at the heart.
> O, what a goodly outside falsehood hath! (*The Merchant of Venice* 1.3.99–103)

Furthermore, Dostoevsky's initial emotional response to Kornilova's crime and her impending trial sounds like the rough draft for his caricature of Fetyukovich's speech on parricide:

> By the way, I imagine how advocates will be defending that stepmother: we shall hear about the helplessness of her situation, and about the fact

that she is a recent bride of a widower whom she married under compulsion or force, or by mistake. We shall have pictures drawn portraying the miserable existence of destitute people, their never-ending work. She, the naive, the innocent, believed when she married, an inexperienced little girl (particularly under our system of upbringing!) that married life brings nothing but joys—and here instead of them—washing of dirty linen, cooking, bathing the child: "Gentlemen of the jury, it is only natural that she started hating the child (who knows, maybe there will appear a 'defense lawyer' who will begin to smear the child and will find in a six-year-old girl some bad and hideous qualities!)—in a moment of despair, in a state of madness, almost without remembering herself, seized the girl, and . . . Gentlemen of the jury, who among you wouldn't have done the same thing? Who among you wouldn't have thrown the child out of the window?" (329; 23:19)

But Dostoevsky had to deny his own words when he took on an impassioned defense of this monster-stepmother, applying the rhetoric of salvation to an attempted filicide. In the Kroneberg case Dostoevsky had defended a child against her father; in the Kornilova case he seemed, at least to his critics, to have completely reversed roles, defending a mother against her child. In *The Brothers Karamazov* "Spasovich-Fetyukovich" makes a reversal as dramatic as the real Dostoevsky's; however, in contrast to Dostoevsky, he defends a father against the child in the Kroneberg case and a child (Dmitry) against the father in *The Brothers Karamazov*. Fetyukovich argues the justification of murder (substituting parricide for filicide) seriously, not ironically, and he oscillates from justification to a rhetoric of salvation in the course of the very same speech. As king of the Russian bar, Fetyukovich becomes the consummate appropriator of the word. He borrows from the Gospels and his literary creator—or, more properly, Dostoevsky gives him his own words, if not his Word. The word (whether in art or law) in and of itself has no intrinsic moral value; its value always depends on intention and goal. Fetyukovich attempts to convince the jury of the soundness of his salvific agenda, just as Dostoevsky had attempted to convince the readers of the *Diary of a Writer* of his.

Fetyukovich's speech calls into question the authority of the word in the real world and in the world of the novel. Dostoevsky excoriates lawyers for unscrupulously discrediting witnesses, but he does the same when he discredits the word of his opposition, whether it be Spasovich or Fetyukovich. But discrediting "witnesses" by poetic convention is fair game for the novelist, a technique that Dostoevsky uses extensively and brilliantly—and judging by the critical response to the novel, with almost universal reader approval. He continually pillories Fetyukovich by exposing the disparity between the lawyer's words and his intentions. Dostoevsky can do this, or assumes he can, only because the novel implies the existence of authoritative and nonauthoritative words and points of view.

But where does the word, the word of the novelist, receive its authority—and thus validity? Which words of the novelist are valorized? Though Vasily Rozanov, Lev Shestov, and D. H. Lawrence have deconstructively questioned the authority of the author's word in *The Brothers Karamazov,* most critics invariably assume and seek the novelist's authoritative word and attempt to distinguish between the false word and unimpeachable authority of the author.[52]

In her study of the authority of the word in *The Brothers Karamazov,* V. E. Vetlovskaya not only assumes the authority of the author's word but uses it as the basis for determining the truth—or relative truth—of all textual statements.[53] If we know that the words of a character agree with those of the author, they ipso facto must be true for the reader. Nina Perlina's brilliant analysis of quotation in *The Brothers Karamazov,* though far more sophisticated than Vetlovskaya's, nevertheless works from the same notion of indisputable authority of the author's voice. The novel presents a universal truth; all that is in accord with it is true, all that diverges from it, however powerful and persuasive it may be, is, in proportion to its divergence, false. In discussing Erich Auerbach's concept of figural interpretation, which she maintains "supplies a key to the entire contextual interpretation of Dostoevsky," Perlina underlines the realm of indisputable truth that provides the standard of all interpretation in the novel.

> All of the novel's characters and their thoughts achieve a wider interpretation (figural in its aesthetic essence) which is possible because all of the characters and the novel itself are placed within and compared to events originating from a highly authoritative realm. The authority of the Bible subordinates and structures the entire sum of individual "moralities" in *The Brothers Karamazov*. In the text of the novel, quotations from Holy Scripture appear as words of *unshakable authority, as ideal models of indisputable truth,* and as a living bond between the eternal

and the temporal. A comparison of a hero's own word to the *undisputed authoritative word of the Bible,* in direct or indirect quotation, is not necessarily an act of willful competition between his own "individual truth" and the Absolute; it is rather his attempt to find and to comprehend universal truth. (emphasis added)[54]

To be sure, few readers of *The Brothers Karamazov* doubt that the Bible is an indisputable word for the author. In *The Brothers Karamazov* the Word of the Gospels, though it can be misused and adulterated, is assumed to be an unimpeachable and authoritative word, vouchsafed, according to Father Zosima, by its mystical and transcendent source. A reciprocal reinforcement of authority is pursued through Father Zosima: the Bible authenticates the word of Father Zosima, and Father Zosima authenticates the biblical Word's validity for the modern world. To give still more weight to Father Zosima's word, Dostoevsky presents Father Zosima's life in the form of a saint's life (written by Alyosha Karamazov), a modern addition to a thousand-year tradition of Russian Orthodox hagiography. Further, Alyosha writes his mentor's "life" (*zhitie*) in partial answer to his brother Ivan's adulteration of the Word in "The Grand Inquisitor," in which Ivan attempts to discredit the Word of the Gospels while at the same time cynically appropriating it for his own agenda. The word remains the same, but the intention and end have been inverted. Just as Dostoevsky attempts to discredit the lawyer through the lawyer's attempt to discredit creditable witnesses (Spasovich's attack on the peasant women in the Kroneberg case), so Dostoevsky attempts to discredit Ivan's world through Ivan's attempt to discredit the Gospels' Word. But the discrediting of discrediting can work only so long as the reader takes the author's word as authoritative, treating it as though it had the same authority that the Word of the Gospels has for a believer. D. H. Lawrence, for one, could not. "And we cannot doubt that the Inquisitor speaks Dostoevsky's own final opinion about Jesus. The opinion is, baldly, this: Jesus you are inadequate. Men must correct you."[55] Was Lawrence not only a resisting reader but also a bad reader?

If *The Brothers Karamazov* does indeed provide a safe haven for the authoritative word, interpretations of "The Grand Inquisitor" and "The Russian Monk" based on the word of the implied author follow an unproblematic, predictable path. Could anything be clearer (despite D. H. Lawrence's demurral) than Ivan Karamazov's subversion of his own word in his contemptuous attitude toward humankind and his desire to reduce people to the state of animals? Or who would attempt to deconstruct the word of Father Zosima, whose sayings constitute an important section of his hagiography? Many commentators, who write almost as hagiographers of Dostoevsky, obediently accept the novelist's word in *The Brothers Karamazov* as unadulterated truth, just as Alyosha accepts the truth of the word from the lips of *his* spiritual father, Father Zosima. Most of Dostoevsky's readers are obedient sons and daughters. Who wants to be on the side of the ultimate profaners of the word, on the side of Fedor Karamazov and Fetyukovich?[56]

But Dostoevsky seemingly understands better than his commentators the problematic nature of the word in the novel, especially its privileged point of view. The privileged word may provide an anchor inaccessible and impossible in the real world, but it also emphasizes, by so doing, the glaring disparity between the function of the word in the novel, in a privileged authoritative text, and the function of the word in the real world, and not only in the real world outside the novel but in the real world described by the novel itself. The novelist's satire tells us enough about the intentions of Fetyukovich to discredit everything that the lawyer says; only the novelist can assume that privileged position with regard to the thoughts and intentions of others. On the other hand, both the prosecutor and defense attorney implicitly question the author-itativeness of the novel in the real world, with each attorney not only questioning the authority of his opponent's novel but even assuming that novels have no authority in real life at all, because they are not un-impeachable evidence but only imaginative fabrications. *The Brothers Karamazov* assumes the uniqueness and authority of the implied author's word in the novel just as it assumes the authoritativeness of the hagiog-raphy and Gospels both in and outside the world of the novel. It pre-supposes that the word of law is intrinsically inferior in authority to the word of hagiography, the Gospels, and even that of the implied author in a nineteenth-century novel. But Dostoevsky, in contrast to most of his commentators, is uncomfortable with these assumptions about "authorial" authority, and he works hard to overcome them.[57]

In a novel, discrediting can undermine the authority of one's oppo-nents' words, but it cannot establish authority. In fact, it can often have self-reflexive, destructive consequences. Zosima's truth, for example, must not so much argue for itself as insinuate. Establishing author-ity demands a different technique than discrediting it. By not directly confronting the "The Grand Inquisitor" but offering instead an alternative mode of being and perception, Zosima's word need not directly discredit the word of the other to achieve its own truth. Dostoevsky attempts artistically to create a world for Father Zosima's Orthodox word (however unorthodox it may have seemed to religious thinkers like Konstantin Leontyev and Vladimir Solovyov). It is a world existing side by side with the world outside the monastery, but it is circumscribed not so much by the walls of the monastery—those walls house the fanatic Father Ferapont as well as Zosima—but by the utopic, hagiographic mode that Dostoevsky uses to set this world off from the secular discourses of the Grand Inquisitor and the Western court.

On 11 June 1879 Dostoevsky writes his publisher, Nikolai Lyubimov, that he intends the world of "The Russian Monk," however Christian and idealistic, to be understood as "not something abstract" but "artistically real, possible" and "right in front of our eyes," and that he is writing "the whole novel . . . for its sake" (31.1:68). Two months later he writes Lyubimov that not only is "The Russian Monk" the "culminating point of the novel" but that it does "not transgress against reality: it is correct not only as an ideal but also as reality" (31.1:102).

Through a wise character, the tutor of the hero in *A Raw Youth* (1875), Dostoevsky expresses his concern that the Russian novel, including the work of Goncharov and Tolstoy, risks becoming more history than novel because of its failure to come to grips with the chaos of the modern world. "The Russian Monk," despite all its attempts to situate itself in the modern world, represents a nostalgia for an imagined wholeness and community more properly associated with the past, especially because it is filtered through the Russian Orthodox hagiographical tradition. Dostoevsky does not present it as a mode of being for some individuals but for Russia as a nation in the international community. He ridicules Fetyukovich when he dismisses mystical experience as not belonging to real life, but Father Zosima's vision, like his brother Markel's, and like Dostoevsky's own vision at the end of his article on the Jewish question, speaks not of the frenetic language of modern chaos at all but the language of mystic union with all creation, the realization of heaven on Earth, and the transfiguration of human life as we know it: "For in the resurrection they neither marry, nor are given in marriage, but are as the angels of God in heaven" (Mt 22:30). One must imagine what kind of "novel" *The Brothers Karamazov* would have been had it ended with "The Russian Monk" and not "A

Judicial Error," had we been left with hagiography rather than with Dostoevsky's vision of the chaos of the word ushered in by the Western court. The word of hagiography is unchallengeable in its own world, but it can be the word of the other world, as Dostoevsky's himself frequently noted, only when the world itself will have been radically transformed. This, of course, is not to deny the importance of the ideal in real life, even the ideal significance of hagiography, but it places in question the authority of the hagiographic word in the world of the nineteenth-century novel. Readers may suspend belief in a medieval tale, but they will be much less likely to do so in the modern world portrayed in much of *The Brothers Karamazov*.

The rhetoric and subject matter of "The Grand Inquisitor" and Fetyukovich's summation speech seem to indicate that the words of the Grand Inquisitor and Fetyukovich exist in different but parallel worlds. Fetyukovich (the stinker) is cast in the role of the bad double of Ivan's Grand Inquisitor, similar to Ivan's devil or even Smerdyakov (another stinker). But "The Grand Inquisitor" section is, in fact, much closer to the "The Russian Monk" than to "A Judicial Error," notwithstanding its being conceived as the "contra" to the "Russian Monk's" "pro," and that Dostoevsky viewed his greatest challenge in *The Brothers Karamazov* to be the refutation, through the "Russian Monk," of Ivan Karamazov's blasphemy in "The Grand Inquisitor." But in "The Russian Monk" and "The Grand Inquisitor" the word has a similar function and type of authority, one diametrically opposite to the function and authority of the word in "A Judicial Error."

The novel presents the word of Father Zosima, as well as Father Zosima himself, as the corn of wheat that falls into the ground to bring forth much fruit. His words inspire Alyosha to write his hagiographic tale about his mentor; later the words of Christ at Cana, read over Father Zosima's body, precipitate Alyosha's mystic experience. Alyosha throws himself down onto the earth, only to rise with renewed faith and strength. In his poem "The Grand Inquisitor" Ivan is equally the creator of Christ and of the Grand Inquisitor. The poem thus reflects the split in Ivan's heart, which, to use Dmitry's formulation, has become a battlefield between the forces of good and evil. To be sure, "The Grand Inquisitor" closely resembles in some ways Raskolnikov's article in *Crime and Punishment* in its argument for exerting power over others, but it differs fundamentally from Raskolnikov's article in its potential salvific function. "The Grand Inquisitor," like Ivan's article on church and state, reflects his passionate need to work out within himself the seeming incompatibility of the moral and spiritual beauty (*obraz*) of Christ with the rationally incomprehensible suffering of the innocent. Ivan's poem is not only a reflection of his spiritual dilemma and suffering but a creative means of confronting the issues affecting his salvation in a typically maximalist Dostoevskian fashion. But, most important, the word in "The Grand Inquisitor," even the Devil's word, has metaphysical significance and universal consequences. It defines a meaningful universe in which good and evil still operate and in which the destiny of the soul depends on an unconditioned moral choice whose terms are negotiated by different narratives of responsibility.

Because the word has ultimate validity in "The Grand Inquisitor," Ivan's fate rests on his response to the words of Christ or the words of the devil. The devil's word implies the existence of the word of the Other, the word of Christ. Though Dostoevsky holds the possibility or even probability that the evil word will win out, he prefers such a risk to the more repugnant possibility of a world in which the word, loosed from ultimate meaning and significance, exists only as a form of manipulation, as a rhetoric that one minute can present the common notion of parricide as a religious prejudice and the very next use the language of Christian salvation to present a case for murdering an unloving father. The world of Alyosha and Father Zosima represents the ideal, the world that we should strive to achieve, however against human nature it may be.[58] The world of Ivan Karamazov represents the world in which Dostoevsky and his fellow Russians had been living for the last forty years or so—a dangerous world, in which people passionately, even fanatically, adopt political and social agendas for which they are willing to sacrifice life and fortune. However Dostoevsky fulminates against his ideological enemies, he presents them as passionately committed to their positions, however wrong-headed and dangerous they may seem. They are as committed to a war of words, which they invest with ultimate significance, as Dostoevsky himself. Ivan Karamazov cannot live without meaning, without the word; the question he faces is to which word must he devote himself; in either case the word will shape his world. The victory of Dostoevsky's ideological opponents may hasten the Apocalypse, but the Apocalypse will restore, not destroy, the Word. I would suggest that Dostoevsky feels at home in the impassioned environment of "The Grand Inquisitor," however nostalgically and fondly he presents the auric peace, harmony, and unity of Alyosha

Karamazov's and Father Zosima's mystical experiences. The world of the Grand Inquisitor is Dostoevsky's existential world.

It is the Western court system that represents Dostoevsky's horrific vision of the Russian future, far worse, though this is difficult for us to imagine, than the cannibalistic Armageddon that he prophesies in the epilogue of *Crime and Punishment* or the degradation of the human race in *The Brothers Karamazov*. Dostoevsky intuits that even the Apocalypse may be wishful thinking, given his fear of the Westernization, secularization, and increasing individualism of Russian society. *The Brothers Karamazov* concludes in 1866 with "A Judicial Mistake" because 1866 marks for Dostoevsky the most crucial date in the implementation of the Western judicial reforms of 1864. *The Brothers Karamazov* signals Russia's entry into the modern world, a development that was accelerating in the 1870s, when Dostoevsky completed the novel. He presents the world of both Father Zosima and the Grand Inquisitor almost as though they were visions belonging equally to the past. (Whether Dostoevsky was right or wrong is not the issue here.) The future, however, belongs to the world of the court, that is, to Western law and jurisprudence. The world of the law is less ecstatic than the world of Father Zosima, less intellectually and emotionally stimulating than the world of the Grand Inquisitor; it is prosaic—even novelistic—but that is the way *The Brothers Karamazov* must end if it is not to become, according to Dostoevsky's own formulation, history, like the novels of Tolstoy and Goncharov, and if it is to reflect the present and prophesy the future. Dostoevsky hates this new world, he rages against it; he greatly prefers the Grand Inquisitor to Fetyukovich, but Dostoevsky recognizes the reality of this world and places that reality where it properly belongs—at the conclusion of his novel, not at the beginning, where Tolstoy places the trial in *Resurrection*. In contrast to *Resurrection* the trial in *The Brothers Karamazov* represents not prelude but finale.

But there is a still more prosaic, but no less ominous, way of looking at Fetyukovich's role in the jury trial. For Dostoevsky, Fetyukovich may also symbolize a new stage in the history of the word—and the law—in which the word is torn loose not only from its former moral and spiritual moorings but from its ideological moorings as well. In Kroneberg, Dostoevsky was bent on revealing the victory of a rational, impersonal, and formal legal system in which human feeling and compassion were trampled on and in which lawyers, compelled to become consciences for hire, became as much victims or prisoners of the legal process as the defendants, witnesses, and jurors. But Fetyukovich is not the champion of his client, he does not care about Dmitry, whom he exploits for his own self-aggrandizement. In both lawyers' summations Dostoevsky shows the dangers of narrative empathy and novelistic art in the courtroom. Fetyukovich uses almost exactly the same empathetic rhetoric that Dostoevsky himself employed in defense of Kornilova. But when we look at the trial against the background of the Zasulich case, we may see another significant transformation. Dostoevsky was disturbed by the politicization of the court, by its use by radicals for advancing their political agendas. But in the context of "The Grand Inquisitor," Fetyukovich's resort to the political may represent a further diminution of the significance of the word. It is politics without conviction, without vision; it is the exploitation of politics, like the exploitation of empathy and art, for purely personal ends. Dostoevsky must prefer the court as a site of real propaganda, where the word is misguided but still taken seriously, to the court as the site of the instrumental word. It is a preference for the Grand Inquisitor (Ivan Karamazov) over the Petty Inquisitor (Fetyukovich), a preference of the immoral over the amoral. Fetyukovich has no real vision, political or otherwise; he represents a word bereft of meaning. When the court is about words and not the Word, it becomes, at least for Dostoevsky, an institution unrelated to truth and justice and will do more to undermine its role as a moral school for the Russian people than any truly political trial. Dostoevsky's fix is to pack the jury with peasants who will simply ignore the attorneys, but if this is the best that can happen in the courts, the judicial system is in serious peril. For Dostoevsky it is probably more disturbing for the court to be irrelevant than it is to attempt to achieve and fail at a higher mission. Better to risk a struggle between God and the devil—and live with the consequences—than to exist in the middle ground. "So then because thou art lukewarm, and neither cold nor hot, I will spue thee out of my mouth" (Rev 3:16).

If one had to give a contemporary example that encapsulates this prediction about the future of the court (and I would suggest that Dostoevsky simultaneously entertains the seemingly mutually exclusive possibilities of Fetyukovich as a liberal ideologue and a self-serving lawyer without ideology), one would not have to look further than the 1995 spectacle-trial of O. J. Simpson, which lasted hundreds of days longer than Dmitry Karamazov's and featured lawyers that, in some respects, could compete with Fetyukovich. Several defense lawyers in the Simpson case knew their client was guilty but took the case on to further their own careers and causes. Alan Dershowitz did not care about Simpson. He saw the trial as a test case for various higher legal principles, such as the exposure of false testimony at criminal trials and the defense of the principle of rational doubt. Because Dershowitz perceived the case from a purely legal standpoint, he more resembled Dostoevsky's judge and lawyer-spectators, for whom Dmitry's guilt or innocence was overridden by more important legal questions. Fetyukovich, of course, more closely resembles Simpson's main attorney, Johnnie Cochran, who saw the Simpson case as a vehicle for enhancing his national reputation by winning the trial of the century. He too focused not on his client's innocence but on the message that the jury should send to the nation. He, in effect, challenged the jurors to acquit his client even if they thought he was guilty. If one assumes that Cochran knew his client had committed the murder, had received special treatment by the police and the press in the past, and had severed his connections to the black community, one might easily conclude that Cochran's performance was purely self-interested. Was he really the champion of his client? Was he really imprisoned by the system in which he was employed to work for his client against the truth? Or did he not self-servingly use the case—including the defendant, the media, the judge (whom he bullied throughout the trial), and the issues—primarily to serve his own interests? Did the system exist essentially to perpetuate itself or for the lawyer who knew how exploit it for his own ends? Moreover, whereas Fetyukovich did not know his jury, the defense team in the Simpson case had for all intents and purposes selected it in the voir dire, determining the outcome of the trial before it even began. If Cochran knew the case was won as soon as the jury was selected, all his histrionics and oratory, all his posturing about the accursed question of race, could have been to only one end: his own self-aggrandizement.[59] After winning the trial of the century, there was no question who was now the king of the American bar. Had Dostoevsky been alive to cover the case, he might have had to concede that real life had simply outdone anything he could have imagined. For Dostoevsky, an ideological novelist, something is worse than a forum for unsound ideas: an institution lacking all conviction, in which ideas are nothing but instruments of individual self-aggrandizement.

# CHAPTER 5

# The Brothers Karamazov

## Russian Justice

If Dmitry's conviction were a mistake or an error, it might be seen as an understandable aberration in an imperfect world (an "affect" [*affekt*]), like Kornilova's temporary insanity), but, as we have seen, Dostoevsky presents the trial as the inevitable consequence of the legal system that arose from the reforms of 1864. He turns the specific error in Dmitry's trial into a miscarriage of justice, characteristic not only of the jury system but of the new world that gave it birth.

*The Brothers Karamazov,* however, goes beyond a vilification of the jury trial; it presents institutional and noninstitutional alternatives to it, much as "The Russian Monk" presents an alternative to "The Grand Inquisitor." "The Russian Monk" had to serve as a counterargument to Ivan Karamazov's "Grand Inquisitor." Dostoevsky explicitly wrote that Ivan's arguments were logically irrefutable and thus he had to confront them by counterexample. "The Russian Monk" presents a countervision as well as an institutional alternative to "the church" of Ivan Karamazov's "The Grand Inquisitor." Similarly, long before the trial takes place, the chapter "So Be It! So Be It!" presents the ecclesiastic court as an alternative to the secular court, one that concerns itself with criminals rather than crime and with the humane treatment of other human beings rather than law (that is, crime and punishment). But Dostoevsky also presents alternative forms of justice within the context of the jury trial itself. In the last chapter of the novel proper, he in effect proposes a system of resistance within the institution itself, in the form of a largely peasant jury that engages in what we might today call jury nullification—a jury that votes its conscience, not the law.[1] Finally, Dostoevsky proposes a soteriological plan for Dmitry that is paradoxically dependent on Dmitry's conviction in a jury trial—that is, on a judicial error—yet supersedes the jury trial by rendering it spiritually and morally irrelevant with regard to justice and truth. I shall first discuss the "people's jury" as a first line of defense against the jury trial, a force that could resist the jury trial from within because it had remained unincorporated intellectually, morally, and spiritually in the legal reforms of 1864. Then I will examine the novel's ecclesiastic alternative to the post-reform court and the soteriological plot that exploits the court and supersedes it at the same time.

### The Jury: Resistance Within

Dostoevsky liked Russian juries, especially when they were made up of representatives of the people. When Russian juries, in his view, returned the incorrect verdict, he could ascribe the verdict to defects in the system. Jurors would tend toward acquittal if conviction automatically incurred a penalty harsher than they thought appropriate. Despite what Dostoevsky may want us to believe, in reality Russian juries usually had the choice, explained in the judge's instructions, of voting for different degrees of culpability and their corresponding punishments. In *The Brothers Karamazov* the jurors rendered the wrong verdict: they convicted an innocent man. But, according to the novel, they did the best they could. They either did not listen to the attorneys or listened to them but rejected their arguments (casuistry). Because they could act only within the judicial system, and because they could never know that Smerdyakov was the real murderer—a privilege granted only to the reader—they could not have in good conscience voted other than they did. The novel implies that the jurors probably voted unanimously for no extenuating circumstances, fully cognizant that the judge could have imposed an even harsher sentence than the twenty years that he did. They went their own way, successfully resisting the pressures of the institution (*Muzhichki nashi za sebia postoiali*). They did what the narrator could never have done, and what Dostoevsky himself implicitly admitted that he too could not do: listen unempathetically. He was in part outraged by the Zasulich trial because he became sympathetic to a defendant whose acquittal was bound to have serious political repercussions. In the end the greatest success of the jurors was to have resisted empathetic narrative, an issue on which Dostoevsky had made a 180-degree turn.

In contrast to the spectators at the trial, the jurors do not become wrapped up in the duel between the lawyers. The spectators seem less concerned about Dmitry's guilt or innocence than about the performance of Fetyukovich and Ippolit Kirillovich. Inane but ironically relevant comments abound. In response to Fetyukovich's speech one official states: "It would be a shame and a disgrace not to acquit him. . . . If I were the defense attorney, I'd have said straight out: he killed him, but he's not guilty, take it or leave it" (751–52; 15:177). Here Dostoevsky makes a sarcastic reference to the speech of the defense attorney in the Zasulich case: "She committed the crime, but should be acquitted, nevertheless." Dostoevsky takes the comments from the parlous to the ridiculous. Some observers wonder how Ippolit Kirillovich will be received by his wife if Dmitry is convicted; others wonder whether Dmitry will smash up the town if he is acquitted.

Dostoevsky uses the very last remarks of the spectators about Fetyukovich's speech as Greek choral truth. He obviously is preparing the reader for the jury's decision:

"The devil? Yes, the devil's in it all right, where else would he be if not here?"

"Eloquence aside, gentlemen, people can't be allowed to go breaking their fathers' heads with steelyards. Otherwise where will we end up?"

"The chariot, the chariot, remember that?"

"Yes, he made a chariot out of a dung cart."

"And tomorrow a dung cart out of a chariot, 'just to suit his needs.'"

"Folks are clever nowadays. Do we have any truth in Russia, gentlemen, or is there none at all?" (752; 15:177)

If the devil, the prince of falsehood, were to appear anywhere, the novel implies, it would be in court. Fetyukovich has made a cart (the court) into a chariot, but if necessary he could the following day, based on his personal agenda of the moment, turn that chariot back into a cart. Having completed his speech, Fetyukovich brags to his supporters that he knew while he was speaking that the jury was his:

Fetyukovich himself was completely certain of his success. He was surrounded, congratulated, fawned upon.

"There are," he said to one group, as was reported afterwards, "there are invisible threads binding the defense attorney and jurors. They begin and can already be sensed during the speech. I sensed that they were there. You can be assured that the case is ours." (751; 15:176)

Dostoevsky undercuts Fetyukovich's remarks first by ironically—and implicitly—comparing the lawyer's feelings about his oneness with the jury with Alyosha Karamazov's mystical experience in Cana of Galilee (15:328), when Alyosha felt completely at one with all creation. Fetyukovich feels "invisible threads [*niti*] binding the defense attorney and jurors" (751; 15:176)[2] His confidence resembles the belief of Stepan Trofimovich Verkhovensky in *The Possessed*, whom Dostoevsky presents as a foreigner in his own land but who claims that no one knows the people better than he.

Although many Russians, perhaps the majority of the public, including the men who desired Dmitry's conviction, believe that Dmitry will be acquitted, some think that the jury might act contrary to expectations. Some even fear that the jurors' lack of education renders them incapable of understanding, much less appreciating, Fetyukovich's arguments. The narrator tells us that he had essentially the same contemptuous attitude toward the jury as everyone else.

> But I do remember who the twelve jurors consisted of: four of our officials, two merchants, and local peasants and tradesmen. In our society, I remember, long before the trial, the question was asked with some surprise, especially by our ladies: "Can it be that the fatal decision in such a subtle, complex, and psychological case is to be turned over to a bunch of officials, and even to peasants? and "What will some ordinary official make of it, not to mention a peasant? . . . Our Skotoprigonevsk tradesmen are almost peasants themselves, they even handle the plow. Two of them were also in German dress, and perhaps for that reason looked dirtier and more unseemly than the other four. So that indeed the thought might well enter one's head, *as it entered mine*, for example, as soon as I took a look at them: "What can such people possibly grasp of such a case?" Nevertheless their faces made a certain strangely imposing and almost threatening impression; they were stern and frowning. (659–60; 15:92–93; emphasis added)

If the public wonders about the capacity of the jurors to understand the complexities of the trial, the lawyers should have as well, especially Ippolit Kirillovich, who is, after all, a resident of the town. Neither lawyer thought that a jury could resist his oratorical powers. By emphasizing that the tradesmen and officials are similar in education and culture to the peasants, Dostoevsky separates the jurors from all the other participants and makes them, comparatively speaking, a bastion of practical wisdom.

What does the jury do? It takes only one hour to find Dmitry guilty of premeditated murder without extenuating circumstances. Although Russian juries did not have to arrive at unanimous verdicts even in criminal cases, their speed in reaching a decision, as I have suggested, probably indicates unanimity. Though the lawyers completely misunderstood the jury, the jury understood the lawyers perfectly. Although the jurors did not understand the literary allusions (most had probably never read a book), the political allegories, and the psychological analyses, they understood the lawyers' intentions. The Russian peasants were traditionally suspicious of the fine talk (the words) of their former masters, and they would have seen that each lawyer was trying to manipulate them in his own way. But the attorneys' rhetoric is completely wasted on them. Fetyukovich at first makes a brilliant case for reasonable doubt. But when he argues that even if his client killed his father, he should not be condemned for parricide, the lawyer probably cuts the few threads that bind him with the jury. Like Ippolit Kirillovich, Fetyukovich asks the jury to send a message, but it is a message that they cannot countenance. Fetyukovich challenges the jury to acquit a man whom he himself believes guilty. Had he not pushed the jurors so far, had he not added insult to injury by cynically justifying an acquittal in terms of Christian salvation, had he not cavalierly presented the case for reasonable doubt, he might, given the leniency of Russian juries in Dostoevsky's estimation, have persuaded the jury to seriously consider extenuating circumstances. Fetyukovich, in effect, forces the jury to send a message of its own: to call a crime a crime and to assert the difference between good and evil. The only way it can do that, given the arguments of the lawyers, is to make the message perfectly unambiguous. Fetyukovich turns out to be the worst possible attorney for Dmitry—or the best, if Dmitry's conviction is seen as part of the author's higher soteriological plan.

## Ecclesiastic Courts

Although both "The Russian Monk" and "The Grand Inquisitor" function as antitheses—or antiworlds—not only in relation to each other but also in relation to the world of the Western court, "A Judicial

Error" has a more direct counterpart or antithesis even earlier in the novel, a virtual "Judicial Correction." Book 2, chapter 6, "So Be It! So Be It!" includes a discussion of Ivan Karamazov's "journal article on the subject of the ecclesiastic courts and the scope of their rights, written in reply to a churchman who wrote an entire book on the subject" (60; 14:56). In this scene the father and all the brothers are preparing to meet with Father Zosima at the monastery. Alyosha is already present when Ivan and Fedor Karamazov arrive, along with a local landowner of liberal sentiments, Miusov. They are soon joined by Father Zosima, the hieromonk Iosif (the monastery librarian), Father Paissy, and another learned hieromonk. Dmitry is yet to arrive. In response to Father Zosima's question regarding the grounds for Ivan's rejection of the separation of church and state, Ivan maintains that although the church and state will probably coexist for a long time, the assimilation of the state should be the ultimate goal of the church. According to Ivan, exactly the opposite is occurring now. Ivan's article looks forward to his poem, "The Grand Inquisitor," an ecclesiastic dystopia—from the author's point of view—in which the boundaries between church and state have been erased. Ivan's journal article focuses on the punishment of crime and the regeneration of the criminal. He speaks the same salvific language as Fetyukovich—or Dostoevsky in the Kornilova case:

> Now, on the other hand, take the Church's own view of crime: should it not change from the present, almost pagan view, and from the mechanical cutting of the infected member, as is done now for the preservation of society, and transform itself [*preobrazit'sia*], fully now and not falsely, into the idea of the regeneration [*vozrozhdenie*] of man anew, of his resurrection [*voskresenie*] and salvation [*spasenie*]? (64; 14:59)

Father Paissy takes issue with the book but for different reasons than Ivan. He rejects the author's position that the church is a kingdom not of this world and therefore the church should have as little to do with this world as possible. He also identifies the assumption of the church by the state, the Roman model, as "the third temptation of the Devil," a temptation to which Ivan's Grand Inquisitor will later succumb. But all this, it turns out, is a preamble for another lecture by Father Zosima in which he presents an alternative to the Western court based on Russian and Orthodox principles: in other words, a *pro* that anticipates the "contra" of "A Judicial Error." Though Zosima agrees with Ivan about the terrible consequences of civil punishment by the courts, he argues for the church that works not through coercion or excommunication but through compassion. Thus Father Zosima offers an alternative to the unacceptable situation of the civil court.

The church, Zosima argues, must focus primarily on reintegrating the convict into the Christian community. The contemporary court not only *mechanically* cuts the convict off from society, it revels in its triumph; once it has finished its business, full of hatred, it becomes completely indifferent to the convict's fate, leaving him in complete despair. It does not understand that the convict is also a brother in Christ. Because the court represents untruth, any compromises that the church makes with the court must undermine its own truth and authority. Although Father Zosima bases his opposition of church and state on different principles than Ivan does, Zosima's polarization of church and state is no less total, no less uncompromising. One bargains with the devil at one's own risk, and one does not bargain with God.

> But the Church, like a mother, tender and loving, withholds from active punishment, for even without her punishment, the wrongdoer is already too painfully punished by the state court [*gosudarstvennyi sud*], and at least someone should pity him. And it withholds above all because the judgment [*sud*] of the Church is the only judgment [*sud*] that contains the truth [*istina*], and for that reason it cannot, essentially and morally, be combined with any other judgment [*sud*], even in a temporary compromise. Here it is not possible to strike bargains. (65; 14:60)

The civil court's reprehensible relationship to the convict, its determination solely to punish and separate, must reinforce the contemporary church's commitment and parental relationship with the convict. Perhaps because of that filial relationship, the criminal will accept the judgment of the church much more willingly than that of the civil court. But more important, Father Zosima's maximalist position regarding truth, and the court as an embodiment of untruth, directs his thoughts away from the phenomenal world of the present to visions of future transfigurations. The resolution of the judicial question will occur when the Jewish question, the Russian question, and the human question are resolved, that is, not in human time but in transfigured time.

"It is true," the elder smiled, "that now Christian society itself is not yet ready, and stands only on seven righteous men; but as they are never wanting, it abides firmly all the same, awaiting its complete transfiguration from society as still an almost pagan organization, into one universal and sovereign Church. And so be it, so be it, if only at the end of time, for this alone is destined to be fulfilled! And there is no need to trouble oneself with times and seasons, for the mystery of times and seasons is in the wisdom of God, in his foresight, and in his love. And that which by human reckoning may still be rather remote, by divine predestination may already be standing on the eve of its appearance, at the door. And so be that, too! So be it!" (66; 14:61)

For all intents and purposes the court (the apotheosis of the state) and the church represent two fundamentally different and irreconcilable realms, with the church representing truth and justice (*istina/pravda* and *spravedlivost'*) and the court representing its exact antithesis, injustice and untruth. The court does not only stand outside the truth; it embodies the lie, "still almost a pagan organization," as any examination of its treatment of the criminal attests. If the church must not compromise Christ's truth by entering into compromises with the court, its truth cannot be realized on Earth while the state holds any power. Thus at the end of the series of articles on the Jewish question, or in his ruminations over his first wife's coffin (20:172–73), Dostoevsky cannot see the realization of the truth in humanity's present state of being, in humanity's present nature; the truth will be realized only when the nature of people will have radically changed: "For in the resurrection they neither marry, nor are given in marriage, but are as the angels of God in heaven" (Mt 22:30). In other words, if it can happen on Earth, then it will happen only at the end of time. Father Zosima considers any temporal considerations—the remoteness of such a transfiguration—insignificant in the presence of the divine truth. Given such views, "a civil judicial error" is a tautology. Dostoevsky presents the second Kornilova trial and the temporary reconciliation of ethnic and religious groups at the funeral of Hindenburg as miracles, like Father Zosima's seven righteous men whose task is not to reform society but to keep the ideal alive in preparation for the miraculous transfiguration when time shall be no more. Thus, by its vary nature, the court, contrary to the statements of both defense and prosecuting attorneys, can hold no hope for Russia. It is the main symbol of the problem, not the solution. Justice and the court are incompatible categories: justice could not have emerged from Dmitry's trial, a trial based on the terrible middle ground of adjudication, compromise, and the resolution of conflict through verbal warfare.

On the other hand, "So Be It! So Be It!" represents a radically different kind of antithesis to "A Judicial Error" than "The Russian Monk" represents for "The Grand Inquisitor." "The Russian Monk" persuades not by its argument but by its iconography, by its hagiography (*zhitie*). Its authority is guaranteed by its genre. Father Zosima's statements and philosophy in "So Be It! So Be It!" however, cannot enjoy the same privilege as they do in his hagiography, for Dostoevsky presents them not as a part of hagiography but as part of a heated argument. Christ does not argue with the Grand Inquisitor, but here, in a sense, Father Zosima does, and he argues a maximalist position in a language that is strikingly similar to Ivan Karamazov's own. Father Zosima steps out of the world of hagiography and enters the world of the novel. Furthermore, he warns against the contamination that the church risks when it becomes associated with the court or with the state. One might argue that this is exactly what occurs when Zosima's word becomes enmeshed in an ideological argument against the courts.[3] "So Be It! So Be It!" may function as an anticipated response to "A Judicial Error," providing a standard against which the court must be judged, but it does not constitute the same kind of hagiographic word that we find in "The Russian Monk," before which all interpretation must bow down—despite the repetition of the hagiographic "So Be It! So Be It!" ("*Budi, budi*"). "The Russian Monk" and "So Be It! So Be It!" also constitute very different antitheses to the world of the court, or the modern world. "The Russian Monk" ecstatically prophesies the realization of truth, "when time will be no more" in the present through mystic experience; "So Be It! So Be It!" utopically prophesies the universal realization of justice in the distant future through humanity's transfiguration. Both must bypass the modern world, and thus also the world of the novel, the world in which the three brothers, who represent humanity in general and Russia in particular, seem at times hopelessly mired.

Some have maintained that Father Zosima's views reflect the influence of Russian Orthodox thinking on Dostoevsky's representation of the law. In his provocative article "The Categories of Law and Grace in Dostoevsky's Poetics," Ivan Esaulov, using a Lotmanian binary paradigm of Russian culture similar to the one discussed in chapter 1, argues that, for the Orthodox, the world has been divided between the incompatible dispensations of law and grace ever since Metropolitan Hilarion's eleventh-century "Sermon on Law and Grace."[4] Once grace superseded the law, the law could have no place in Christian society. The moral world is thus by its very nature antinomical to the legal world. The law may in fact refuse to defer to grace, but it should, and where it does not, the soul of the world is in great jeopardy. Because for Dostoevsky all "legal space" is alienated from grace, "the predominance in human relationships of juridical (legal) criteria to the detriment of relations based on Grace as understood in the Gospels, is an unfruitful and dangerous return of humanity to the pre-Christian state of the world."[5] Esaulov quotes the Orthodox theologian N. Afanasyev to bring home his point:

> By its very nature, Grace excludes the law [*pravo*] just as Grace, having overcome it by fulfillment, excluded the Old Testament [*zakon*]. . . . The end of the Old Testament law [*zakon*] is at the same time the end for the secular law [*pravo*]. . . . Christianity proclaimed the surmounting of the law in human relationships in a new life in Grace. . . . This was not a new Law based on legal principles, since what Christ said in the Sermon on the Mount does not and cannot be fitted into a concept of law. . . . The acknowledgment of law [*pravo*] is a rejection of Grace by which the members of the Church live in Christ. . . . It is a *return to the law* [*zakon*], and if there is justification by law, then Christ died in vain.[6]

It is not surprising that almost all of Esaulov's examples come from *The Brothers Karamazov*, in which Dostoevsky takes direct aim at the legal reforms of 1864. Esaulov, however, glosses over the counterevidence before *The Brothers Karamazov*. Contrary to not recognizing or valuing Russian legal space, we have seen that Dostoevsky supported the 1864 legal reforms and in 1867 stated that the spiritual regeneration of the Russian people depended on the speedy implementation of the new Russian courts. In the Kornilova case Dostoevsky came close to likening the proceedings of the court to a Russian Orthodox religious service. *The Brothers Karamazov* reflects Dostoevsky's disillusionment with the jury trial arising from the Zasulich affair and the political trials directly preceding it. Esaulov can make such a strong case for his views precisely because he relies on *The Brothers Karamazov*, where his argument finds substantial validation. We may infer from Zosima's theology that the ecclesiastic "courts" are not a solution to the rampant juridical hegemony of the modern world but an alternative that must be resorted to until true theocracy can be achieved, at which time the state will be incorporated into the church and the law will completely give way to grace. All the attempts that are being made to adapt the jury trial to the people's religious and moral values and sensibilities are in vain. The jury trial is not only antithetical to truth and justice, it is in Dostoevsky's world worse: it is irrelevant.

### Dmitry, Salvation, and the Court

Dostoevsky, as we have seen, offers a jury of representatives of the people, at best, as a negative alternative for achieving justice. It can reach a more just verdict, relatively speaking, only by actively resisting the powers of the court, by acting in a way that baffles all those who have accepted the court as the most reasonable, civilized, and equitable means of achieving justice. It also convicts a legally innocent man. The ecclesiastic court is presented as a positive alternative but a hypothetical one at best and one that can be achieved only when the state is incorporated into the church, when law as we know it ceases to exist. Dostoevsky knows that no state would willingly cede all "legal" authority to the church. And Dostoevsky himself would probably have rejected any theocracy achieved and maintained through the coercion proposed by Ivan Karamazov. For Dostoevsky such a theocracy is, in fact, an example of the church absorbed by the state, not the state absorbed by the church. In any case, such a solution of "one universal and sovereign Church" is not of our time, and it could never affect any of the characters in Dostoevsky's novel. Father Zosima implies, as Dostoevsky does elsewhere ("The Jewish Question"), that the solution may need to await the complete transformation of humankind. For Dostoevsky the truly righteous man, Dr. Hindenburg, can miraculously unite the disparate nationalities and religions of the borderlands through Christian acts of charity. But he can do so only for a moment. The duty of all Christians is to have faith that a time will come when society will be completely transformed, when heaven will come down on Earth, when justice and truth, one and the same, will rule forever. But this utopic ("no place") "no time" is the stuff of hagiography, not of the novel. When there is "no time," there will be no story. Where there is a perfect coincidence of word and truth, there can be no irony, no novel.[7]

But Dmitry exists in novelistic time. Whereas we all may be saved together at the end of time, individuals may be saved—*The Brothers Karamazov* implies—in community with others, in novelistic time. And so may Dmitry. And if Dmitry, then everyone. A place and time must be given for Dmitry's personal salvation outside Father Zosima's vision of a final transfiguration, outside a universal church, and, of course, outside the court. The last line of the novel proper talks about Dmitry's complete ruin in terms of the legal system. "And so they have finished off our Mitya [*I pokonchili nashego Miten'ku*]." But this is the limited and flawed view of the spectators at the trial. The novel implies that the verdict presages not Dmitry's ruin but the beginning stage, or one of the beginning stages, of Dmitry's road toward *potential* salvation. Dostoevsky adumbrated a similar regeneration for the hero in the epilogue of *Crime and Punishment*. But the circumstances and character of the protagonists in *Crime and Punishment* and *The Brothers Karamazov* differ so radically that Dostoevsky requires a very different resurrection plot for Dmitry than he did for Raskolnikov, preferably an "out-of-court settlement" that would paradoxically exploit the court to achieve its extralegal, mystical ends. But just as Dostoevsky does not present a counterargument to the "Grand Inquisitor" but a counter-story (Father Zosima's hagiography), so he does not present a counterargument to "A Judicial Error" but a counterplot. It is a soteriological plot, exactly the opposite, of course, of the salvation plot imagined by Dmitry's lawyer, Fetyukovich. But before we can fully understand the court's role—or lack of it—in Dmitry's fate, we need to trace the evolution of the "other" plot.

Judging from his notebooks, Dostoevsky was seriously contemplating the ideas of parricide, mistaken conviction, terrible suffering, and resurrection from the dead as early as the 1850s. The first chapter of *Notes from the House of the Dead* includes a story based on the life of Dmitry Ilyinsky, a twenty-two-year-old ensign from the nobility. Invariably jovial and thoughtless, Ilyinsky talks about his murdered father with such levity and insensitivity that the narrator can only assume some unknown constitutional defect of character. On the other hand, the narrator says he "never noticed any particular cruelty in him" and he "did not believe in that crime. . . . But people from his town who knew all the details of his story told me all about his case. The facts were so clear that it was impossible to doubt them [*Fakty byli tak iasny, chto nevozmozhno bylo ne verit'*]" (4:16).

It turned out that Ilyinsky was unjustly convicted. He was released after serving ten years of a twenty-year sentence.[8] Only while writing the second part of *Notes from the House of the Dead*, in 1862, did Dostoevsky learn of the prisoner's innocence. In part 2, chapter 7, the author included the following note:

> The publisher of *Notes from the House of the Dead* has recently received information from Siberia that the criminal was actually innocent and suffered ten years' penal servitude in vain [*desiat' let stradal v katorzhnoi rabote naprasno*]; that his innocence was officially recognized by the court; that the real criminals were found and have confessed and that the unfortunate man [*neschastnyi*] has already been released from prison. The publisher cannot doubt the reliability of this report. (4:195)

Because Ilyinsky was convicted in 1847, almost two decades before the implementation of the jury trial in Russia, he was "tried" in front of a commission, not a jury. Thus the original judicial error was not even made by a court. Nevertheless, the Ilyinsky case was fully investigated: there are seven extant volumes of materials relating to the case (4:284).[9] Had the real culprits not been found, Ilyinsky would have had to serve out his full term. Given his character—at least as described in the novel—he would probably have survived his imprisonment. Dmitry's twenty-year sentence thus does not necessarily presage his ruin.

With regard to Ilyinsky, in *Notes from the House of the Dead* Dostoevsky places his narrator (and himself as well) in the same unprivileged, unknowing position as he places the characters and the jury in *The Brothers Karamazov*. He is perplexed by the glaring disparity between Ilyinsky's levity and his horrible deed. The narrator believes and does not believe in the crime at the same time. Because he writes that "the facts were so clear it was impossible to doubt them," we can assume that had the reform court been in place at the time of the original conviction, and had the narrator been a juror, however much he may have disbelieved that this man was guilty, he would have had to convict. He would have acted as the jury did in *The Brothers Karamazov* because "it was impossible to doubt" the facts of the case—just as the jury does not doubt the facts in either *The Brothers Karamazov* or the parricide case of Peter Nazarov, from Staraia Russa, the site of Dostoevsky's summer home in the 1870s.[10]

Of course, Dostoevsky's attitude toward Ilyinsky's and Dmitry's innocence differs significantly. The editor-narrator of *Notes from the House of the Dead* states that the falsely accused prisoner had suffered in prison for ten years in vain (*naprasno*). His fate was profoundly tragic because he had been crushed by his horrible (*uzhasnyi*) sentence while still a youth. From the perspective of 1862 the wrongly convicted parricide not only did not benefit from his prison experience, he probably was permanently crippled by it. Dostoevsky implicitly contrasts the fate of the narrator at the end of the novel, who sees himself resurrected from the dead ("Resurrection from the dead. What a glorious moment! [*Voskresen'e iz mertvykh . . . Ekaia slavnaia minuta!*]" (4:232) with that of Ilyinsky, who has suffered in vain, tragically lost his youth, and now faces an uncertain future.[11] Although Dostoevsky recalls that the most unendurable part of his prison experience was the common convicts' hostility toward all members of the nobility, class does not seem to be an issue in the prisoners' attitude toward Ilyinsky. "The other prisoners despised him not for the crime, which was never mentioned, but for his foolishness, his inability to behave properly" (748; 4:16).

Dostoevsky's 12 September 1874 notebook entry for a new novel reveals a radically new conception of the Ilyinsky prototype. The plan includes a rivalry between brothers (but only two) as well as enmity between father and son. But the salvation plot that had been tied exclusively to the narrator in *Notes from the House of the Dead* migrates to the unjustly convicted older brother, who is serving a twenty-year sentence for killing his father.

> A scene in prison. They want to kill him [*ego khotiat ubit'*]. Administration. He doesn't betray. The convicts swear fraternity to him. The commandant of the prison reproaches him for killing his father.
>
> Twelve years later the brother comes to see him. Scene, where they *silently* understand each other. Another seven years pass. The younger brother has attained rank and position, but is tormented, depressed. He reveals to his wife that he is the murderer. I killed him. "Why did you tell me?" He goes to his brother. The wife also runs to him. On her knees the wife asks the convict to remain silent, to save her husband.

The convict says: "I've gotten used to it [*Ia privyk*]." They are reconciled. "Even without that, you are punished," the older says.

The younger brother's birthday. The guests have gathered. He comes in: "I am the murderer." They think he has had a stroke.

The end: the other has returned. The younger brother is at a transport point. He is being sent away. The younger brother asks the older brother to be a father to his children.

"You have gone on the right path."[12]

The younger brother, the real parricide and falsifier of the evidence, combines plot and personality traits of both Ivan Karamazov and the mysterious stranger who visits Father Zosima. The older brother, like Raskolnikov in *Crime and Punishment*, initially experiences the enmity of his fellow inmates but later undergoes a radical transformation in the first year in prison. Soon all the prisoners swear fraternity to him. After nineteen years the older brother has gotten used to prison and is willing to forgive his younger brother, who, he understands, has suffered on the outside as much as he has suffered on the inside. The sentence of twenty years remains unchanged to the very end.

Because the older brother is presented very much like Dmitry, the transformation that takes place in prison is especially significant for *The Brothers Karamazov*. Despite what Alyosha, Ivan, Katerina Ivanovna, Grushenka, and Fetyukovich say about Dmitry's inability to bear his suffering in Siberia for twenty years, all the earlier allusions to Dmitry's fate project his survival in prison. The 1874 notebook outline even increases the incarceration from ten to twenty years. On the other hand, Dostoevsky does not "sentence" Dmitry to life imprisonment (*vechnaia katorga*), which was the sentence meted out in 1875 to the parricide Peter Nazarov.[13] Such a sentence would have deprived Dmitry of all possibility of regeneration, which entails eventual reintegration into the community.

These early plans do not predict Dmitry's path, but they at least show Dostoevsky as entertaining a view diametrically opposite to those who reject the possibility of Dmitry's resurrection in prison. Without a salvation plot—that is, the possibility of Dmitry's salvation in Siberia —the trial scene makes little sense: at best it would be a brilliant Juvenalian satire, at worst a serious artistic lapse. But there have been many Dmitry doubters in and outside the novel, and their doubts are not unfounded psychologically. The doubts grow out of Dmitry's character.

Although Hingley blithely comments that "Dmitry is not afraid of twenty years in the mines," in reality Dmitry is deeply divided about what would be in his best interest.[14] R. P. Blackmur emphasizes the ephemerality of Dmitry's dreams and intentions, comparing Dmitry's dream of the babe unfavorably ("a lower version") with Alyosha's dream of Christ at Cana: "Dmitry is one of those for whom rebirth is not permanent, but only a deeper form of a New Year's resolution . . . an onion for the moment."[15] Ronald Hingley implies that for Dmitry to suffer twenty years in prison so defies common sense that not only will Dmitry have to escape to America but that Dostoevsky is wise to give Dmitry that way out.[16] And Nathan Rosen, despite his relatively favorable presentation of Dmitry's moral ideal, states that Dmitry "may instead accept the unheroic destiny urged by Alyosha of escaping with Grushenka to America. Dostoevskii leaves this deliberately open as if he could not come to a decision himself."[17] Some critics formulaically emphasize that Dmitry must suffer for his sins and the sins of others and leave the matter at that.[18] But Alyosha, Ivan, and Katerina Ivanovna also believe, or want to believe, for their own reasons that Dmitry will not survive such a severe sentence. That is why they are actively engaged in arranging Dmitry's escape to America. Alyosha offers the following casuistic justification for Dmitry's escape. It is, of course, the same one that Fetyukovich uses:

> Listen, brother, once and for all. . . . Listen, then, you're not ready, and such a cross is not for you. . . . You wanted to regenerate another man in yourself through suffering; I say just remember that other man always, all your life, and wherever you escape to—and that is enough for you. That you did not escape that great cross will only serve to make you feel a still greater duty to yourself, and through this constant feeling from now on, all your life, you will do more for your regeneration, perhaps, than if you were *there*. (763–64; 15:185)

But at times Dmitry also does not believe that he will have the strength to bear his sentence; rather than rising from the underground mines, he says, he will turn bitter and curse his fate.

> "And here's something else I wanted to tell you," Mitya continued in a suddenly ringing voice, "if they start beating me on the way, or *there*, I won't let them, I'll kill someone, and they'll shoot me. . . . I'm not ready!

Not strong enough to take it! I wanted to sing a 'hymn,' yet I can't stand the guards' talking down to me! I'd endure anything for Grusha, everything . . . except beatings, that is. . . . But they won't let her go *there*." (763; 15:185)

Dmitry also does not know how he will survive his sentence if Grushenka is not permitted to accompany him. "And without Grusha what would I do there underground with a sledgehammer? I'll take the sledgehammer and smash my own head with it!" (595; 15:34). Dostoevsky takes away the salvific helper that he gave Raskolnikov in *Crime and Punishment*: a Sonya Marmeladova.

But lest we lend too much weight to the position that Dmitry is unequal to his punishment, we must remember that it is Fetyukovich who makes the most convincing argument regarding Dmitry's inability to bear his suffering in Siberia. If his client is sent to Siberia, Fetyukovich argues, he will lose his only chance for moral regeneration; it will mean his certain destruction. Fetyukovich makes for Dmitry exactly the same argument, almost word for word, that Dostoevsky made for Kornilova. Has Dostoevsky made Fetyukovich the ultimate authority on Dmitry Karamazov's expiatory suffering and spiritual renewal?

Moreover, Dostoevsky presents the escape to America, especially to his contemporary readers, as not only completely inappropriate for Dmitry but, literarily speaking, patently ridiculous. Dmitry represents Russian earth; he cannot receive salvation by watering with his tears the soil of America, the quintessential symbol of materialistic individualism. In *Crime and Punishment*, going to America means committing suicide, as Svidrigaylov makes explicit.[19] All those planning Dmitry's escape have their own reasons for not wanting Dmitry to go to Siberia, but Dmitry understands that these reasons are not and should not be his. If he has to escape, he must do so for himself, not for Katerina Ivanovna or Ivan, or even for Alyosha. Besides, to escape because others think he cannot bear the burden is demeaning; it would force Dmitry to assume the role that Ivan inscribes for him in "The Grand Inquisitor" as the archetypical representative of the multitudes who, no longer able to bear the "gift" of their suffering and freedom, must be relieved of their burden for their own good. Hearing Alyosha's rationalizations for escape, Dmitry laughs; he accuses his brother of reasoning like a Jesuit, for he sees that Alyosha's words are essentially a paraphrase of the devil's (Fetyukovich's) words on spiritual resurrection.

Too honest to conceal the truth, Alyosha answers Dmitry's smile with one of his own.

"'That's how the Jesuits talk, isn't it? Just as we are doing?' 'Yes,' Alyosha smiled gently" (724; 15:186).[20] Dmitry has already told Alyosha his feelings about responsibility and suffering:

> But on the other hand, my conscience? I will be running away from suffering. I was shown a path—and I rejected the path; there was a way of purification—I did an about-face. Ivan says that a man "with good inclinations" can be of more use in America than under the ground [that is, forced labor in the mines of Siberia— G.R.]. Well, and where will our underground hymn take place? Forget America, American means vanity again. A sign has come, I reject the sign. I have a way of salvation and I turn my back on it. And there's a lot of swindling in America, too, I think. To run away from crucifixion! (595; 15:34)[21]

Dostoevsky implicitly disparages the plan for escape even more by making it almost identical to the plot of Nicholas Chernyshevsky's *What Is to Be Done?*, which he had devastatingly parodied in both *Notes from the Underground* and *Crime and Punishment.* Lopukhov, one of the heroes of *What Is to Be Done?* escapes to America with his wife, makes a fortune, and returns to Russia incognito. Because in Dostoevsky's lifetime *What Is to Be Done* was far more popular and influential than any of his own novels, every contemporary reader would have recognized the parodic intent of Dmitry's hypothetical escape to America.

Moreover, the novel shows that everyone is wrong about Dmitry's potential, even Dmitry. Dmitry's potential is something that can never be known—or at best only retrospectively—especially by the court. The trial cannot be as relevant to him as it was for Kornilova; it cannot embody a form of Russian justice—even despite itself. Alyosha is ashamed of his lack of faith in Dmitry's ability to bear his suffering in Siberia, especially because he has just written a hagiographical account of Father Zosima's dissolute youth uncannily similar to that of Dmitry's, in which a terrible blow, again similar to the one experienced by Dmitry, turns Father Zosima's life around. The charge of parricide provides the shock that precipitates Dmitry's dreams of the starving babes, in which he implicitly acknowledges his responsibility not only for the death of his father—which he wished and willed, and for which he prepared the way—but for all suffering, especially for the starving peasant mothers and their children. Richard Peace calls the dream the expression of Dmitry's parricidal guilt.[22]

Dmitry's dream goes directly back to the vision of Father Zosima's brother, who, like Dmitry, wonders why everyone does "not embrace and kiss," does not "sing joyful songs" (507; 14:458).

"Why are they blackened with such black misery, why don't they feed the wee one?" . . . And he feels within himself that, though his questions have no reason or sense, he still certainly wants to ask in just that way, and he should ask in just that way. And he also feels a tenderness such as he has never known before surging up in his heart, he wants to weep, he wants to do something for them all, so that the wee one will no longer cry, so that the blackened dried-up mother of the wee one will not cry either, so that there will be no more tears in anyone from that moment on, and it must be done at once, at once, without delay, with all his Karamazov unrestraint. (507–08; 14:456–57)

Dmitry explicates the meaning of this dream to Alyosha on the day before the trial:

Why did I have a dream about a "wee one" at such a moment? "Why is the wee one poor?" It was a prophecy for me at that moment? It's for the wee one that I will go. Because everyone is guilty for everyone else. For all the "wee ones," because there are little children and big children. All people are "wee ones." And I'll go for all of them, because there must be someone who will go for all of them. I didn't like father, but I must go. I accept! All of this came to me here . . . within these peeling walls. (591; 15:31)

Dmitry may have doubts about whether he will be "strong enough to take it . . . to sing a hymn" in prison (763; 15:185). That he will is presented as a mystery. "But it is possible, it is possible: the old grief, by a great mystery of human life, gradually passes into quiet, tender joy; instead of young, ebullient blood [*iunaia kipuchaia krov'*] comes a mild, serene old age" (292; 14:265). Certainly, when Zosima mentions the riotous blood of youth, he is not speaking of Job—or of Alyosha and Ivan—but of himself and the Karamazov brother that most resembles him in youth, Dmitry.

Moreover, the more we see Dmitry's court sentence in symbolic (and mystical) rather than psychological terms, the less literally we are asked to take those twenty years. The twenty years remain solely a physical and psychological reality only when seen as *chronos*. When seen as a higher form of *kairos,* or in chiliastic or millennial time— that is, as part of a divine plan, a part for which Dmitry is predestined —Dmitry's sentence and fate appear otherwise. Father Zosima again provides the foundation for this kairotic interpretation of Dmitry's fate in his millenarian vision of truth's victorious reign on Earth.

> And there is no need to trouble oneself with times and seasons, for the mystery of times and seasons is in the wisdom of God, in his foresight, and in his love. And that which by human reckoning may still be rather remote, by divine predestination may already be standing on the eve of its appearance, at the door. And so be that, too! So be it. (66; 14:61)

Because the characters in *The Brothers Karamazov,* including, at times, Dmitry himself, look at the long sentence in psychological and phenomenal categories, they cannot but view it as a terrible waste. Indeed, Dostoevsky himself had reacted to the news about Ilyinsky's vindication in much the same way. Seen from the perspective of Father Zosima, Dmitry's sentence of twenty years becomes a spiritual unity, not a long series of meaningless moments. The meaning of "times and seasons" is beyond our ken; it is a mystery and cannot be understood, only believed in. Fetyukovich argues everything mystical—all that cannot be understood by reason, all that belongs to religion and is accepted on faith—must remain outside the realm of real life. Zosima asserts the opposite: The most important things in life can be understood only otherwise, that the highest form of understanding is faith, acceptance of God's plan. In Mikhail Bulgakov's *The Master and Margarita,* Pontius Pilate is compensated kairotically by his final reconciliation with Jesus. He suffers nineteen hundred years for a murder he did not commit but for which he is responsible.

The role that incarceration will play in Dmitry's fate is partly worked out within the novel itself. The first vision of mutual responsibility for innocent suffering comes to Dmitry during the interrogation. But his realization that he also needs to take responsibility and suffer for the murder of his hated father, a crime he did not commit, comes to him only while in prison. There is no doubt that the first year or the first years of Dmitry's incarceration, especially without Grushenka, will be hard; Dmitry also seems an unlikely character to play the Russian Job. But that is the salvation plot that Dostoevsky needs him for. Dmitry's salvation is not meant for him alone; it is part of a much larger project. For Dostoevsky, Dmitry's ability to play this role is essential not only to his own salvation but all of Russia's. If Dmitry can endure his suffering he will not only "disprove" "The Grand Inquisitor" more effectively than the "Russian Monk"—he will demonstrate the strength of the Russian people. Dmitry must not only take on the suffering of others, he must come to understand the "justice" of his punishment and reject the judicial idea of commensurate punishment and suffering: punishment that fits the crime, the foundation of almost all law. Like Job, Dmitry must bear his suffering with a song of praise from the bowels of the earth. Dostoevsky, like God, delivers Dmitry up to the devil to be tested. The punishment therefore cannot be understood in terms of rational commensurability—it is by definition irrationally commensurate and mystical; it is beyond explanation and beyond psychology. According to Zosima, the greatness of Job's story lies in:

> this very mystery—that the passing earthly image and eternal truth here touched. In the face of earthly truth, the enacting of the eternal truth is accomplished. . . . "And Job praising God, does not only serve him, but will also serve his whole creation, from generation to generation and unto ages of ages," for to this he was destined [*ibo k tomu i prednaznachen byl*]. (292; 14:265)

Dmitry's symbolic and typological role as a representative of the Russian nobility provides another reason for Dostoevsky's differential treatment of Dmitry and Kornilova: why Dmitry must suffer for a crime he did not commit and why she should be acquitted of a crime she did commit. Dostoevsky argues for her acquittal because he thinks that penal servitude will bring about the ruin of her child and effectively eliminate the possibility of her spiritual renewal and her reintegration into the community. Although Mikolka, the peasant in *Crime and Punishment* who confesses to Raskolnikov's murder, shows that the cult of suffering—of taking on the suffering of others—has deep roots in the Russian people, Dostoevsky conceives of the representatives of the people in these trials as victims still suffering from the effects of hundreds of years of serfdom, still victimized by the upper and educated classes of Russian society. They must not undergo any additional suffering; they are the suffering mothers and babes that lead Dmitry to an understanding of his responsibility to other human beings. They are the ones that the Dmitrys must suffer for, in expiation, for the centuries-long exploitation of mothers and babes by the Karamazovs. Dostoevsky presents Kornilova's acquittal as a social action by which the jurors, understanding their debt to the people, transcend their class and cultural interests and take responsibility for their past by giving one of the people a chance for resurrection. Father Zosima's spiritual renewal begins when he strikes his servant a blow to his face for a trivial reason, thus understanding his brother Markel's words urging all men to act *as servants to their servants.* Dmitry badly humiliates the clerk Snegiryov. He also traumatizes Snegiryov's son, Ilyusha, by beating up his father in his son's presence, an incident that may have precipitated Ilyusha's death from consumption. Dmitry must suffer not only for himself but for his class and for his country.

Dostoevsky's real polemic with the law, then, and not only in "A Judicial Error," centers on the issue of responsibility. Invariably, the contrast is made between Father Zosima's idea of universal responsibility and the Grand Inquisitor's of absolute relativism. Though radically different ideas about justice ensue from these notions, they ultimately derive from the same premise: the inadequacies relating to crime and punishment under the law. Part of Ivan's purpose in telling Alyosha about the atrocities committed against innocent children is to show that there can be no commensurate punishment, human or divine, for these crimes, no punishment that can or should satisfy us. In his narration about the little boy who is torn apart in front of his mother's eyes by a landowner's dogs, Ivan compels Alyosha to agree to mete out justice in the real world.

> "I believe the general was later declared incompetent to administer his estates. Well . . . what to do with him? Shoot him? Shoot him for our moral satisfaction? Speak Alyoshka!"
>
> "Shoot him!" Alyosha said softly, looking up at his brother with a sort of pale, twisted smile. (243; 14:221)

But Ivan mocks this retribution: "To shoot him for our moral satisfaction." There can be no commensurate punishment for such an atrocity. Ivan postulates atonement of the child's suffering but cannot understand how it possibly could be done—on Earth or in heaven.

> Not worth it, because her tears remain unredeemed [*neiskuplennye*]. They must be redeemed otherwise there can be no harmony. But how, how will you redeem them [*iskupish'*]? Is it possible? Can they be redeemed by being avenged [*otomshcheny*]? But what do I care if they are avenged, what do I care if the tormentors are in hell, what can hell set right here, if these ones have already been tormented? . . . I do not, finally, want the mother to embrace the tormentor who let his dogs tear her son to pieces. (245; 14:223)

Ivan pushes the issue so far that he obliterates the category of incommensurability. It is not a question of the punishment's not fitting the crime; the whole idea of punishment in the face of such crimes is itself an affront, a sop for our moral feelings. The Russian word for atonement, at least here, suggests the idea of compensation, of paying for a crime. Given Ivan's view about divine justice, it is not surprising that he views the law almost as a satanic joke. He relates a court trial in which a father is accused of beating his child—it is essentially a variation of the Kroneberg trial—and is eventually acquitted. It is hard to imagine a more intolerable situation. Not only is the torturer acquitted —there is no punishment for the crime—he is hailed by the public.

The law cannot play a role in Ivan's world because there can be no conceivable commensurable relationship between crime and punishment, given the nature of the crimes that are committed against children. On the other hand, Zosima must accept the concept of commensurability because he must believe that all crimes can be atoned for. Zosima would agree with Ivan that it is impossible to understand rationally how this could be so, but he chooses to believe that what is an obvious affront to reason is entirely possible, for nothing is impossible for God. But however much, in contrast to Ivan, Zosima believes in the commensurability of crime and punishment, he, like Ivan, sees the law as essentially irrelevant. For the law the relationship between crime and punishment must be rational—and to a certain extent impartial, standardized, formal, and codified—in order for society to be satisfied that justice is being done. For Zosima the nature of the commensurability is a mystery, not something that can be worked out rationally in a court of law. What Dostoevsky does in the trial scene in

*The Brothers Karamazov* is to create an experiment to validate Father Zosima's position regarding the mystery of responsibility and, conversely, to present a case against both Ivan's rejection of commensurability and the law's idealization and dependence on it. To see how Dostoevsky performs this mystical experiment, we need to compare how differently he handles the category of responsibility in *The Brothers Karamazov*, from the earliest trial he created (*Crime and Punishment*) to one of the last he reported on (the Kornilova case).[23]

Dostoevsky's desire to address the question of crime and redemptive punishment was probably quickened by the radical critique of responsibility and free will propounded in the works of radical thinkers like Nikolay Chernyshevsky and Dmitry Pisarev. In both *Notes from the Underground* and *Crime and Punishment*, Dostoevsky reacted directly to Chernyshevsky's thesis in *What Is to Be Done*, that human beings have no free will and therefore it is absurd, even stupid, to hold them responsible for their behavior. *Crime and Punishment* dismisses the temporary insanity defense put forward by Raskolnikov's lawyers as the most insidious argument against responsibility. If it can be argued that all murder is committed in a condition of temporary insanity, the whole notion of crime is undermined: everybody who commits a crime is in some state of diminished capacity. And if perpetrators of "crimes" are not responsible for their acts, then it makes no sense to "punish" them, although it may be necessary to incarcerate them for the safety of the general public—on the condition, of course, that one can reasonably argue that another attack of temporary insanity might occur.

But in *Crime and Punishment* Dostoevsky makes a perfectly rational argument against Chernyshevsky's relativist ideas regarding responsibility. Raskolnikov plans a crime for which at first he wishes to take full responsibility, for if it is successful, it will prove to him that he is a Napoleon. But once he bungles the murder (he is lucky to escape undetected), he begins to dissociate himself from his crime, refusing, until the very end of the epilogue, to take responsibility for a murder that he meticulously planned and committed.

> He judged himself severely. Yet his hardened conscience did not find any particularly horrible deed in his past, except perhaps for a simple *blunder*, which could happen to anyone. He was most ashamed because he, Raskolnikov, had perished so blindly, hopelessly, and stupidly through some sentence of blind fate and had to submit and humble himself

before the "senselessness" of this sentence if he wanted to attain any peace. (6:417)

Raskolnikov thinks that he can find peace if he submits to a senseless decree, but Dostoevsky shows that Raskolnikov's resentful submission to blind fate is the very antithesis of what he must do in order to achieve spiritual renewal. Only when he begins to understand, through his frequent nightmares, the implications of his actions and his own responsibility for these actions does he intuit the path of expiational suffering that will lead to spiritual rebirth.

Though Dostoevsky presses the issue of responsibility on almost every page of *Crime and Punishment,* he does not problematize the notion of responsibility itself, nor does the novel imply that responsibility is something mystic in origin or operation. The main obstacle to Raskolnikov's moral regeneration is simple: his stubborn refusal to take responsibility for a murder for which he is entirely responsible. The novel presents a criminal who commits a premeditated murder and who intuits his full responsibility for what he has done only at the very end. Neither the reader nor any of the characters, with the exception of Svidrigaylov and Raskolnikov himself, have any doubt about the hero's responsibility for the crime.

In the Kornilova case about ten years later, Dostoevsky is already working with a much more mystical notion of responsibility. Kornilova commits a terrible act, but, fortunately, her stepdaughter, whom she threw from the window, escapes uninjured. In contrast to Raskolnikov, Kornilova abhors her act from the beginning; she never tries to defend what she did. She immediately reports her action to the police and accepts full responsibility for her crime before God and the community. "She fully confessed that she was a criminal guilty of everything of which she had been accused" (531; 24:39). She also understands that the community has every right to punish her.

Kornilova at times seems to dissociate herself from the crime, to look upon the person who committed the crime as someone who took possession of her soul against her will. Dostoevsky encourages this impression because he initially argues that the Kornilova who committed the crime was, as it were, not the real Kornilova but an aberrant Kornilova.[24] He attempts to resolve this apparent disjunction of selves—and the problem of responsibility it poses—by maintaining that the self that committed the crime and the self that dissociated itself from the crime both belong to Kornilova. The "real" Kornilova is no less responsible for the crime than her "temporary evil self." Though Dostoevsky maintains that Kornilova cannot be held as responsible in the same way—at least in terms of punishment—as she should have been had she not been pregnant and thus temporarily insane, he also implies that only the community, not Kornilova, may look at her crime in terms of diminished capacity. In fact, the court must make this distinction between the two Kornilovas only on the condition that she herself does not—that is, only if she continues to consider herself a criminal, to take responsibility for her actions, and to ask forgiveness publicly of the community against which she sinned. The court can accept the temporary insanity defense only if the perpetrator rejects it. Kornilova's acquittal and redemption necessitate full responsibility for an action for which she was not completely responsible.

Dostoevsky takes this concept of responsibility to its extreme conclusion in Dmitry Karamazov. The differences between Raskolnikov and Dmitry in terms of responsibility are especially relevant. Raskolnikov is a murderer who is tried and convicted of several crimes for which he refuses to take responsibility. Because of legally understood extenuating circumstances, including what may have been temporary insanity, he is given a rather short sentence, considering the severity of his crime: seven years of hard labor in Siberia. By contrast Dmitry is tried for a murder he did not commit. Both Fetyukovich and Dmitry reject temporary insanity as a defense. Dmitry is found guilty with no extenuating circumstances. He is given a twenty-year sentence.

All those close to Raskolnikov understand that he has committed a terrible crime and urge him to take responsibility through confession and expiation. Alyosha, Ivan, and Katerina Ivanovna attempt to persuade Dmitry that he is too weak to survive Siberia and encourage him to escape. Until the very end, Raskolnikov refuses to acknowledge his responsibility for the crimes that he has committed, and he does not understand why he should suffer other than for his incompetence and stupidity. Dmitry acknowledges his responsibility for a crime he did not commit, understands that he needs to atone for it and that he needs to go to Siberia to do so. Raskolnikov will have the angelic Sonya, his Beatrice, to lead him onto the correct path. Dmitry will have to survive a much longer sentence without the benefit of Grushenka.

Raskolnikov's crime was premeditated. Kornilova committed a crime when she may have been mentally incapacitated. Dmitry does not even commit the crime.[25] But until Dmitry acknowledges his responsibility for the murder he did not commit, accepts it as his own, and suffers for it, he too cannot achieve spiritual redemption. To a Fetyukovich, and probably to most of Dostoevsky's contemporary readers, such an understanding of responsibility and redemption smacks of religion and mysticism and thus should be not be the concern of the court, which can and must deal only with "real life." For Dostoevsky, because the mystical can never become a part of the secular court, or of the world that is defined by Western law, the legal system can never deal adequately with the most significant aspects of crime and punishment.[26] When the court does what is best for an individual, it is presented as only accidental or a miracle, as in the Kornilova case. Dostoevsky withholds that possibility for the court in Dmitry's case, for the author needs to show the unbridgeable divide between legal and mystical notions of responsibility, crime, and punishment.

*The Brothers Karamazov* presents the mystical realization of universal responsibility as essential to spiritual regeneration, but it is only the initial stage. Responsibility contains another mystery: it is not only mystically revealed, it must be actively assumed through the acceptance of suffering. This is the significance of Dmitry's sentence of twenty years.[27] Fetyukovich looks upon this "ancient" view of suffering and its relation to redemption as irrational and mystical, something that again belongs in neither the court nor real life. Dostoevsky uses Fetyukovich again to argue his point apophatically.

> Oh, of course, there is another meaning, another interpretation of the word "father," which insists that my father, though a monster, though a villain to his children, is still my father simply because he begot me. But this meaning is, so to speak, a mystical one [*misticheskoe znachenie*], which I do not understand with my reason, but can only accept by faith, or, more precisely, *on faith* [*na veru*], like many other things that I do not understand, but that religion nonetheless tells me to believe. But in that case, let it remain outside the sphere of real life [*vne oblasti deistvitel'noi zhizni*]. While within the sphere of real life, which not only has its rights, but itself imposes great obligations—within this sphere, if we wish to be humane, to be Christians finally, it is our duty and obligation to foster only those convictions that are justified by reason and experience [*rassudkom i opytom*], that have passed through the crucible of analysis, in a word, to act sensibly [*razumno*], and not senselessly as

in dreams or delirium, so as not to bring harm to a man, so as not to torment and ruin a man. Then, then it will be a real Christian deed, not only a mystical one [*misticheskoe*], but a sensible [*razumnoe*] and truly philanthropic deed. (744–45; 15:170–71)

As might be expected, the spectators applaud Fetyukovich's attack against mysticism and his equation of rationalism with true Christian thinking. "At this point loud applause broke out in many parts of the courtroom" (745; 15:171). Fetyukovich gets support for his position but not from the most trustworthy sources in the novel: Fedor Karamazov and Kolya Krasotkin. In "Over the Brandy" Fedor Karamazov tells Alyosha how he would deal with monasteries and mysticism. "But still I'd put an end to that little monastery of yours. Take all this mysticism and abolish it at once all over the Russian land, and finally bring the fools to reason. And think how much silver, how much gold would come into the mint" (133; 14:123). Fedor also tells Alyosha how he tried to eliminate his mother's mysticism. "She especially kept the feasts of the Mother of God, and on those days she would drive me away from her to my study. I'd better knock this mysticism [*mistika*] out of her, I thought" (137; 14:126). Kolya Krasotkin tells Alyosha, who seems to be the addressee of most of these remarks: "I've long learned to respect the rare person in you. . . . I've heard you are a mystic and were in the monastery. I know you are a mystic, but . . . that hasn't put me off. Contact with real life will cure you. . . . With natures like yours it can't be otherwise" (553; 14:499). Here Kolya anticipates the remarks not only of Fetyukovich but the prosecutor, Ippolit Kirillovich, who hopes that Alyosha's youthful idealism will not degenerate into "gloomy mysticism [*mrachnyi mistitsizm*]" (697; 15:127). The apophatic rhetoric of the text is clear: mysticism is not only part of life but its essence. The implication is that the court should be left out of real life. To Dostoevsky the mystery of redemptive suffering through the assumption of responsibility for other human beings lies at the heart of what it means to be human. It preserves for human beings a view of agency— no less, in the end, a mystical concept than responsibility—that makes possible the only moral world in which Dostoevsky's heroes will consent to live.

Dostoevsky, on occasion, could express his mystical view of suffering and responsibility in what might seem to some a half-serious or even joking manner. In his fifties he befriended the young philosopher

Vladimir Solovyov. During one of Solovyov's visits Dostoevsky noticed that his friend was depressed and gave him the following advice about Siberia, hard labor, and suffering:

> I know what you want to tell me, I understand your situation perfectly. I experienced it myself. Listen, my friend, you need to do something with yourself, otherwise it will end badly. . . . I was just telling you that at that time fate came to my aid, forced labor saved me, I became a completely different person. When I arrived in prison, I thought that it was the end for me, I thought that I would not last three days, but somehow I settled down. . . . Oh, what great fortune that was: Siberia and forced labor! They talk about how terrible it is, how one becomes embittered, about the inevitability of such embitterment. That's absolute rubbish. My friend, only there did I live a healthy and happy life, only there did I come to understand myself. I came to understand Christ and man. I began to feel that I also was a Russian, that I was part of the Russian people. I thought all by best thoughts then, they are only beginning to return now, and not quite as clearly. You know, you really might benefit from some time in forced labor.[28]

On another visit, after praising Solovyov, Dostoevsky added:

> "I haven't finished. I want to add to my praise that you would do well to have about three years of forced labor."
> "Good Lord! Whatever for?"
> "Because you are not good enough: but then, after forced labor you would be a completely beautiful and pure Christian."[29]

It is difficult to know how seriously Dostoevsky meant his suggestion, and in what sense. But he was perfectly serious about the role that suffering played in his own life. In his remarks to Solovyov, Dostoevsky was actually taking the idea of crime and punishment, responsibility and suffering one step further than he would in *The Brothers Karamazov*. Solovyov not only did not commit a crime, he did not even contemplate one. He was, in many ways, an exemplary young man. He needed to suffer for himself and the sake of others because suffering was inherently good for him and for others. And it is best when one consents to it, takes it on of one's own free will. That Russia's greatest theologian, who had a mystical side of his own, was shocked to hear such advice may be some measure of the peculiar nature of Dostoevsky's idea of responsibility and suffering.

Dostoevsky's strategy in confronting the court and the law is to try to present them as inconsequential and irrelevant. The law is ephemeral, superficial, and of this world only. Whatever importance it has achieved in contemporary life is illusory. The drama in the court is a tragicomic sideshow to the real story, the salvation plot of Dmitry Karamazov. "The Russian Monk" does not directly confront "The Grand Inquisitor," but it is in immediate juxtaposition to it in the actual text; by contrast, the salvation plot is in progress all throughout the trial, though it is almost entirely under the surface: it asserts itself apophatically as the implied antithesis of the workings of the court, as the inversion of the salvation plot that Fetyukovich proposes for Dmitry. Undoubtedly, the jury trial scene is an attack on the untoward and unforeseen consequences of the legal reforms of 1864. But sub specie aeternitatis the reforms are not the issue, for there really is no significant difference between the law before and after 1864. Dostoevsky attempts to have his cake and eat it: he attacks the specific legal reforms implemented after 1864 at the same time that he implies there is little significant difference between the old and new systems and that both systems are irrelevant to living life.

Because Dostoevsky focuses his attack on the post-1864 legal system, one might assume that the pre-reform legal system is presented, at least implicitly, less negatively. To the extent that the new court, as Dostoevsky believed, was miseducating the Russian people and that it was being exploited for radical causes, it could be interpreted as worse than the egregious system it replaced. But with regard to the salvation plot, there can be no significant difference between the two. Dostoevsky gives us a devastating portrait of the investigatory process, during which Dmitry is humiliated by his interrogators. But no one in Russia thought that defendants were better treated under the old system.[30] And Dostoevsky himself was always outraged by mistreatment of prisoners, including the prisoner who was beaten on the order of the governor of St. Petersburg—the central issue in the Zasulich trial. One also must not lose sight of the significant difference between nineteenth- and twentieth-century European legal systems, especially with respect to the discovery process, the prosecutor's investigation of the crime, and the restricted rights of defense lawyers. Despite what Dostoevsky makes the reader think—we know that Dmitry did not commit the crime and the author loves him—Dmitry is not treated badly at any time during the pretrial, trial, and post-trial proceedings. As Ilyinsky shows, innocent men were convicted under the old system; Dmitry Ilyinsky would have served his full term if by some stroke of fortune the real killers had not confessed. Dmitry Karamazov is convicted not because of the new system. Few legal systems would not have found Dmitry guilty. It is not a question of not having had DNA analysis in 1866. Dostoevsky created a scenario that made it impossible for the court of 1866 to acquit his hero. Had he written the novel in a different time and place, he would have invented an equally unfortunate judicial error.

But does the salvation plot work, artistically? Of course, it does not need to work if *The Brothers Karamazov* is merely an attack on the Russian legal system. Dostoevsky depicts a "legally" innocent man who does not even play a central role in his own trial. He is exploited by the lawyers for their own ends, and no one in the courtroom is interested in seeing justice done. The experts are interested in the technical aspect of the case, and the spectators are caught up entirely in the courtroom melodrama. But if the salvation plot is to supersede the legal process and make it seem irrelevant, it must have strong novelistic support. It must be convincing and ultimately impervious to deconstruction. Almost all the characters think that the author's salvation plot is psychologically unconvincing, because, as Dostoevsky would have it, they do not think mystically. But they do not think that it is novelistically convincing, either, for it does not belong to what they understand as real life: the proper domain of the contemporary novel. Is Dmitry's salvation plot, in the end, any more artistically satisfactory than Alyosha's hagiographic account of Father Zosima's life? It was Dostoevsky, after all, who wrote that the validity of his answer to "The Grand Inquisitor" depended on the artistic success of his portrait of Zosima. Then what about the validity of his salvation plot vis-à-vis "A Judicial Error"?

There are those who think that Dostoevsky failed to create the Zosima that he intended. Zosima is the stuff of hagiography and not of the novel. Because hagiographic reality is static and for the ages, it seems, paradoxically, outside nineteenth-century novelistic time. In order for Dostoevsky's salvation plot for Dmitry to succeed, the author needs to create a reader (the author's reader) who will accept his kairotic plot for Dmitry; Dostoevsky also needs to create a text that is basically impervious to the kind of deconstruction to which I have subjected his

re-creation of the Kornilova trial. And what, indeed, if it were successful? What if he had, indeed, created an undeconstructible text in
which the author's word was essentially unchallengeable? Would not
such a monologic approach entail significant artistic costs? This is a
question that obviously cannot be resolved without directly addressing perhaps the most complex artistic question in *The Brothers Karamazov*, the nature of the novel's narrative authority. That, in the end,
is what the trial is about. Each of the lawyers understands the importance of narrative authority for his case and makes a special point of
directly addressing the issue. The author of *The Brothers Karamazov*
tries to make us unresisting readers, to persuade us to take his word
as unchallengeable, unchallengeable as hagiography, that is, to put his
word out of play. But before we take a closer look at how the author
attempts to establish the authority of his word over all other words and
to compel us, as dutiful filial readers, to repeat after Father Zosima "So
be it? So be it?" we need to consider more thoroughly the possibilities
of reading Dmitry's fate otherwise.

I have tried to show that the novel requires that Dmitry serve his
sentence in Siberia. Dostoevsky attempts to make the alternative of
escape to America thematically, symbolically, and literarily improbable
and unworkable. I have mentioned Svidrigaylov's equation in *Crime
and Punishment* of going to America and committing suicide, but even
more to the point, Svidrigaylov offers the same solution of escape to
America to Raskolnikov that Ivan and Alyosha offer Dmitry—it is
part of Svidrigaylov's attempt to win over Dunia, Raskolnikov's sister.
Dunia and Sonya, however, are insistent that Raskolnikov confess his
crime and serve his sentence—which he does. The only major characters in Dostoevsky's works who make it to America are Shatov and
Kirillov in *The Possessed*. Tough, ideologically driven young men, they
go to America to experience the very harshest social conditions, but
the dog-eat-dog competitive American environment is too much for
them, and they return to Russia. Shatov remarks: "Well, we worked,
sweated, suffered, and exhausted ourselves. Finally, Kirillov and I just
left—we fell ill. We just couldn't take it any more" (10:180). Shatov
implies that it was the less the harshness of the conditions and more
the experience of spiritual alienation that forced this odd couple to
return to Russia.

Of course, we do not know for sure what happens to Dmitry after
his conviction; we only know where the novel's rhetoric wants to take

him. Because the reader learns of Dmitry's potential for salvation, not its inevitability, the question of Dmitry's fate, Dmitry's life beyond the novel proper, has often been the subject of debate. Having speculated about the legal, penal, and moral consequences of Dmitry's serving his sentence in Siberia, we need—to be fair—to consider what these consequences might be for the deconstructive alternative: Dmitry's escape to America. I call this alternative deconstructive because it goes against the rhetoric of the novel—the imputable intentions of the author— and exploits the building blocks that Dostoevsky himself provides so that the reader can reconstruct an antithetical interpretation, here one based on an alternative that is depreciated by the author.

If Dmitry escapes to America, his punishment must be entirely internal, probably from the guilt that he will feel from running away from what he viewed as condign punishment. The idea that America is as good a place to suffer as Russia is based on the anguish that Dmitry thinks he must experience, knowing that he is not being legally punished and that he is not suffering for others. But before speculating about Dmitry's suffering, we need to deal with the other implications of Dmitry's escape to America. *The Brothers Karamazov* presents the judicial process, both pre- and post-reform—or, more broadly, Western rationalist law—as essentially irrelevant to human spirituality. But Dmitry's escape makes not only the strictly legal consequences irrelevant—whether he is convicted and sentenced or not—but all the discussions relating to Dmitry's and Russia's suffering, and salvation— and not only the lawyers' analyses but Alyosha's, Ivan's, and Father Zosima's views as well. Though the lawyers are exploiting the burning Russian questions of the day for their own personal agendas, the novel never implies that the issues of personal salvation and Russia's fate are not the most important problems for the novelist as well. But everything that happens during the court proceedings—that is, not only the legal issues—becomes irrelevant if these proceedings entail no consequences, if they can be sidestepped by a simple escape, which can be easily arranged if there is enough cash. Escape to America more than removes Dmitry from the realm of the legal; it transfers him to an entirely different world, which has no relevance for Russian reality. It is a world in which all is truly permitted (*vse pozvoleno*) because in America nothing Russian is binding, because in America there are no ties to Russian history, culture, family life, spirituality, suffering, and salvation. For Russians, according to the novel, it is a spiritual and moral vacuum. What relevance do Zosima's watering the earth with tears and Dmitry's starving babes have in America? Or, for that matter, what relevance does the world of the Grand Inquisitor, a disguised form of socialism, have in the land of ruthless individualistic capitalism? For *The Brothers Karamazov* America is not only an escape from the Russian legal system, or the legal system in general; it is an escape from both the world of Father Zosima and the world of the Grand Inquisitor. It is the most complete deconstruction of every aspect of the novel. For it is not only the legal system that becomes irrelevant with Dmitry's escape but the antithetical moral and theological counterpoints to the legal system of Father Zosima and Ivan Karamazov. Dmitry is central to both Father Zosima's and Ivan Karamazov's worldviews, particularly to their ideas of human redemption. Once Dmitry escapes to America, once their central symbol is gone, these worldviews become as inconsequential as the legal system. When critics view Dmitry's escape to America as a viable alternative, they are probably thinking in terms of law and psychology: he did not commit the crime, so he should not go to prison and he should not be forced to undergo useless vain suffering as did Ilyinsky, Dmitry's prototype. But to think strictly in these terms is to treat the novel's theological, cultural, and philosophical concerns as disposable rhetorical entities.

We also need to examine the deconstructionist argument of escape to America more concretely by speculating about what would Dmitry do in America, and how he would live there as a moral being. Dostoevsky is very specific about the salvation plot. He himself lived part of it, he used a real-life prototype for it, and he left fictional examples of the plot in *Notes from the House of the Dead* and *Crime and Punishment*. Furthermore, in *The Brothers Karamazov* itself, the plot is adumbrated in numerous variations (the life of Father Zosima, the story of "The Mysterious Stranger," and the tribulations of Job) and discussed at length by almost all the major characters. For the reader it is not a question of what the author's salvation plot is but whether it is appropriate for Dmitry. There is nothing comparable to this specificity for the escape plot. The novel includes only parodic allusions to the escape plot, such as Lopukhov's escape to, and successful business career in, America, worked out by Chernyshevsky in *What Is to Be Done*. Dmitry, as a successful Russian businessman in America, following, as it were, in his father's footsteps, would be more burlesque than parody. Dmitry offers another alternative: working the land, but he makes fun of it himself. He and Grusha will find an isolated spot inhabited only by wild bears and perhaps some Indians. There they will plow the soil and study English grammar. After mastering English grammar in three years, they will speak English as well as any Englishmen (not to mention, Americans), and so they will be able to return to Russia as disguised American citizens (this part of the plot is parodically borrowed from Chernyshevsky). In three years both Dmitry and Grushenka will have so changed that no one will recognize them. And if they do recognize him and send him to Siberia, he will accept that too; that is, the American escape plot falls apart and the author's salvation plot returns. Here is how Dmitry represents this plot to Alyosha, who has come to visit him in prison after Dmitry has been convicted and is waiting transport to his Siberian prison:

"So this is what I've decided, Alexei, listen!" he began again, suppressing his excitement. "Grusha and I will arrive there—and there we'll immediately set to work, digging the land, with the wild bears, in solitude, in some remote place. Surely there must be remote places there. People say there are still redskins there, somewhere on the edge of the horizon, so we'll go to that edge, to the last Mohicans. And we'll immediately start on the grammar, Grusha and I. Work and grammar—about three years like that. In three years we'll learn Engullish as well as any downright Englishman. And as soon as we've learned it—good-bye America! We'll flee here, to Russia, as American citizens. Don't worry, we won't come to this little town. We'll hide somewhere far away, in the north or the south. I'll have changed by then, and so will she; a doctor there, in America, will fabricate some kind of wart for me; it's not for nothing that they are all mechanics. Or else I'll blind myself in one eye, let my beard grow a yard long, a gray beard (I'll go gray thinking of Russia), and maybe they won't recognize me. And if they do, worse luck, let them exile me, I don't care. Here, too, we'll dig the land somewhere in the wilderness, and I'll pretend to be an American all my life. But we will die in our native land. That's my plan, and it will not be changed. Do you approve?" (764–65; 15:185)

Dmitry presents this version of the escape plot as ridiculous, but Alyosha too could hardly take seriously a plot that has Dmitry spending three years in America, learning English perfectly from a grammar book, and then returning to Russia as an American. But just as the salvation plot does not require Dmitry to be the main prognosticator of his own fate, perhaps Dmitry simply is unable to conceive of a spiritually productive life that he might lead in America. Perhaps he will not retreat to the wilds but settle on a farm in South Dakota with Grushenka, grow Russian winter wheat, gradually learn English, and become a respected member of the community, maybe even sit on an American jury weighing an accused parricide. If Dmitry's tilling the soil like a peasant seems a little farfetched, how about an alternative taken from *The Brothers Karamazov* itself? Dmitry escapes to America in 1866. When in 1867 America takes possession of Alaska from Russia, Dmitry heads north to prospect for gold, where he makes a fortune (this, of course, is a variation of Madame Khokhlakova's gold mine plot, transferred from Siberia to Alaska). He then uses the influence of his new fortune to persuade a Russian official in the Ministry of Justice to vacate his sentence on a technicality, as in the Kornilova case. Then Dmitry can freely return to Russia with Grushenka. If one wants, one can freely imagine a more sober or prosaic American escape plot based on Dmitry's character.

Of course, the problem with imagined escape alternatives is that they are artistically unconvincing. They do not constitute persuasive deconstructions of any of the novel's major structural centers; they do not offer alternative reconstructions as convincing as the implied author's. For some readers Dostoevsky's salvation plot for Dmitry may be wanting, however much Dostoevsky attempts to support it textually in *The Brothers Karamazov*, and however much extratextual evidence can be found in Dostoevsky's own life and in the real-life prototype of Ilyinsky. But uneasiness with the fate implied for Dmitry does not make alternative fates for Dmitry necessarily better aesthetically, especially escape to America, the only alternative discussed in the novel itself. Although we may reject deconstructive reconstructions of "The Grand Inquisitor" that argue that the author sides with the devil or at least makes a better case for the devil than for Christ, it is still not hard to see that *The Brothers Karamazov* provides the building blocks from which such interpretations can be derived. Dostoevsky himself had doubts about his ability artistically to refute Ivan's arguments against God. A convincing deconstructive counterplot involving Dmitry that would undercut the legal, philosophical, and religious Weltanschauung of *The Brothers Karamazov* would make it an even richer text. But Dmitry's escape to America is not such an alternative. Once we see the escape to America as a conscious parodic variation of the plot of Chernyshevsky's *What Is to Be Done*, it becomes clear that America is not really a choice but a device that the author consciously deploys to bolster his own salvation plot, a sort of ruse to demonstrate that there is no alternative to the author's design for his hero. As soon as one considers the legal, psychological, philosophical, national, and theological implications of escape to America, as I have tried to do, one is forced to acknowledge that suffering in Siberia is the only possibility for Dmitry as a character in Dostoevsky's novel—like it or not.

# Conclusion

## The Court and the
## Authority of the Word

---

*The Brothers Karamazov* opposes to Western law several versions of Russian justice: jury nullification, the ecclesiastic courts, and Dmitry's expiational suffering. In the Kornilova case, in which Dostoevsky took an active role, he presents the triumph of Russian justice, Kornilova's acquittal, as having occurred not because of the court but despite it. Because Dostoevsky had come to see the court as home to the adulteration of the word, he presents Kornilova's acquittal as a miracle. One can, however, use his descriptions to construct an equally credible but opposite interpretation—a deconstruction—of Kornilova's acquittal, one in which she is saved from a terrible fate in Siberia because of the Western court and not despite it. Where else but in court could Kornilova have seen that she was forgiven by other Russians, including representatives of all classes? Dostoevsky's article in the *Diary of a Writer* turned the secular court into something like an imagined ecclesiastical court and the court proceedings into a church service. The Kornilova case may be seen in terms of Father Zosima's and Father Paissy's vision of the state's being incorporated, if only for a moment, by the church, but one can make just as good a case for the incorporation of the church by the court.

Deconstructing the trial scene in *The Brothers Karamazov* constitutes a more formidable task. Dostoevsky seems to have written "A Judicial Error," after realizing that it was possible to read his article on the Kornilova case as a validation of the Western jury trial and court. And that is exactly what Fetyukovich does, or that is what Dostoevsky has Fetyukovich do. *The Brothers Karamazov* seems to be Dostoevsky's attempt to prevent a recurrence of that "artistic error." He exegetically

232

plugs almost every loophole of ambiguous interpretation relating to the judge, lawyers, jurors, public, experts, witnesses, details of the final decision, and, most of all, Dmitry's salvation.

For Kornilova the public trial was essential because her salvation depended on the confession of her guilt before the entire community and on experiencing the forgiveness of people of all classes. That could happen only at a jury trial, where she could physically stand before and receive forgiveness from those against whom she had sinned. Under the old system she would have been summarily sentenced to many years of hard labor. The old court would hardly have said: "Go and sin no more," which, in effect, the new court did. Her case would have received no publicity, it would not have been part of the public record, and no Dostoevsky would have written an article that made it possible—again, through the court—for Kornilova to go free.

On the other hand, Dmitry's trial plays almost no role in his spiritual awakening or potential salvation. There is little that the jury trial makes possible for Dmitry that was not possible under the old legal system. Just like Father Zosima, Dmitry needed a shock to turn his life around. He is subjected to a humiliating investigation at the place of his carousing on the night of his father's murder. He is asked to strip so the prosecutor's officers can inspect his clothing. Here he has his dream of the starving babes and begins to understand his responsibility for himself as well as for others. But the soul's journey through hell (*khozhdenie dushi po mytarstvam*), which he would have experienced under the old system, could easily have provided him with a sufficient salvific shock. Dmitry's prosecutors behave decently, if insensitively, despite Dostoevsky's attempt to make us feel otherwise.

Unlike the Kornilova trial in *The Diary of a Writer*, the Karamazov courtroom resembles popular theater more than a church service. The lawyers are interested in Dmitry solely as a legal phenomenon, and the public is more interested in the lawyers than in the defendant. The spectators and actors in the court drama do not constitute a community that could extend forgiveness to Dmitry or be the recipient of his confession of universal responsibility. Any confession that Dmitry could make regarding responsibility would have been viewed as irrelevant to the proceedings of the court. Dmitry is not chastened by the court proceedings, he does not see justice done. Dmitry says he has learned a great deal about himself from each lawyer, but it is insignificant by comparison with what he has learned in his dream of the babes.

One might argue that the post-reform court functions as an instrument of a higher purpose: God works in mysterious ways. But Dmitry would have received approximately the same sentence in a pre-reform court; the real Ilyinsky, after all, was serving a twenty-year sentence for a parricide he also did not commit. Dostoevsky's conservative critique of the post-reform court is clear, but it has little to do specifically with Dmitry's salvation plot.

But although Dostoevsky consciously does everything he can to discredit the court, and to foreclose the opportunities for reading otherwise, it is not impossible to deconstruct the trial, to show that the trial can, on the basis of Dostoevsky's own presentation, be interpreted in a way diametrically opposite from the author's obvious intentions. We have seen the precedent for this procedure in interpretations of "The Grand Inquisitor" by Rozanov and others. Lawrence was never in doubt about what Dostoevsky had intended to do, but he argued that Dostoevsky made a much better case for the view that he was trying to undermine.[1] Dostoevsky's statement that Ivan's argument about the unjustifiable suffering of little children was irrefutable, of course, lends support to this position. But it lends support to the arguments of Ivan, not those of Fetyukovich, who argues that children have the right to murder unexemplary fathers. Thus, while making "The Grand Inquisitor" relevant for Ivan's regeneration, Dostoevsky provides no basis for making the trial relevant for Dmitry's regeneration. He also undermines any foundation for crediting the word of Fetyukovich, his most powerful opponent, who is unambiguously labeled as a corrupter of thought.

But there is another deconstructive possibility. Even if it is difficult to make a good case for the efficacy of the jury trial or for the various positions of Fetyukovich, I hope to show that the novel both implicitly and explicitly challenges the author's point of view. Such an interpretation implies, however, a resisting reader, a reader who sees the voice of the author compromised in the text precisely in his attempt to compromise the voices of others. A resisting reader might also take more seriously some of the defense attorney's arguments regarding Dmitry's salvation, especially when they resemble what Dostoevsky himself wrote on other occasions. Further, the resisting reader may view the trial as a heavy-handed attempt of the author to impose his ideology on the text, an authorial strategy that might encourage a resisting reader to react as negatively to the author's word as to the lawyer's word, even to look beyond the personality and motives of the lawyer and seriously consider some of his cogent arguments regarding Dmitry's salvation. The text offers support for such an approach: the author not only seems anxious about the authority of his word but the text dramatizes these doubts in several long discussions about narrative authority.

## The Validation of the Authorial Word

We have seen that the author attempts to establish his authority in part by discrediting the voices of those who are adulterers of thought. The idea of adulteration, however, is meaningless without the presupposed existence of the Word, the Word that in the beginning was with God, the Logos. By discrediting the adulterers, the authorial voice apophatically aligns itself with the truth, that is, defines itself, in the Orthodox tradition, in terms of what it is not or in terms of its antithesis. Dostoevsky uses a similar apophatic technique with his narrator, from whose "narrative word" he dissociates himself early in the novel. Most of the psychological explanations of behavior are given over to characters in the text (including the lawyers) and to his observer-chronicler narrator. The psychology that undergirds the characterization of the brothers is independent of the narrator; it arises through the brothers' conversations, writings, and the experiences—dreams (Dmitry), hallucinations (Ivan), and mystic ecstasy (Alyosha)—conveyed, in a style consonant with the experience, primarily by the omniscient narrator. In order to maintain an authority greater than the phenomenal world of the events, Dostoevsky abandons the persona he occupied in the Kornilova trial. But that is not enough—he needs to eliminate as many traces of his narrative persona as possible in order not to be subject to Fetyukovich's epistemological attacks against psychological narrative. The observer-narrator is sometimes insightful, but his psychological commentary and analysis exist on the same plane as that of the lawyers and other characters. The author cannot be seen arguing in a court of law, or a close substitute for it, as in the Kornilova case, without placing himself on the same level as the lawyers and having his authority tainted by association.

In chapter 5, I tried to show how Dostoevsky attempts to bolster the authority of his word positively, unapophatically, by associating it as closely as possible with the unadulterated Word of biblical and hagiographical narrative. On the simplest level the author's attack against the adulterated word makes him apophatically into a defender, knight, or champion of the unadulterated Word. But Dostoevsky as author also creates his own unapophatic narratives as alternatives to the narratives of the lawyers. He attempts to establish himself as author in the original sense of creator or Logos, and not as an equal partner in a dialogue among autonomous narrative voices. Being the author of a hagiography is presumably something quite different from being the author of a novel (*roman*). Solovyov saw Dostoevsky engaged in the creation of religious narrative of the future. Alyosha Karamazov is ostensibly the author of the hagiography devoted to Father Zosima, but few readers will fail to see Dostoevsky guiding Alyosha's pen.

Dostoevsky uses the hagiography of Father Zosima, among other things, to validate the salvation plot for Dmitry. Dostoevsky incorporates into Father Zosima's "Life" a whole section based on the Book of Job and devoted to the aesthetics and epistemology of biblical narrative. The Old Testament is key here, because it is the part of the Bible most devoted to narrative. And although the New Testament is supersessionist, it paradoxically derives its own authority, at least in part— and this reflects the early debate in the church about whether to accept or reject the Old Testament—from the predictions (prefigurations) in the Old Testament, including the messianic salvation plot for humanity, the story of Jesus, a scion of the House of David. The epistemological aesthetics of Bible narrative, as Father Zosima explains, are not the same as those of the nineteenth-century novel. Father Zosima first talks about the impression that the Book of Job, read right before Easter, made on him as a boy. This is Father Zosima's Cana of Galilee:

> Mother took me to church [*Khram Gospoden'*] by myself (I do not remember where my brother was then), during Holy Week, to the Monday liturgy. It was a clear day, and, remembering it now, I seem to see the incense rising from the censer and quietly ascending upwards, and from above, through a narrow little window in the cupola, God's rays pouring down on us in the church, and the incense rising up to them in waves, as if dissolving into them. I looked with deep tenderness, and *for the first time in my life I consciously received the first seed of the word of God* [pervoe semia slova Bozhiia] *in my soul*. A young man walked out into the middle of the church with a big book, so big that it seemed to me that he even had difficulty carrying it, and he placed it on the

analogion, opened it, and began to read, and suddenly, then, for the first
time I understood something, for the first time in my life I understood
what was read in God's church. . . . Lord, what a book, what lessons!
What a book is the Holy Scripture, what miracle, what power are given
to me in it! Like a carven image of the world, and of man, and of human
characters, and everything is named and set forth unto ages of ages. And
so many mysteries are resolved and revealed: God restores Job again,
gives him wealth anew; once more many years pass, and he has new
children, different ones, and he loves them—Oh, Lord, one thinks, "but
how could he so love those new ones, when his former children are no
more, when he has lost them? Remembering them, was it possible for
him to be fully happy, as he had been before, with the new ones, however dear they might be to him?" But it is possible, it is possible: the old
grief, by a great mystery of human life, gradually passes into quiet, tender joy. (291–92; 14:264–65)

The first time that Zosima consciously received the seed of God's
word in his heart is directly associated with his listening to the Word
in the form of biblical narrative. This is why Richard Weisberg's notion
that the word is in itself corrupt, and that silence is the only form
of truth, goes against the aesthetics and rhetoric of the novel.[2] Silence
can be the silence of Christ, but it can also be the silence of evil
(Smerdyakov). And as Robin Feuer Miller has shown, the word as seed
occupies the metaphorical center of *The Brothers Karamazov*: it is the
"dissemination" of the Word that promises resurrection from the dead.
"The seeds of the epigraph find another manifestation as words in the
novel."[3] And as Zosima implies, the seed of God's word (*semia slova
Bozhiia*) reveals itself in its most powerful form as narrative. But it is
a special kind of narrative. It is not ruled by the aesthetics of the modern psychological novel. It is not addicted to normal psychology. "But
how could he love those new ones when those first children are no
more, when he has lost them?" Normal psychology cannot explain Job's
faith and trust in God. The Bible is a miracle. The greatest mysteries
of creation can be revealed to people only through mystical narrative.[4]

And just as Dostoevsky creates ("authors") authoritative religious
biography based on the older hagiographic tradition and achieves
authority by working in the same genre, if not the same narrative mode,
so does he go back to the Old Testament, to the favorite narrative
of Zosima, to establish the authority for a new Jobian plot for his hero,

whose story relies as much on mystery and miracle as it does on nineteenth-century novelistic psychology. The authority for Dmitry's salvation is doubly authorized: it derives first from the hagiography that Dostoevsky creates from Father Zosima's "Life" and then from the Old Testament plot that Father Zosima cites as the greatest moment of biblical narrative, the moment when he first consciously received the seeds, the Word of God.

## Challenging the Authorial Word: The Resisting Lawyer

Practically speaking, readers whose religious views are close to Dostoevsky's will be more receptive to "The Russian Monk" and to the idealized portrait of Alyosha than the nonbeliever will. But "New Critical" readers who are interested in fitting together all parts of the aesthetic puzzle of *The Brothers Karamazov* have been equally receptive to the text's religious echoes, symbolism, and plot structures. But Dostoevsky is not only preaching to the choir in *The Brothers Karamazov*. He knew that he would be facing resisting readers in his own time, and he tries to incorporate them into the text, often casting them in uncomfortable roles as bad readers or readers who are limited by popular psychology (the determining role of environment) and phenomenal reality (the dismissal of the mystical). Fetyukovich is of course the best example of a resisting reader, someone who refuses to grant a place for the religious and the mystical in everyday life, especially in a court of law, where matters of life and death are being adjudicated. Just as in *The Idiot*, where Dostoevsky casts the resisting reader in the role of Ippolit Terentyev, someone who cannot overcome his belief in natural law and thus accept the resurrection, he casts the resisting reader in *The Brothers Karamazov* in the role of Fetyukovich, who cannot understand the mystical bases for human experience.

But Dostoevsky understands that Fetyukovich is not his only resisting reader. As we have seen, most of the other characters do not accept his salvation plot for Dmitry, either. In the end Dostoevsky must rely on his art. In an article about *The Merchant of Venice*, Thomas Moisan argues that from a strictly rational point there is much to be said for Shylock's position, given the Christians' complicity in his daughter's abduction and Antonio's continual harassment of his rival on the Rialto.[5] But Shakespeare so bathes his positive characters in an aura of magnificent poetry that only those unreceptive to the music of Belmont are still thinking about Shylock in act 5.[6] Poetry trumps rational argument and all the issues that Shakespeare problematizes in the previous four acts. Dostoevsky knew he could not easily manipulate the resisting reader by argument, nor could he cast the reader in an abhorrent role. He knew, as his remarks about "The Russian Monk" clearly show, that he had to win over the reader by poetry. If he could not accomplish that, all was lost. And poetry, Dostoevsky would probably have asserted, is something "mystical," like the Bible, that we cannot argue about. Some readers will always be as entranced with Zosima and Alyosha as Dostoevsky was, others will see them as unsuccessful attempts to create positive religious heroes in the modern novel.

Although Dostoevsky attempts to establish authority for his word by discrediting the prosaic word of the opposition (in particular, the lawyers) and by associating his own word with the Russian religious tradition, he nevertheless willy-nilly gives voice to those who implicitly challenge his authority as novelist. The lawyers are so negatively portrayed, and their word so persistently compromised by contradictions, misreadings, and outrageous contentions, that one is hardly predisposed to credit their word about anything. Who is going to agree with Fetyukovich on authorship after he argues that one has the right to kill an unexemplary father? And who is going to take seriously the lawyers' arguments about the novel in the face of their interpretations and rewriting of *Dead Souls*? But the lawyers' discussion about authority in the novel, especially Fetyukovich's, is curiously much more sound—another mystery—and ultimately more dangerous for Dostoevsky's position as author than anything else they say. If a crack exists in the text within which a deconstructive analysis can work, it is certainly in the trial scene, where Dmitry's fate—which plot is most suitable for him—rests on the readers' conclusions about the aesthetics of the novel. The trial, which, from one point of view, has been reduced to almost complete irrelevance because it has nothing to do with the real plot involving Dmitry's salvation, again becomes the most important thing in the novel because it broaches the issue of authority on which the salvation plot must squarely rest.

Each lawyer sets out to destroy the idea of the novel as an authoritative narrative. By ridiculing the lawyers' attempt to undermine the novel, Dostoevsky tries, as elsewhere, to restore the value of that which has been falsely discredited. If Dostoevsky is successful in repulsing the

attack against authority in the novel—and, by implication, his authority as implied author—then he again apophatically will have asserted
his authority over the text and ipso facto over the lawyers, the court,
and, in the end, the law itself. He will have gained control over the
word, the most powerful weapon of the modern world, and demonstrated the difference between words as mere relative signifiers and the
Word as an unchallengeable signifier of ultimate truth.[7]

Nevertheless, Fetyukovich has counterarguments that cannot be dismissed out of hand. To see where and how Fetyukovich's attack against
authority arises, we need to go back to Ippolit Kirillovich's disparage-
ment of Dmitry Karamazov's venture into novel writing and the prosecutor's attempt to create a superior novel from the facts of the case.
Ippolit Kirillovich begins his critique of narrative authority, which
Fetyukovich later takes to its extreme conclusion, when Ippolit Kirillovich offers an alternative salvation plot for his client.

First, in his summation Ippolit Kirillovich ridicules Dmitry's alibi
about the money he spent in Mokroe a month before the crime. Dmitry
maintains that he spent only fifteen hundred rubles rather than the
three thousand that the prosecutor needs in order to demonstrate that
Dmitry robbed and murdered his father.

> The examination angers him, but also encourages him: the full three
> thousand is not found, only fifteen hundred. And, of course, only in this
> moment of angry silence and denial does the idea of the amulet jump
> into his head for the first time in his life. *He himself undoubtedly sensed*
> *the utter incredibility of his invention, and he was at pains, terrible pains,*
> *to make it more credible, to spin a whole plausible novel out of it.* [Bez
> somneniia, on chuvstvuet sam vsiu neveroiatnost' vydumki i muchitsia,
> strashno muchitsia, kak by sdelat' ee veroiatnee, tak sochinit', chtob
> vyshel tselyi pravdopodobnyi roman.] (720; 15:148; emphasis added)

Ippolit Kirillovich accuses Dmitry of approaching his alibi as literature. Because Dmitry senses the improbability of his invented story,
he must to do everything in his power to make it more verisimilar, to
create a completely believable novel. That is his only hope. Dmitry creates his novel solely to deceive, to gull the jury into accepting appearance for reality. But, fortunately for us all, the prosecutor implies,
Dmitry is an awful novelist; he may try to carry us away by his grand
invention, but he overlooks the most significant realistic details and

thus fails to convince us. Nothing could be less verisimilar than the explanation he gave for the three thousand rubles.

> Gentlemen of the jury, I have already made known to you why I con-sider all this invention about money sewn into an amulet a month ear-lier, not only an absurdity, but also the most implausible contrivance that could have been hit upon in this situation. If one bet on whether anything more implausible could have been said or imagined, even then it would be impossible to invent anything worse than that. Here, above all, the triumphant novelist can be brought up short and demolished by details, those very details in which reality is so rich, and which are always neglected by such unfortunate and unwilling authors, as if they were utterly insignificant and unnecessary trifles, if indeed they even occur to them. (721; 15:149)

Had Dmitry been a better novelist—that is, taken care of the super-fluous details à la Tolstoy—he might have fashioned a far better alibi, perhaps sowing the seeds of doubt in the minds of the jurors. The prosecutor brings his skills as literary critic to expose the untenability of Dmitry's alibi. The truth that Dmitry tells about the amulet be-comes, through Ippolit Kirillovich's narrative critique, an artistically deficient, incredible story that cannot constitute valid evidence for the court. But the prosecutor cannot leave the matter at that, he cannot leave the jury and the Russian public with Dmitry's bad novel. He tries, as he has done throughout the summation, to create a better, more credible (*pravdopodobnyi*) psychological novel with all the requisite details, a novel that his readers, the jury, can accept.

The prosecutor obviously is treading on thin ice here. He hints that Dmitry resorted to the novel in the first place to deceive the jury. How could a better novel be more reliable in a court of law, when, as Ippolit Kirillovich argued, Dmitry resorted to the novel only to lead the jury astray? Would not one need to be even more wary of Ippolit Kirillovich than of Dmitry, because, as the better of the two novelists, he could more easily deceive the jury by his convincing realistic details?

But for some reason Ippolit Kirillovich thinks the only way he can persuade the jury is to create a more convincing psychological novel than the defendant and the defendant's lawyer. He looks foolish because he errs precisely in the area of his vaunted expertise: he is wrong precisely about the realistic details. As a result, his larger picture becomes—for the reader—even more far-fetched and distant from the truth than Dmitry's completely improbable—although true—story. Nothing is inherently wrong with the prosecutor's psychological analysis. It really is in accord with the canons of verisimilitude; it just happens to be false. The story of Job, which represents the highest of all truths, is, as Father Zosima points out, completely improbable, almost beyond psychological understanding. It is an affront to rational, psychological explanation, but it is true. Ippolit Kirillovich is successful; his "better novel" convinces the jury of the improbability of the truth and is largely responsible for convicting an innocent man. But it gets worse. In the concluding part of his summation Ippolit Kirillovich leaves the world of details he so admires and launches into a sermon, transforming himself from realist novelist into novelist-seer. He thinks he can improve, novelistically, not only on Dmitry Karamazov but on Gogol himself. He presents himself to the Russian public as a new, improved Gogol, riding on a revamped and redirected troika. But all Ippolit Kirillovich's venture into the novel does is apophatically reinforce Dostoevsky's authoritative voice as implied author.

Moreover, Ippolit Kirillovich has to become somewhat disenchanted with his foray into the novel when Fetyukovich rips his novel apart in his summation. Because his novel has no authority guaranteeing its validity, Ippolit Kirillovich must, in his response to Fetyukovich's speech, completely reverse direction, attacking the novel form, which had just been the backbone of his case. Fetyukovich's presentation, according to the prosecutor, is even worse than a novel—it is even worse than poetry in the Byronic style; it is a sphinx, a mystery:

> We are reproached with having invented all sorts of novels. But what has the defense attorney offered if not novel upon novel? The only thing lacking is poetry (*stikhi*). Fyodor Pavlovich, while waiting for his mistress, tears up the envelope and throws it on the floor. Even what he said on this remarkable occasion is quoted. Is this not a poem (*poema*)? And where is the proof that he took out the money, who heard what he was saying? The feebleminded idiot Smerdyakov, transformed into some sort of Byronic hero revenging himself for illegitimate birth—is this not a poem (*poema*) in the Byronic fashion? And the son bursting into his father's house, killing him, and at the same time not killing him, this is not even a novel, not a poem, it is a sphinx posing riddles, which, of course, it will not solve itself. (748–49; 15:174)

Ippolit Kirillovich is of two minds about the novel. To maintain his position he must argue that Fetyukovich has written a far-fetched, unbelievable novel, in some respects outdoing Dmitry Karamazov. Rather than writing a realistic novel, he has written something like a Byronic narrative with respect to Smerdyakov and, with respect to many other things, something that approaches mysticism. On the other hand, Ippolit Kirillovich has to point out that if novels are the problem, then his opponent is even more guilty in this respect than Ippolit Kirillovich is, because his adversary has written several novels, not just one.

Ippolit Kirillovich misses the point. Fetyukovich is not really interested in writing a novel at all, only in questioning the presuppositions regarding narrative authority. He constructs counterplots not to persuade his audiences (the jury, the spectators, and the Russian public) to accept one or another narrative but to show that an almost limitless number of narratives can be "created" to account for the same "facts" of the case, and in most instances one can come to the opposite conclusions on the basis of the very same evidence. There are no authoritative, privileged narratives given the facts of Dmitry's case. Fetyukovich never says that he prefers or even believes his own alternative hypotheses; he merely argues that the evidence can lead to different conclusions of equal probability, and one must not convict a man of premeditated murder when reasonable doubt exists. Fetyukovich does not try to write a counternovel because he knows it will be no less vulnerable to deconstruction than his opponent's; he merely uses his imaginative powers to demonstrate that more or less equally convincing counternovels could be written, none of which can be disproved.

> I myself, gentlemen of the jury, have resorted to psychology now, in order to demonstrate that one can draw whatever conclusions one likes from it. *It all depends on whose hands it is in.* (728; 15:156; emphasis added)

And because one can create so many alternative narratives, one must be suspicious of them all. They are fanciful creations that are much more dangerous than the most "malicious and preconceived attitudes" and thus obviously must be kept out of the courtroom. The more imaginative the plot, the more dangerous it is.

> But there are things that are even worse, even more ruinous in such cases than the most malicious and preconceived attitude towards the

matter. Namely, if we are, for example, possessed by a certain, so to speak, artistic game, by the need for artistic production, so to speak, the creation of a novel [*sozdanie romana*], especially seeing the wealth of psychological gifts with which God has endowed our abilities. (726–27; 15:154)

Fetyukovich harps on Ippolit Kirillovich's novel creation, continually referring to his opponent's psychological conclusions as being more appropriate to imaginative fiction:

"We thereby enter the realm of novels [*oblast' romanov*]" (730; 15:157).
"Is it not a fantastic, is it not a novelistic [*romanicheskoe*] suggestion?" (731; 15:158).
"And with such novels are we prepared to ruin a human life [*I takimi-to romanami my gotovy pogubit' zhizn' chelovecheskuiu*]" (731; 15:158).
"The prosecution liked its own novel [*sobstvennyi roman*]" (731; 15:158).
"Well and what if the thing went quite differently, what if you created a novel [*sozdali roman*] around quite a different person?" (732; 15:158–59).
"Is this proved? Is this not also a novel? [*Uzh ne roman li eto*]" (734; 15:161).

The most important conclusion that Fetyukovich reaches is that, in the court, novels are far from innocent imaginative creations; they can destroy a person's life. Fetyukovich cannot know that he himself is in a novelistic plot in which he is being undermined by his creator. But at times one gets the impression that Fetyukovich is not so much arguing against Ippolit Kirillovich but against the author's plot, protesting the fate about to overtake him, arguing with his creator that what is being done to him is arbitrary, unfair, and unjustified, motivated solely by the author's fear of losing the authority over his own creation.

Fetyukovich's arguments are, of course, not meant as purely theoretical; they are as self-serving as the prosecution's. His argument that many equally plausible narratives could be invented to account for the facts of the case is correct but disingenuous. He knows that the prosecution has been dealt a far better hand, and there is much more evidence in support of the prosecution's narratives. Dostoevsky manufactures the circumstantial evidence in such a way that almost any jury would have been more receptive to the prosecutor's arguments than to the defense attorney's. Not having facts to support his position,

Fetyukovich is compelled to undermine narrative interpretations of the evidence or to use narrative only to cast suspicion on the validity of narrative. He must turn the argument from the specific to the general, from the practical to the theoretical, from narrative to rhetoric. Because he knows that he cannot persuade the jury to acquit his defendant either on the evidence or on narrative, he needs a jury nullification, that is, he needs the jury to disregard the evidence, disregard narrative, and be persuaded by rhetoric based on moral suasion. He then attempts to persuade the jury that no real crime was committed even if his client killed his father; he further argues that if the jurors acquit his client, they will be responsible for the salvation of his soul— à la Dostoevsky and Kornilova. Dostoevsky could easily point to the Zasulich case, in which the perpetrator was never at issue, and in which the lawyer asked for acquittal based on the character and motivation of his client. And as we have seen, through Fetyukovich, Dostoevsky offers a criticism of his own rhetoric in the Kornilova case. He is not implying that he should not have written the article in the *Diary of a Writer* otherwise, but he understands much better than he ever could have before that the method he used could be easily exploited to serve the interests of the lawyers and the political platforms of his ideological enemies.

## Challenging the Authorial Word:
## Salvation and the Resisting Reader

Dostoevsky cannot present rhetoric itself as adulteration of the word, having used it himself in the Kornilova case. Instead, he imposes on Fetyukovich so extreme a form of rhetorical excess that it appears qualitatively different from the rhetoric used by the participants (lawyers and *substitute lawyers*) in the Kornilova (Dostoevsky) or Zasulich (Aleksandrov) affairs. And herein lies the problem for the author. As we have seen, in order to discredit the discreditor, Dostoevsky uses the same techniques as Fetyukovich when the lawyer adulterates the word, including exaggeration, sarcasm, and ridicule. When a lower form of word is used, must the reader judge that too only by its source? If the author's word gains authority because of its association with the biblical Word, is it not bound to lose authority when it becomes associated with the lawyer's word, regardless of motivation? This is not a moral but an aesthetic issue. To discredit the lawyer Dostoevsky must become a contestant in the very world from which he wishes to withdraw. First, Dostoevsky builds Fetyukovich up as a brilliant deconstructionist who casts doubt on every prosecution witness and who subverts the reliability of narrative reconstructions. But so intent is Dostoevsky on bringing down the reigning king of the Russian bar that the author fobs off on his enemy a patently ridiculous argument about sons who have the right to kill less than perfect fathers.

This reduction of Fetyukovich comes at a price; it draws the implied author back into the world of the novel. He begins to merge with his narrator and become more a point of view within the experiential world of the novel than above it. In *The Brothers Karamazov*, as I have suggested before, Dostoevsky appears to dissociate himself from his narrator in order to maintain a superior, unchallengeable point of view, leaving the commentary to the characters and his narrator. Technically, of course, everything that Fetyukovich says is merely reported, or at least summarized, by the narrator, who was present at the trial. But here the author is not just paring his nails above the world of the novel, dispassionately observing the forces he has let loose through the internal dynamics of the plot; he has entered the fray and does everything that he can to destroy the word of the defense attorney, not only to save his plot for Dmitry and scuttle Fetyukovich's but also to undermine Fetyukovich's arguments about the relativity of narrative: that all narratives are permissible because the Word does not exist. Dostoevsky is trying to preserve and defend authorial omniscience but at the same time understands its shaky foundations. For Solovyov, who sees Dostoevsky as the precursor of the religious literature of the future, Dostoevsky is the true progressive, but in terms of both the history of the novel and Dostoevsky's earlier novels—especially *The Idiot* and *The Possessed*—*The Brothers Karamazov* looks backward, seeking authority for narrative in hagiography and the Bible, when the nineteenth-century novel was increasingly moving toward "realism" (verisimilitude) in point of view. *The Brothers Karamazov* assumes the uniqueness and authority of the author's word in a novelistic world where every word is contested and where no basis exists for authoritatively assessing the value of any word. Without the existence of an authority that guarantees the word of one over the other, all words and plots are contestable. By pressing his point of view so hard—the chapter title, for example, "The Adulterer of Thought"—Dostoevsky cannot avoid foregrounding the issue of authorial control, especially when it is openly discussed and debated in court and before all Russia.

Dostoevsky builds in protection against equating his salvation plot with Fetyukovich's by dismissively treating similar alternatives elsewhere. When Alyosha contests his brother's conclusion that all is permitted, Ivan blurts out that Dmitry's version, parricide (his salvation scenario before the actual murder), is not such a bad interpretation after all.

> "You mean 'everything is permitted'? Everything is permitted, is that right, is it?"
>
> Ivan frowned, and suddenly turned somehow strangely pale.
>
> "Ah, you caught that little remark yesterday, which offended Miusov so much . . . and that brother Dmitry so naively popped up and re-phrased?" He grinned crookedly. "Yes, perhaps 'everything is permitted,' since the word has already been spoken. I do not renounce it. And Mitenka's version is not so bad." (263; 14:240)

The novel asks the reader to weigh the alternatives when there is no superhuman authority, that is, when real authority no longer exists. But this move is not so easily transferable to Dmitry's salvation plot. The alternative plot that Fetyukovich suggests may, after all, be a viable alternative even though he is the one that offers it. Does not Dosto-evsky often express some of his most cherished ideas through despi-cable characters, including Svidrigaylov and Lebedev? In *The Idiot* Lebedev's views coincide with those of the implied author, although he is a scoundrel and his actions invariably stand in stark contrast to his ideas.[8] And the salvation plan that Fetyukovich offers is, after all, ex-actly the one that Dostoevsky worked so ardently to attain for Kornil-ova. And here the reader's special knowledge works as much against Dostoevsky's plan as for it. What is so bad about Fetyukovich's plan when we as readers know better than anyone in the world of the novel that Dmitry did not kill his father? Will not the shock be enough for Dmitry as it was for Father Zosima and Kornilova? Can one authori-tatively say it will not? If the trial took place not in 1866 but in 1879—that is, contemporaneous to the writing of the novel—Fetyukovich certainly would have intoned: "It is not only I who believe the acquit-tal of Dmitry is the surest way to achieve his moral and spiritual renewal, one need only refer to the articles and personal intercession of one of our greatest writers, Fedor Dostoevsky, who, though given to

a bit of mysticism, in 1877 advocated the same resolution for a defendant who, in contrast to my client, actually committed and confessed
to a serious crime." Could Dostoevsky have resisted such a move?

> Along with that you will destroy the still-possible man in him, for he
> will remain wicked and blind for the rest of his life. No, if you want to
> punish him terribly, fearfully, with the most horrible punishment imag-
> inable, but so as to save [*spasti*] and restore [*vozrodit'*] his soul for-
> ever—then overwhelm him with your mercy. You will see, you will hear
> how his soul will tremble and be horrified: "Is it for me to endure this
> mercy, for me to be granted so much love, and am I worthy of it?" he
> will exclaim! . . . But overwhelm such a soul with mercy, give it love, and
> it will curse what it has done, for there are so many germs of good in
> it. The soul will expand and behold how merciful God is, and how beau-
> tiful and just people are. He will be horrified, he will be overwhelmed
> with repentance and the countless debt he must henceforth repay. And
> then he will not say, "I am quits," but will say, "I am guilty before all
> people and am the least worthy of all people." In tears of repentance and
> burning, suffering tenderness he will exclaim: "People are better than I,
> for they wished not to ruin but to save me!" (747; 15:173)

If the word of the author is not completely authoritative, is it not possible to say, paraphrasing Ivan, that "Fetyukovich's version is not so
bad either?" It is certainly better than Alyosha's, Ivan's, and Katerina
Ivanovna's plan for Dmitry's escape to America. But perhaps the most
important unintended effect of the trial is that by opening up the question of authority, it also opens up, undetermines, Dmitry's fate, providing textual justification to resist the author's salvation plot. What
the author wants the trial to tell Dmitry is that he must resist all the
narratives offered in court that attempt to define him and lay out their
way for his salvation. On the contrary, he must accept his responsibility for the death of his father and suffer in Siberia for the sins of others, that is, he must accept the author's plot. But once the authority of
the author is subject to question, the author's salvation plot for Dmitry
itself becomes problematized; it becomes another plot that Dmitry
must consider, but it cannot be constrained, lest the author seem to be
assuming the position of the Grand Inquisitor against Christ. Moreover, the author's salvation plot is not a supernatural force working
its way through the phenomenal world unbeknown to the characters

themselves. Dmitry knows his creator's plot all too well, as is obvious from his passionate speech in prison before the trial:

> "Rakitin wouldn't understand it," he began, all in a sort of rapture, as it were, "but you, you will understand everything. That's why I've been thirsting for you. You see, for a long time I've been wanting to say many things to you here, within these peeling walls, but I've kept silent about the most important thing: the time didn't seem to have come yet. I've been waiting this last time to pour out my soul to you. *Brother, in these past two months I've sensed a new man in me, a new man has arisen in me! He was shut up inside me, but if it weren't for this thunderbolt, he never would have appeared. Frightening! What do I care if I spend twenty years pounding out iron ore in the mines, I'm not afraid of that at all, but I'm afraid of something else now: that this risen man not depart from me! Even there, in the mines, underground, you can find a human heart in the convict and murderer standing next to you, and you can be close to him, because there, too, it's possible to live, and love, and suffer! You can revive and resurrect the frozen heart in this convict, you can look after him for years, and finally bring up from the cave into the light a soul that is lofty now, a suffering consciousness, you can revive an angel, resurrect a hero! And there are many of them, there are hundreds, and we're all guilty for them! Why did I have a dream about a 'wee one' at such a moment? 'Why is the wee one poor?' It was a prophecy to me at that moment! It's for the 'wee one' that I will go. Because everyone is guilty for everyone else. For all the 'wee ones,' because there are little children and big children. All people are 'wee ones.' And I'll go for all of them, because there must be someone who will go for all of them. I didn't kill father. But I must go. I accept! All of this came to me here . . . within these peeling walls.* And there are many, there are hundreds of them, underground, with hammers in their hands. Oh, yes, we'll be in chains, and there will be no freedom, but then, in our great grief, we will arise once more into joy, without which it is impossible for man to live, or for God to be, for God gives joy, it's his prerogative, a great one. . . . Lord, let man dissolve in prayer! How would I be there underground without God? Rakitin's lying: if God is driven from the earth, we'll meet him underground! It's impossible for a convict to be without God, even more impossible than for a non-convict. And then from the depths of the earth, we, the men underground, will start singing a tragic hymn to God, in whom there is joy! Hail to God and his joy! I love him!" (591–92; 15:30–31; emphasis added)

Reading otherwise, we might say that although the dream of the babes tells Dmitry that he must take responsibility for others, the trial tells him that he must also take responsibility for himself in the sense that he must write his own script and resist all the attempts of others, including the author, to impose their agendas on him. Dmitry takes the author's salvation plot seriously, but something in Dmitry rebels against this plot as artificial, as though he senses that, like other plans for him, it is being used to advance someone else's agenda—though, of course, he cannot know that it is his creator's agenda. Dostoevsky presents Fetyukovich as exploiting Dmitry for his own political and personal ends, but the author uses Dmitry in much the same way that Fetyukovich does—albeit for a very different purpose. He needs Dmitry, as a sacrificial victim, to redeem Russia through his suffering. The rhetoric of the novel is designed to make Dmitry serve in the author's plot, not Fetyukovich's. But until Dmitry chooses the author's plot of his own free will, the plot, novelistically speaking, will remain the author's plot, not Dmitry's choice.

When we see Dmitry, in the second chapter of the epilogue, he is not only seriously considering his author's plot but also rebelling against it. Dmitry does not care that others—Alyosha, Ivan, and Katerina Ivanovna, for example—think that the author's plot is not for him (everybody is aware of the author's plot through Dmitry); he needs to make the decision by himself and for himself before he can make it for others.

> "And here's something else I want to tell you," Mitya continued in a suddenly ringing voice, "if they start beating me on the way, or *there,* I won't let them, I'll kill someone, and they'll shoot me. And it's for twenty years! They've already started talking down to me here. The guards talk down to me. I was lying here all night judging myself: I'm not ready! Not strong enough to take it! I wanted to sing a 'hymn,' yet I can't stand the guards' talking down to me! I'd endure anything for Grusha, everything . . . except beatings, that is. . . . But they won't let her go *there.*" (763; 15:185)

The narrator's salvation plot for Dmitry will also suffer once the reader loses confidence in the kairotic time propounded by the author. The mystical foundation of the salvation plot is validated by the sayings of Father Zosima regarding the difference between chronological and kairotic time and the relevance of Job for modern man. The author's idea is that Dmitry may initially rebel against the master plot, but with time a miracle will occur: he will accept his creator's plan, he will be purified by suffering and understand its existential, national, and mystical purpose. But Zosima's statements and ideas are reported in the neo-hagiography written by the author. Once the author places himself on the same level and in the same court as Fetyukovich, we may question the authority of the hagiography that he pens and the salvation plot that he uses Father Zosima to validate. Fetyukovich cites "authorities," including the Gospels (of course mangled) and Dostoevsky (almost exactly but with a change of context) in order to validate his propositions. Fetyukovich says, as it were, "It is not only I who say this, but Dostoevsky, my creator, says so, too." Dostoevsky uses the same technique for himself. It is not only I who have created this plot for Dmitry, it is part of the hagiographical tradition. But, of course, Dostoevsky is the author of the very hagiographical text that he uses to bolster his authority.

If authorial authority is problematic, the law and the court cannot be seen only in terms of the author's salvation plot for Dmitry. The presupposition of the author's plot is that the jury trial is irrelevant, not because it is a creation of the reform court but because all legal solutions are inadequate in the face of the mystery of life. The same thing would have happened, albeit through different procedures, in the old court. The twenty-year sentence is part of a divine plan whose meaning we can never completely fathom but that we take on the authority of the author. But if the authorial plot becomes subject to doubt or dispute, Dmitry's twenty years immediately become something very different. If the divine plan remains in effect, the court becomes a tool of the author, not only for Dmitry but for all Russia. But if the author's plot is not validated by the text, then Dmitry's sentence of twenty years for a crime he did not commit serves no purpose, just as Ilyinsky's twenty-year term, in Dostoevsky's own view, was a terrible mistake serving no purpose whatsoever. To remove the higher purpose of the author's master plot for Dmitry returns the plot of *The Brothers Karamazov* to its early prototype—and to the court.

The worst mistake that the court can make—sentencing Dmitry to twenty years of hard labor—makes the best possible material for the author's salvation plot. But if the master plot is called into question, the trial can no longer be dismissed as irrelevant, just as Ilyinsky's "trial" was never irrelevant. The judicial error will turn into a catastrophe. The decision of the court would be absurd. Without the master plot—or even with a somewhat discredited master plot—Dmitry is no longer a sacrificial lamb but the victim of a terrible, impersonal, rational machine called the jury trial, through which an innocent man gets convicted and a whole nation is exposed to the worst of all possible moral educations. Under such a scenario *The Brothers Karamazov* comes to resemble the pessimism of *The Idiot,* where the salvation plot also fails, with Nastasya Filippovna murdered, Myshkin gone insane, and Rogozhin sentenced to twenty years of hard labor. It would mean the ruin of Russia (Dmitry) and the complete triumph of the law (Fetyukovich). Fetyukovich would have lost the battle (the trial) but won the war—his real aim from the very beginning.

Thus the novel presents us with a typical Dostoevskian maximalist choice. Because Dostoevsky forecloses any possibility that the jury trial in *The Brothers Karamazov,* as jury trial, will play any rational role in Dmitry's salvation, he asks us to either buy into his master plot for Dmitry and Russia or resign ourselves to a life ruled by the court and law, through which Dmitry is impersonally and rationally dispatched for the so-called good of us all.[9]

Dostoevsky attempts to discredit the modern world through the court, the center of the adulteration of the Word. There are other dangerous adulterations of the Word, such as the Grand Inquisitor's, but Dostoevsky fears them less because they are closer to the Word, even when they are on the side of the devil. There is always hope for a prodigal son. He attempts to persuade the reader that his salvation plot for Dmitry is the only one possible for Russia and the world, and he places resisting readers in the position of those of little faith, denizens of the accursed middle ground, lukewarm spewed-out Laodiceans, the Miusovs, and Rakitins, who view everything as permissible and possible but find no place in life and the court for the mystical sources of our being. There is no middle that can be occupied. Dostoevsky takes away the possibility that he extended to Kornilova, and which he himself once envisioned for the Russian people, salvation through the court. Those who resist both "The Russian Monk" and "The Grand Inquisitor" are condemned to live in an empty world, signifying nothing. It is certainly difficult being a resisting reader of *The Brothers Karamazov,* left to defend the law and the court against the ostensible rhetoric of the novel. But this is the fate of all deconstructionist readers of *The Brothers Karamazov.*

I say *all* somewhat ironically. The truth is that there have been relatively few resistant readers of *The Brothers Karamazov* of late.[10] There are those who hold that Zosima, and especially Alyosha, are some of Dostoevsky's most successful artistic achievements. Others are swept away by Dostoevsky's art. Art trumps rational argument in the novel as much as Dostoevsky argued it does in court. And it is no consolation that we know that we lead most of our lives in the middle ground and that however we may rage against the law and lawyers, we will be the first to turn to the law and the courts when we need to resolve our disputes with others. Dostoevsky would use lawyers himself when in need of them, though he remained somewhat contemptuous of their tactics.[11] But until the next dispensation, he would say that there is no other way.

And so the persistently resisting reader must struggle against the rhetoric of the novel, ready to defend the most pessimistic and legal ending of Dostoevsky's most optimistic and religious novel. For *The Brothers Karamazov*, after all, is not only Dostoevsky's most optimistic novel, it is also his most monophonic novel. For the more essential Dostoevsky, for the most ambiguous, polyphonic, and dialogic novelist, the reader probably needs to turn to novels of greater tragic vision, *The Idiot* and *The Possessed*. In *The Brothers Karamazov*, instead of exploring the world of ultimate ambiguity—the world of law symbolized by the jury trial—Dostoevsky chooses the opposite path, attempting to bypass the world of law almost entirely, presenting it in the end as not so much evil as irrelevant. Dostoevsky does not fall into the same trap as Tolstoy and Goncharov. He does not write history, but the avoidance of the chaos so brilliantly described in *The Idiot* and *The Possessed* leads him at times into the world of allegoric hagiography no less distant from the modern world than Tolstoy's Napoleonic invasion of the early nineteenth century. The law is silent at the end of *The Brothers Karamazov*, but it is a destabilizing silence. There is a price, an artistic price, to be paid for stifling its voice. But that price will be felt only by those who insist on the primacy of the novel. For those more hagiographically inclined, all that will be heard are the final words of Alyosha, as supreme scout leader, inspiring the next generation at Ilyusha's grave, and, of course, the echo of Father Zosima's words: "So be it! So be it!"

# Notes

## Introduction

1. The novel was published before the reforms were enacted. Jury trials began in St. Petersburg in November 1866. But aspects of the new reform, such as the examining magistrate (*sudebnyi sledovatel'*)—Porfiry Petrovich in the novel—were already being introduced in the early 1860s.

2. Theodore Ziolkowski, *The Mirror of Justice: Literary Reflections of Legal Crises* (Princeton, N.J.: Princeton University Press, 1997), 16.

3. Ziolkowski writes: "It is a commonplace of legal anthropology that, at the beginning of their evolution, law and morality are not yet separated and the development of law amounts to a process of continual dissociation of those two social forces" (*The Mirror of Justice*, 14). By contrast, in the earliest stages of civilization, law and morality (religion)—even lawyers (lawgivers) and priests—are not easily separable. See Uwe Wesel, *Juristische Weltkunde. Eine Einführung in das Recht* (1984; reprint, Frankfurt am Main: surhkamp taschenbuch, 1993), 194–202.

4. Richard A. Posner, *Law and Literature: A Misunderstood Relation* (Cambridge, Mass.: Harvard University Press, 1988), 13.

5. Although law and literature is frequently called a movement, school, or enterprise within legal studies, its representatives cover the entire map of modern and postmodern hermeneutical positions, from New Criticism to deconstructionism. Theorists such as Michel Foucault, Jacques Derrida, Paul de Man, Andrea Dworkin, Stanley Fish, and Richard Rorty have been especially influential in the area of interpretation: law-as-literature or discourse. Fish poses the same questions about the interpretation of law and its authority as he does about the interpretation of literature, applying his well-known concept of interpretative communities to both disciplines. Through the 1980s law and literature scholars distinguished between law-in-literature and law-as-literature, but although this distinction is still widely used, it has been increasingly contested. Legal scholars who have adopted the postmodern view of law and literature as texts, as coterminous narrative discourses, argue against any real separation. Works like Kafka's

*Trial* are seen not as pure imaginary creations but as virtual legal texts, from which we can learn as much about the law as from studying the U.S. Constitution.

6. Robert Weisberg, "The Law-Literature Enterprise," *Yale Journal of Law and Humanities* 1, no. 1 (1988): 1.

7. See Guyora Binder's discussion of the trope of law-as-narrative, "The Law-as-Literature Trope," in Michael Freeman and Andrew D. E. Lewis, eds., *Law and Literature* (New York: Oxford University Press, 1999), 72–76. In the late 1980s both Richard Posner and Robert Weisberg expressed their dissatisfaction with the scholarly work done in law-as-literature. Robert Weisberg writes:

> As for the other side of the coin, law-as-literature, I will argue that most of this work has also yielded fairly skimpy intellectual benefits. Most of it has sought to exploit the analogy between legal and literary texts by treating legal texts as consciously created works of prose that can be appreciated and criticized in terms of explicit or implicit intended meaning. As such, though it has helped to demonstrate some of the rhetorical artistry of great lawyers, it has bumped up against the obvious, fundamental fact that lawmaking is an intellectual act conditioned by formal political constraints that do not apply to literary expression" ("The Law-Literature Enterprise," 3).

Ironically, today the law-as-literature movement is viewed as being more central to the concerns of the profession and is consequently drawing most of the attention of legal scholars.

8. J. M. Balkin and Sanford Levinson, "Law as Performance," in Freeman and Lewis, *Law and Literature,* 729.

9. Posner writers, "The study of law and literature seeks to use legal insights to enhance understanding of literature, not just literary insights to enhance understanding of law" (*Law and Literature,* 1988, 1). In the latest edition of his work Posner recognizes the more practical reality of law and literature scholarship: "That the edifying school has struck a responsive chord with legal scholars of literary bent should come as no surprise. The ratio of normative to positive scholarship is higher in law than in most other fields. Law is not a contemplative discipline and the aesthetic outlook does not come easily to its disciples. If they bring literature into law it is to contribute to what they perceive to be the normative mission of legal scholarship" (*Law and Literature,* 2d ed. [Cambridge, Mass.: Harvard University Press, 1998], 308).

10. The trial scene in act 4 of *The Merchant of Venice* may be the most famous of all literary trials, but it hardly resembles a modern jury trial at all. The situation regarding the bond is farfetched (it is as literary a device as the caskets), there are no lawyers, and the judge (Portia) is an impostor who outwits Shylock by hoisting him by his own literalist, legalistic petard.

11. Justifying his book on literary analyses of law, Ziolkowski writes: "Laws, and systems of laws, have changed profoundly over time. The record of that change, of the forces that have produced that evolution, can often best be observed not in

the law books but in literature. What many masterpieces of world literature mirror are not simply the workings of the law but, more compellingly, the moments of crisis when society discovers that its laws have become problematic. . . . Literature provides a faithful mirror of justice that shows, moreover, that the finest literary works (the 'canon') more often challenge than support the prevailing ideology" (*The Mirror of Justice*, x).

12. The same may be said of the numerous articles written about Kafka's *The Trial*, Dickens's *Bleak House*, and Shakespeare's *The Merchant of Venice* and *Measure for Measure*. Richard Posner's insightful article on the theme of revenge in Elizabethan literature and Boyd White's interesting analysis of *Richard II* do not seem to benefit from their authors' legal expertise. I am not contesting that articles by legal experts on law in literature can be as insightful as those of literary critics. But other than interest and passion, there is probably little that a specialized knowledge of the law per se will add to the analysis of literary texts, even where the law figures prominently. The insight of literary criticism written by lawyers and legal scholars is related to their perspicacity as literary critics, not expertise on the law.

13. Posner, *Law and Literature*, 1998, 19–20. Furthermore, as Ziolkowski points out, the vast majority of works that deal with the law do not question its authority or validity; they invariably concern themselves with "the determination of the facts within its framework" (*The Mirror of Justice*, 16).

14. As we shall see, Dostoevsky did have a model for the twenty-year sentence. The convict Ilyinsky, whom Dostoevsky portrays in *Notes from the House of the Dead*, was sent to hard labor in Siberia for twenty years for killing his father. He was exonerated after having served ten years. But his sentence was meted out under entirely different conditions, that is, long before the new reform courts, based on the legal reforms of 1864, began to operate.

15. The legal reforms of 20 November 1864 are a complex subject to which many monographs, dissertations, and articles have been devoted. For an insightful review of the literature on the 1864 reforms, especially that relating to the introduction and implementation of the jury trial from 1864 to 1881, see Girish Narayan Bhat, "Trial by Jury in the Reign of Alexander II: A Study in the Legal Culture of Late Imperial Russia, 1864–1881" (Ph.D. diss., University of California, Berkeley, 1995). The only study to date that attempts to link the legal reforms to Dostoevsky's work in detail is David Lee Keily's "The Brothers Karamazov and the Fate of Russian Truth: Shifts in the Construction and Interpretation of Narrative after the Judicial Reform of 1864" (Ph.D. diss., Harvard University, 1996). Keily asks many of the right questions about Dostoevsky's portrayal of the trial in *The Brothers Karamazov*, but he does not treat the trial in the context of Dostoevsky's journalism, nor does he offer answers to the questions he poses.

16. This is a very widely held notion. Literature "can better educate lawyers" (Ian Ward, *Law and Literature: Possibilities and Perspectives* [Cambridge: Cambridge University Press, 1995], ix). "Fiction stimulates the reader's capacity to imagine other people in other universes. . . . After a lawyer or law student reads

Charles Dickens's *Bleak House,* he can never again be completely indifferent or 'objective' towards the client across the desk" (C. R. B. Dunlop, "Literature Studies," *Cardozo Studies in Law and Literature* 3, no. 1 [1991]: 70). "In this understanding, law and literature is much like the movement for medicine and literature: a use of literature as a humanizing device" (Peter Brooks and Paul Gewirtz, eds., *Law's Stories: Narrative and Rhetoric in the Law* [New Haven, Conn.: Yale University Press, 1996], 15). "It was hoped that the study of literature might create more rounded people and therefore more sensitive and thoughtful lawyers, leading in turn to the hope of justice and ethics in the operation of the legal system" (John Morison and Christine Bell, eds., introduction to *Tall Stories? Reading Law and Literature* [Aldershot, U.K.: Dartmouth Publishing, 1996], 2).

Another often discussed aspect of "literature-for-law" concerns the education of law students. Some lawyers with literary interests openly acknowledge that they find teaching and writing about literature more interesting than analyzing the standard dry-as-bones case studies and statutes. If given the opportunity in a course on criminal law, they will use *The Brothers Karamazov.* But more often they cite practical reasons: Students prefer literary to legal texts in learning about the law, and they can learn better from the literary texts. Ward writes: "To lawyers like myself, in general, and certainly too often, there seems precious little fun in the law, or in learning about it. Literature, on the other hand, can be fun. . . . Law need not be like sawdust. . . . Students might better enjoy, and thus, inevitably, better understand the origins of English constitutional thought by reading *Richard II,* the inadequacies of rape law by reading *The Husband's Tale* and the psychology of English property law just by looking at the pictures in *The Tale of Peter Rabbit*" (*Law and Literature,* ix).

Christine Bell maintains that literary texts that address legal issues engage students more than legal texts. Kafka's "Penal Colony," for example, can stimulate discussion of corporal punishment and the role of body in terms of punishment (Bell, in Morison and Bell, introduction to *Tall Stories?* 13–16). In her preface to her anthology of critical essays and literary texts relating to law, Lenora Ledwon writes: "A second reason for the growth in Law and Literature studies is that, quite, simply, it's wonderful, mind-expanding stuff" (*Law and Literature: Text and Theory* [New York: Garland, 1996], 10). On the use of literature in the law curriculum, see also Robin West, *Caring for Justice* (New York: New York University Press, 1997), 181.

17. Richard Weisberg, "Coming to Age Some More: 'Law and Literature' Beyond the Cradle," *Nova Law Review* 13 (1988): 121.

18. Robin West, *Narrative, Authority, and Law* (Ann Arbor: University of Michigan Press, 1993), 263. The moral aesthetics of law is the animating force of such studies as Richard Weisberg's *Poethics, and Other Strategies of Law and Literature* (New York: Columbia University Press, 1992), and Martha Nussbaum's *Poetic Justice: The Literary Imagination and Public Life* (Boston: Beacon, 1995). Weisberg writes: "Poethics in its attention to legal communication and to the plight of those who are 'other' seeks to revitalize the ethical component of law" (*Poethics,* 46).

Posner writes convincingly of the dubious practice of resorting to literature for moral support. Kevin Crotty recognizes the problem of literature as a moral guide; he is content to use it a way of seeing the law in its concrete and problematic manifestations in real life (*Law's Interior: Legal and Literary Constructions of the Self* [Ithaca, N.Y.: Cornell University Press, 2001], 15–16). Some doubt has crept in even among those who apply law and literature comparisons.

19. The interest of legal scholars in literature has encouraged a comparable phenomenon among literary scholars: the examination of literary texts through the lens of the law or legal system, which is seen as central to the fictional universe of many writers. Kieran Dolin writes: "It seems clear that despite the apparent opposition of the discourse of literature and law fostered by professional specialization, that a contextualized study of the fictional representations and appropriations of law, and of the institutions of writing and legal practice will materially enhance our understanding of nineteenth-century culture and its dominant genre, the novel" (*Fiction and the Law: Legal Discourse in Victorian and Modernist Literature* [Cambridge: Cambridge University Press, 1999], 4). Because literature represents the private sphere and law the public, works in which legal issues are present will be seen as an attempt to achieve a dialogue between private and social cultural spheres. Dolin cites dozens of studies that "underline the formative importance of law in nineteenth-century culture" (7). They are all, in various ways, products of the "return to history" in literary criticism, that is, greatly influenced by new historicism.

20. Weisberg, "The Law-Literature Enterprise," 52.

21. Crotty writes, "Indeed, an important feature of our legal system is that it extends to all aspects of social life, so that for every conceivable situation there exists a case precedent that is at least arguably relevant. There are few subjects, it seems, on which the law is wholly silent. . . . Law, like language, reflects the irreducibly social aspect of our nature" (*Law's Interior,* 1, 2).

22. Ibid., 11, 21.

23. Robert M. Cover, "*Nomos* and Narrative," *Harvard Law Review* 97 (1983–84): 4.

24. See, for example, Peter Brooks's attempt to use literature, including Dostoevsky's *The Brothers Karamazov,* to arrive at a better understanding of confession in legal proceedings (*Troubling Confessions: Speaking Guilt in Law and Literature* [Chicago: University of Chicago Press, 2000], 9).

25. Vladimir Nabokov, who had a similarly unflattering view of Chernyshevsky's work, nevertheless recognized its tremendous power for nineteenth-century readers. Even Turgenev and Tolstoy, far more popular than Dostoevsky, could not make as powerful an impression on their contemporaries as *What Is to Be Done.* See Vladimir Nabokov, *Sobranie sochinenii russkogo perioda,* 5 vols. (St. Petersburg: Simpozium, 2002), 4:453.

26. Paul Gewirtz writes, "But for others the interest in narrative may actually reflect . . . a turn to analyzing form and structure and rhetoric that arises from a frustration with the capacity of substantive legal arguments to change the real

world as one would like, or perhaps even a loss in substantive reform itself" ("Narrative and Rhetoric in the Law," in Brooks and Gewirtz, *Law's Stories*, 12).

27. Or, as Guyora Binder writes: "The law-as-literature trope is understood to imply that left to lawyers, law is mere letter: dry, abstract, artificial, unyieldingly rigid, naively formalistic, cynical, calculating, contentious, profane. Literature, by contrast, is a redemptive spirit or unrepressed feeling, anarchic play, or unembarrassed faith" ("Law-as-Literature Trope," 68).

28. Peter Goodrich, *Law in the Courts of Love: Literature and Other Minor Jurisprudences* (London: Routledge, 1996), vii. Richard Weisberg writes: "Poetics in its attention to legal communication and to the plight of those who are 'other' seeks to revitalize the ethical component of law" (*Poethics*, 46).

29. According to Weisberg, "Much of this work assumes that law is naturally, or has become viewed as, mechanistic, abstract, rule-like, and that to appreciate, apply, or reform law, the abstracted professional, rationalist voice must be replaced or at least complemented by something like a more human voice" (*Poethics*, 17).

30. Robin West is as skeptical now about the literary representation of outsiders, especially women, as she is about the status of women in the law. Now we need to be wary, she argues, that "misrepresentations of women in law will only be magnified . . . by the misrepresentations of women in literature and other high forms of culture." The shared communality of literature and law "is an obstacle to overcome in the quest for true equality, not an overlooked reason for wedding the two" (*Caring for Justice*, 185). For West, continuing to see law as a humanity can very well halt the real need for reforming the law. Those taken up with the law as literature sometimes see law too much in terms of aesthetics and insufficiently in terms of justice (188, 185). Indeed, like Weisberg, West is suspicious of the word as a historically perfected tool of oppression (for West, patriarchal oppression). In that, she comes close to the earlier work of French feminist psychoanalytic critics like Hélène Cixous, Luce Irigaray, and Julia Kristeva.

31. Toni M. Massaro, "Empathy, Legal Storytelling, and the Rule of Law: New Words, Old Wounds?" *Michigan Law Review* 87 (1988): 2001. Lynne Henderson, a proponent of this view, writes that "the ideological structures of legal discourse and cognition block affective and phenomenological argument" (quoted in Massaro, "Empathy," 2102). For arguments in favor of empathy in legal proceedings, see Kim Scheppele, "Forward: Telling Stories," *Michigan Law Review* 87 (1988): 2073–98; Richard Delago, "A Plea for Narrative," *Michigan Law Review* 87 (1988): 2411–41.

32. Michael Ryan, "Meaning and Alternity," afterword to Martha Minow, Michael Ryan, and Austin Sarat, eds., *Narrative, Violence and Law* (Ann Arbor: University of Michigan Press, 1992), 68.

33. Massaro, "Empathy," 2113. It was common in the nineteenth century, as it is today, for lawyers to argue the law when the facts were not on their side and to appeal to the emotions of jurors when the law was not on their side. "Indeed, it is a truism of trial practice that when the defense lawyer cannot prevail on

categorical legal issues, she will use jury arguments to tell a sympathetic, usually deterministic story of her client's life and conduct" (Weisberg, "The Law-Literature Enterprise," 19). Complaints about the attempt of defense attorneys to manipulate the emotions and prejudices of jurors were universal in the nineteenth century and were used as the basis of arguments for placing limitations on the jury trial or even eliminating it altogether.

34. Gewirtz writes, "But storytelling is an activity available to all individuals and groups, and in law a decision maker usually must choose amongst competing stories. . . . Surely we cannot assume that just because a story is told by an outsider it is any more true or complete than a story told by an insider" ("Narrative and Rhetoric in the Law," 6). Gewirtz addresses in detail the problems of storytelling in the court (2–13), noting the many ways narrative at trial differs from literary narrative: "In short, a trial consists of fragmented narratives and narrative multiplicity" (8). But even more problematic, the notion of narrative that legal scholars use in applying narrative to court proceedings differs radically from the use of narrative in fiction; it is often narrative in its simplest storytelling function.

35. For a discussion of the differences of common law and civil law in this regard, see A. G. Chloros, "Common Law, Civil Law and Socialist Law: Three Leading Systems of the World, Three Kinds of Legal Thought," in Henry W. Ehrmann, ed., *Comparative Legal Cultures* (Englewood Cliffs, N.J.: Prentice-Hall, 1976). "It was in resolving disputes, rather than in laying down principles, that the English judge could see justice done" (85). Whereas in literary interpretation, author, reader, and text each play important roles in the interpretative process, in legal interpretation judges, given the real life consequences of their decisions, are often the main focus of concern. Their interpretations are performative. This is sometimes reflected in law-in-literature texts, as in Portia's role as a judge in *The Merchant of Venice*. On the other hand, minority groups can always test the system for a sympathetic hearing. As Ehrmann notes, minority groups have traditionally attempted to take advantage of judicial discretion. "In some countries, including the United States, certain minority groups which lack electoral strength find it more profitable to resort to litigation rather than to legislation" (*Comparative Legal Cultures*, 10).

36. Ward, *Law and Literature*, 42.

37. Weisberg, "The Law-Literature Enterprise," 52, 53, 55.

38. In the latest edition of his book on law and literature, Posner has added a new chapter ("The Edifying School of Legal Scholarship") critiquing those who assess the value of literature by the moral values that it purportedly espouses or those who wish to use literature as a means of advancing their moral, social, and political positions. See Posner, *Law and Literature*, 1998, 306–44.

39. White and Dworkin have at times advanced an idealistic equation of aesthetics and morality in which judges and lawyers can be viewed as political artists. See, for example, James B. White, *The Legal Imagination: Studies in the Nature*

*of Legal Thought and Expression* (Boston: Little, Brown, 1973), xxiv–xxv. Robin West has accused White and Dworkin of attempting to resurrect an old American nineteenth-century ideal laid out by Robert A. Ferguson, who shows that, for the nineteenth century, the ideal lawyer was at once an attorney and a person of letters, a lawyer-writer in whom law and culture were not separate entities but a continuous web (*Law and Letters in American Culture* [Cambridge, Mass.: Harvard University Press], 1984).

40. Despite the increasing scholarly production in the field of law and literature, questions continue to arise about the utility of harnessing literature for the causes of legal studies—and sometimes from unexpected quarters. In particular, Robin West seems to have become less sanguine about the efficacy of the law and literature movement to effect the kind of radical legal changes that she advocates, even suggesting the peripheral nature of the entire literature and law enterprise. "Enthusiasm for the law and literature renaissance we are presently experiencing must be tempered: surely by any objective standard, law and literature is a marginal movement, which, although healthy, is viewed by everyone but its practitioners as voicing peripheral concerns to the overall pedagogical and scholarly missions of the legal academy" (West, *Caring for Justice*, 180).

41. See also Dostoevsky's articles on the Jewish question in *Diary of a Writer* for March 1877.

42. See Bhat, "Trial by Jury," 44. For an informative summary of the Russian judicial system before the reforms of 1864, see Samuel Kucherov, *Courts, Lawyers, and Trials Under the Last Three Tsars* (New York: Praeger, 1953), 1–19.

43. A. F. Koni points out that whereas there were great disagreements about the emancipation of the peasants, everyone was in essential agreement regarding the inadequacy of the old judicial system and the need for substantial changes. See Koni, *Sobranie sochinenii*, 8 vols. (Moscow: Iuridicheskaia literatura, 1967), 4:201–3.

44. Richard Pipes, *Russia Under the Old Regime* (New York: Scribner's, 1975), 288–89. For further details see pp. 295–97.

45. Compared to his counterparts in contemporary common and civil law systems, the defendant in the reformed Russian courts lacked many pretrial rights. The defense lawyer did not see the case against his client until it was completed for trial by the prosecutor's office, the arm of the state. The Russian system, which was based on French and other civil law models, reflected its contemporary counterparts in this regard. Toward the end of the century, in France and other Western European countries, steps were taken to give defendants greater pretrial rights. But because of the limited access of the defense to pretrial investigation, an increased burden was placed on the defense attorney, especially his summation.

46. Bhat writes, "Familiar in its essentials to modern-day inhabitants of common and civil law countries, controversial procedure is governed by the presumption of innocence, the overriding importance of orality in adjudication, and an official adherence to codified, rigorous standards of proof in evaluating testimony and material evidence" ("Trial by Jury," 46).

47. According to Michael T. Florinsky, the most important elements of the legal reform in general were:

> Equality of all before the law; access to an impartial tribunal and the right to be heard; acceptance of the maxim *nullum crimen, nulla poena sine lege,* that is, no action is punishable unless adjudicated, after a fair trial, as a violation of the law; uniformity and relative simplicity of judicial procedure; separation of the judicial from the legislative and executive power; irremovability of judges, except for misconduct in office; publicity of proceedings; representation of the parties in civil cases and of defendants in criminal cases by qualified members of the bar; trial by jury; election of judges of the lower courts; preliminary investigation of criminal offenses by examining magistrates (*sudebnyi sledovatel',* the French *juge d'instruction*) instead of by the police. (*Russia: A History and an Interpretation,* 2 vols. [New York: Macmillan, 1953], 2:903–4)

One must also admit that in fact there was a transition from one system to another. Just as some of the unfortunate aspects of the old system were carried forward into the new, some of the improvements noticeable in the new system had already been initiated earlier, such as the investigatory pretrial procedures as amended in the Svod zakonov of 1857. See Bhat, "Trial by Jury," 64–65. Bhat concludes: "In its broad outlines and principles, then, the 1864 jury trial system may properly be considered 'adversarial' according to the tendencies of common law procedure, but in its daily functioning this system proved to be a striking composite of pluralistic, almost communitarian judicial tendencies and more traditional praxis along the lines of older, pre-Reform inquisitorial modes" (165).

48. A. I. Gertsen, *Byloe i dumy* (Leningrad: GIKhL, 1947), 102.

49. A. F. Koni, *Na zhiznennom puti* (Moscow, 1912–13), 2:168–69, quoted in Kucherov, *Courts, Lawyers and Trials,* 3.

50. Quoted in Kucherov, *Courts, Lawyers and Trials,* 4.

51. Herbert Spencer, *Social Statics; or the Conditions Essential to Human Happiness Specified, and the First of the Them Developed* (New York: Appleton, 1875), 289.

52. Most historians, though more critical than their counterparts in the nineteenth century, still have considerable praise for the 1864 judicial reforms. See, for example, Nicholas Riasanovsky, *A History of Russia,* 5th ed. (Oxford: Oxford University Press, 1993), 376–78; W. Bruce Lincoln, *The Great Reforms* (DeKalb: Northern Illinois University Press, 1999); Ben Eklof, John Bushnell, and Larissa Zakharova, eds., *Russia's Great Reforms: 1855–1881* (Bloomington: Indiana University Press, 1994), passim. Contemporary Russia is still working on jury reform. Since 1994 experimental trials have been held in about 10 percent of the country. Under the new criminal code passed in 2002, all serious crimes are to be tried by jury. For an insightful assessment of the state of the jury trial in late 2003—with discussion of actual trials and interviews with defendants and jurors—see Peter

Baker's 21 Sept 2003 article in the *Washington Post,* entitled "Russia Tests Juries by Trial and Error."

53. Quoted in Kucherov, *Courts, Lawyers and Trials,* 98–99.

54. The new courts opened in St. Petersburg on 17 April 1866 and in Moscow on 23 April 1866.

55. Bhat, "Trial by Jury," 21, 42.

56. For a discussion of the polemics in *Vremia* and other prominent journals of the time on the issue of the impending (and newly implemented) judicial reforms, see V. S. Nechaeva, *Zhurnal M. M. i F. M. Dostoevskikh "Vremia": 1861–63* (Moscow: Nauka, 1972), 110–25; V. S. Nechaeva, *Zhurnal M. M. i F. M. Dostoevskikh "Epokha": 1864–65* (Moscow: Nauka, 1975), 42, 56–59; T. S. Karlova, *Dostoevskii i russkii sud* (Kazan': Izd. Kazanskogo universiteta, 1975). Especially important are the articles by P. N. Tkachev in *Vremia,* "Nashi budushchie prisiazhnye," and in *Epokha,* "Byt' ili ne byt' sosloviiu advokatov," in which Tkachev discusses the advantages and disadvantages of creating a Russian bar. In general, Dostoevsky's journals are rather eclectic in their representation of the reforms, with conservatives and even radicals (Tkachev, for example) contributing major articles.

57. F. M. Dostoevskii, *Polnoe sobranie sochinenii,* ed. V. G. Bazanov et al., 30 vols. (Leningrad: Nauka, 1972–90), 20:180. Hereafter Russian citations from Dostoevsky's works will be taken from this edition and cited directly in the text with just volume and page numbers. All translations from the Russian are mine unless otherwise indicated.

58. A. G. Dostoevskaia, *Vospominaniia* (Moscow: Mezhkniga, 1971), 170.

59. Citing the lawyer who worked on the "civil" case against Prince Myshkin, Ganya, who has taken up the case for the Prince, reports to a large gathering: "Everyone was completely sincere, and although Chebarov may indeed be a great scoundrel, in this business he acted as any petty, sharp, scheming lawyer would have under the circumstances" (6:234). Evgeny Pavlovich recalls, humorously, another unscrupulous lawyer. "It reminds me . . . of a recent, well-known case in which a defense lawyer cited the poverty of his client as the reason for murdering and robbing six people. He concluded that 'It was quite natural that my client, because of his poverty, decided to murder six people; for who would not have committed this crime in his place?'" (8:236). Lizaveta Prokofyevna responds: "No, Evgeny Pavlovich, if, as you stated yourself just now, a defense attorney said in open court that there was nothing more natural than to murder six people on account of poverty, then the world must be entering its last days. I had not heard anything like that before. Now it is all clear to me" (8:237). And Lebedev resorts to the services of a clever lawyer to have Myshkin declared insane. "However, Lebedev did not lose heart; he consulted with a clever lawyer, a respectable old man, a friend, one might even call him his benefactor. The lawyer concluded that it was completely possible to bring it off, if only he could get competent witnesses of Myshkin's mental derangement" (8:487).

60. The alternatives to evil are most explicit in *Crime and Punishment,* but even there they play a minor role or are relegated to the future.

## 1. The Imprisonment of the Law

1. All translations from the *Diary of Writer* are from the Brasol edition, F. M. Dostoievsky, *The Diary of a Writer*, trans. Boris Brasol (New York: Braziller, 1954); they have been checked against the original in F. M. Dostoevskii, *Polnoe sobranie sochinenii*, ed. V. G. Bazanov et al. (Leningrad: Nauka, 1972–90), vols. 22–23. The pagination for the three cases that will be discussed in this and following chapters are as follows: the Kroneberg case (22:50–73); the Kairova case (23:5–20); and the Kornilova case, in four sections (23:136–41, 24:36–43, 25:119–21, 26:92–110). Henceforth, references to the English and Russian editions of the *Diary* will appear in the text; the Russian volume and page number follow the English, separated by a semicolon.

2. The description of Rogozhin's trial in *The Idiot* resembles that of Raskolnikov's trial in *Crime and Punishment*. "He [Rogozhin] gave straightforward, accurate, and completely satisfactory testimony on every point, and because of it from the very beginning the Prince was not involved in the court proceedings. Rogozhin was silent during the trial. He did not contradict his sharp and eloquent lawyer, who clearly and logically tried to prove that the cause of the crime was inflammation of the brain, a condition that had long predated the crime and that had been caused by his client's misfortunes" (8:507).

3. Dostoevsky's deontological position in this passage, a position that he maintains fairly consistently throughout the Kroneberg article, is, however, not particularly characteristic of his ethics. For Dostoevsky the psychologist, and particularly for Dostoevsky the Russian Orthodox Christian, motivation is usually the most important moral measure of action. And, in fact, the more psychology comes to play an important role, as in his other legal articles in *Diary of a Writer*, the more Dostoevsky as motivist comes to the fore. It is generally far easier for Dostoevsky—as it would be for most of us—to take a deontological position when he does not take a personal interest in the accused. For one of the classic arguments for Dostoevsky as motivist, see the analysis of *The Idiot* by E. H. Carr, "The Ethical Ideal," in *Dostoevsky: 1821–1888* (London: Allen, Unwin, 1962), 162–64.

4. The last name of the defendant is Kronenberg. That is the name in the court records and the name reported by the papers that first followed the trial. But in the latest issues of the *Voice* (Golos), the paper giving the trial the most detailed coverage, the defendant is called Kroneberg. In his notebooks Dostoevsky uses the form *Kronenberg*, but he then switched to *Kroneberg* in the article in the *Diary of a Writer*. See 22:346. Except in this instance, I will be using *Kroneberg* throughout.

5. For similar passages in the article, see pp. 220, 226, 230.

6. O. O. Gruzenberg, *Ocherki i rechi* (New York: N.p., 1944), 138.

7. As we shall see later, Russian juries often did not feel terribly constrained by the letter of the law, nor were they required to follow it.

8. Dostoevsky often calls the young girl *mladenets*, baby or infant, to further underline the contrast.

9. K. D. Kavelin, a moderate liberal, argued that Dostoevsky's view of the truth—and the Slavophile and Russian Orthodox views of truth, of which he believed it derivative—could only dissuade people from actively and creatively participating in social life ("A Letter to F. M. Dostoevskii," in Marc Raeff, ed., *Russian Intellectual History: An Anthology* [New York: Harcourt, 1966]). Because pious Orthodox Christians thought that a moral and Christian life could not be led in a corrupted world, they often renounced the world for the salvation of their souls. Dostoevsky's idea that social and civic ideas must derive from the "idea of absolute personal self-perfection" was really a confusion of personal morality with civic ideas. But civic ideas or ideals, Kavelin pointed out in his critique of Dostoevsky's famous Pushkin speech, have little to do with individual personal morality and much more to do with "the practical concrete necessity of ordering" man's "coexistence in society in such a way that each and every one will be as safe, free, and generally comfortable as possible and able to look after his affairs in peace" (317). Kavelin agreed entirely with Dostoevsky's personal moral ideal, but he believed it to be a self-defeating ideal when elevated to an inflexible evaluative norm for social life. Further, Kavelin believed that the improvement of social life facilitated the achievement of moral self-perfection.

10. N. K. Mikhailovskii, "Zhestokii talant," in A. Dmitrieva, ed., *Dostoevskii v russkoi kritike* (Moscow: GIKhL, 1956), 311–12.

11. Using similar observations, Gary Saul Morson comes to a very different conclusion, arguing that Dostoevsky decreases aesthetic, but not moral, distance: The reader remains a voyeur ("Prosaics, Criticism, and Ethics," *Formations* 5, no. 2 [1989]: 77–82).

12. The Kroneberg article provides many other examples of Dostoevsky's personal, existential representation of children and their psychology. Equally effective passages relate to children's memory (223; 22:61), the behavior of a five-year-old boy dying of scarlet fever (229; 22:66), and the psychology of what seems to be Dostoevsky's own daughter at six years of age (235; 22:70–71).

13. Girish Narayan Bhat, "Trial by Jury in the Reign of Alexander II: A Study in the Legal Culture of Late Imperial Russia, 1864–1881" (Ph.D. diss., University of California, Berkeley, 1995), 230.

14. Fyodor Dostoevsky, *The Brothers Karamazov*, trans. Richard Pevear and Larissa Volokhonsky (San Francisco: North Point, 1990), 245. All translations from *The Brothers Karamazov* are from this edition. Hereafter the English pagination will precede the pagination from the Russian Academy edition.

15. In an article on the aesthetics of moral perception in literature, Martha Nussbaum emphasizes the ethical price—the detachment from life—that writers often pay for their special perceptions. Using Strether from *The Ambassadors* as an example, she argues that artists often achieve ethical insight at the expense of their own emotional and ethical development ("Perceptive Equilibrium: Literary Theory and Ethical Theory," in Ralph Cohen, ed., *The Future of Literary Theory* [New York: Routledge, 1989], 58–85). On the contrary, Dostoevsky emphasizes in the Russian women the unity of action and moral-aesthetic perception (83).

16. Dostoevsky is obviously not arguing that lawyers have no freedom at all but rather that their freedom, for all practical purposes, is taken away if they abide by the "ethics" of their profession. He cites the example of a French lawyer to make this point: "Once, a long time ago I read about a certain lawyer in France who had become convinced in the course of the trial of the guilt of his client. When the time came for him to make his defense speech, he rose, bowed to the court and then silently took his seat. In our midst, I believe, this could not happen [*U nas, ia dumaiu, etogo ne mozhet sluchit'sia*]" (218; 22:56).

17. When Dostoevsky was charged with illegally printing material in the *Citizen* (*Grazhdanin*) of which he was the editor, he confessed that he was guilty but was told by his attorney "that not only was I not guilty but that I was absolutely innocent, and that he was firmly determined to defend me by all means" (214; 22:53). In a later article I hope to show more of Dostoevsky's ambivalence toward the role of defense attorney. A year later Dostoevsky himself would usurp the defense lawyer's role in the Kornilova case, in which a woman was, according to Dostoevsky, wrongly convicted of a *crime for which she could not be held responsible*.

18. Samuel Kucherov has argued, for example, that Spasovich was a court-appointed lawyer who did his job well. Gruzenberg realized that "the disclosure of the negative features of the girl's character was necessary so as to mitigate Kroneberg's guilt, that Spasovich, as his counsel, was bound to bring out all the circumstances which could extenuate his guilt, and that Dostoyevsky's compassion belongs to the field of sentiment and philosophy" (*Courts, Lawyers, and Trials Under the Last Three Tsars* [New York: Praeger, 1953], 178). Dostoevsky was well aware of this, although it is true that he does not place as much weight on this as Kucherov. Dostoevsky's statement has a definite tinge of irony: "Mr. Spasovich was appointed as defense-attorney by the court and consequently, he took on the defense, so to speak, under a certain coercion" (212; 22:52). On the other hand, Kucherov sounds like a parody of Fetyukovich when he implies that sentiment and philosophy should be kept out of legal procedures.

19. The noted literary critic Iu. Aikhenval'd argues that Dostoevsky disliked lawyers not so much because they were hired consciences but because of their superficial attitude toward crime, which they remove from the human soul like a hat (*Siluety russkikh pisatelei*, 3 vols. [Moscow: Slovo, 1923], 2:117).

20. M. E. Saltykov-Shchedrin, *Sobranie sochinenii*, 20 vols. (Moscow: Khudozhestvennaia literatura, 1965–77), 15.2:228.

21. Ibid. Here is not the place to engage in comparative studies, but Saltykov's position is one fairly close to the most generally accepted view of the role of the lawyer in the United States today, a view that first gained currency, not incidentally, around 1870. The late Abe Fortas, for example, wrote the following about legal agency: "Lawyers are agents, not principals; and they should neither criticize nor tolerate criticism based upon the character of the client whom they represent or the cause they prosecute or defend. They cannot and should not accept responsibility for their client's practices. Rapists, murderers, *child-abusers*, General Motors, Dow Chemical—even cigarette manufacturers and stream polluters—are entitled to a

lawyer; and any lawyer who undertakes their representation must be immune
from criticism for so doing" (Abe Fortas, "Thurmond Arnold and the Theatre of
the Law," *Yale Law Journal* 79 [1969–70]: 1002; emphasis added). The opposite
point of view, closer to Dostoevsky's own, is represented by that of Richard
Wasserstrom, who waxed indignant at the behavior of Richard Nixon's lawyers
during the Watergate affair:

> What is characteristic of this role of a lawyer is the lawyer's required indif-
> ference to a wide variety of ends and consequences that in other contexts
> would be of undeniable moral significance. Once a lawyer represents a
> client, the lawyer has the duty to make his or her expertise fully available
> in the realization of the end sought by the client, irrespective, for the most
> part of the moral worth to which the end will be put or the character of the
> client who seeks to utilize it. Provided that the end sought is not illegal, the
> lawyer is, in essence, an amoral technician whose peculiar skills and knowl-
> edge in respect to the law are available to those whom the relationship is
> established. ("Lawyers as Professionals: Some Moral Issues," *Human Rights*
> 5 [1975]: 5–6)

It should be mentioned that American trial lawyers often refer to themselves as
hired guns.

22. The Russians followed the Europeans in not binding the jury in any way.
Whereas in the English system jurors are supposed to be bound by the evidence,
in the Russian and other European systems juries are permitted to vote their consciences. The jury is twofold a prisoner of the system. First, its judgment is con-
stricted by legal rules; second, it is subject to the talent of the lawyer, which, as
we shall see, is also subverted to the purposes of the system. "And it stands to reason that a juror, too, would understand this, had he the time and desire to think
and reason; but he has no time for reasoning: he is under the sway of the irre-
sistible pressure of talent; he is dominated by the grouping; the case does not
revolve around any individual fact but, so to speak, a cluster of facts. And say what
you wish, these insignificant facts, grouped together in a bunch, at length create,
as it were, a hostile feeling toward the child" (223–24; 22:61).

23. In Russia, however, judges had far less flexibility in sentencing than English judges.

24. For a detailed analysis of the Kairova case in terms of gender and sexual-
ity, see Harriet Murav, *Russia's Legal Fictions* (Ann Arbor: University of Michigan
Press, 2001), 144–53.

25. As for most of us in real life, Dostoevsky does not make strict distinctions
among ethics focused on action (motivist, consequence, or deontological) nor
does he often separate action from virtue ethics. He reacts so strongly against the
jury system, because, as in the Kroneberg case, it prevented duty and compassion
from acting in concert in the determination of guilt and innocence. He would
never have seen duty and compassion, as Max Horkheimer did, as different moral

impulses. Horkheimer saw duty as being more characteristic of the nineteenth century, when men still looked upon themselves as free subjects, and compassion as being more characteristic of the twentieth, when men saw themselves more as objects of forces beyond their control (Max Horkheimer, "Materialismus und Moral," in Alfred Schmidt, ed., *Kritische Theorie: Eine Dokumentation* [Frankfurt: Fischer, 1968], 183–86). See also Martin Jay's discussion of Horkheimer's views in his *Dialectic Imagination* (Boston: Little, Brown, 1973), 51–53.

26. Dostoevsky is probably closer to what today in American law might be called an "anti-advocacy" position, similar to that of David Hoffman, who wrote in 1836 with respect to his client, whom he thought guilty:

> I shall not hold myself privileged, much less obliged, to use my endeavors to arrest, or to impede the course of justice, by special resorts to ingenuity—to the artifices of eloquence—to appeals to the morbid and fleeting sympathies of weak juries, or of temporizing courts—to my own personal weight of character—nor finally, to any of the overweening influences I may possess, from popular manners, eminent talents, exalted learning, etc. Persons of atrocious character, who have violated the laws of God and man, are entitled to no such special exertions from any member of our pure and honorable profession; and indeed, to no intervention beyond securing to them a fair and dispassionate investigation of the facts of their cause, and the due application of the law; all that goes beyond this, either in manner or substance, is unprofessional, and . . . sets a higher value on professional display and success, than on truth and justice, and the substantial interests of the community. (quoted in Henry S. Drinker, *Legal Ethics* [New York: Columbia University Press, 1953], 340–41)

Dostoevsky's position is, in fact, the opposite of that of the contemporary American bar. See, for example, American Bar Association, *Model Rules of Professional Conduct and Code of Judicial Conduct* (Chicago: American Bar Association, 1989), 15. He is against advocacy: the practice of arguing with zeal for cases in which one does not believe; he is for vouching: the practice of becoming personally involved on behalf of one's client in cases in which one strongly believes. The problems of advocacy and vouching are endemic to the bar and are not really amenable to solution, a fact often dramatized by such television popularizations as *L.A. Law*. Donna C. Burchfield praises *L.A. Law* for its positive presentation of advocacy, that is, its presentation of lawyers as "champions of their clients" ("Appearance Versus Reality: 'L.A. Law,'" *National Forum* 71, no. 4 (1991): 22). But the vouching of some lawyers on the program is also presented quite positively.

27. In terms of the Tolstoyan moral aesthetic, Spasovich's defense of Kroneberg, in its ability to persuade and infect the jury, is unquestionably art, but in its antagonism to correct morals, it is, by definition, bad art. Precisely because it is art, and therefore affectively moving, bad art is potentially far more dangerous than nonart, which, however moral, always fails to move.

28. Gruzenberg takes issue with Dostoevsky on this point, among other things, writing that "although textbooks on belles-lettres may call them [court oratory—*sudebnye rechi*—G.R.] one of the forms of art, it is a great mistake to do so. . . . The tendentious can never be art" (*Ocherki*, 139).

29. Dostoevsky implicitly compares Spasovich to Alphonse Lamartine, who "was a poet, and a man of talent" (217; 22:55). Like Spasovich, Lamartine was a prominent liberal and, of course, an even greater artist of the word than Spasovich. Dostoevsky is clearly pointing here to the misuse of art, that is, "bad art" in the Tolstoyan sense.

30. The article is replete with similar examples: "The whole trick comes to this" (223; 22:60–61). "This is an old and well-known device" (224; 22:61). "Later you will see how skillfully Mr. Spasovich turned the taking of a prune without permission into a theft of banknotes" (225; 22:62). "Mr. Spasovich is skillful: under no circumstance would he state this in express terms" (226; 22:63). "Yes, this is skillful" (226; 22:63). "Is it permissible to deceive us to such an extent?" (229; 22:65–66). "He makes a determined attempt to lead us astray" (229; 22:66).

31. In his discussion of the prostitution of talent, Dostoevsky does not lose the opportunity to link talent and capital. Talent, like capital, can easily get the upper hand over ethics. In relating an incident in which a son valued his capital over his own mother, Dostoevsky comments: "So he gave nothing to his mama, and she was dragged into the insolvent debtor's jail. Please take this allegorically and equate talent with capital" (218; 22:56).

32. The boy here is almost certainly a corrupted house servant, past puberty.

33. Bogdan Kistyakovsky, "In Defense of the Law: The Intelligentsia and Legal Consciousness," in *Landmarks*, trans. Marian Schwartz (New York: Howard, 1977), 113.

34. Ibid., 115.

35. Ibid., 121–23.

36. This is actually a corollary of the idea of the Russian philosopher Peter Chaadaev (1794–1856), who had argued in the late 1820s the compensatory advantages of Russian backwardness. "I am sure that in a little while the great ideas, once they have reached us, will find it easier to realize themselves in our midst and to incarnate themselves in our individuals than anywhere else, because here they will find no deep-rooted prejudices, no old habits, no obstinate routines to fight" (308). "I believe that if we have come after the others, it is so we can do better than the others; it is so that we may not fall into their faults, their errors, their superstitions" (314). Or, to use more "judicial terms": "In a way we are appointed, by the very nature of things, to serve as a real jury for the many suits which are being argued before the great tribunals of the human spirit and of human society" (314). All quotes are from "Apology of a Madman," quoted in Thomas Riha, ed., *Readings in Russian Civilization*, 3 vols. [Chicago: University of Chicago Press, 1964], 2:304–14.

37. Kistyakovsky, "Defense of the Law," 123–25.

38. Ibid., 117.

39. Ibid., 132.

40. Iurii M. Lotman and Boris A. Uspenskii, "Binary Models in the Dynamics of Russian Culture (to the End of the Eighteenth Century)," in Alexander Nakhimovsky, ed., *The Semiotics of Russian Cultures* (Ithaca, N.Y.: Cornell University Press, 1984), 32.

41. Ibid., 31.

42. Ibid., 32.

43. Ju. M. Lotman, "'Agreement' and 'Self-Giving' as Archetypal Models of Culture," in Ju. M. Lotman and B. A. Uspenskij, *The Semiotics of Russian Culture*, ed. Ann Shukman (Ann Arbor: University of Michigan Press, 1984), 127.

44. Ibid. For a Western knight, by contrast, it was dishonorable not to keep one's word, even if given to Satan (128).

45. For a study of the liberal pro-legal tradition in nineteenth-century Russia, see Andrzej Walicki, *Legal Philosophies of Russian Liberalism* (Notre Dame, Ind.: University of Notre Dame Press, 1992).

46. In the original this reads: "Vlast' t'my, ili 'Kogotok uviaz, vsei ptichke propast'.' Drama v piati deistviiakh." The play, full of folk expressions and wisdom, is based on an actual criminal trial involving the murder of a child (L. N. Tolstoi, *Sobranie sochinenii*, 20 vols. [Moscow: GIKhL, 1963], 11:29).

47. A. P. Chekhov, *Sobranie sochinenii*, 12 vols. (Moscow: GIKhL, 1960–64), 8:128.

48. Ibid., 8:171.

49. "Pravda odna. Net dvukh pravd. Trudno zhit' bez pravdy libo s oskolochkami, s chastitsei pravdy, s obrublennoi, podstrizhennoi pravdoi. Chast' pravdy—eto ne pravda" (Vasilii Grossman, *Zhizn' i sud'ba* [Moscow: Knizhnaia palata, 1988], 619).

## 2. Dostoevsky and the Kornilova Case

1. For a discussion of Dostoevsky's interest in contemporary court cases, see Harriet Murav, "Legal Fiction in Dostoevsky's *Diary of a Writer*," *Dostoevsky Studies* 1, no. 2 (1993): 155–74. For a specific analysis of the Kroneberg cases, see Gary Rosenshield, "The Imprisonment of the Law: Dostoevskij and the Kroneberg Case," *Slavic and East European Journal* 36 (1992): 415–34; Gary Rosenshield, "Western Law vs. Russian Justice: Dostoevsky and the Jury Trial, Round One," *Graven Images* 1 (1994): 117–35.

2. Harriet Murav is certainly correct in arguing that Dostoevsky seems to be assuming the role that Spasovich took in Kroneberg (*Russia's Legal Fictions* [Ann Arbor: University of Michigan Press, 2001], 131–36), but Dostoevsky was keenly aware of what he was doing before he was pilloried in the press for doing so. What was most important for Dostoevsky, as we shall see, was that Kornilova confessed to her crime.

3. The medical expert from Moscow who testifies in Dmitry Karamazov's defense in *The Brothers Karamazov* uses essentially the same argument of temporary insanity (15:104).

4. Dostoevsky was much less disturbed by the judicial error in the Kornilova case than by the vindications in the Kroneberg and Kairova cases. At least in the Kornilova case the jury did not take crime lightly; it pronounced crime to be crime. At no time during the trial, as far as we know, did the defense lawyer try to present Kornilova's crime as though it were something anyone would have done in her circumstances, as something justifiable, though he probably did argue for extenuating circumstances. The sentence of two-and-one-half years' hard labor and permanent exile, not the harshest sentence that could have been given, probably shows that the jury took into consideration extenuating circumstances even in the first trial.

5. Whereas in the Kroneberg case Dostoevsky used every weapon at his disposal, including his own experiences at hard labor, to prove that the father had "tortured" his daughter, in the Kornilova case Dostoevsky attempts to refute all the accusations made against the stepmother, including a cruel beating that Kornilova had given the little girl for a night-time accident. Dostoevsky says that, unfortunately, the common people still as a rule deal harshly with such accidents and that the young wife was merely meting out the accepted punishment for this type of unacceptable behavior. Kroneberg's beating of his daughter, however, left no visible marks, whereas Kornilova's beating left some nasty welts; in fact, Kornilova's husband thought the beating so excessive that he in turn beat Kornilova for punishing the child so harshly (919–20; 26:97).

6. The formal reason for the annulment of the verdict was the illegal questioning of the same person as an expert and a witness in the same case (24:395–96). The editors of the Academy edition note that Dostoevsky himself made this mistake in *The Brothers Karamazov*.

7. Dostoevsky did not initiate the visits to Kornilova. An official of the Ministry of Justice, K. I. Masliannikov, was so moved by Dostoevsky's article about Kornilova in the October 1876 issue of the *Diary of a Writer* that he wrote Dostoevsky asking him to meet Kornilova and persuade her to make an appeal for clemency. Dostoevsky immediately went to the district attorney's office to seek permission to see Kornilova. Permission was granted for several visits. See 24:394–95.

8. These questions are interesting for the future of Dmitry Karamazov as well as for the past of Dostoevsky himself. Dostoevsky maintained that he experienced a rebirth in prison. His semiautobiographical *Notes from the House of the Dead* supports this claim. Dmitry Karamazov is not Kornilova, so Dostoevsky's words here cannot be glibly applied to Dmitry. Nevertheless, Dmitry is preoccupied with his capacity for surviving exile and hard labor. Other characters (Ivan, Alyosha, and Katerina Ivanovna, for example) doubt Dmitry's ability to endure.

9. A good example is Dostoevsky's description of the poor Jewish family in his article about the Jewish question (656–59; 25:90–92).

10. The twenty-seven-year-old Anna Kirilova shot and killed her lover, whom she found with another woman. On hearing the verdict, Kirilova fell down and suffered an attack of hysterics. See the Academy edition notes to the December 1876 *Diary* article (24:394).

11. Although he does not disclose it here, Dostoevsky reveals in his last article about the case that the prosecutor and presiding judge both announced publicly during the retrial that Dostoevsky's article in the *Diary of a Writer* had led to the voiding of the conviction and the call for a new trial with a fresh jury (914; 26:92).

12. See note 3 for a similar use of "insanity" in *The Brothers Karamazov*. Also see Harriet Murav's interesting discussion of gender bias in Russian determinations of temporary insanity. Because women were thought to be subject to forces beyond their control, they could not, it was argued, be held to the same standards of responsibility as men (*Russia's Legal Fictions*, 134).

13. For a detailed discussion of Dostoevsky's critique of the Western adversarial system, see Rosenshield, "The Imprisonment of the Law."

14. The main lawyers were probably both of German origin. The name of the prosecutor was Kessel, that of the defense attorney Vilgelm Iosifovich Lyustikh (1844–1915). Dostoevsky was sufficiently impressed by Lyustikh to hire him to settle the problems arising from his aunt's inheritance (24:395).

15. A police officer testified that when Kornilova appeared at the station to confess her crime, she said that she had been planning for six months to kill the child and that for the past two weeks she had been preparing to carry out her plan. Dostoevsky wrote to Masliannikov (see note 7) that Kornilova vehemently denied that she ever made such a statement to the police. She told Dostoevsky: "That's untrue. I could never have said such a thing" (24:395).

16. Dostoevsky states that the jury came in with an acquittal after less than fifteen minutes, but *Peterburgskii listok*, the only newspaper that ran an account of the retrial, notes that the jury came in with the acquittal after a lengthy deliberation (*prodolzhitel'noe soveshchanie*; 25:410).

17. Dostoevsky's Kroneberg article and various statements in his letters show that he generally had a high opinion of Russian juries—except of course in cases where they were excessively lenient—and thus it is not surprising to see the jury coming to the right decision and so quickly (Rosenshield, "The Imprisonment of the Law," 418). We do not know whether the previous jurors had wanted to acquit but could not vote their consciences, either because of their special charge or because of the way the question to the jury was originally formulated. Obviously, the jury at the second trial confirmed Dostoevsky's high regard for the moral standards of Russian juries. The peasant jurors in *The Brothers Karamazov* have a much more difficult case, from almost every point of view, but manage to deliver a rather reasonable decision, given the evidence against Dmitry. They listened to all the evidence, were not overawed by the histrionics of the lawyers, and in the end voted their consciences.

18. Dostoevsky reacts indignantly to the terrible charge (*strashnoe obvinenie*) of the critic of the *Northern Messenger* that Dostoevsky is defending a torturer

against the child. He refers in his defense to his thirty years' work as a writer, to the many articles about children in the *Diary of a Writer,* and to his defense of the child, the victim, against the father, in the Kroneberg case (932; 26:107–08). Dostoevsky would, of course, revisit the issue of cruelty to children in *The Brothers Karamazov.*

19. Dostoevsky does not mention a June visit, but he says in reference to his last meeting, which was on Christmas, that it was about six months since he had last seen the Kornilovs (927; 26:103).

20. Neither Kornilova's lawyer nor Dostoevsky had expected an acquittal (929; 26:104).

21. Dostoevsky maintains the differences between Kornilova and his fictional heroines even though he later argues that simple people experience the very same feelings as their more educated and cultured counterparts. "These ignorant people do not know how to express all this in our way, in our tongue; but quite often they feel as deeply as we do, the 'educated people,' and experience these feelings of theirs with the same happiness or with the same sorrow and pain as we" (934; 26:109).

22. The passages in question read, "And these are they which are sown among thorns, such as hear the word. And the cares of this world . . . choke the word, and it becometh unfruitful. And these are they which are sown on good ground; such as hear the word, and receive it, and bring forth fruit, some thirtyfold, some sixty, and some an hundred" (Mk 4:3–20). "And that which fell among thorns are they, which when they have heard, go forth, and are choked with cares and riches and pleasures of this life, and bring no fruit to perfection. But that on the good ground are they, which in an honest and good heart, having the word, keep it, and bring forth fruit with patience" (Luke 8:14–15).

23. For a booklength analysis of the metaphor of the seed in *The Brothers Karamazov,* see Robin Feuer Miller, *The Brothers Karamazov: The Worlds of the Novel* (New York: Twayne, 1992).

24. This is an example of what V. V. Zenkovsky calls Dostoevsky's "Christian naturalism": his "faith in the goodness of man and human 'nature'" despite his appreciation and revelation of "the darkest impulses of the human soul" ("Dostoevsky's Religious and Philosophical Views," in René Wellek, ed., *Dostoevsky: A Collection of Critical Essays* [Englewood Cliffs, N.J.: Prentice-Hall, 1962], 130, 140).

25. See especially in the *Diary of a Writer,* "But Long Live Brotherhood" (No da zdravstvuet bratstvo!), "The Funeral of a 'Universal Man'" (Pokhorony "*Obshchecheloveka*"), and "An Isolated Case" (Edinichnyi sluchai) (651–60; 25:86–92). See Gary Saul Morson's discussion of the increasing monophonic treatment of the diary selections during the course of Dostoevsky's writing the *Diary of a Writer* in Morson's introduction to Fyodor Dostoevsky, *A Writer's Diary,* trans. Kenneth Lantz (Evanston, Ill.: Northwestern University Press, 1993), 1:1–117.

26. Nikolai Berdyaev, "Philosophic Truth and the Moral Truth of the Russian Intelligentsia," *Landmarks,* trans. Marian Schwartz (New York: Howard, 1977), 19–22.

27. I. S. Aksakov, *Sochineniia* (Moscow: Volchaninov, 1886–87), 4:656.

28. Ibid., 98–99.

29. See *Sudebnye ustavy 20 noiabria 1864 goda*, Decree 41476, *Ustavy ugolovnogo sudoproizvodstva*, article. 666. Quoted in Girish Narayan Bhat, "Trial by Jury in the Reign of Alexander II: A Study in the Legal Culture of Late Imperial Russia, 1864–1881" (Ph.D. diss., University of California, Berkeley, 1995), 96.

30. Quoted in Bhat, "Trial by Jury," 97.

31. Bhat, "Trial by Jury," 97.

32. Ibid., 98. In the twelfth-century apocryphal work *The Descent of the Virgin into Hell*, the Virgin asks the Archangel Michael about the sinners "who are immersed in the fiery flame up to their necks." Michael replies: "They are those, Lady, who holding the cross, have sworn falsely. Such is the power of the cross that it is worshiped with awe by the angels and they tremble before it. And so, when a man swears by the cross and then lies, he is punished by such a torment" (Serge A. Zenkovsky, ed., *Medieval Russia's Epics, Chronicles, and Tales* [New York: Dutton, 1974]), 155.

33. See the note to art. 443 of the *Ustavy ugolovnogo sudoproizvodstva*.

34. *Ustavy ugolovnogo sudoproizvodstva*, art. 705. Quoted in Bhat, "Trial by Jury," 114–15.

35. *Ustavy ugolovnogo sudoproizvodstva*, article 705. Quoted in Bhat, "Trial by Jury," 116.

36. Bhat, "Trial by Jury," 124.

37. The relative disadvantage of the defense in trial proceedings in the nineteenth century was characteristic of all trial systems based on the French model. Toward the end of the nineteenth century, most European countries but not Russia, did a great deal to restore the balance between the strengths and rights of the defense and the prosecutor's office, a change, by the way, that reflected English and American practice.

38. Bhat, "Trial by Jury," 69.

39. Ibid., 71–72, 80–81, 84.

40. A. F. Koni, *Vospominaniia o dele Very Zasulich*, in *Izbrannye proizvedeniia* (Moscow: Gos. izdat. iur. lit, 1956), 565.

## 3. The Perils of Narrative Empathy

1. For an ingenious attempt to see the Kornilova case less as a legal case and more as a form of authorial self-expression, in which Dostoevsky plays now father, now child, and now peasant, see Harriet Murav, "Legal Fiction in Dostoevsky's *Diary of a Writer*," *Dostoevsky Studies* 1, no. 2 (1993): 155–74.

2. The Mumia Abu-Jamal case is still, in 2003, the subject of bitter controversy. On 5 April 2001 Mumia was named an "Honorary Citizen of Paris." Several websites promote his case. See *Mumia Abu-Jamal's Freedom Journal*, http:// www.mumia.org/freedom.now (28 September 2003); *The Mobilization of Free*

*Mumia Abu-Jamal,* http://www.freemumia.org (28 September 2003); *Millions 4 Mumia,* http://www.mumia2000.org (28 September 2003).

3. Victims are often permitted to confront in court those who have committed crimes against them or their family, and in some capital cases relatives of victims have chosen to be present at executions.

4. Evans D. Hopkins, serving a fourteen-year sentence for armed robbery, writes:

> The throw-away-the-key fever really took off in 1988, when George Bush's presidential campaign hit the Willie Horton hot button, and sparked the tough-on-crime political climate that continues to this day. The transformation was nearly complete when President Clinton endorsed the concept of "three strikes and you're out" in his 1994 State of the Union address. And when Congress outlawed the Pell grants for prisoners later that year the message became clear: We don't really give a damn if you change or not. . . . Still, what really bothers me is knowing that many thousands of the young men entering prison now may *never* get that "last chance to change," which I was able to put to good use—in an era that, I'm afraid, is now in the past. And more disturbing, to my mind, are the long "no hope" sentences given to so many young men now—they can be given even to people as young as thirteen and fourteen. Although I personally remain eligible for parole— and in all likelihood will be released eventually—I can't help thinking of all the young lives that are being thrown away. I know if I had been born in another time I might very well have suffered the same fate. ("Lockdown: Life Inside Is Getting Harder," *New Yorker* 24 February 1997, p. 70)

5. Largely in response to *Brief against Death,* Ronald E. Calissi, the son of the New Jersey prosecutor who won Smith's conviction, wrote a book about the trial (*Counterpoint: The Edgar Smith Case* [Hackensack, N.J.: Manor, 1972]) that defends his father's conduct as prosecutor. Calissi gives all the evidence against Smith, including testimony and photographs, and provides detailed summaries and quotes from many of Smith's appeals to the state and federal courts.

6. Buckley writes, "Assuming he had actually killed the girl: is it more reasonable that he did so unprovoked than provoked? Murder resulting from a 'wrongful act or insult' is mandatory second-degree murder" ("The Approaching End of Edgar H. Smith, Jr.," *Esquire,* November 1965, p. 120). Buckley was also perplexed by Smith's seeming lack of concern for finding the real killer, that is, for establishing his innocence. Smith did not ask for Buckley's belief in his innocence, only for his doubts about his guilt.

7. Buckley, "The Approaching End," 116–20, 178. Buckley appended the following note to his *Esquire* article: "Edgar Smith has no funds to retain counsel, without which he cannot complete the final legal appeals that stand between him and the electric chair. A fund for this purpose has been started: donations should

be earmarked 'Edgar Smith Fund' and sent [immediately] to Mr. James Williams, Treasurer, New York Yearly Meeting of Friends, Oakwood School, Poughkeepsie, New York [a tax-deductible foundation]. Any surplus will be returned after the final disposition of the case. The author's fee for this article has been turned over to the fund" (183).

8. Edgar Smith, *Getting Out* (New York: Coward, 1972), 12–14.

9. William F. Buckley Jr., "The Return of Edgar Smith," *National Review,* 21 January 1977, p. 111.

10. Smith, *Getting Out,* 165.

11. In California at the time of Smith's crime (1976), those convicted of kidnapping with intent to rape could not be sentenced to life imprisonment without possibility of parole. Smith, therefore, wanted to argue that not only his kidnapping of Ozbun but also his earlier crimes were sexually motivated.

12. Hiemer is quoted in Miles Corwin, "Celebrity Convict's Myth Exposed: Admitted Killer's Possible Parole Prompts Protests," *Los Angeles Times,* 5 July 1989, pp. 1, 17.

13. Buckley, "The Return of Edgar Smith," 111.

14. Although keeping the judicial system honest was not the focus of his *Esquire* article, Buckley wrote that the issue of constitutional rights "transcends guilt and innocence" ("The Approaching End," 117).

15. Mark Royden Winchell, *William F. Buckley, Jr.* (Boston: Twayne, 1984), 96.

16. For the technical reasons for annulling the conviction, see 24:394–95. For Dostoevsky's letters to Masliannikov, see 29.2:129–32, 29.2:133. For Masliannikov's letters to Dostoevsky, see "Pis'ma chitatelei k F. M. Dostoevskomu," *Voprosy literatury,* no. 9 (1971): 193–95.

17. For a detailed account of Kovner's life and his correspondence with Dostoevsky, see Leonid Grossman, *Confession of a Jew,* trans. Ranne Moab (New York: Arno Press, 1975). Kovner also wrote Dostoevsky that if Kornilova's stepdaughter had died, Dostoevsky would have had far less sympathy for the mother, despite her pregnancy and confession to the police (29.2:280). Dostoevsky, of course, interprets the unharmed child as a miracle, a sign of divine favor, grace, and intervention.

18. Dostoevsky's need personally to assure himself that Kornilova was worth the great risk of acquittal pervades all his articles on the Kornilova case. See the discussion of this in Gary Rosenshield, "Death and Resurrection at the Russian Bar: Dostoevsky and the Kornilova Case," *Canadian-American Slavic Studies* 31 (1997): 1–32.

19. Dostoevsky could not have found out too much more about Kornilova's slow progress of renewal, for she died on 6 June 1878, just more than a year after her acquittal in April 1877. After her death Dostoevsky never mentioned Kornilova again.

20. Abbott lived in a string of foster homes before being sent to reform school at twelve, and he spent all but nine and a half months of his life after the age of

278           Notes to Pages 116–117

twelve in reformatories and prison. At nineteen he was sentenced to five years for forgery and forced entry; at twenty-one he had a longer sentence added for fatally stabbing another inmate. Five years later he escaped from prison and robbed a bank; he was apprehended and given nineteen more years. Abbott spent many of his prison years in solitary confinement. During one term of solitary he slashed his wrists and afterward assaulted the doctor who stitched him up.

21. Norman Mailer, interview by David Frost, *The David Frost Special*, PBS, 24 January 1992.

22. Jean Malaquais, "Reflections on Hipsterism," introduction to Norman Mailer, *The White Negro* (New York: City Light, 1969), 21.

23. Or as Mailer has said elsewhere: "Social violence creates personal violence as its antithesis" (*Pieces and Pontifications* [Boston: Little, Brown, 1982], pt. 2, p. 28).

24. Many who have commented on Mailer's involvement in the Abbott affair have linked it to Mailer's valorization of violence in contemporary American society, his romanticization of the criminal, and his faith in the redemptive powers of literary talent. As Michiko Kakutani has written: "It was the wishful impulse to see Mr. Abbott's life as a story not just of crime and punishment, but of crime and punishment and redemption; and it was the fervently held belief that talent somehow redeems, that art confers respectability, that the act of writing can somehow transform a violent man into a philosopher of violence" ("The Strange Case of the Writer and the Criminal," *New York Times Book Review* 20 September 1981, p. 38).

25. Mailer, *The White Negro*, 15.

26. Mailer used this phrase at a press conference after the Abbott trial. (See Lance Morrow, "The Poetic License to Kill," *Time*, 1 February 1982, p. 82). As Michael André Bernstein argues—and as Mailer has since acknowledged—such a position involves much more than a little risk (Bernstein, *Bitter Carnival: Ressentiment and the Abject Hero* [Princeton, N.J.: Princeton University Press, 1992]). According to Bernstein, for the last two centuries our culture, often with disastrous consequences, has romanticized and championed the behavior of romantic outsiders who, poisoned by ressentiment, act out what we believe to be our repressed selves. For Bernstein, Mailer hardly constitutes an exception: "I believe it is the rhetoric of revolutionary apocalypse indulged in by a large contingent of Western academics and intellectuals that is the truly conventional gesture, in ready harmony with the pieties of the day" (183). Bernstein takes this idea to its extreme conclusion in the last chapter of his book, where he suggests that, for many, even Charles Manson could do service as an icon of the repressed (157–84).

27. Perhaps Mailer assumed that the more violent the criminal, the greater his artistic and revolutionary potential.

28. Abbott, *In the Belly of the Beast* (New York: Random House, 1981), 126. Can anyone doubt that Dostoevsky would have somehow incorporated Abbott into *The Brothers Karamazov*, had Abbott been living in Russia in the 1870s?

29. Abbott, *In the Belly*, 100.

30. Mailer is quoted in Kevin Cullen, "Litigants Enter Belly of Beast; Jury Awards \$7.5m in Abbott Case," *Boston Globe*, 18 June 1990, p. 5.

31. In the debate about whether Abbott was released because of Mailer or the parole board, the parole board defended its decision by arguing that prisons are always squeezed for space and that Abbott, like a lot of men, was paroled to make room for others. Further, his case was not that different from those of others who had committed similar crimes. Ready or not, thousands of hardened convicts are routinely released from prison every year. As James Young, spokesman for the New York State Parole Board, puts it: "A convict has to do something really bad in prison to serve his full term. . . . People don't realize that maximum sentences don't really mean anything. But it sounds good for public consumption. It's good public relations for judges and prosecutors" (quoted in John Phillips, Domestic News [a Reuters agency], 29 January 1982).

32. Wendell Rawls Jr. reports: "As he was driven to jail, he said that he was surprised to learn how well his book had been doing. He had heard nothing about it since he left New York, and he had been afraid to enter a bookstore and look at his work for fear someone would recognize him from the picture of the author" ("Trail of Convict-Author Eluded Police for Month," *New York Times*, 25 September 1981, p. B3).

33. In his review of Abbott's *In the Belly of the Beast*, Terrence des Pres writes that "we must be grateful to him [Mailer] for getting these letters into publishable form and—a job more difficult—for helping to get Abbott out on parole" ("A Child of the State," review of *In the Belly of the Beast* by Jack Abbott, *New York Times Book Review*, 19 July 1981, p. 3).

34. For example, Lance Morrow acidly writes: "A judge of Solomonic gifts might condemn Abbott and Mailer to be shackled together with molybdenum chains, inseparable ever after, like Tony Curtis and Sidney Poiter in *The Defiant Ones*, to clunk, snarling, from one literary dinner party to another" ("Poetic License to Kill," 82). Jerzy Kosinski was more open than Mailer in admitting his responsibility for Abbott's murder of Adan: "By toasting him, I endorsed his philosophy," he says. "If I had voiced a doubt about his sanity, maybe he would have had less of an emotional license to kill. Why did I go to embrace him? . . . Had Abbott proposed the Nazi solution, we would not have embraced him. There is a tendency to believe violence on the left is somehow justifiable. Had Jack Abbott substituted for the phrase Marxist-Leninist, Hitlerian-Mussolinian, I do not think Mailer would have written the introduction to his book, I do not think we would have gone to toast his success" (quoted in Kakutani, "The Strange Case," 39).

35. Morrow, "Poetic License to Kill," 82.

36. Cullen, "Litigants Enter Belly of Beast," 5.

37. Norman Mailer, introduction to Abbott, *In the Belly*, xii.

38. By the time of the wrongful death suit against Abbott by Adan's widow, Mailer had sensibly cut himself off from his former protégé. To be sure, he could still argue that writers should continue to take risks for causes and persons they believed

in—Mailer still wanted to hold out the possibility of defending if not Abbott another unfortunate—but he did not take up the case of Jack Abbott again: then specifically, he did not actively support any of Abbott's numerous requests for parole.

39. William Styron, *This Quiet Dust: And Other Writings* (New York: Random
House, 1982), 112–26. The article, "The Death-in-Life of Benjamin Reid," appeared
in the February 1962 issue of *Esquire*, where three years later Buckley would publish his equally effective defense of another inmate on death row, Edgar Smith.

40. Styron, *Quiet Dust*, 137. For a criticism of Styron's defense of Ben Reid, see
Jack Henry Abbott, "Dear William Styron," *My Return* (Buffalo: Prometheus,
1987), 167–78.

41. Styron, *Quiet Dust*, 135.

42. Ibid., 122.

43. Ibid., 128.

44. Ibid., 137. Likewise, Dostoevsky's article in the *Diary of a Writer* influenced
an official from the Ministry of Justice to overturn the conviction of Kornilova,
who, Dostoevsky argued, would have lost the possibility of redemption had she
been sentenced to hard labor in Siberia with her newborn child.

45. Styron writes, "Remembering one's own Elysian childhood in juxtaposition
with that of Reid and of Abbott, I think it is fair to say that a concern for either
of those wretched felons has to do less with romanticism than with a sense of justice, and the need for seeking restitution for other men's lost childhoods" (Styron, *This Quiet Dust*, 141).

46. Ibid., 135.

47. Ibid., 132.

48. Ibid., 138.

49. Ibid.

50. Ibid., 139.

51. Ibid., 121–22, 142.

52. Styron says, "I haven't lost faith in him. I hope to be able to walk through
New York City with him some day soon" ("Protégés in Prison: Writers Debate
Mailer's Support for Abbott," combined wire service story in the *Washington Post*,
21 January 1982, p. D1.

53. In another context the narrator of *Sophie's Choice* explains his odd behavior by referring to "the Presbyterian ethic," which "still exercised some vestigial
hold on me" (*Sophie's Choice* [New York: Vintage, 1992], 15).

54. Though Styron seems to have read *Notes from the House of the Dead*, he
was probably not acquainted with the *Diary of a Writer*.

55. Styron, *Quiet Dust*, 135.

56. See note 17 for Kovner's comments about the survival of the child.

57. Robert Satter, *Doing Justice: A Trial Judge at Work* (New York: Simon and
Schuster, 1990), 15.

58. Perhaps the most famous example of this idea is Raskolnikov's bowing
down at the crossroads. Raskolnikov's act, however, contains more masochistic
humiliation than it does humility.

4. *The Brothers Karamazov* I

1. "Na stsene budet ne zrelishche, ne igra, a urok, primer, nazidanie" (Pss 26:54).

2. The quotations are from Dostoevsky's analysis of the case of General Hartung, who committed suicide after being convicted of embezzlement (*Diary of a Writer*, October 1877).

3. Fetyukovich, Dmitry Karamazov's lawyer, will "quote" these remarks out of context at Dmitry's trial.

4. Leonid Grossman has pointed out some of the more striking similarities between the Zasulich and Karamazov trials ("Dostoevskii i pravitel'stvennye krugi 1870-kh godov," *Literaturnoe nasledstvo* 15 [1934]: 101–3).

5. Other radicals planned an attempt on Trepov's life, but Zasulich managed to beat them to it.

6. Jay Bergman, *Vera Zasulich: A Biography* (Palo Alto, Calif.: Stanford University Press, 1983), 40. Bergman is an excellent source on the political aspect of the trial. See also Iu. S. Karpilenko, *"Delo" Very Zasulich: Rossiiskoe obshchestvo, samoderzhavie i sud prisiazhnykh v 1878 godu* (Briansk: Izdatel'stvo Brianskogo gosud. ped. instituta, 1994).

7. Bergman, *Zasulich*, 50-51; A. F. Koni, "Vospominaniia o dele Very Zasulich," *Izbrannye sochineniia* (Moscow: Gos. izdat. iurid. literatury, 1956), 569. Koni's memoirs of the trial remain the best and most detailed account of the proceedings.

8. When Pahlen fell from power as a result of the jury's failure to deliver a guilty verdict in the Zasulich trial, Dmitry Nabokov, Vladimir Nabokov's uncle, was chosen as minister of justice, probably because he had the reputation of a characterless bureaucrat who would follow orders. He wanted to pursue Zasulich's extradition after her flight, but the tsar's ministers thought another trial would be unwise. (See Bergman, *Vera Zasulich*, 57). Dmitry Nabokov was committed to an independent jury and held the line as much as he could against efforts to gut the reform. Conservative attacks on him led to his dismissal in October 1885, when Pobedonostsev replaced him with a protégé. Dmitry Nabokov was the only one to argue for a fair proceeding for those suspected of terrorism. His position outraged even centrists.

9. Michael T. Florinsky, *Russia: A History and an Interpretation* (New York: Macmillan, 1953), 1081. Bergman writes: "Thus, the Zasulich trial revitalized the revolutionary movement and inspired its more extremist wing to turn to terrorism as a means by which to change the status quo" (*Vera Zasulich,* 58). It is interesting to note in light of what actually happened after the acquittal that one juror wrote anonymously to the Third Section that the jurors felt compelled not to convict Zasulich, fearing that it would have been far worse for the government had she been convicted. See A. A. Kukl', "Vokrug dela Very Zasulich," *Katorga i ssylka,* no. 38 (1928): 62–63. Zasulich later wrote an article, published in the *Social Democrat* in 1890, that rejected terror as a counterproductive method of achieving socialist aims. See V. I. Zasulich, *Revoliutsionery iz burzhuaznoi sredy* (Petersburg, Russia: Gos. izdatel'stvo, 1921).

10. V. I. Zhukovsky, the first choice, declined for personal reasons. S. A. Andreevsky, the second choice, refused to try the case on the government's terms. Kissel was "a man whom many prominent figures, most notably Pobedonostsev, considered ill equipped for the task" (Bergman, *Vera Zasulich,* 42). After the trial Zhukovsky and Andreevsky were forced to resign.

11. Pss 30.1:273–74. During a break in the trial Dostoevsky told the liberal journalist K. G. Gradovsky (1842–1915) that the court did not have the proper means for dealing with a situation like Zasulich's and that the court might turn her into a hero (K. G. Gradovskii, *Itogi* [Kiev, 1908], 18).

12. Richard Pipes, *Russia Under the Old Regime* (New York: Scribners, 1974), 296. Though the government probably excised some of the defendants' speeches from the court records, what was left out was printed secretly and achieved even greater effect. But it is generally agreed that the great trials of 1877 and 1878, which the government used to arouse public opinion against the revolutionaries, failed miserably, in the end arousing sympathy for them as well as providing them with a public forum from which they could denounce the autocracy. See also Avrahm Yarmolinsky, *Road to Revolution* (New York: Collier, 1962), 201–5.

13. Relatively little has been written about the trial. In her book on Dostoevsky and the Russian court, T. S. Karlova hardly mentions the trial scene at all (*Dostoevskii i russkii sud* [Kazan': izd. Kazanskogo universiteta, 1975], 142–59). For studies that focus on the trial, or at least parts of the trial, see Grossman, "Dostoevskii i pravitel'stvennye krugi 1870-kh godov"; Wolfgang W. Holdheim, *Der Justizirrtum als literarische Problematik* (Berlin: De Gruyter, 1969); G. Shchennikov, "Sud i pravosudie v 'Brat'iakh Karamazovykh' i idealy Dostoevskogo," *Russkaia literatura 1870–1890 gg.* Sverdlovsk Sb. 7 (1974): 34–49; V. D. Rak, "Iuridicheskaia oshibka v romane 'Brat'ia Karamazovy,'" *Dostoevskii: Materialy i issledovaniia,* 2 (Leningrad, 1976), 154–59; Victor Terras, *A Karamazov Companion* (Madison: University of Wisconsin Press, 1981), 399–437; Richard H. Weisberg, *The Failure of the Word: The Protagonist as Lawyer in Modern Fiction* (New Haven, Conn.: Yale University Press, 1984); 54–64; Robin Feuer Miller, *The Brothers Karamazov: Worlds of the Novel* (New York: Twayne, 1992), 125–31; Wolfgang W. Holdheim, "On the Genealogy of the Judicial Error," *Cardozo Studies in Law and Literature* 7, no. 2 (1995): 125–29; David Lee Keily, "*The Brothers Karamazov* and the Fate of Russian Truth: Shifts in the Construction and Interpretation of Narrative After the Judicial Reform of 1864" (Ph.D. diss., Harvard University, 1996); N. G. Mikhailovskaia, "Sudebnaia rech' v romane F. M. Dostoevskogo 'Brat'ia Karamazovy,'" *Russkii iazyk v shkole* (November–December 1997): 57–65; Daniel J. Solove, "Postures of Judging: An Exploration of Judicial Decisionmaking," *Cardozo Studies in Law and Literature* 9, no. 2 (1997): 173–227; Joseph Frank, *Dostoevsky: The Mantle of the Prophet, 1871–1881* (Princeton, N.J.: Princeton University Press, 2002), 684–96.

14. Terras maintains that the term *sudebnaia oshibka* is better translated as "judicial error" than "miscarriage of justice," although the implications of a miscarriage of justice are certainly present (*A Karamazov Companion,* 399).

15. Dostoevsky is obviously recalling the applause "even in the places for the judges" at the Zasulich trial. Koni recalls the especially enthusiastic applause of someone right next to him (*nad samym ukhom moim*): "I turned around. Major-general G. A. Barantsov, a flushed, grey-haired and heavy man, was clapping enthusiastically. When he met my glance, he stopped and smiled with embarrassment, but hardly had I turned away when he began to applaud again" (*Vospominaniia,* 569).

16. Dostoevsky emphasizes the absurdity of the testimony by having the experts focus their arguments not only on Dmitry's entrance into the courtroom but also on the relationship of that entrance to his "present psychological condition." The experts are supposed to focus on Dmitry's presumed mental condition before and during the crime, not months after—especially if *temporary* insanity is the issue. In fact, after the crime Ivan deteriorates mentally far more than Dmitry does. As we have seen, having the Moscow doctor testify for Dmitry was an afterthought of Katerina Ivanovna's; the doctor was brought in to assess Ivan's deteriorating mental condition.

17. Actually, Dostoevsky first brings up the issue of the legal status of Dmitry's temporary insanity in one of the comic riffs of the flighty Mme. Khokhlakov. She notes that the condition of temporary insanity (she uses the word *affekt,* the same word that the Moscow doctor uses to describe Dmitry's temporary insanity, and the same word Dostoevsky used to describe Kornilova's temporary insanity) was discovered as soon as the new courts of law were opened, so temporary insanity must be a blessing (or more properly the good deed) of the new courts (*blagodeianie novykh sudov;* 577; 15:17–18).

"Listen, what is a fit of passion [*affekt*]?"

"A fit of passion?" Alyosha said in surprise.

"A legal fit of passion [*sudebnyi affekt*]. A fit of passion for which they forgive everything. Whatever you do—you'll be immediately forgiven." (577; 15:17–18)

18. The portrait of Dr. Hindenburg is taken from a letter from one of Dostoevsky's Jewish correspondents, Sofya Lurye (Sof'ia Lur'e). Lurye writes:

He has been practicing in M. for fifty-eight years and how much good he did during that time. If you only knew, Fedor Mikhailovich, what a man this was! He was a doctor and an obstetrician; his name will live here in posterity; legends about him are already being told. All the common people called him "father," they loved and adored him, and only when he died did they comprehend what they have lost in this man. While his body lay in the coffin (in the church), I think there wasn't a single person who did not come up to weep over him and to kiss his feet, particularly the poor Jewesses whom he has helped so much; they wept and prayed that he be taken straight to Paradise. (*Diary of a Writer* 655; 25:89)

19. See Dostoevsky's letter to his niece (28.2:251) in which he expresses his fear that one cannot create a perfectly beautiful man in literature without making him somewhat ridiculous. Christ remains the only exception. "I shall mention that of the beautiful figures in Christian literature, Don Quixote is the most complete. But he is beautiful solely because he is also ridiculous."

20. Herzenstube is thus used as both an expert and a witness. This was illegal, according to article 693 of the Russian criminal code. It is difficult to establish whether Dostoevsky knew that the conviction in Kornilova's first trial was vacated precisely because of *this* technicality. See Rak, "Iuridicheskaia oshibka," 154–59. Terras suggests that Dostoevsky may be using Herzenstube as a secret "legal" weapon for Dmitry's post-trial defense: Dmitry will have the basis for an appeal (*A Karamazov Companion*, 404, 429). But in Kornilova's case her intercessor (Masliannikov) used the technicality as a ploy to force a new trial. It seems less likely that any highly placed official would have intervened for a parricide.

21. I shall discuss the problem of the relationship between truth and authority later in this chapter and in even more detail in the last chapter.

22. In the Dmitry Ilyinsky parricide case of 1845, on which the Dmitry Karamazov plot is partly based, Ilyinsky's brother, Aleksandr, was expected to give whatever information he may have had about their father's murder, however incriminating it might have been. A letter of inquiry addressed to Aleksandr stated: "However, you did not agree to his opinion and ordered the wood to be taken from the first pile. So after this did you not notice anything in your brother's appearance or have you no information that might serve as evidence against your brother or any other persons involved in the case? If such you have, you are bound by *conscience and filial duty* to expose the murderers of your father and disclose all details concerning the said question. April 17th, 1845" (Boris Fedorenko and Irina Yakubovich, "Ilyinsky—Karamazov: A Key to a Character," *Soviet Literature* 6 [1976]: 137). The evidence that Aleksandr gave against his own brother played a crucial role in Dmitry's conviction. The state's pre-reform attitude toward testifying against one's relatives seems to have differed significantly from post-reform procedure. Perhaps the obligation to testify against one's kin was considered one of those abuses of the old system that the new system had to redress.

23. Throughout "his whole life" (*vsiu zhizn'*) Ivan recalls slipping out of his father's house on the day of the murder. The narrator repeats the phrase "his whole" three times in one sentence: "Afterwards, his whole life, he would refer to this 'action' as 'loathsome,' and his whole life, deep within himself, in the innermost part of his soul, he considered it the basest action of his entire life" (14:276). There are several other similar statements.

24. Girish Narayan Bhat, "Trial by Jury in the Reign of Alexander II: A Study in the Legal Culture of Late Imperial Russia, 1864–1881" (Ph.D. diss., University of California, Berkeley, 1995), 77.

25. Dostoevsky encourages readers to compare the women's view of Dmitry with the jury's by linking their positions linguistically: the women stood up for

Dmitry (*stoiali za Mitiu*); the members of the jury stood up for themselves (*za sebia postoiali*; 15:178): that is, the women took sides based on sentiment, whereas the jury remained true to its principles.

26. Dostoevsky himself greatly admired, and was inspired by, the wives of the Decembrists. He incorporates the Decembrist model into the epilogue of *Crime and Punishment*, where Sonya accompanies Raskolnikov to hard labor in Siberia. For Dostoevsky's moving description of his meeting with some of the wives of the Decembrists, who greeted Dostoevsky and other prisoners on their way to prison, see his letter to N. D. Fonvizina, 20 January 1854 (28.1:175–77). Images and plots in Dostoevsky, however, invariably derive their positive or negative charge from context.

27. The author's deflationary sarcasm is obvious. The chapter in which Ivan Karamazov presents the causes of his rebellion against God is entitled "Rebellion" (*Bunt*).

28. As Grossman notes, Dostoevsky grossly exaggerates the publicity and public presence that a trial like Dmitry's would have received ("Pravitel'stvennye krugi," 102). It is unlikely that prominent government officials and intellectuals would have attended an unpolitical parricide trial in a provincial backwater. Dostoevsky is simply transferring these aspects of the Zasulich trial to the provinces for greater effect.

29. See note fifteen of this chapter.

30. "Spasovich was justly called the 'king of the Russian bar.' But with his death, it is impossible to cry out: 'the king is dead, long live the king!' There will be no other king" (S. A. Andreevskii, *Zashchititel'nye rechi* [St. Petersburg: Pravo, 1909], 587). The "obituary" also includes a brief defense of Spasovich vis-à-vis Dostoevsky.

31. I am focusing on the narrator as a device, a tool of the author. For more general discussions of narration in the novel, see, especially in terms of structure, Terras, *A Karamazov Companion*, 100–10; Ralph Matlaw, *The Brothers Karamazov: Novelistic Technique* (The Hague: Mouton, 1957); Robert Belknap, *The Structure of The Brothers Karamazov* (The Hague: Mouton, 1967), 77–105; V. E. Vetlovskaia, *Poetika romana "Brat'ia Karamazovy"* (Leningrad: Nauka, 1977).

32. Furthermore, it is not always possible to distinguish the older narrator from the omniscient or implied author.

33. Because of readers' privileged position, their view of the trial must differ significantly from the views of the various actors and participants. But the evidence is really overwhelmingly against Dmitry, and no jury, especially one made up of peasants, would have acquitted him. As Dmitry says himself: "Who else could have done it if I didn't?" Fetyukovich himself believes Dmitry did it. Fetyukovich is, of course, wrong, but he is not stupid. He simply does not believe his own arguments, which are convincing to the reader only because the reader knows by artistic convention that Dmitry is innocent.

34. It is also possible that the prosecutor knows that he has a tougher jury than

most spectators assume. It is made up of peasants, who are not going to respond warmly to either psychology or high-blown rhetoric. Furthermore, although many, if not most, of the educated males in the town dislike Dmitry (he has managed to insult almost everyone), the peasants have a soft spot in their hearts for Dmitry and consider him one of their own.

35. The first mention of Fetyukovich occurs in a remark by Alyosha to Grushenka a day before the trial. Alyosha says he met Fetyukovich the day before for the first time. In book 12, chapter 2, we learn that Fetyukovich probably arrived only three days before the trial. "Furthermore, everyone immediately noticed with pleasure that during his brief stay with us, perhaps in only three days' time, he had managed to become surprisingly well acquainted with the case, and had 'mastered it in the finest detail'" (663; 15:96).

36. N. V. Cherkasova, *Formirovanie i razvitie advokatury v Rossii* (Moscow: Nauka, 1987), 51–53. Quoted in Bhat, "Trial by Jury," 208. In Russia summations enjoyed a life outside the courtroom, becoming a popular genre in Russian literature and culture. Many prominent attorneys published their summations. They were often republished during the Soviet period when the jury had been abolished. See, for example, M. M. Vydri, *Sudebnye rechi izvestnykh russkikh iuristov* (Moscow: Iuridicheskaia literatura, 1956); P. M. Zakharov, ed., *Rechi izvestnykh iuristov* (Moscow: Iuridicheskaia literatura, 1985).

37. I've kept "amulet" as the translation for *ladonka*. However, it is probably closer, at least here, to "a little pouch."

38. Dmitry's case must be based, as we might say today, on reasonable doubt, which Fetyukovich does a brilliant job of arguing.

39. Although there are crude "journalistic" passages in Ippolit Kirillovich's speech, other passages could be taken from the finest moments in Dostoevsky's fiction. The passage relating to the man about to be executed closely resembles one of Myshkin's stories in *The Idiot* and, of course, Dostoevsky's own experience.

40. America knows this strategy all too well from the O. J. Simpson trial, where in his summation the defense attorney Johnnie Cochran in effect told the jurors that the guilt or innocence of his client was secondary to the message that they needed to send to American society. It was the jury's civic duty, as American citizens, to make a statement about the most important issue facing American society: ingrained white racism, exemplified by the police lieutenant Mark Furhman, who became, as far as the defense was concerned, the true defendant, and who permitted Johnnie Cochran to reverse roles and play, like Ippolit Kirillovich, the prosecuting attorney.

41. To prove a similar point Fetyukovich cites Ippolit Kirillovich's explanation of Dmitry's calculation regarding the servant Grigory, on one hand, and his careless handling of the envelope containing the money, on the other (727, 732–33; 15:155, 159).

42. Holdheim *(Justizirrtum,* 17–19) sees them as two forms of rationalism in opposition to the spiritual understanding of Father Zosima.

43. The invasion fears recall the bureaucrats' ridiculous fears about a foreign

invasion in the opening scene of Gogol's *Inspector General*, fears that the mayor, still in possession of his faculties, dismisses derisively.

44. Holdheim sees Fetyukovich almost more like a skeptical, perspectivist epistemologist than a trial lawyer: "a philosopher arguing . . . the impossibility of knowledge" ("On the Genealogy of the Judicial Error," 127).

45. In his excellent article on "art" in *The Brothers Karamazov*, Terras emphasizes the artistic powers of Fetyukovich and attributes his superior reconstruction of the crime to the quality of his imagination ("The Art of Fiction as a Theme in *The Brothers Karamazov*," *Dostoevsky: New Perspectives* [Englewood Cliffs, N.J.: Prentice-Hall, 1984], 193–205). But the facts, as Terras recognizes elsewhere, are irrelevant to the author's higher plot regarding Dmitry's salvation, so Fetyukovich's superior imagination is equally irrelevant. Moreover, as Dmitry argues, the art of Sodom and Gomorrah can be as powerful as the art of the Madonna. And this is exactly why Dostoevsky feared the misuse of artistic talent in the courtroom.

46. Speaking purely on a practical level, given the preponderance of the evidence —the blood, the witnesses against Dmitry, and Dmitry's own behavior—it is of course possible that Fetyukovich sees his reconstruction of the crime as an inadequate defense, that is, he thinks that he will not win on the basis of reasonable doubt.

47. Fetyukovich might have benefited from contemporary specialists in jury analysis. But one wonders whether he (as the character Dostoevsky created) would have sacrificed his rhetoric just to appeal to a peasant jury.

48. Thus I would dispute Victor Terras's claim that Fetyukovich "certainly does his best to save Dmitry" ("The Art of Fiction," 201).

49. There is a glaring inconsistency in Dostoevsky's presentation of Fetyukovich's justification of parricide. Ippolit Kirillovich's speech is presented in many instances as an example of the high-flown and overwrought rhetoric characteristic of the courtroom in high-profile cases in Dostoevsky's time. Most of Fetyukovich's narrative, by contrast, is much more down-to-earth, matter-of-fact, and prosaic. As we shall see, Fetyukovich not only attempts to deflate his opponent's venture into novel creation, he also attempts to attack his rhetorical style. But at the end of his speech, in his justification of parricide, Fetyukovich indulges in the same kind of rhetorical excess as his opponent. Dostoevsky obviously does this to place him, as elsewhere, in the same moral space as Ippolit Kirillovich, but this ploy falls somewhat flat given Fetyukovich's strategy of attacking Ippolit Kirillovich on this very issue. Robin Feuer Miller notes the uncharacteristic stupidity of such a move: "Fetyukovich becomes a true blockhead, for at the moment when he should have concluded his argument, he launches into a theoretical justification for negating filial bonds" (*Worlds of the Novel*, 130). For an analysis of the rhetoric of the attorneys' speeches, see N. G. Mikhailovskaia, "Sudebnaia rech'," 57–65. V. V. Vinogradov suggests that the rhetoric of legal summations was influenced by literature and also that the influence was mutual: The rhetoric of the post-reform court may have left its trace on the literature of its time (*O teorii khudozhestvennoi rechi* [Moscow: Vysshaia shkola, 1971], 150). For an attempt to show the influence of the new courts on the literature of the time—with *The*

*Brothers Karamazov* as a prominent example—see Keily, *"The Brothers Karamazov* and the Fate of Russian Truth."* Lawyers often thought of themselves as artists.

   50. The passage crucial to my argument in this section of the chapter reads in full:

Along with that you will destroy the still-possible man in him, for he will remain wicked and blind for the rest of his life. No, if you want to punish him terribly, fearfully, with the most horrible punishment imaginable, but so as to save and restore his soul forever [*spasti i vozrodit' ego dushu naveki*]—then overwhelm him with your mercy [*miloserdiem*]! You will see, you will hear how his soul will tremble and be horrified: "Is it for me to endure this mercy [*milost'*], for me to be granted so much love, and am I worthy of it?" he will exclaim! Oh, I know, I know that heart, it is a wild but noble heart, gentlemen of the jury. It will bow down before your deed [*podvig*], it thirsts for a great act of love, it will catch fire and resurrect forever [*voskresnet naveki*]. There are souls that in their narrowness blame the whole world. But overwhelm such a soul with mercy [*miloserdie*], give it love, and it will curse what it has done, for there are so many germs of good in it. The soul will expand and behold how merciful [*miloserd*] God is, and how beautiful and just people are [*prekrasnye i spravedlivye*]. He will be horrified, he will be overwhelmed with repentance [*raskaianie*] and the countless debt [*dolg*] he must henceforth repay. And then he will not say, "I am quits," but will say, "I am guilty before all people and am the least worthy of all people [*Ia vinovat pred vsemi liud'mi i vsekh liudei nedostoinee*]." In tears of repentance [*v slezakh raskaianiia i zhguchego stradatel'skogo umileniia*] and burning suffering tenderness he will exclaim: "People are better than I, for they wished not to ruin but to save [*spasti*] me!" Oh, it is so easy for you to do it, this act of mercy [*miloserdie*], for in the absence of any evidence even slightly resembling the truth, it will be too difficult for you to say: "Yes, guilty [*Da, vinoven*]." It is better to let ten who are guilty go, than to punish one who is innocent—do you hear, do you hear this majestic voice from the last century of our glorious history? Is it for me, insignificant as I am, to remind you that the Russian courts exist not only for punishment [*kara*] but also for the salvation of the ruined man [*spasenie cheloveka pogibshego*]! Let other nations have the letter and punishment [*bukva i kara*], we have the spirit and meaning [*dukh i smysl*], the salvation and the regeneration of the lost [*spasenie i vozrozhdenie pogibshikh*]. And if so, if such indeed are Russia and her courts, then—onward Russia! And do not frighten us, oh, do not frighten us with your mad troikas, which all nations stand aside from in distrust! Not a mad troika, but a majestic Russian chariot [*velichavaia russkaia kolesnitsa*] will arrive solemnly and peacefully at its goal. In your hands is the fate of my client, in your hands is also the fate of our Russian truth [*pravdy russkoi*]. You will save it [*spasete ee*], you will champion it, you will prove that there are some to preserve it, that it is in good hands! (747–48; 15:172–73)

Again, the invasion fears recall the bureaucrats' ridiculous fears about a foreign invasion in the opening scene of Gogol's *Inspector General,* fears that the mayor, still in possession of his faculties, dismisses derisively.

51. Terras is correct in maintaining that Fetyukovich's justification of Dmitry's murder degenerates into travesty: "It begins to remind one of Mme. Khokhlakov's tirade in Book Eleven" (*A Karamazov Companion,* 433). Indeed, the chapter is closer in some respects to the *Diary of a Writer* than it is to Dostoevsky's earlier (pre-1875) fiction.

52. See D. H. Lawrence, "The Grand Inquisitor," in Edward Wasiolek, ed., *The Brothers Karamazov and the Critics* (Belmont, Calif.: Wadsworth, 1967), 78–85; Vasily Rozanov, *Dostoevsky and the Legend of the Grand Inquisitor,* trans. Spenser E. Roberts (Ithaca, N.Y.: Cornell University Press, 1972), 175–78; and Lev Shestov, *Dostoevsky, Tolstoy and Nietzsche* (Athens: Ohio University Press, 1969), 221–23. Saul Bellow wrote: "Dostoyevsky wrote to one of his correspondents that he must now attempt, through Father Zosima, to answer Ivan's arguments. But he has in advance all but devastated his own position" (Bellow, "Where Do We Go from Here: The Future of Modern Fiction," in A. L. Bader, ed., *To the Young Writer,* Hopwood Lectures, second series [Ann Arbor: University of Michigan Press, 1965], 146). To argue that Dostoevsky is on the side of the Grand Inquisitor is to question the authority of the voice of the "author." Terras expresses the view of most: "This and a number of similar passages make it clear that Dostoevsky was on Christ's side, not the devil's. Any interpretation of *The Brothers Karamazov* which reaches the opposite conclusion disregards not only the direct meaning of the novel, but also Dostoevsky's professed intent. The evidence is overwhelming that Dostoevsky at the time he wrote *The Brothers Karamazov* was a Christian, secure in his faith, and anxious to convey his faith to others" (*A Karamazov Companion,* 39–40).

53. Vetlovskaia, *Poetika romana.* See, especially, the section entitled, "Otnoshenie avtora k slovam geroia," 52–142.

54. Nina Perlina, *Varieties of Poetic Utterance* (Lanham, Md.: University Press of America, 1985), 13. Perlina argues that M. M. Bakhtin is essentially in accord with Erich Auerbach regarding the ideal of authority in the novel and its relation with the author's (and of course, not necessarily, with the narrator's) voice. Perlina quotes from Bakhtin's *The Dialogic Imagination*: "'The authoritative word demands that we acknowledge it, that we make it our own. It binds us, quite independently of any power it might have to persuade us internally; we encounter it with its authority already fused to it. The authoritative word is located in a distanced zone; it is felt to be hierarchically higher'" (*The Dialogic Imagination,* ed. M. Holquist, trans. Caryl Emerson [Austin: University of Texas Press, 1981], 342).

55. Lawrence, "The Grand Inquisitor," 79.

56. Bakhtin does not maintain that the voices of the characters are equal to that of the author. The belief that he does has led Holdheim, for one, to suggest that Dostoevsky may be not only on Ivan's side but also on Fetyukovich's, even though he attempts to prove that Fetyukovich is the purest representation of nihilism—

moral and aesthetic—in the novel (*Justizirrtum*, 41). To maintain that "the author" is on Fetyukovich's side clearly cannot be substantiated. As I will show later, it is difficult enough to support a deconstructive interpretation in defense of Fetyukovich, that is, to argue that the rhetorical structures of the novel may be used to establish an interpretation diametrically opposite to the one intended by the author. On the other hand, Terras, who contrasts those in the novel with and without artistic imagination, takes a relatively sympathetic view of both Fedor Karamazov and Fetyukovich, because both are imaginative artists, and as such are thus closer to the truth than those without imagination (Terras, "The Art of Fiction," 193–205).

57. In my conclusion I will try to assess to what extent Dostoevsky is successful in creating authority for his word and what might be the artistic consequences of such a success.

58. In 1864 Dostoevsky had already conceived of the ideal of Christ as something contrary to human nature but something toward which all human beings were obligated to strive. The failure to strive (*stremlenie k idealu*), not the failure to achieve, results in sin (20:172–75).

59. Recently, Johnnie Cochran has published a book in which he writes about the importance of the Simpson case not so much for the country or the legal profession but for himself personally: for launching his career as a national and even international celebrity. See his *A Lawyer's Life* (New York: St. Martin's Press, 2002).

### 5. *The Brothers Karamazov* II

1. Such a practice was entirely in accordance with the reform statutes of 1864, something that Dostoevsky finds in his interest to conceal.

2. The narrator uses the following words to describe Alyosha's mystical experience: "It was as if threads (*niti*) from all those innumerable worlds of God all came together in his soul" (14:328). Here the defense attorney is using in court the same language that Dostoevsky uses to describe Alyosha Karamazov's mystical experience. Dostoevsky thus emphasizes the contrast of the most prosaic and utilitarian with the mystical and transcendent.

3. Dostoevsky risks the contamination of "The Russian Monk" by "So Be It! So Be It!" Once Zosima's word is seen as one voice among others in a larger debate, his statements in "The Russian Monk" may be perceived in the same way, undermining the authority of his hagiography.

4. Ivan Esaulov, "The Categories of Law and Grace in Dostoevsky's Poetics," in George Pattison and Diane Oenning Thompson, eds., *Dostoevsky and the Christian Tradition* (Cambridge: Cambridge University Press, 2001), 116–33.

5. Ibid., 120.

6. Ibid., 118.

7. Wolfgang Kayser, *Entstehen und Krise des modernen Romans*, 2d ed. (Stuttgart: Metzler, 1955).

8. The original sentence, specified by Nicholas I himself, was for life. But it seems to have been commuted to twenty years after the ascension to the throne of Alexander II. The evidence against Ilyinsky was not especially strong. Nicholas knew that but wrote against the recommendation that Ilyinsky be reduced to the ranks, maintaining that someone under suspicion of parricide should not be serving in the army. See Boris Fedorenko and Irina Yakubovich, "Ilyinsky-Karamazov: A Key to a Character," *Soviet Literature* 6 (1976): 131–47.

9. The seven volumes comprise more than three thousand pages and include Ilyinsky's own handwritten statement reporting his father as missing. See Fedorenko and Yakubovich, "Ilyinsky Karamazov." Fedorenko and Yakubovich show many striking similarities in situation and character between the two Dmitrys. It is clear that Ilyinsky must have provided Dostoevsky with a great deal more information about his case and his relationship with his father and brother than the narrator in *Notes from the House of the Dead* reveals. For further information about the Ilyinsky case, see B. G. Reizov, "K istorii zamysla *Brat'ev Karamazovykh*," Zven'ia 6 (1936): 545–73; Robert Belknap, *The Genesis of The Brothers Karamazov* (Evanston, Ill.: Northwestern University Press, 1990), 57–63.

10. See M. L. Reinus, *Dostoevsky v Staroi Russe* (Lenizdat: Leningrad, 1969), 44–45.

11. The introduction to *Notes from the House of the Dead* tells us that the narrator died soon after his release. But this is probably just a narrative ploy. See Gary Rosenshield, "The Realization of the Collective Self: The Rebirth of Religious Autobiography in Dostoevsky's *Notes from the House of the Dead*," *Slavic Review* 50, no. 2 (1991): 317–27.

12. F. M. Dostoevskii, *Sobranie sochinenii,* 10 vols. (Moscow: Gos. izd. khud. lit, 1958), 10:466–67.

13. See Reinus, *Dostoevsky v Staroi Russe,* 44–45.

14. Ronald Hingley, *The Undiscovered Dostoyevsky* (London: Hamilton, 1962), 212.

15. R. P. Blackmur, *Eleven Essays in the European Novel* (New York: Harcourt, 1964), 223.

16. Hingley, *The Undiscovered Dostoyevsky*, 213.

17. Nathan Rosen, "Why Dmitrii Karamazov Did Not Kill His Father," *Canadian-American Slavic Studies* 6 (1972): 424. Another doubter of Dmitry's ability to bear his cross, Maurice Friedman, states that Dmitry opts for America, because, although he has great breadth, he does not have the requisite depth (Friedman, "Martin Buber's *For the Sake of Heaven* and F. M. Dostoevsky's *The Brothers Karamazov*," *Comparative Literature Studies* 3 [1966]:164). Robert Louis Jackson does not preclude the possibility of Dmitry's salvation through suffering in Siberia, arguing that such a salvation promises "a hope of no small consequence for mankind," but he remarks that Dmitry's "desire to suffer, his yearning to bear the cross and to sing a 'tragic hymn' to God, turns out to be more symbolic than real" (Robert L. Jackson, "Dmitrij Karamazov and the Legend," *Slavic and East European Journal* 9 (1965): 266, 264). Soviet criticism, as one might imagine, did not look favorably on the American alternative. See, especially, Ia. E. Golosovker, *Dostoevskii* (Moscow: Akademiia nauk, 1963), 29–30: "The secret of escape to

America, that is, the decision to renounce suffering, purification, the hymn, immortality, God—turns out to be the invention of the devil, 'the devil's secret'" (30).

18. Luigi Pareyson writes, "Dmitri is willing, indeed anxious, to go to Siberia for 'the little child.' He must do something for the little child. And the only way to do this is to suffer and, although innocent, go to Siberia. Suffering from this perspective is the only way to redeem the suffering of the child, to heal the pain of all since 'we are all guilty and must answer for the sufferings of others'" ("Pointless Suffering in *The Brothers Karamazov*," *Cross-Currents* 37 [1987]: 280).

19. Even Shatov and Kirillov, no mollycoddles, could not survive the rigors of life in America and were forced to return to Russia.

20. In *Crime and Punishment* Svidrigaylov, who knows that Raskolnikov committed the murder, offers to save him—as Ivan does Dmitry—by engineering Raskolnikov's escape to America. But later Svidrigaylov uses the expression of going to America as synonymous with committing suicide.

21. Dmitry makes other statements about his desire to suffer for his sins. He is by far the most garrulous of the brothers. "I accept the torment of the accusation and of my disgrace before all, I want to suffer and be purified by suffering. . . . I accept punishment not because I killed him, but because I wanted to kill him, and might well have killed him" (509; 14:458). For an interesting attempt to justify Dmitry's going to America, see Paul Contino's application of casuistry and Bakhtinian situational ethics (*prosaics*) to Dmitry's dilemma ("Dostoevsky and the Ethical Relation to the Prisoner," *Renascence* 48.4 (1996): 271–76.

22. Richard Peace, *Dostoyevsky: An Examination of the Major Novels* (Cambridge: Cambridge University Press, 1971), 284.

23. As we have seen, the trial in *Crime and Punishment* is not a jury trial. But as a transitional legal procedure, it did include important elements of the 1864 legal reform. Before *Crime and Punishment* Dostoevsky occasionally mentions "cases" (*dela*), but these are strictly procedures relating to the old courts. As early as *Poor Folk* (1846), Dostoevsky's first novel, he refers to a case that led to the dismissal of Gorshkov, Devushkin's fellow impoverished lodger, from his job. The court (*sud*) subsequently absolves Gorshkov of all charges.

24. Creatively interpreting the fourth edition of the *Diagnostic and Statistical Manual of Mental Disorders* (*DSM-IV*, 1994), we could probably say that Kornilova experienced an episode of autoscopic depersonalization disorder, a psychological condition in which subjects feel that they are watching their own physical and mental behavior as though it were the behavior of another person. In her book on criminal responsibility and multiple personality disorder—or what is now called dissociative identity disorder—Elyn R. Saks argues that those suffering from depersonalization disorder should almost always be held accountable for their criminal actions, in contrast to those suffering from multiple personality disorder, who, she maintains, are seldom responsible (*Jekyll on Trial: Multiple Personality Disorder and Criminal Law* [New York: New York University Press, 1997].

25. In fact, most critics view Ivan Karamazov, who also did not commit the crime, to be far more guilty of his father's murder than Dmitry. Ivan is the "mentor" and

"creator" of the murderer, Smerdyakov, whom he infected with his doctrine of permissibility. Although he was staying with his father to protect him from Dmitry, Ivan abandoned the house at Smerdyakov's suggestion, leaving the field open for Smerdyakov to commit the murder. Ivan's mental breakdown at the end shows the extent to which he believes himself more responsible for his father's death than Dmitry, perhaps even more than his half-brother Smerdyakov. See, for example, Ernest J. Simmons, *Dostoevsky: The Making of a Novelist* (New York: Vintage, 1940), 354; Edward Wasiolek, *Dostoevsky: The Major Fiction* (Cambridge, Mass.: MIT Press, 1964), 175–77; Peace, *Dostoyevsky*, 239–42, 279–80; Hingley, *The Undiscovered Dostoyevsky*, 200; Konstantin Mochulsky, *Dostoevsky: His Life and Work*, trans. Michael A. Minihan (Princeton, N.J.: Princeton University Press, 1967), 598. But, as Peace points out, Smerdyakov is as much Dmitry's instrument as Ivan's (260–61).

26. Father Zosima suggests religious courts as a better alternative to secular courts. See book 2, chap. 5, "So Be It! So Be It!" Dostoevsky argues similarly about responsibility whenever environment and responsibility—determinism and free will—are at issue. In *Notes from the Underground* the Underground Man, the quintessential proponent of free will, argues that the only thing that a human being can do to guarantee his humanity, to prove that he is a human being and not a piano stop, is to assert his free will against all the deterministic (environmental) evidence. Here free will becomes an article of faith, something that must be believed in—for without that belief life becomes unlivable. In a typically maximalist move the Underground Man takes responsibility for the laws of nature, the very laws to which he ascribes all his ills and misfortunes. It is a masochistic solution, for he becomes responsible for all that afflicts him, but he would rather assume responsibility, and thereby preserve his freedom—and humanity—than be the innocent victim of forces beyond his control: to be a piano stop and not a human being.

27. For an excellent analysis of the relationship between suffering and redemption in *The Brothers Karamazov*, see E. H. Carr, *Dostoevsky: 1821–1881* (London: Allen, Unwin, 1962), 222–31. Carr argues that the main theme of the novel is "the redemption of Dmitri through sin and suffering" (220). For an attempt to summarize the various interpretations of redemptive suffering in the novel, see Geir Kjetsaa, *Fyodor Dostoyevsky: A Writer's Life* (New York: Viking, 1987), 344–49. Whereas Carr treats Dostoevsky's mystical view of suffering in *The Brothers Karamazov* with considerable sympathy, Hingley, obviously more at home in Chekhov than in Dostoevsky, adopts a far more skeptical, Western view:

Dmitry is thus the embodiment of one central message of the novel, that man should cultivate and distend to its ultimate limit the feeling of guilt inside him and find relief in purification and suffering. As Dostoyevsky knew himself, this doctrine runs contrary to common sense. The logic on which this is based is "not of this world." It operates as interpreters have explained, on a "heavenly" or "metaphysical" level and it is not susceptible

of discussion in everyday terms. . . . It is possible to be a sincere admirer of
Dostoyevsky's art without being at all a disciple of Dostoyevskianism. To
enjoy *The Brothers Karamazov* one does not have to be obsessed with a
desire to purify oneself by suffering. One does not even need to feel that this
is a serious concept. (212)

Dostoevsky obviously goes beyond Paul: "The evil that I would not, that I do." He
sees suffering not only as a *consequence* of sin (thoughts and actions that separate
us from God) but as a positive force that we voluntarily must take upon ourselves
for our own sake as well as for the sake of others. For another fervent apology for
the novel's view of suffering, see Pareyson, "Pointless Suffering," 271–286. I should
like to emphasize that Dostoevsky does not present all suffering as good or beneficial. There is, among other things, the suffering that arises from pride and
wounded vanity.

28. V. E Vatsurov, ed., *F. M. Dostoevskii v vospominaniiakh sovremennikov*, 2
vols. (Moscow: Khudozhestvennaia literatura, 1990), 2:212.

29. D. I. Stakheev, "Gruppy i portrety," *Istoricheskii vestnik*, January 1907, trans.
(Kostalevsky, *Dostoevsky and Soloviev*, 59). Maria Kostalevsky, *Dostoevsky and
Soloviev: The Art of Integral Vision* (New Haven: Yale University Press, 1997), 59.

30. See A. I. Gertsen, *Byloe i dumy* (Leningrad: GIKhL, 1947), 102.

### Conclusion

1. This position is very different from that of M. M. Bakhtin, who asserted
the relative autonomy of the voices of Dostoevsky's main characters but assumed
the primacy of the author's voice. For Bakhtin the author was at worst a primus
inter pares. Vasily Rozanov actually represents an earlier, more psychological, version of the deconstuctionist hypothesis. Deconstruction presupposes an intended
point of view and argues for an interpretation against intention. Rozanov posits
a divided, ambivalent author who consciously argues one position but uncon-
sciously and more deeply sympathizes with the other. Georgy Lukacs made this
very argument with Balzac, and dozens have made virtually the same argument
with regard to Milton's Satan.

2. Alyosha's "incipient downfall is expressed even more significantly in the
*form* of his concluding statement, a long narrative which fittingly closes the book.
Never before has Alyosha been so wordy; his usual stance of saintly, tacit veracity, has always avoided the verbosity of false formulators around him. His uncharacteristic garrulousness is thus a surer sign of the evil he foresees . . . than is the
substance of his closing remarks. His two paragraphs of advice to the children
. . . mark his initial break with Father Zosima's teachings." See Richard H. Weisberg, *The Failure of the Word: The Protagonist as Lawyer in Modern Fiction* (New
Haven, Conn.: Yale University Press, 1984), 81. But, in fact, Father Zosima is far
more garrulous than Alyosha.

3. Robin Feuer Miller, *The Brothers Karamazov: The Worlds of the Novel* (New York: Twayne, 1992), 31.

4. We know that Father Zosima's life is not traditional hagiography: it is neo-hagiography. Alas, hagiography can no longer be written in the old way. To some Orthodox thinkers neo-hagiography might be a heretical notion. But Dostoevsky, as Solovyov remarked, was blazing a trail for the religious narrative of the future, in which religious narrative could no longer be identical to the religious literature of the past.

5. In "Which Is the Merchant Here? And Which the Jew? Subversion and Recuperation in *The Merchant of Venice*," in Jean E. Howard and Marion F. O'Conner, eds., *Shakespeare Reproduced: The Text in History and Ideology* (New York: Metheun, 1987), 202, Thomas Moisan argues that in *The Merchant of Venice* art trumps ideological contradictions: "The play manages to transcend the issues its text problematizes to render a dramatically, theatrically satisfying experience."

6. This depends a great deal on the director's interpretation of Jessica in act 5. Modern performances have begun not only to emphasize her melancholy but implicitly associate it with her own responsibility for her father's fate.

7. The Grand Inquisitor's system is based not on compulsion but authority, authority that is gained through the possession and exploitation of the Word. Without the misappropriated Word—control over the great text—the Grand Inquisitor acknowledges that he could not rule, for he would not possess the authority necessary to rule.

8. Dostoevsky has a soft spot in his heart for Lebedev because although Lebedev acts badly, he is conscious that he is acting badly; he just cannot control himself. He would never try to justify his behavior, although he would take masochistic pleasure in reveling in his guilt.

9. Ivan gives the example of the Swiss murderer, Richard, who was rationally sacrificed—that is, executed—for the good of the community.

10. Under the Soviets, of course, it was often expected of critics to read otherwise, but otherwise always in the same way.

11. In the 1870s Dostoevsky's maternal aunt's estate was being contested within his family. Dostoevsky was legally entitled to more of the estate than he knew he was morally entitled to, but he, in effect, gave permission to his wife, who looked after his financial interests, to deal with the lawyers. For one of the most interesting accounts of the squabbling that occurred over the Kumanin inheritance and its reflection in *A Raw Youth* and *The Brothers Karamazov*, see E. H. Carr, *Dostoevsky: 1821–1881* (London: Allen, Unwin, 1962), 191–94.

# Index

Abbott, Jack Henry: as author, 116, 117–18, 119; civil case against, 119, 123; criminal record of, 116, 277n20; facts of case, 116; Mailer's relationship with, 116–19; as media celebrity, 154; recidivism of, 118

Adan, Richard, 118

adversarial system, 26–27, 55, 173; as amoral, 178; medical expert witnesses and, 81–82; *vs.* partnership, 84; truth and, 133; *vs.* unanimity of Russian justice, 101

advocacy, 269n26

Afanasyev, N., 204

Aikhenval'd, Iu., 267n19

Aksakov, I. S., 21–23, 96

Aksakov, Konstantin, 63

Aldershot, 258n16

Aleksandrov, P. A., 135, 179

Alexander the Second, 23

alienation of the artist, 49–50

America: emigration to equated with suicide, 226; escape plot in *Brothers Karamazov*, 210–12, 226–31, 292nn19–20; redemption in culture of, 108; as spiritual and moral vacuum, 227–28

Andreevsky, S. A., 282n10

"anti-advocacy" position, 269n26

art: abuse of, 17, 27, 55–56, 161, 166–69, 184, 193, 244–45; exploitation of, 12, 14, 121, 244–45; good and bad art in Dostoevsky's works, 6, 269n27, 270n29; judges as political artists, 261n39; lawyers as artists, 27, 55–56, 184, 261n39; talent as potentially evil, 16; talent exploited by criminals, 121

audience: Dostoevsky's awareness of his readers, 59–60, 239, 245–46; Dostoevsky's effort to restore compassion in, 38, 59–60; juries as, 180; for Kornilova articles, 70–71, 103–4; readers as spectators at trial, 38, 155–56, 285n33; resisting readers, 234–35, 238, 245–46, 252–53. *See also* spectators at trials

Auerbach, Erich, 289n54

authority: Abbott on, 119; of authorial word, 235–38; *Brothers Karamazov* and narrative authority, 239–45, 246–47; discrediting of, 188–89; Dmitry as rebelling against author's plot, 250–51; Dostoevsky's authority, 38–40, 43, 59, 181, 223, 236–37, 289n52, 294n1; Fetyukovich's appropriation of, 181, 185; the Gospels and, 235–36, 246; narrative authority, 6, 31, 226, 239–47; prison as

297